Good Government?
Good Citizens?

Law and Society Series

W. WESLEY PUE, GENERAL EDITOR

A list of the books in this series appears at the end of this book.

Good Government?
Good Citizens?

Courts, Politics, and Markets in a Changing Canada

W.A. BOGART

UBCPress · Vancouver · Toronto

15 14 13 12 11 10 09 08 07 06 05   5 4 3 2 1

Printed in Canada on acid-free paper

Library and Archives Canada Cataloguing in Publication

Bogart, W. A.
    Good government? Good citizens? : courts, politics, and markets in a changing Canada / W.A. Bogart.

(Law and society, ISSN 1496-4953)
Includes bibliographical references and index.
ISBN 0-7748-1164-1 (bound); ISBN 0-7748-1165-X (pbk.)

    1. Political participation – Canada – History. 2. Political culture – Canada – History. 3. Citizenship – Canada. 4. Canada – Politics and government – 1984-1993. 5. Canada – Politics and government – 1993- 6. Canada – Social conditions – 1971-1991. 7. Canada – Social conditions – 1991- I. Title. II. Series: Law and society series (Vancouver, B.C.)

JL186.5.B64 2005   306.2'0971   C2005-900721-4

Canadä

UBC Press gratefully acknowledges the financial support for our publishing program of the Government of Canada through the Book Publishing Industry Development Program (BPIDP), and of the Canada Council for the Arts, and the British Columbia Arts Council.

This book has been published with the help of a grant from the Canadian Federation for the Humanities and Social Sciences, through the Aid to Scholarly Publications Programme, using funds provided by the Social Sciences and Humanities Research Council of Canada.

Printed and bound in Canada by Friesens
Set in Arrus and News Gothic by Artegraphica Design Co. Ltd.
Copy editor: Judy Phillips
Proofreader: Deborah Kerr
Indexer: Patricia Buchanan

UBC Press
The University of British Columbia
2029 West Mall
Vancouver, BC V6T 1Z2
604-822-5959 / Fax: 604-822-6083
www.ubcpress.ca

For my sisters:
Jo-Ann, Ellen, Pat, and Debbie

And to the memory of Chris – she had many gifts;
a long life was not among them.

"Strength and honour are her clothing;
and she shall rejoice in time to come"

— PROVERBS 31:25

Contents

Acknowledgments

A good many people helped this book along its way, though, of course, I alone am responsible for its shortcomings.

Randy Schmidt at UBC Press and Wes Pue, the general editor of the Law and Society Series, were enthusiastic about the manuscript from the start and masterfully guided it through all stages. I received very helpful comments from three anonymous reviewers and from the Publications Board. Darcy Cullen provided careful editorial guidance.

I would like to thank all my research assistants: Leanne Fasciano, Michael Haraschuk, Daniel McNamara, Kurt Pereira, Lilli Ripandelli, and Kate Sellar. Many colleagues read or discussed parts of *Good Government? Good Citizens?* and others supported grant applications: Jeff Berryman, Bob Brym, Sandra Burt, Charles Epp, Scott Fairley, Maureen Irish, Dick Moon, Jacqueline Murray, Wes Pue, Greg Richards, Len Rotman, Peter Russell, Billy and Sharon Sammon, Austin Sarat, Elisabeth Scarff, and Myra Tawfik. Kent Roach was very generous and read the entire manuscript. He registered disagreement with parts of the book even as he provided many insightful comments. My secretary of many years, Annette Pratt, lent terrific administrative assistance to the project.

Dean Bruce Elman supported this project in many ways. He was forever asking encouraging questions (including as to when the book would be finished). His enthusiasm for scholarship and for my institutional home is truly inspiring.

Financial grants from the following made this book possible: the Centre for Innovation Law and Policy; the Law Commission of Canada (LCC) through its Virtual Scholar in Residence Program; the Ontario Law Foundation through its Block Grant to the Faculty of Law, University of Windsor; the Social Sciences and Humanities Research Council of Canada (SSHRC); and the University of Windsor Research Grant Program. The SSHRC and the LCC grants both released me from teaching obligations; the pace at which I could proceed with the book was substantially increased. All this assistance is most gratefully acknowledged.

I discussed the ideas in *Good Government? Good Citizens?* in several places: a meeting of partners and associates at Weir and Foulds; a seminar for the Justices of the Court of Appeal for Ontario; a dinner meeting of the Ontario Bar Association, Constitutional Civil Liberties and Human Rights Section; a meeting at the Department of Justice; a talk at the Legal Studies Institute, University of Wisconsin; a conference sponsored by the Policy Research Initiative, "Instrument Choice in Global Democracies"; a meeting of the Judges of the Ontario Court of Justice; a conference sponsored by the International Consortium for Intergenerational Programmes, "Global Challenges – Future Directions"; and the 2004 Ontario Justice Summit. I thank all participants for their helpful reactions.

Finally, thanks to my household. Nanette Flores for keeping us all going. My daughter, Ab, for all her encouragement that so inspires me. My wife – and editor – Linda Bertoldi, who ever demonstrates that corporate law, love of literature, fine Italian cooking, and civic works make a wonderful combination. Linda Bertoldi: the good citizen.

As I finished this book I was in the country. It was winter. One night I awoke to a beautiful sight: the full moon, a still, clear sky, and a fresh blanket of snow. The cold, the clarity, the serenity made me think of Canadians' pact with the land; a constant in this ever changing world. There was a reassuring moment of tranquility in nature as I ended a project about our rambunctious human affairs.

W.A. Bogart
"Raspberries," Lake Kawagama
January 2005

Introduction

Inspirations for books come from many sources. Sometimes it is a single idea that the author feels passionately about. Sometimes it is a series of conversations, prompting the writer to work through her views on an issue in extended form, or it is the culmination of a group of articles developing a perspective that requires full-length treatment.

Sometimes one book inspires another. So it is with this one. I have long been interested in assessing the interaction of law and social issues. There are many aspects to this interaction. An important one is the growing influence of rights and the ascendance of courts as arbiters of myriad issues confronting postindustrial societies. While at work on my last book, I read Michael Schudson's *The Good Citizen: A History of American Civic Life.*[1]

The Good Citizen is an eloquent but disturbing account of the widespread turning to the courts in America as a reaction to the decline of popular politics. As the title suggests, the book recounts the different understandings of what has constituted desirable roles for individuals in public life at different periods in the history of the United States. The colonial period was associated with a citizenship founded on social hierarchy; the nineteenth century emphasized mass political participation; the Progressive Era's ideal was the informed citizen. What is most relevant for our purposes is Schudson's assertion that the latest era is that of the "rights-regarding citizen." In this depiction, the decline in voting, the lack of trust in government, and the dissatisfaction with popular politics are indicators not of the enervation of public life but, rather, of its transformation; "rights and rights-consciousness have become the continuous incitements to citizenship in our time."[2]

Schudson's book is important for many reasons, and I return to a discussion of it in Chapter 2. Its message jolted me. Yes, it was a depiction of the citizen in America – and maybe not an accurate assessment for even that society. Still, what does it mean for the idea of the citizen to be bound up in rights claiming? How does such a concept of the citizen actually work in terms of the necessary adjustments, modifications, and trade-offs that societies inevitably face as they navigate the complex world of the twenty-first century?

Rights are a good and noble thing. Yet, whether a society should so immerse itself in rights and in going to court that the concept of citizenship, the very notion of what constitutes public life, becomes embodied in rights-regarding individuals, is a question that needs urgent attention. After much study and writing a very long book, I concluded that such discussion probably comes too late for American society – its commitment to courts is just too strong.[3] A society that believes an effective response to crime is tort suits against gun manufacturers has likely gone too far down the litigation path.

My strong reaction to Schudson's book prompted me to contemplate to what extent his account was applicable to Canada. Is our society being transported on the "wing of rights"?[4] Has "rights-consciousness place[d] the courtroom along-side the polling place in the practice of public life"?[5] My drive to answer these questions was made more intense because, about ten years previously, I had written a book warning of over-reliance on litigation in tackling the hard questions faced by Canadian society.[6] Schudson's eloquent and disturbing depictions compelled me to look at what had happened to Canada in the last decades of the twentieth century and what is occurring as the new century unfolds.

This book's title reflects its focus on what constitutes the "good citizen" in a rapidly changing Canadian society. The title also underscores a central argument of this book: that the founding words of this society regarding "peace, order, and good government" are goals that are still critical in the life of the "good citizen" in this country.[7] *Good Government? Good Citizens?* is written by a political moderate, one who believes that good public goods are foundational for civic society.

A number of significant institutional changes have occurred in Canada over the last few decades. There is no doubt that a turning to litigation and an assertion of rights in courts, as well as in the legislatures, the media, and the streets, have been an important part of the transformation of this society. A comparative study has characterized litigation and related developments under the *Charter* as "Canada's Dramatic Rights Revolution."[8] Judges are asked to respond to complex issues even as their stature in the eyes of the public reaches new heights. But there have been other powerful forces at work that have fundamentally altered Canadian society.

The roles not only of courts but also of politics and of markets have been transformed and have changed the concept of the individual and her place in society. Technology, particularly the communications revolution, has spelled the "death of distance." There are boasts about technological capacities, from turning knowledge into an inexhaustible resource to enabling direct democracy.[9] Representative democracy is suffering a loss of confidence in many countries. Canada has its own tale of dishevelment of popular politics. In 2002 almost 70 percent of those who were asked agreed that government in this country is "corrupt."[10] This spurning of politics and its agents is establishing the citizen as an exerciser of choice in the marketplace and as a bearer of rights against government.

The state is now suspect – as a mangler of free markets and as a denier of constitutionalized rights. Courts and markets have overtaken representative politics and government in the determination of many fundamental choices for society. Courts and markets advance in an uneasy alliance. Their core functions are, of course, different: courts focus on the creation of rights; markets on the creation of wealth. Yet, both can deliver the same fundamental message: Government can't be trusted.

How has Canadian society actually been transformed? Is the state truly in retreat? Do individuals, in fact, have a fundamentally altered sense of their relationship to the government and to each other? Have courts and markets supplanted representative politics regarding the expression of basic values? Must judicialized protection of human rights and minority interests mean a diminished concern for the common good on the part of representative politics? To what extent should markets and representative politics maintain a role in the protection of human rights and minority interests? Will popular politics ever hold the public trust again?

Good Government? Good Citizens? responds to these questions. It does so by examining the altered roles of courts, politics, and markets over the last two decades. It evaluates the roles of these three institutions. It then examines a number of areas in order to gauge the extent of the evidence of changes that have occurred because of these altering roles. There are chapters on the First Peoples, cyberspace, education, and an ageing Canada. The book concludes with reflections on the "good citizen" at the dawning of the new century.

Good Government? Good Citizens? does not assert that the judges are primarily responsible for the fundamental issues we face as a society, that our quandaries can simply be attributed to "rights talk." The problem is not that we have a *Charter* and an enlarged role for the judiciary. The dilemma that confronts us is that we have the *Charter,* greater judicial power, and more rights talk at the same time as we have expanding markets and a marked decline in faith in representative politics' capacity to forge the common good.

Consider the First Peoples (discussed in detail in Chapter 5). Three main positions are advanced regarding Aboriginals. First, there are those who urge assimilation: both Aboriginals and the rest of the country would be best served by the First Peoples being treated essentially the same as other citizens.[11] They ought to be integrated into mainstream society. Aboriginals are expected to cease their demands for special treatment and recognize the futility of dreams of a separate, land-based economy. They should take their place in Canada's globalizing market economy.

Second, there are those who view First Peoples as primarily belonging to nations: the governments of Canada should recognize the status of Natives by honouring treaties, affirming constitutional rights, and conferring other legal entitlements.[12] Their hope is that courts and legislatures will recognize rights guaranteeing Aboriginals' claims to nation status and to necessary remedial measures.

Third, in between these two positions, are those who see the First Peoples as "citizens plus": Aboriginals are citizens of this society; their historical mistreatment and the horrible conditions of life experienced by many Aboriginals justify programs of support intended to enable First Peoples to take their full place in this country.[13] This view is based on the belief that representative politics can reflect understandings of the good citizen.

What will these three, largely irreconcilable positions lead to in the initial decades of this century?

There is a role for courts, for markets, and for cyberspace in the making of the good citizen. Markets are necessary to create wealth; courts, to protect fundamental freedoms; and the Internet, to exploit knowledge as the inexhaustible resource. The problem is with the "myth of exit." The market, courts, and cyberspace are touted as offering alternatives that can be turned to as the population resiles from dishevelled politics. Yet, for most people, these alternatives do not respond to many important issues in their daily lives. Education is a public good that must be supplied by representative politics and its agencies (an issue I discuss in Chapter 7). Claims that courts, markets, or technology can do this are corrosive fables.

Consider the Internet, a revolutionary development that has become widely available over the last decade (see Chapter 6). Despite its origins in government-sponsored research, the Net is now being propelled largely by the market.[14] Because of its facility in linking users directly, the Internet can result in disintermediation – the reduction or elimination of agents.[15] One of the claims made on behalf of cyberspace is that it will result in direct democracy: citizens will no longer be dependent on politicians to forge and implement policy.[16]

Even enthusiastic boosters of the communications revolution admit that its claims about direct democracy are unlikely to be fully realized, and they acknowledge the harms that could occur if they did.[17] Yet, even more modest forms of disintermediation and other effects of the Internet pose problems for representative politics.[18] The greatest danger may be not that they offer a real alternative to deliberative politics but that they *seem* to. Such apparitions can lure people farther away from a representative politics that is already in tatters.

A vibrant role for politics with a reinvigorated sense of its representative capacity and its ability to forge consensus is essential. Yet, renewing politics is not an easy task.[19] There are two important points of departure. One is recognizing the limits of the judicial role and that "rights are not enough."[20] A rights activist has recently charged that "the critique of judicial activism in Canada ... is the expression of deep anguish by the stakeholders of a world view in demise."[21] I will talk a great deal about "judicial activism" in a number of places in this book. But it is the phrase "world view in demise" that I found striking – and disturbingly ambiguous. Which world view?

The world view in which only a handful of people were politically empowered and in which many – women, Aboriginals, the disabled, and others – were marginalized, was one that needed to go. It is little wonder that rights claiming should have focused on such exclusion. Yet, for many, another world view, the one that promoted a temperate politics in Canada in order to produce an internationally recognized record for respect for human rights, universal health care, and a commitment to achieving excellent public education, basic income entitlement, and a stewardship of the environment, needs to be reinvigorated. If it is that world view that is being referred to as "in demise," some of us will plead guilty to an "expression of deep anguish." The angst is that judicial activism and extravagant rights claiming in the courts, legislatures, media, and streets have rightly helped to banish the former world view even as they have enervated the latter one.

The other point of departure for attaining a vibrant role for representative politics and proactive government must be a widespread insistence that markets cannot be hostile to shared entitlements such as excellent health care, quality education, an adequate social safety net, a healthy environment, and vigorous protection of human rights. Wealth creation and governments that provide a wide range of services are not inevitably opposed.[22] The market is essential. It creates the wealth that is a reward for individual achievement and that is a precondition for the provision of good public goods. It is the market triumphant, with its relentless demands to be the sorter and distributor of everything, that needs to be resisted.

Good citizens forging good government and relying on it should be a central goal of Canadian society at the beginning of the new century. This will not be easily accomplished. A critical place to begin is to acknowledge that representative politics still has a vital role to play in our lives. Lives that are about more than rights bearing and consuming.

PART 1
The Society That Was

1 Before the Transformation

Erna Paris's award-winning book *Long Shadows* is a study of "the ways that those happenings we call history can be shaped by selection or manipulation."[1] The book underscores the importance of a society remembering its past as it faces its future. *Long Shadows* does not address this nation's story. Paris chose to explore other societies and their pasts. Nevertheless, she reminds Canadians that "when it comes to historical memory we have no shortage of material."[2]

To understand the effects that the changing role of courts, markets, and politics is producing, one must first have an appreciation of Canada before such transformations. In our rush to grapple with the changes that are all about us, we need to engage historical memory, to remember the society that was. Representative politics is now in disarray. We are in danger of forgetting its many past achievements as we are exhorted to exit from popular politics and embrace other mechanisms for fundamental decision making, such as courts and markets.

There is no precise point of demarcation, no sudden break with the past. However, three events occurred in the 1980s and 1990s that make those decades a watershed. The first was the entrenchment of the *Charter of Rights and Freedoms*. This document enhanced the power of the courts to nullify legislation. It also ushered in an era of "rights talk" not only in the courts but also in the media and on the streets. The second was the intensification of free trade. There have always been debates about trade policies and their promotion. Canada took giant steps to liberalize the exchange of goods and services, including becoming part of NAFTA (and the earlier FTA). Such agreements, and their connections to the broader forces of globalization, promote commerce beyond the nation's borders. These activities produce a range of outcomes that have effects on Canadian society. Beyond such effects, NAFTA has become a lightning rod symbolizing the embrace of market forces as the distributor of wealth and the promoter of individual choice and responsibility.

The third was the failure of the Meech Lake and Charlottetown accords. These aborted attempts to reformulate federal and provincial powers damaged the belief in the capacity of representative politics to find solutions to complex issues through negotiation and compromise.

These three events and their implications in transforming Canada are addressed in Part 2 of this book. This chapter will canvass Canada's defining attributes before such fundamental changes to our nation. Often these attributes were underscored by comparing this society with that of America. The influence of such attributes and the comparisons with the United States are not free of controversy. Still, in 1975, a leading political scientist contrasted us with the Americans and their affiliation with "self evident principles and universal rights." He described our political and legal thought as "pragmatic and empirical"; the approach "which is truest to our experience ... is that of Edmund Burke, not John Locke."[3] The Burkean ideas of order, responsibility, and gradual change consistent with working out of community needs is concisely reflected in important words of our founding document. The American Declaration of Independence claims for the individual "life, liberty and the pursuit of happiness." In contrast, section 91 of our *Constitution Act, 1867,* admonishes the powers that be to strive for "peace, order, and good government." Citizens were to be involved in a complicated relationship with government. Their rights, liberties, and happiness, however comprehended, did not stand apart from the state but were linked to it. They were to be "good citizens" enjoying "good government."

Good Citizens? Good Government?

What attributes of this society were the foundation of "good government"? of "good citizens"? Canada was, since its beginnings, a society ever in search of itself.[4] There was a mixture of political ideologies, tensions between the regions and Central Canada, clashes between the founding languages and cultures, and a long struggle for recognition by the First Peoples. It was a society that tolerated concentration of wealth, lacked economic competition, and had a need for elitism and an attraction to authoritarianism.

Yet, it was a society that showed compassion for its less fortunate members and that committed itself to the creation of public goods for its citizens – education, a social safety net, and universal health care among them. In the 1990s, the UN Development Program began to rank 160 countries in terms of life span, literacy, educational and health care systems, and absence of discrimination and violent crime. Canada has consistently been at the top. That achievement did not occur suddenly. It was the product of a long history using representative politics to build the society. It was "a dance of adjustment":[5] much questioning, many foibles, a search for shared goals. "Good government" for "good citizens"?

Mixed Ideology

Canada began to form when Americans took to arms against Great Britain. The United States was said to be Whig, classically liberal with its attendant antistatism, populism, egalitarianism, voluntary religions, and veneration of individualism. Canada, outside of Quebec, reflected the values of Toryism, with its statism, deference to authority, curbing of the individual, and hierarchical religions.[6]

These differences were not as extreme as they are sometimes drawn.[7] Nevertheless, comparisons with the United States are an important clue to how Canada sought its identity. Margaret Atwood put it, graphically, if pathologically: "If the national mental illness of the United States is megalomania, that of Canada is paranoid schizophrenia"[8] and Seymour Martin Lipset observed that "Much of what Canadian intellectuals, both scholars and creative artists, write about their own country is presented in a comparative context – that is, with reference to the nation to the south. They frequently seek to describe what Canada is about by stressing what it is not: the United States."[9]

It has been argued that overseas European societies, including both the United States and Canada, were in the main settled by the middle class and so were "fragment cultures" with neither the aristocracy nor the peasantry of Europe. Hartz noted the presence of Toryism in Canada as a reaction to the American Revolution. He contended, however, that the countries were far more united in their similarities and the true differentiation was as against the older European societies.[10]

In contrast, Horowitz insisted that liberal ideology in Canada did not completely dominate.[11] He found in Canada the presence of Tory and socialist ideas that allowed for differences in ideology. This combination was closer to that of the European countries, which have accommodated liberalism while retaining these other ideologies.[12] In a famous quote, he maintained that "here Locke is not the one true god; he must tolerate lesser tory and socialist deities at his side."[13] This basic assertion of mixed ideology made us more committed "to collective provision"[14] – again, especially when compared with the United States. Such assertions were by no means beyond controversy.[15] Yet, what may have been critical was the insistence that while "Canadian practice may be not as much better as many of us believe ... the important point is that this is seen as a difference worth preserving."[16]

Two important consequences for Canada came from this collectivist strain, fed by both the left and the right. First, it gave the political terrain a left of centre, communitarian cast. All political parties supported government intervention and programs to a marked degree, whether that involved the railway and canal building of the nineteenth century or public enterprises such as the CBC, Air Canada, Ontario Hydro, and Petro-Canada. There was broad-based political support for the elaborate network of social and welfare programs of the twentieth century. The building of a system of health care providing universal access was long and difficult. The health care structure that we now know took almost forty years to establish from its limited beginnings in one province. It is a story of turbulence, the overcoming of elite and self-interested opposition, jerky adjustments between the federal and provincial governments, and many compromises: representative politics at its best, flawed though it might be.[17]

Second, no strong right-wing political party (with the possible exception of the Social Credit in British Columbia) ever developed in Canada up to the 1980s.[18] This is not to say that strains of business liberalism, as described above, are not found in the Liberals and Progressive Conservatives. The impulse to deregulate, celebrate the market, and proclaim the rights of property and contract was found repeatedly throughout Canadian history. And when combined with Tory hierarchy and elitism, it produced a tolerance for privilege and inequality that, at times, was simply undemocratic, whether found in the Family Compact or the privileges of the Toronto establishment.[19]

Yet, it was ideological diversity that was depended on, sometimes to a fault, to forge solutions to the many challenges of the twentieth century: "Canada was in its origins and is still a country of rich ideological diversity ... the explicit expression and acknowledgement of these differences gives our country a much greater chance to resolve the question of the kind of social life we wish to share as fellow citizens."[20]

Identity and Nationalism

Canada's expression of nationalism was as linked to a search to define itself as to anything else. One view saw our disappearance, as we merged with the United States, as inevitable. Economic integration first, then political integration over time.[21] Another saw the uncertainty and tentativeness of the country as part of what it could be: "Canada was from its depths experimental and conditional."[22]

Nationalism attempted to portray the country as something separate from the United States.[23] This differentiation from the giant to the south found expression in many places, including literature. The vast unpopulated territory of Canada and the coming to grips with it, particularly as a northern country, became a frequent theme.[24] Frye's imposition of the natural world on the Canadian psyche,[25] Atwood's theme of survival,[26] and Moss's exploration of isolation through what he calls the "geophysical imagination"[27] all pushed us to consider whether "any other national consciousness has had so large an amount of the unknown, the unrealized, the humanly undigestable, so built into it."[28]

Canada was compared with other countries of the north sharing such characteristics as "reticence, pragmatism, wariness of public display" and social democratic liberalism.[29] Robertson Davies, speaking directly about Canadian literature and the influence of the North on it, characterized writing in this country as being more closely connected with Scandinavian countries than with America: "I like to think that Canada's greatest writers are Ibsen and Chekhov [he said, laughing]. When I go to Scandinavia and step off the plane, I ask myself if I've really left home. There is that very powerful sunlight and the wind-torn pine trees. The real Canadian is a Northerner. I'm a great believer in the influence of the climate and the land in plays and novels."[30]

In the economic arena, nationalism spurred government intervention to foster investment and develop resources for Canadians. The establishment of the Canada Development Corporation (1971), the Foreign Investment Review Agency (1973), and the National Energy Program (1980) were prominent endeavours. The 1970s and 1980s also saw the intensifying of nationalism in social and cultural matters. The enhancement of the power of the Canadian Radio-television and Telecommunications Commission (CRTC) to control broadcasting in terms of its ownership and content, measures to control domination of universities by foreign academics, and the regulation of the publishing industry to control foreign content and to stimulate works by Canadians are but some examples of this intensification.

However, the rise of Mulroney's Progressive Conservatives, their antagonism to government intervention in general, and their victory concerning free trade with the United States in the 1980s challenged these impulses of economic and other forms of nationalism. Many of these programs would be dismantled.[31] The continuation of Canada as a separate country would resurface as an issue as the twentieth century ended.

The Economy and the Government

From the railroad and nation-building programs of John A. Macdonald[32] to the Macdonald Commission, which reported in 1985,[33] there was a government presence in the economy. It has been contended that Canadian elites employing the state so broadly in economic issues was actually the source of Tory ideology, and not the reverse.[34] A related aspect was that the Canadian economy was so resource-dependent. A land rich in resources has a source of wealth that individuals can do very little to alter.[35] As a result, there was an anti-risk-taking ethos, compounded by the massive amount of foreign ownership:[36] "We are not an entrepreneurial country and never have been ... there is a feeling in the Canadian establishment that it is a little bit vulgar to go after things too hard."[37]

Further, whether cause or effect, there was tolerance for concentration of wealth. For much of the twentieth century, there were only six Canadian chartered banks, in contrast to something like fifteen thousand in the United States. In the early 1980s, only nine families controlled 46 percent of the shares of the companies on the Toronto Stock Exchange. In the United States, the one hundred largest companies controlled only 15 percent of the total, nonfinancial, industrial assets; in Canada, the hundred largest controlled 34 percent.[38] Moreover, there was not the popular hostility to this concentration, despite the strength of unions and left-wing groups. In opinion polls during the 1980s, more Americans than Canadians (by about a 10 percent margin) believed that "many of our largest companies ought to be broken up into smaller concerns."[39] These and other factors led to the characterization of Canadian society as one of "economic passivity."[40]

A 1982 study revealed that, of the leading twenty-five financial institutions, nine were federally owned or controlled.[41] On a percentage basis, Canadian subsidies to business and employment in public enterprise during the 1970s were each five times that of those in the United States. The Canadian subsidies just referred to were below the norm for members of the Organisation for Economic Co-operation and Development (OECD).[42] Nonetheless, governments' relationship with leading business figures was pronounced: "most of Canada's most successful businessmen have been those who've figured out how to get what they want out of government; it was said of former Dome Petroleum chairman Jack Gallagher 'he did his best exploration in Ottawa.'"[43]

At the same time, this image of the Canadian economy as bureaucratic, concentrated, foreign-owned, and heavily dependent on government compared with America's must be tempered.[44] First, Canadians were becoming more entrepreneurial in the 1970s and 1980s. Canadians' investment in the United States in those decades grew extensively: "Although Canada is one-tenth the size of the United States in population, the ratio, in absolute terms of American investment in the north to Canadian investment in the south decreased from five to one in the early 1970's to three to two as of the early 1980's to par or above by the latter years of the decade. More Canadian capital is moving to the United States than is being invested by Americans in Canada."[45]

Canadians were also reclaiming ownership of corporations. Among all nonfinancial companies in Canada, the value of assets under foreign control decreased from 36 percent in 1970 to 26 percent in 1981; in manufacturing, the decline was from 58 percent in 1970 to 41 percent in 1983.[46]

Second, despite governmental presence in enterprise, Canada regulated the economy less than did the United States. America was more committed than Canada was to policies "to reduce pollution, to help preserve scarce environmental resources, and to deal with a range of related concerns."[47] For the regulation that existed, those enforcing it in Canada had more discretion. Regulation in Canada "tends to trust the public service to use its expert judgment to protect legitimate interests"; in contrast, that in America is "usually public, contentious and combative, with stricter and less discretionary enforcement."[48]

The most blatant absence of regulation of the economy concerned competition policy. Several incarnations of anticombines legislation existed over the decades. However, they were weak and sporadically enforced; the few litigated cases received a hostile reception in the courts. I return to this issue of lack of competition later in the chapter.

Deference

Before the 1980s, Canadian society had a strong element of elitism and hierarchy.[49] This attitude assumed that stratification in society was the inevitable result of some having greater endowments than others. Such hierarchy was said to be a good thing. It allowed those best able to lead to do so.[50] When aligned with a collectivist sense, it meant that those who rule should do so for the public good and should exercise their power as a trust. In exchange, there was to be a strong deference to this authority.[51]

The unification of the colonies in British North America was brought about by conservatives who were Empire oriented. They feared American expansion. They were opposed to reform-minded "pro-American" frontier settlers who favoured local autonomy. A strong central government, in Canada, was empowered to disallow provincial laws. The opening of the Canadian frontier was achieved with caution in contrast to America and its Wild West: "it was the established tradition of British North America that the power of civil authority should operate well in advance of the spread of settlement."[52]

Authoritarian modes of thinking in Canada have also been traced to religion. Ecclesiastical traditions in Canada bolstered values of elitism and order. A powerful bond existed at one time between church and state in Canada; religious development was less subject to fundamentalism and experimentalism, particularly compared with the United States. Thus, interdependent, conservative elements could be found at the pinnacle of class, church, and political structures.[53]

These elitist and hierarchical values instilled in our society had implications for civil liberties. These values chilled the development of a populism that produced the political intolerance associated with McCarthyism, Coughlinism, and the Ku Klux Klan in the United States. Yet, this comparative political tolerance also resulted in less freedom: "examination of the American community ... would probably reveal that, in spite of witch hunts in that country, the people of the United States enjoy in fact a much greater degree of freedom than do the people of Canada."[54] At the same time, tolerance was often not extended to minorities. Discrimination was a sorry legacy for too much of Canadian history.[55]

The Liberal government invoked the *War Measures Act* during the FLQ crisis in 1970. There was substantial public support for this action, though it appeared, even then, to be unjustified in light of the overwhelming majority in Quebec disavowing violence.[56] The *War Measures Act* was ultimately repealed. Yet, as late as 1989, a poll indicated that more Americans than Canadians – 56 versus 49 percent – opposed the federal government's capacity to "remove all civil rights" during "times of crisis." This difference increased when the comparison was confined to Americans and anglophone Canadians. Of French Canadians, 67 percent were opposed, but such opposition shrank to 45 percent among anglophones.[57]

The West, the East, and Central Canada

Vast and sprawling, with tracts of land cold and forbidding for much of the year, and settled by a ribbon of population stretched from coast to coast, this country's mass had a great influence on what we became. Ontario and Quebec may have had much that separated them, but they were united in viewing themselves as the heartland, the core that regarded itself as the focus of the nation. The rest of Canada was the hinterland that had to be coordinated – and dominated – when necessary. Regionalism in Canada defied a modern trend toward greater centralization.[58] In fact, change in this country led to a more robust regionalism in Canada.[59] By the 1980s this country was more decentralized than any other industrialized nation; since the 1960s there was a clear trend to such decentralization, as measured by spending and tax shares.[60] Much of this decentralization was related to a sense of regional identity and a wariness that the federal government too easily identified the national interest with that of Central Canada: Quebec and Ontario. The diversity among the various regions is an important factor in explaining the dominance of Quebec and Ontario.

Such differences were important in the Atlantic provinces. The French and English of New Brunswick were located in different economic and geographic segments; Cape Breton and the remainder of Nova Scotia had to deal with deep and long-standing divisions.[61] As well, there were substantial economic variations among the four Atlantic provinces. Central Canada dominating the economy became a well-developed theme in this region. The contention was that Atlantic Canada's poor economy was not a consequence of the region's lack of valuable natural resources nor of its geography.[62] In the nineteenth century there were industries that prospered in Atlantic Canada, but Confederation brought the exertion of control by Central Canada, and the Depression resulted in the collapse not only of industry but of the important trades of forestry and fishing.

The federal government from the early 1960s onward established programs to stimulate the economy, for example, the Agricultural Rehabilitation and Development Agency (1961) to the Atlantic Canada Opportunities Agency (1987). The failure of such programs to achieve lasting economic improvement was often attributed to federal governments acceding to pressures to provide like funding to all other regions, even Ontario and Quebec.[63] Other criticisms targeted the inappropriateness of such programs, their inefficiency, and their inadequate funding. A too typical Atlantic province response was to react with daring but implausible schemes, such as New Brunswick's Bricklin car.

Although Yukon and the Northwest Territories comprise about 40 percent of this country's land mass, into the 1980s, only about eighty thousand people lived there.[64] However, by the 1970s there was an assertion that the North was not just a repository of resources but, rather, a home, however large and foreboding, to the Inuit, Indians, and whites. This assertion produced a "no development" reaction. In the 1980s, some need for – and benefit from – development was acknowledged. The focus was on enterprises that minimized the effect on the way of life of those who had a long-standing relationship with the North. Training, employment opportunities, and joint ventures carried the potential for Native peoples to enjoy the tangible benefits from such projects.[65]

British Columbia is part of the "West" – geographically and in terms of its resentment of Central Canada. And yet, it is different from the three Prairie provinces. It has relied on mining and lumbering rather than wheat farming as its base industry, and its economy has been tied to large corporations from Central Canada and the United States. In the 1970s it was argued that British Columbia differed in two fundamental ways: it was part of the Pacific Rim, and an embrace of the "new right" ideology had taken hold.[66] The electorate was often polarized, creating swings in support between the right-wing Social Credit Party and the left-wing NDP.[67]

Although British Columbia was linked as part of the "West," the core of that sense of regionalism belonged to the three Prairie provinces, where alienation waxed and waned even as the economy gyrated in boom and bust. Financial stability and a secure share of political power were possible but never securely grasped; the course of life was determined elsewhere.[68]

The economic domination of the West by the centre was buttressed by political rule. In 1905, Alberta and Saskatchewan became provinces. Yet, the boundaries were those designed by federal politicians. Before the Prairie provinces obtained control of natural resources in 1930, the Dominion's Department of the Interior shaped settlement and development. It was against legislation of western provinces that the federal government most frequently used its powers of disallowance.[69]

Central Canada controlled the West through classic mercantilism: the hinterland is confined to production of staple products exported from it in a raw or semi-finished state; it is required to buy the manufactured goods of the heartland; its capital development is controlled by institutions of the heartland; and so forth.[70] A provocative example of such control was the ill-fated National Energy Program, a major source of alienation in the 1980s. In Central Canada, cultural duality became the linchpin; other concerns needed to be suspended until a firm balance was struck between the French and English. To the West, such claims were destructive of the Confederation they presumed to sustain.[71] Instead, there was growing demand in the Prairies that national powers be exercised in ways conducive to western interests.[72]

Quebec and the Rest of Canada

Quebec and its continuance within Canada at times brought the nation to a precipice. It was part of the Central Canada that the rest of the country resented. At the same time, it was different from all the rest of Canada because of its linguistic, political, and cultural heritage. The matter was further complicated because English Canada was increasingly heterogeneous in its composition culturally, tone of skin, and even linguistically. Especially in the West, many settlers' first language was not English; often it was a language of Eastern Europe. In the 1970s and 1980s there was a large influx of immigration from Third World countries, particularly to large urban areas.[73] In English Canada, multiculturalism became a separate force in the society; it was the official policy of the federal government since the 1970s.[74]

Preserving the French identity and yet having Quebec coexist with the English became the federal government's dual and often contradictory mission. By the 1830s, Lord Durham's solution to the isolationist French was to have them disappear through assimilation. His vehicle for this was legislative union of the two Canadas. Such equality was intended to swallow the French: the English of Upper Canada would join with the English minority of Lower Canada to frustrate the furtherance of the goals of the French majority of Lower Canada. But such a simple solution was not to succeed; the French were far more cohesive than the English.[75]

This French-English duality in government was the premise for Confederation negotiations. Many of the Fathers of Confederation would have preferred a unitary government, but to the French-Canadians such an arrangement was unacceptable.[76] Aspects in which the two groups differed most were assigned to provincial authority.[77] Still other sections of the *Constitution Act, 1867*, related to cultural-linguistic duality.[78] Quebec and the rest of Canada settled into a coexistence, the framework of which endured for almost one hundred years, until the beginning of the 1960s. There was strife concerning the treatment of French-Catholic minorities outside Quebec and over external affairs where the English prevailed. These battles made Quebec a prominent defender of provincial rights.[79] Yet, for a number of reasons, French-English relations were stable during this long period.[80]

The 1960s and Quebec's Quiet Revolution witnessed the agreement coming apart. The established institutions were ill-suited to a changing, industrializing North America; the Catholic Church as the focal point of society was weakening. The federal government respected less and less federal-provincial boundaries of legislative action, and entered into areas initially reserved for local governance. The Quiet Revolution drastically altered the bases of the stabilized relationship between the rest of Canada and Quebec.[81]

The instability became apparent in a number of ways. First, by the 1960s, the government in Ottawa had invaded areas that were initially used by Quebec to foster the francophone culture. Conversely, Quebec governments came to see survival as dependent on the province's control of its own economic development. Second, there was a breakdown in institutional segregation. The new Quebec middle class that had arisen in response to urbanization and industrialization had an orientation that was democratic, secular, and materialistic. Third, antistatism ended. The emerging middle class came to see the state as a powerful means for transforming Quebec. The church's grip (especially in welfare, education, and health issues) was broken as the governmental sector exerted its influence. Fourth, elite accommodation of French-English relations became complicated. Alternatives from cooperative federalism to revolutionary separatism were vigorously debated. Lastly, the concept of a fundamental compact broke down. The prevailing attitude became that Quebec had failed to have the rest of Canada accept the compact theory of two founding, separate nations; thus, the province should distance itself from the theory and achieve its goals by other means.

Canada now had two modernized linguistic communities. The federal government pursued the recommendations of the Royal Commission on Bilingualism and Biculturalism. Whatever results such efforts produced, they did awaken the antagonism of the English, particularly in the West, against the French.[82]

Meanwhile, the primary political vehicle for the new middle class so closely related to the state was the Parti Québécois (PQ). The coming to power of the PQ in 1976 had much to do with the magnetism of René Lévesque and his ability to gather support from those who did not support independence. Yet, the defeat of the plebiscite, the disenchantment with the governing of the PQ, the resignation and subsequent death of Lévesque, and the flaccid term of leadership of Pierre-Marc Johnson all suggested the decline of that party. The election in 1985 of the resurrected Bourassa suggested a mandate to roll back the Quebec state to accommodate the French and English business elite. Yet, the indépendantiste project was not spent.[83] It would be part of the volatile mix of Canadian society in the late 1980s and 1990s.

Politics, Markets, and Courts

The defining elements of Canadian society played out in complex ways. From the country's birth until the 1980s, the watchwords were "peace, order, and good government." That phrase, taken from section 91 of the *Constitution Act, 1867*, reflected a pact: individuals acknowledged the authority of government in exchange for maintenance of a civil society in which the state was expected to play a wide-ranging role. Canada was a nation that showed compassion for its less fortunate members, constructed a system of universal health care and many other social programs, and shared resources among its regions. It struggled to recognize the distinctive aspects of the French even as it insisted that Quebec was to have the same status in Confederation as the other provinces. It had an international reputation for respecting human rights – subject to dark exceptions. It had a liking for elitism, an attraction to authoritarianism, and a lack of economic competition. It was a society without constitutional protection of rights; the legislature was the ultimate source of law. Women, the disabled, Aboriginals, gays and lesbians, among others, were mostly excluded from power. This complicated arrangement was manifested in politics, markets, and courts.

Politics – and the Growth of Government

In that society, representative politics held sway. There was no entrenched bill of rights empowering courts to bound legislative action. The market had an important role, but one which accepted (and sometimes sought) a notable governmental presence in many areas. By the end of the Second World War, social Keynesianism, with its role for government in many aspects of the economy, became the prevailing orthodoxy.[84]

If representative politics was central, so too were its agents. The twentieth century witnessed in Canada and other Western nations a massive growth in regulation. This increase in governmental activity was often accomplished through various agencies, commissions, and tribunals. A study done in the late 1970s that focused only on permanent agencies (thus excluding specifically appointed commissions, public inquiries, and so on) reported that, by that decade, more than 640 government agencies existed in Canada. A survey of similar bodies in Ontario also done in the late 1970s identified thirty-six regulatory bodies, forty-four licensing appeal tribunals, eight compensation boards, nineteen arbitral agencies, and ninety-five advisory boards.[85]

Such growth often led to complex and contradictory demands: "the voices which complain about the overpowering anonymity, control, and impenetrability of bureaucracy are often the same as those demanding the regulations, the controls, and the productivity which are the daily concerns of bureaucracy."[86] Nevertheless, on the whole, such increases were received more positively in this country than expansions in the United States. Generally, commentators in America were skeptical of any augmentation of administrative powers. Such questioning was consistent with the liberal philosophy of minimalism, an underpinning of that society. Canadian scholarship, focused on the extent and cause of the growth of government, was "generally characterized by a much more sympathetic attitude towards governmental intrusions in society."[87]

At one level, such openness to regulation is explained by the pragmatism for which Canadians were famed.[88] There were jobs to do and institutions to build, and if governments could accomplish the goals, so be it; "no Delphic phrases and fundamental philosophies about government preoccupy our thoughts on the nature of governmental institutions."[89] That openness can also be explained by the mix of ideologies discussed above. Government intervention was consistent with both Tory and socialist notions of the legitimacy of restraint of the individual and the use of government to achieve common ends. Pragmatism reflected a much more complex set of ideas about how society ought to function than that depicted by the minimalist state of liberalism, particularly as manifested in the United States.

In addition, government played a vital role in nation building: "the role of the state in the economic life of Canada is really the modern history of Canada."[90] To make the country coalesce, government had to exert a strong influence from the start. Because of the vastness of the subcontinent, the imperial sweep of settlement after 1867, and the speedy reaction to industrialization, government was forced to and encouraged to act.[91] Other countries allowed the administrative state to develop as a brake on the rapacious aspects of capitalism. In Canada, this factor was present also but joined with the need to make a nation.[92] Ideology was not seen as bounding the state in the achievement of that purpose; "in a period where laissez-faire policies were at their peak of respectability, the Canadian attitude to the question of public versus private enterprise was purely pragmatic. In the vital field of railway transportation there was not generally any clear view on the merits of public versus private action so long as the railways were actually built."[93]

For America, regulation performed, at bottom, a policing role guaranteeing that economic activity reflected competitive market conditions. The usefulness of regulation was a function of it achieving efficiency.[94] Not so for us. Regulation and its activity were largely traced to what was called the "three Ps": policing, promoting, and planning, and all this mostly in aid of constructing the country.[95] Freight rates and airfares were set at least partly to foster national unity. Agricultural marketing boards were created in a deliberate attempt to transfer income from consumers to producers.[96] In performing such functions, Canadian agencies, unlike many of their American counterparts, were less "independent." They were, at least in part, much more controlled by executive action, reflecting the fact that they were meant to carry out these larger governmental policies: "the instrumental and, indeed, beneficent role of bureaucracy as the core of modern government is a theme which is well developed in the literature of public policy and administration."[97]

But a large role for government and its agencies costs money. The accumulated public debt in the 1970s and beyond was a main factor in transforming representative politics. By the 1980s, all parties were decrying various aspects of the sad state of governmental finances and the troubled economy that was experiencing both high rates of inflation and unemployment. The pact supporting "social Keynesianism" had broken down.[98] The administrative state and the public goals it enhanced would soon become targets in the austerity scramble.

Markets and Timid Competition

A substantial presence of the government in the economy, a tolerance for large entities, acceptance of concentration of wealth, and resource-dependent industries that were not innovative, made for an enfeebled market. The vigour of capitalism in producing wealth for the entire society may have been saluted; the reality was often otherwise. Canada's attitude to competition was indicative of the actual state of the market in this society.

Competition is the engine that drives free markets. But unleashing competition and letting it work its economic wonders were often not part of the Canadian way. Political reticence, acceding to strong opposition to reform from the business community, resulted in law and policy that was "a national joke ... a saga of delays and procrastination."[99] As a result, producers' interests often dominated those of consumers, leading to high tariffs, production inefficiencies, and extensive foreign ownership.[100]

They may have had different reasons for their positions, but neither the Liberals nor the Conservatives demonstrated enthusiasm for a strong anti-combines policy.[101] At mid-twentieth century, the Liberal government was going out of its way to reassure influential financial interests: "the deferential tone used by King and others defending [weak] anti-combines legislation indicated that the business community had little to fear."[102] The administration of the relevant legislation was poorly funded and understaffed; rigorous enforcement was impossible. The courts demonstrated attitudes similar to those of the politicians. Whether through creating and interpreting their own common law rules,[103] or bounding the federal power by limiting it to criminal sanctions as a matter of constitutionalism,[104] or blunting provisions addressing conspiracies to restrict competition,[105] judges almost always rendered decisions which deflected whatever attempts were made by the politicians to create vigorous anticombines policies. The situation in America, with its vigorous antitrust laws and courts that were receptive to such policies, was in marked contrast. Attacks on mergers and large corporations, the enthusiasm of the judiciary for antitrust, and the heavy use of the private court action all served to effectively distinguish the United States from this country in terms of attitudes toward competition.[106]

W.T. Stanbury, a prominent student of competition law, writing in the 1970s, summarized our attitudes: "There does not exist in Canada any fundamental belief in the virtues of competition as the method of allocating scarce resources and of diffusing economic and political power."[107] There was some limited reform in that decade.[108] Nonetheless, it was said that there is "no larger blot on the public policy record than our failure to come to terms with competition policy."[109] A national study in the late 1980s came to similar conclusions. It charged that, among such problems was the high concentration of foreign-controlled firms that perform little research and development or sophisticated production in Canada.[110]

Those supporting a vigorous economy increasingly came to the view that the best way to bolster the market was to expose Canada to global forces.

More energy should be put into bringing about free trade and the agreements necessary to facilitate such exchange.[111] The hope was that these agreements could be realized on a multilateral basis involving many countries. After a number of forays on the part of Canada, it became clear that other nations were reluctant parties, while the United States was more than willing to enter a pact. Thus, the stage became set for fundamental changes to Canadian markets – and to its society.

Courts: A Marginal Role

Courts had a limited role in Canadian society before the 1980s. They resolved disputes, punished criminals, and patrolled the blurred boundaries of federal and provincial authority. No one but a handful of lawyers and academics looked to the judges to solve complex social and economic problems. Courts were the repository of established and elitist values. They were dominated by traditional liberal values: celebration of an unfettered market and self-regarding behaviour and minimum state involvement in social policies. This influence was reflected in civil litigation – the active parties, the passive judge, and a costs regime that rewarded winning litigants by making losers pay the winners' costs.[112]

There were many instances of courts refusing to recognize claims that questioned established social and economic arrangements. Such opposition was apparent in litigation that protested the restricted role of women.[113] Movements to improve conditions of workers, such as claims for compensation and for the right to organize collectively, were spurned by courts. So, too, were attempts to curb discriminatory behaviour.[114] Administrative agencies could be scrutinized through judicial review to ensure they were not operating outside their limits. That review, largely of the courts' creation, was used to blunt the effectiveness of the agencies.[115] The dominant ideology of tort suits (the type of litigation most generally concerned with compensation) was rooted in individualism and individual responsibility based on fault.[116] Surveying the judicial record over an extensive period, a prominent legal academic asserted, "The courts utterly failed to deal with the most significant legal repercussions of the Industrial Revolution in the nineteenth century and with the revolution of rising expectations in the twentieth."[117]

The courts supported lack of economic competition by blunting any legislative attempts at such a policy, as I discuss above. In so doing, they echoed values of the established economic order: a celebration of free markets in the abstract, while bounding their scope. In the anticombines area, the courts reflected the values of established Canadian society at least as much as they were defying any statutory authority.

Respect for order and deference to authority, supported by the general population, were reflected by the courts in their role in the administration of criminal justice. The judiciary was influenced by the crime control model, with its emphasis on the suppression of crime and on convictions even at the risk of infringing on due process for the accused. Our courts stood in contrast to American ones, which were more attracted to the due process model, which emphasized procedural safeguards (right to counsel, protection from self-incrimination, right to a speedy trial, and so on) to protect against abuses by the state even at the risk of some guilty not being convicted.[118]

Federalism, the tug between the provincial and federal governments, has been an insistent theme throughout our nation's history. There have been two very different aspects to this tension: regionalism and its competition with Central Canada in a hinterland/heartland debate, and the struggle between Quebec and the rest of Canada. Both are discussed above. Federalism litigation was a direct product of such disputes. The courts were active in dealing with these issues; on a few occasions they used their powers to protect minority interests in the provinces.[119] From the 1950s to the 1970s, the norms of cooperative federalism moved federalism litigation and the influence of courts to the margins. That litigation revived in the 1970s. As cooperative federalism broke down, representative politics was deflected away from the necessary adjustments in federal-provincial relations, which had been essential to make the Dominion work.[120]

After the Second World War, there was increasing dissatisfaction, particularly in the legal community, with the fact that Canada had no entrenched bill of rights protecting constitutional entitlements of individuals. There was the belief that a bill of rights would go a long way in safeguarding citizens, especially minorities, and would move the courts away from their preoccupation with established and privileged interests. A pale version of a bill of rights, not entrenched, was legislated by the Diefenbaker government in the 1960s. It was quickly neutralized by the courts. This evisceration made the clamouring louder for an entrenched rights document that would be ambitious in scope. With the election of Trudeau, rights' advocates and the man who was dedicated to bounding Quebec nationalism would soon make a pact. Constitutionalism, the courts, and Canadian society would never be the same.

Conclusion

The last two decades of the twentieth century and the early years of the twenty-first would see momentous change in Canada. What were the historical characteristics of that society against which these alterations might be compared?

Representative politics was central in the Canada that was, one that was ever in search of itself; "a story of a nation bearing questions in its heart."[121] That politics was forceful yet also diverse. It was dominated by liberalism but enriched by social democracy and Toryism. It celebrated individualism – within the community. Even its "Conservatives" were "Progressive." Markets had a critical role in wealth creation. However, they were not seen as a prime vehicle for addressing many central social issues. Courts were important but, on the whole, their role in tackling complex public issues was marginal. They decided civil disagreements, enforced the criminal law, and set (shifting) limits on federal and provincial constitutional authority.

The country was conditional, a work in progress. Northrop Frye once remarked that "Canada is the Switzerland of the twentieth century, surrounded by the great powers of the world and preserving its identity by having many identities." Yet, he went on to say that a statue emblematic of Canadian patriotism would depict "someone holding his breath and crossing his fingers."[122]

Canadian society was elitist and authoritarian. It treated Aboriginals shamefully, and discriminated against racial minorities, gays and lesbians, people with disabilities, and others in many ways. It excluded women from the corridors of political and professional power. It produced painful divisions between Central Canada and the East and the West. There were deep cleavages between the English and the French. It was economically uncompetitive, relying too much on government, too often.

Yet, it was tolerant of some elements of its diversity – linguistic, cultural, and geographical. It developed a world-class reputation for respecting human rights as then understood. It devoted large resources to developing an array of public goods: in education, health, social services, and the environment. Its citizens had a real opportunity for productive, healthy, and long lives – the UN Development Program and its results for Canada attest to those possibilities. It was masterful at the "dance of adjustment."[123]

In the last decades of the twentieth century, much changed. Faith in representative politics was shaken. The public became deeply suspicious of legislators and their agents. By 2002, almost 70 percent of those asked thought that the political system was "corrupt."[124] Meanwhile, the role of markets increased noticeably. Globalization, tackling debts and deficits, the ideology of right-wing parties, technology (most prominently the Internet), and the influence of a variety of policies in the United States were all factors that pushed this society toward the embrace of more pervasive markets. At the same time, the courts were in the ascendant. The introduction of the *Charter* was central to judges having more influence. But the importance of other kinds of litigation also increased, law became more pervasive, and "rights talk" not only in the courts but also in the media, the legislatures, and the streets became a habit of mind for reacting to myriad issues.

The days of "peace, order, and good government" as the watchwords for the "good citizen" faded away. "Choice!" became the cry. Individuals became bearers of rights, consumers, and unbounded communicators in cyberspace.

The reality of their day-to-day lives in all this was often pushed to the side-lines. The capacity of courts, markets, and cyberspace to deliver goods and services for ordinary men and women and their children made for a very different existence than promised. Myths were at work. But they were powerful myths, strong enough to make the public believe that the rubble of representative politics could be ignored. Where was the "good citizen" in all of this? Frye's statue appeared ever more anxious.

PART 2

Courts, Politics, and Markets
in a Society in Transition

2 The Ascendance of Courts

One of the most dramatic transformations in Canadian society over the last two decades has been in the role of courts. Historically, judges were seen as peripheral to the development and implementation of public policy. They were the referees of federalism, requiring the provinces and the federal government to stay within their jurisdictional boundaries. But in a parliamentary system with no entrenched bill of rights, the courts had no means of striking down legislation that they judged violated fundamental freedoms. The courts' primary role was to punish criminal wrongdoers and to decide individual disputes that those in conflict could not resolve themselves. The common (and civil) law was developed, as necessary, along the way.[1]

No longer. Judges are now involved in an array of important public policy issues. Limits on pornography, gay and lesbian rights, protection of the environment, the right to assisted suicide, and special provisions for medical care for the disabled are but a few issues on a lengthening list of topics that are now being brought to the courts for resolution. In addressing a multitude of questions, those involved in reflecting and shaping public opinion – legislators, public officials, the media – keep a watchful eye on judges.

How has this fundamental change happened? What outcomes have been produced? What is the impact on the forging and implementation of public policy? What are the effects on other institutions of society? The legislatures and administrative agencies? The markets?

The introduction of the *Charter* and the enhanced role it gives to the judges is the biggest factor influencing this change. However, explanations extend beyond the *Charter* to the increased importance of other kinds of litigation, to the growth of law, and to the habit of mind focused on "rights talk" in the courts, the media, and the streets. Courts and markets advance in an uneasy alliance: courts create rights, markets create wealth. Both can deliver messages that government cannot be trusted or relied on. Representative politics recedes for a number of reasons, including being upstaged by the judges. All the while there are complex issues about using lawsuits to forge and implement policy. In particular, litigation is an unsure means for achieving social change. Such unsteadiness is especially disappointing for progressives who have had high hopes for using courts to effect reform.

Rights are a noble idea. That idea is a powerful one for those long excluded from politics and other forms of power. But the myth of rights and exaggerated claims about the capacity of courts are bound to disappoint. Such myths come in a variety of forms. Together, these fables draw people away from representative politics, dismembering it further. Courts and rights should not be blamed for this society's discontents. Yet, the myth of rights is a powerful magnet pulling us away from the hard work of making representative politics work on a day-to-day basis. The dishevelment of popular institutions continues.

The Rise of Rights

A Turning to Law

Many trace the increased importance of the courts to the introduction of the *Charter*. The *Charter* is of fundamental significance for a number of reasons. Other factors have also been at play. Other forms of litigation – federalism review, judicial review of administrative action, and class actions – have also turned the spotlight onto the courts.[2] What is more, the activities of judges are encased in the larger society, one that sees rights talk as a way of tackling complex issues and one that has increasingly turned to all manner of law to address complicated questions.[3]

One of the hallmarks of post-Second World War societies is their invoking of law to mediate a wide variety of issues. The role for law as the regulator of the industrialized state had emerged by the early decades of the twentieth century. Yet, it was given impetus by the Depression and the reaction to the excesses of unregulated markets.[4] The Second World War only added to expectations that law could be harnessed to articulate and implement societal values.[5]

The decades since the Second World War have seen an embrace of law that has dwarfed the otherwise significant experiences with regulation in the previous fifty-odd years. This period witnessed extensive and complex intrusion of regulation into multiple facets of daily life. A prime method by which such activity has been achieved has been through agencies and commissions performing a vast range of tasks and implementing an array of policies.[6]

One reaction to this growth of law – and government – was to support politicians pledging to cut back on such expansion. During the 1980s, Thatcher and Reagan symbolized efforts to curtail regulation and to curb governmental agencies. Such developments came later in other countries, including Canada, but were in place in some of the provinces by the 1990s.

In many respects, legal regulation became identified as both cause and effect of the huge debts and deficits weighing down governments in the last decade of the twentieth century. The impetus to use regulation as a response to an array of issues did abate, and some programs were eliminated as "privatization" and "deregulation" became the new watchwords.[7] Nevertheless, it is by no means true that regulation uniformly shrank even in the United States and England under conservative, market-oriented governments. A survey of regulation in Canada in the late 1990s did point to some areas where there had been deregulation, for example, in fields such as transportation, energy, and telecommunications. But it concluded that overall, regulation, including of the marketplace, had continued to grow.[8]

In any event, many who support limited government involvement in the economic sphere can be boosters of regulation of personal or moral behaviour.[9] Those who cry out for deregulation and privatization can also be the ones leading the charge for laws governing all sorts of other behaviour, from crime control to pornography to intimate personal relations such as domestic partnerships between gays and between lesbians.

Along with the growth of law have come lawyers. The legal profession is growing even as it is stratifying and performing an array of tasks for increasingly diversified clients.[10] In many ways, the increase of lawyers is a worldwide phenomenon for industrialized countries and even for some that are in the process of industrializing.[11] In England and Wales, the two branches of the profession (barristers and solicitors) increased about 147 percent from the early 1960s to the mid-1980s.[12] In the United States during approximately the same period, the number of lawyers grew 129 percent.[13] Canada led the way, in terms of percentage increase, with growth of the legal profession during the same period (mid-1960s to mid-1980s) expanding by 253 percent.[14] Total spending on civil legal services in Canada grew from $1.9 billion in 1973 to $11 billion in 1993.[15] These expenditures easily outpaced consumer spending generally. While per capita income rose on average about 1.5 percent from 1982 to 1992, the growth in legal services spending rose, in most sectors, by nearly 5 percent per year.[16] More specifically, money spent on legal aid services in Canada increased enormously during the 1980s. In Ontario, the province where the growth of such expenditures was possibly the greatest, the total cost of legal aid rose almost 500 percent between fiscal years 1980 and 1990.[17] Despite this galloping increase, the cost of legal aid in that province went on to almost double between fiscal 1990 and 1995.[18] It was then reorganized in the face of a fiscal crisis.[19]

With increased numbers of lawyers and increased expenditures has come an increase in the amount of law.[20] There is no shortage of claims that we are being engulfed in a legal morass.[21] Nevertheless, because statistics on the legal system and empirical studies of its functioning are not what they should be, such expansion is difficult to establish systematically and uniformly. However, figures and other evidence are available that document a qualitative and quantitative shift in the way that some societies are invoking law.

In 1960, the annual output of the Dominion Law Reports, a main service for publicizing judgments of Canadian courts, was five volumes, with 3,902 pages. By 1989 it was eleven volumes with 8,448 pages.[22] Between 1960 and 1985, general law reviews grew from 65 to 186; specialized increased from 6 to 140. From 1958 to 1980 in Canada, the number of law journals increased by 175 percent.[23] Moreover, such statistics from printed sources scarcely do justice to an intense level of activity. Online databases, which first appeared in the 1970s, have increased access to a vast range of legal material, both published and unpublished.

With more lawyers and more law come increased legalization in a complicated array of human activity. Labels warn about dangers, instruct regarding use, and provide details for complaints if the consumer feels aggrieved. Notices in restaurants, on airline tickets, and at swimming pools invite use while limiting claims for loss. The lines between popular and legal culture have become blurred: the two collide and interact.

Marc Galanter, examining "law abounding" in Canada, Great Britain, and the United States,[24] observed that there has been an extension of law to whole areas of activity that were previously not regarded to be in need of such structuring.[25] Health care is provided in very different ways in Canada, Great Britain, and the United States. Yet, it has undergone legalization in important aspects in each: entitlement to treatment has undergone substantial regulation, with users increasingly turning to law for recourse for alleged deficiencies.[26] More generally, there is a pattern of legal norms and institutions as the common language of addressing problems. This pattern exists whether individuals experience difficulties with intimates or faceless entities. It occurs in such diverse areas as the environment, safety regulation, health care, employment, and sports:[27] "[There is a] popular perception of the ubiquity of law and its intrusion into areas previously immune from its infringement."[28]

Rights Talk

It is not just the growth of law in a quantitative sense that is important. It is the way that legal issues have come to be debated and thought about over the last decades that is so notable. Now, many issues having legal implications are discussed in terms of rights. Most obviously, rights can be implicated in lawsuits, especially those invoking the *Charter*. I will come to the significance of that document in a moment. But beyond the courts, a whole habit of mind has developed that seeks to determine a complex array of societal quandaries by invoking "rights talk." To come to grips with that phenomenon we need to briefly survey developments in the land of rights – the United States.[29]

Any number of progressives throughout the twentieth century saw legislation as a means of social, political, and economic reform. Statutory and regulatory interventions were seen as the great counterweight to the excesses of market capitalism for the protection of workers (for example, occupational health and safety, collective bargaining, and minimum wages), safeguarding the environment, guarding against anticompetitive practices and fraud, providing minimum security from poverty, and so forth. However, sometime after the Second World War, in the United States, many progressives took another tack regarding the use of law to achieve particular agendas. The core of that strategy was the claiming of rights.[30]

If laws are meant to recognize certain claims, there is a role for rights in that recognition. Someone injured in a motor vehicle accident (perhaps especially because of the negligence of another) should have a "right" to recover. When Canada implemented a program of universal access to health care, it was vital that individuals have a "right" to receive treatment based on need. However, the rights revolution, especially in America, aimed to recognize interests, individuals, and groups primarily through litigation.[31] There were many goals for this transformation, but a primary one was to gain, legally, recognition that had not been obtained politically.

Such use of litigation was especially compelling, at least at the theoretical level, for those who have long been denied opportunities in society. Patricia Williams, a prominent African-American woman, puts eloquently the case for rights: "'Rights' feels so new in the mouths of most black people. It is still so deliciously empowering to say. It is a sign for and a gift of selfhood ... The concept of rights, both positive and negative, is the marker of our citizenship, our participatoriness, our relation to others."[32]

At the same time, rights claiming in an array of areas proceeded apace.[33] A confederacy of progressives (activists, lawyers, academics, some media admirers – aided, for at least a period, by sympathetic courts) was determined to invoke rights to transform a politics which, at least in their view, was not responsive: "court majorities with an expansive view of the judicial role, and their academic admirers, propelled each other, like railway men on a handcar, along the line that led to the land of rights."[34]

By the 1960s, in the United States, one could talk about a public interest/rights movement. Law was to become an instrument of progressive change, as exemplified by the work of Ralph Nader. By the 1970s, there were public interest law firms representing a host of interests, including environmentalists, consumers, women, the disabled, minorities, children, and prisoners, as these groups pressed their agendas largely through the claiming of rights in the political, legislative, and administrative processes but most prominently through actual or threatened litigation.[35]

In rights talk, it is claimed, the vulnerable and the powerful share a common view: "the language of the law enables lawyers to reform client problems in terms of broad standards of American law and culture and, thus, to convey the plight of the have nots in terms that maximize the likelihood for a sympathetic response culturally as well as legally."[36] With rights claiming, even our sense of language is transformed: "Legal rights, then, should be understood as the language of a continuing process rather than fixed rules ... [as] language we use to try and persuade others to let us win this round ... [we can take] the aspirational language of the society seriously and ... promote change by reliance on inherited traditions."[37]

Yet, there are progressives who contend that the meanings given to "rights" in law are problematic.[38] There is no neutral standpoint from which to identify those who are to be the recipients of such rights. There is no uncontroversial means of determining the scope and nature of each particular right. There is no method that can be used to fairly adjudicate a clash of competing rights. What is more, the costs of such rights and the associated demands for resources that could be directed elsewhere are rarely carefully examined.[39] The implications for goods supplied by the political process – public education and health care, welfare, public parks, and urban cores – are not related to the cost that rights can impose:[40] "First, constitutional and legal symbols are not likely to be particularly useful for rallying those most in need. Second, with litigation at its core, mobilization tends to be divisive ... The net effect is to pit have not segments of the society against one another in a zero sum struggle over scarce resources."[41]

Defenders of rights claiming in the United States have responded to these misgivings in two ways. The first attacks the idea of community, a concept that is often asserted to blunt the expansion of rights. "Community" has too many ill-defined meanings to be a foundation for a worthy politics. In its worst manifestations, community can be a prescription for tyranny, stifling individualism, choice, and freedom. The American South once had a highly developed sense of community – one that was oppressive and exclusionary toward blacks.[42]

The second insists that there never was a time of a model politics. Instead, what constitutes good citizens and worthy political involvement has changed over the decades, with each stage having its attractions and its foibles. The rights-bearing citizen is the most recent manifestation of such transformations. Such change cannot be addressed by decrying it and wishing for the return of the "long civic generation" that, in fact, probably never existed. Schudson is particularly eloquent in pleading for a coming to terms with this new way of conceiving of politics, of law, and of the citizen: "A rights-regarding citizenship does not 'answer' democracy's discontents, but it is a necessary part of any answer. Moreover, it automatically implies respect for the rights of others and the willingness to engage in public dispute according to public norms and a public language. We have to recognize that the claiming of rights, though it should not be the end of a citizen's political consciousness, is an invaluable beginning to it."[43]

Nevertheless, there are insistent questions as to how effective "rights" are in facilitating the goals of such claimants. Complex issues arise about the effectiveness of litigation, especially in achieving progressive reform, a matter I return to below.

The Great Litigation Experiment

Canada has had its own version of rights talk, largely prompted by the introduction of the *Charter*. The myth making surrounding the *Charter* obscures the reality that its coming was by no means preordained. There was no widespread abuse of human rights to which it responded. To the contrary, Canada enjoyed an international reputation for its vigilance in respecting basic freedoms. Nor was the *Charter* a product of a broad movement among citizens.[44] Rather, it was part of that massive turning to law that has just been described.

It was born as a device to shore up the centralizing tendencies of Pierre Trudeau. Centralization was thought to be critical to enhancing Quebec's stake in the country and to containing the forces of separation in that province.[45] The *Charter*'s terms were negotiable in order to make a deal to repatriate the Constitution from England and to address other federal-provincial issues.[46] Trudeau declared that there must be a strong federal government and that language rights had to be enshrined. The rest was up for grabs – "a classic example of raw bargaining."[47] Given that process, a depiction of the *Charter* as indispensable for governance, with judges as its inevitable guardians, is romantic at best.

Yet, the *Charter* has taken hold. After some hesitation, Canadian courts have warmed to the task, involving themselves in questions relating to abortion, mercy killing, assisted suicide, language rights, and an array of issues relating to the administration of criminal justice, to name but a few.[48] So noticeable has been this alteration in the role of the judiciary that a 1998 study comparing the role of the supreme courts in four countries, including the United States, has characterized the shift in Canada as "a Great Experiment" and the result as "Canada's Dramatic Rights Revolution."[49]

The "Great Experiment," the "Dramatic Rights Revolution," resulted from a number of factors. First was the prominence of *Charter* claims in litigation itself. Though not overwhelming in sheer numbers, *Charter* cases are very influential, given the kinds of issues they raise.[50] In addition, there developed a support structure for litigation brought by individuals and invoking the *Charter* and other claims. These developments included rights advocacy organizations, sources of funding (particularly government-provided aid), lawyers and academics as rights advocates, and compliant government agencies. Thus, the foundation for the "rights revolution" was laid. Such developments "supported a steadily growing number of rights cases ... they developed the scholarship that supported a vigorous judicial role in interpreting the Charter, and they brought new cases under the Charter that provided the judges with the opportunities to enforce, expand, and create the new rights."[51]

Meanwhile, the rights talk accompanying the enactment of the *Charter* was second to none. The myth making proceeded apace. The Canadian public was continually bombarded with claims about the importance of the *Charter* and, indeed, of all litigation. Within some legal circles, it was a self-evident proposition that we were "litigating the values of a nation"[52] and that "as the Charter evolves so evolves Canada."[53] Spectacular claims appeared in the popular media, documenting a "rights revolution" in which the "courts lead the charge."[54] A front-page story in a national newspaper, entitled "Top Court Becomes Supreme Player," included a four-column picture of the then Chief Justice and quoted him as saying that the introduction of the *Charter* has been nothing less than "a revolution ... like Pasteur's discoveries. Medicine was never the same after. Like the invention of penicillin, the laser."[55] Another member of the Court talked about judges who "govern [the public's] lives," who are "custodians of the Charter," and who render "a supreme public service."[56]

At the same time, there was talk among legal academics of the rational ("conversations of justification")[57] and of the uplifting ("moments of possibility"),[58] and of the perennial for progressives ("consciousness raising").[59] Section 33 was "an alien feature in any Charter."[60] All issues of justice housed in the *Charter* should receive responses that were "ultimately adjudicable."[61]

Such extravagance promised all but the moon. Yet, what has been the effect of turning to litigation to address an array of complex issues? One alleged consequence is the convergence of Canadian and American societies. The contention is that as Canadians turn to the courts for solutions to complicated social, economic, and political questions, they will develop the same appetite for litigation as their neighbours have. They certainly developed a similar hype about constitutional lawsuits.

What is more, the fear is that entrenched rights will make Canadians less communitarian and less inclined to use political and administrative processes to forge and implement solutions particularly regarding fundamental goods: health care, education, the social safety net, and so forth. In 1989, Seymour Martin Lipset, in a study of the two countries, pointed to the *Charter* as the greatest force pushing Canadian society in the direction of America: "The Charter makes Canada a more individualistic and litigious culture ... The greater institutional emphasis on individualism ultimately should be reflected in the country's values ... Whether [Canada] can continue to be ... a deferential welfare state, will be its basic issue for the 21st century."[62] How accurate are Lipset's assertions?

A 1997 study examined the specific issue of the judicialization of politics – the extent to which the courts were becoming involved in issues that might otherwise be expected to be addressed by the legislative process.[63] The study assessed possible convergence by using a number of measures, litigation activity, jurisprudential influence, and so forth. It found that the amount of rights-based litigation in the Supreme Court of Canada was approaching levels in the US Supreme Court. The Canadian Supreme Court had become more open to relying on US authorities; such reliance both reflects and facilitates convergence. The Canadian Court had also broadened its capacity for scrutinizing governmental action by adopting substantive review inspired by US precedents. The study contended that the evidence "broadly supports" the conclusion that Canada is converging with the United States in the judicialization of politics.[64]

However, the study reached different conclusions on the substance of judicial policy making. It examined two areas, equality and political participation, where both Courts had rendered decisions having implications for marginalized groups. In these areas, the Canadian Court exhibited much more solicitude for those claiming disadvantage than its American counterpart: "while the U.S. court has returned to a formal, intent-based, individual-rights orientation towards equality rights issues, the Canadian court has embraced a substantive effects-based, group-rights orientation."[65] The study suggested that this policy divergence was attributable to cultural, textual, and political factors. In contrast to the position taken by Lipset, the study asserted that the collective values in Canadian society were influencing rights discourse (rather than the other way around). Such values were bolstered by the text of the *Charter,* which protects the collective rights of linguistic minorities, Aboriginal peoples, and multicultural groups.

These policy divergences should be good news for those seeking to use the courts for progressive social change.[66] Any number of activists in Canada see the *Charter* as a prime vehicle for effecting reform on behalf of the disadvantaged. But such hopes bring us to another way of looking at the consequences of increased turning to litigation and to rights. How effective are the courts in bringing about social change?

Litigation and Social Change

Assessing the Impact of Litigation

Politicians can point to the ballot as the source of legitimacy for their actions: their power rests on the democratic process. The source of authority for courts is more complex. The power they exercise can, by definition, be antimajoritarian; thus, those espousing an ambitious judicial role have to offer a rationale that does not depend on popular will or authority. Advocates of courts usually assert arguments about the improvement of society – however judged – as the benefit to put against the loss to democracy.[67]

Political progressives are called upon to justify vigorously the judicial enterprise, since so many of them, over the last decades, have been so optimistic about the intervention of courts in a range of issues. Thus, progressives emphasize the ways in which litigation and the acknowledgments of rights will empower the marginalized so as to respond to a political process that an unyielding majority has blocked. But just how effective have the courts been in bringing about social change? What evidence exists to answer this question?

Movements in several countries have sought to employ litigation to bring about social and political transformation.[68] Such efforts have been most prominent in the United States.[69] Courts are especially powerful in terms of judges' capacity, because of an entrenched bill of rights, to nullify the laws of elected officials and to negate regulatory orders: "the United States is the outlier in the extraordinary power that its ... courts exercise in reviewing the constitutionality of legislation."[70] Progressive reformers (in America, "liberals") had the highest confidence in the courts' willingness and ability to respond to their demands.[71] Thus, this section of this book and the next one concentrate on the use of litigation in the United States to effect social and political change. That experience is one important indicator of what may lie in store for Canadian society over the next decades. True, the experiences of the republic cannot just be mapped onto this society; neither should they be ignored.

I should begin with some fundamentals. The argument is not that litigation has no effects. Individuals and organizations constantly use litigation (or threaten to) as they assert myriad claims (and defences). The effects produced by such lawsuits raise important questions related to the outcomes of differentials of financial power, repeat involvement with litigation, and so forth.[72] The focus here is the ability of lawsuits to effect major social change. The contention is that litigation can produce such change only under limited circumstances that are not often present.

Gerald Rosenberg, in his book *The Hollow Hope,* focuses on the Supreme Court of the United States and its role in social transformation. He describes both the potential and limits of litigation to "cause" change.[73] Rosenberg concludes that courts can be effective causes of change only under specific limited conditions. These are that (1) there is ample legal precedent for change; (2) there is support for change from substantial numbers in Congress and from the executive; and (3) there is support from some citizens or at least minimal opposition from all citizens and (a) positive incentives are offered to induce compliance, or (b) costs are imposed to induce compliance, or (c) court decisions allow for market implementation, or (d) key administrators and officials are willing to act and see court orders as a tool for leveraging additional resources or, conversely, as a screen to hide behind.[74]

The Hollow Hope ignited controversy for several reasons, not the least of which are the conclusions Rosenberg reaches:[75] "U.S. courts can *almost never* be effective producers of significant social reform."[76] Although major victories in the courts can be cited, Rosenberg concludes that, almost always, their impact over time was minor. He asserts that there is evidence that litigation may actually galvanize opponents. Courts give rise to the "fly-paper" phenomenon. Litigation is a "lure" that induces groups and organizations to employ it: they hope to provoke responses from bureaucracies, to counter the advantages of the better endowed in the legislative processes, and to force recalcitrant majorities to desist from their unprincipled ways. Instead, these groups expend resources that could have been better spent in the electoral, legislative, and administrative processes to achieve the sought-after ends.

In response, some assert that Rosenberg is simply wrong about the ineffectiveness of courts. These critics, examining areas as diverse as prison reform,[77] school financing,[78] and the availability of sexually explicit material,[79] contend that courts have been responsible for substantial change. Moreover, there is skepticism regarding Rosenberg's set of conditions to be used to judge the effectiveness of the courts.

Shuck, in his review of *The Hollow Hope,* criticized the analysis as basically incomplete.[80] Rosenberg nowhere tackles the meaning of the concept of causality; indeed, he expressly disclaims any such attempt.[81] He is also accused of neglecting the repetitive, dialogic nature of the interactions between courts, legislatures, agencies, and other social processes. Further, he gives excessive weight to whether litigation advances the avowed agendas of public interest litigators and too little weight to more modest reform goals.

Finally, it is alleged that Rosenberg does not differentiate between constitutional litigation and lawsuits turning on statutory interpretation. Administrative agencies can have a fundamental role in implementing statutory schemes of regulation designed to deal with social and political problems. In any event, in Shuck's view, there is no account of the judicial enterprise that will adequately describe how courts exert their influence: "the many threads of causality are simply too tightly knotted to disentangle."[82] He urges that students of courts confess that "we ... are guided more by our professionally honed, often intuitive grasp of an elusive social reality than by any robust scientific theory worthy of the name."[83]

Yet, Shuck, in his eagerness to demonstrate the incompleteness of Rosenberg's framework and its conclusions, has underscored the latter's most fundamental point: those that place faith in litigation to effect change have only that faith. They cannot, in fact, demonstrate any such capacity. If the fundamental conclusion is that there is no theory to account for the impact of courts, no sensible way to analyze cause and effect relating to their decisions, then, equally, any claims about their capacity to achieve change must surely be thrown on the scrap heap as well. Most importantly, if the effects of litigation reflect, as Shuck insists, an "elusive social reality," what is the normative basis for an ambitious judicial role? A role that undermines the basic democratic legitimacy that elected officials can claim?

The Complexities of Assessing Impact – The Legacy
of *Brown v. Board of Education*
A discussion of a specific case will help illustrate the complexities of assessing the impact of litigation. There have been some attempts to evaluate the effects of court decisions in Canada; I discuss some of those efforts in Part 3. Nevertheless, in this country, most discussion of the enabling power of litigation,

particularly among proponents, proceeds at an abstract level. Such eloquent vagaries pave the way for an inflated sense of the capacities of courts.

In the previous section I discussed the controversy over the impact of litigation in the United States to effect social change. In that country, studies have been conducted that examine the effects of litigation in a number of areas.[84] The specific instance that I discuss here is the aftermath of possibly the most famous decision of the US Supreme Court: *Brown v. Board of Education*.[85] This discussion will illustrate the difficulty of assessing the outcomes of lawsuits and, in particular, demonstrating their effectiveness in bringing about progressive change.

Conventional views hold that it was the courts, most prominently through the *Brown* decision, that were the catalyst for the civil rights movement in the United States. Even the most uninformed are likely to have heard of *Brown*. They know the legend of how, in one fell stroke, the Supreme Court of the United States ended the shame of segregation. One Canadian commentator, writing during the early days of the *Charter* about the effects it would have, characterized the case as "such a moral supernova in civil liberties adjudication that it almost single-handedly justifies the exercise."[86]

Yet, a set of opinions confronts these claims. It is contended that *Brown* and subsequent decisions had a much lesser role in recognizing and implementing civil rights and in addressing underlying problems.[87] These controversial effects are illustrated by a discussion of litigation of educational issues, especially desegregation, during the decades since *Brown*.

Rosenberg asserts that in the ten-year period after that decision (1954 to 1964), almost nothing happened to end segregation in public schools (or other discriminatory practices regarding voting, transportation, and accommodation). As late as 1964, ten years after *Brown*, only 1.2 percent of black children in the South attended school with whites.[88] Rosenberg argues that it was only after the enactment in 1964 of the *Civil Rights Act* that any real progress was made toward desegregation: by 1971, 85.9 percent of black children in the South were attending desegregated schools (the measure of success and the quality of the education they were receiving are matters pursued below). Thus, it was not the Supreme Court but, rather, Congress and the executive branch that achieved any desegregation.[89]

If Rosenberg's account of what caused desegregation were to be accepted, an entirely different response would be to contend that it was the decision in *Brown* that propelled the awakening of civil rights. The argument would be that *Brown* altered the way race relations were viewed so that the legislation and other government action which did begin to end discrimination followed. Thus, *Brown* may not have been the immediate cause, but it was the ultimate one in terms of vanquishing discrimination.

Rosenberg also responds to this argument. His research, examining the structure of civil rights organizations, press reaction, and public opinion polls, found no evidence that the judgment mobilized concern for civil rights or was influential in moulding opinion. Instead, he contends that, after the holding, the press did not devote more attention to civil rights issues, and organizations failed to use *Brown* as a basis for fundraising or membership recruitment. What is more, civil rights legislation of the 1950s and 1960s proceeded with few references to the decision.[90] What did occur was the galvanization of opposition by a hard core familiar with attempts to promote civil rights, including through the courts. After *Brown* there was an increase in the membership and activities of pro-segregation groups such as the White Citizens Councils and the Ku Klux Klan.[91]

Still, Sunstein points out that the principles of *Brown* may have been deeply internalized by blacks so as to profoundly alter their sense of entitlement.[92] He suggests that, if in fact the decision was rarely mentioned in the press, this may have been because the Court's holding was so right that people did not see the need to refer constantly to it. Further, Martin Luther King referred to Supreme Court decisions and to the Constitution, and from this Sunstein conjectures that *Brown* must have been an unmentioned moral force. Others contend that there was a relationship, if a complicated one, between the decision and the activities of civil rights groups and other forces.[93]

Rosenberg's main target is the contention that *Brown* specifically effected change in civil rights. He admits that, following congressional and executive action in the 1960s, the courts did play a significant role in the battle to achieve civil rights.[94] Other studies substantiate the argument that the judiciary supported black progress in some areas. Court decisions seem to have bolstered antidiscrimination laws concerning employment of blacks and their earnings.[95] Courts also appear to have played a role in the 1930s in improving segregated schools. They supported the National Association for the Advancement of Colored People (NAACP) and certain philanthropic organizations that worked to improve black education.[96] Rosenberg admits that courts can effect change when they are acting in concert with other political institutions and social forces. The problem for those wishing to use the courts to promote change is that this conjunction too rarely occurs. In 2004, the fiftieth anniversary of *Brown,* a number of books appeared on the subject, several of them written by African-Americans.[97] The books have a depressing tone regarding what had actually been accomplished in the wake of *Brown:* "How could a decision that promised so much and, by its terms, accomplished so little, have gained so hallowed a place?"[98]

Whatever the contribution of *Brown* and related decisions, those scrutinizing judicial activity on educational issues and the plight of blacks in the last three decades of the twentieth century report decidedly mixed results. A study examining civil rights litigation in a number of areas, including education, from the late 1960s to the late 1980s concluded that "litigation ... should be seen as ... extremely complex, problematic and contingent both on external events and intraorganizational developments."[99] There is evidence that some state courts have achieved "dramatic results" for the school finance systems.[100] But even the study investigating the aftermath of such litigation would not stipulate the conditions under which such results will occur.[101]

Reformers hoped that desegregation, often implemented through court-ordered busing, would rescue black children from inferior schools. Even in 1984 it was being argued that even more aggressive techniques should be used to desegregate public education.[102] Yet, a study reported in 2003 that black and Latino students are now more isolated from their white counterparts than they were three decades ago before many of the overhauls from the civil rights movement got under way.[103] Complex factors are at play: big increases in enrolment by black, Latino, and Asian students; continuing white flight from urban centres; housing patterns that isolate racial groups; and the termination of many court-ordered desegregation plans.[104]

In any event, the effects produced by any desegregation that has occurred have been disappointing at best. Judicial fiats, particularly involving busing, can cause much public resentment. Even more importantly, desegregation does nothing in itself to provide access to quality education and may in certain circumstances actually work against that goal.[105] To have a good education a child must have access to good educational programs. Nonetheless, an exhaustive study of the effects of court-ordered desegregation emphasizes that this apparent point has been obscured by those insisting that desegregation must occur at any price. Desegregation is an important goal. Yet litigation, the language of the law, and unyielding antagonists have so narrowed the terms of the debate that desegregation, including through busing, has been turned into *the* issue in much litigation alleging discrimination. Meanwhile, the overarching question of access to quality programs has been largely sidelined.[106]

Sunstein does take issue with Rosenberg for being too unqualified in his conclusions. Yet, he recognizes the vigour of *The Hollow Hope* in confronting those who assert simplistic conclusions regarding the effects of litigation: "[Rosenberg] has shown that there is room for much uncertainty about this matter [of consequences]. In any case, he has put into question the assumption of people who now believe ... that litigation is an especially promising approach to social reform."[107] Still, it might be said that in the United States there was no choice but to turn to the courts: the caste system promoting such racism was just too embedded. That society had to be shown the path that only an independent judiciary could create: "[*Brown*] raised a standard of justice in the treatment of Americans with dark skin. It aroused African-Americans in the South to demand that justice."[108]

This is possibly so. But when courts become substantially implicated, public policy may pay dearly. A litigious approach to complicated social problems may create possibilities for change. It is more likely that the range of responses will be constrained.[109] It is this prospect that needs to be pondered as "Canada's Dramatic Rights Revolution," its "Great Experiment," proceeds apace.[110]

The Courts and Representative Politics

Whatever the impact of litigation on specific issues, what effect has the enhanced role of courts had on representative politics? This section tackles that question. It does so by examining different images of courts, litigation, and of rights: as "dialogue," as "the court party," and as the "wing of rights." Each of these three depictions approaches the images of courts, litigation, and rights from different perspectives. Yet, they have a common theme. Representative politics is being moved from centre stage in the life of the nation. Courts, litigation, and rights are a major force in this displacement. In all of this, what has become of the "good citizen"?

Litigation as "Dialogue"

Recently in Canada, defenders of rights litigation have increasingly focused on the effects that these lawsuits have on democratic processes as a basis for justifying the expansion of the courts' power. Advocates assert that judicialization of rights, far from blunting representative politics, actually enlivens it through "dialogue." In this conception, curial review has a critical role to play in energizing democratic discourse.[111]

Judges have an important say in defining rights. Nevertheless, the *Charter* promotes a role for legislatures as well, in modifying or even reversing judicial pronouncements. Thus, there can be dialogue between these two institutions on fundamental entitlements. This depiction of the role of judges is in contrast to the hype surrounding the courts in the initial decades of the *Charter*.[112]

The *Charter* is said to facilitate this dialogue in four ways. First, section 33, through its "notwithstanding" provision, permits legislatures to override the courts' decisions. Second, section 1 allows legislatures to implement means of achieving important objectives other than those favoured by courts, because that section recognizes "reasonable limits." Third, some rights, such as those specified in section 8 forbidding "unreasonable search and seizure," are internally qualified; they do not constitute an absolute prohibition on certain actions. Fourth, the *Charter* contemplates a variety of remedial measures short of the legislation being struck down.

Advocates of "dialogue" maintain that such "conversations" are occurring, in terms of actual responses by the legislatures to court judgments. A study in 1997 examined sixty-five cases in which a court had struck down legislation on *Charter* grounds.[113] In 80 percent of the cases, there was a legislative sequel – "some action by the competent legislative body" – in response to the court decision nullifying the act. Moreover, the response was prompt. In a sizable majority of cases, legislatures acted either before any appeal was concluded or within two years of the legislation being struck down. As a result of this record, the study concluded that the *Charter* "can act as a catalyst for a two-way exchange between the judiciary and the legislature on the topic of human rights and freedoms, but it rarely raises an absolute barrier to the wishes of the democratic institutions."[114] Not surprisingly, judges have found this dialogue metaphor attractive.[115] In such a depiction the courts do not threaten democracy but are responsible agents of its redefinition, as rights are infused into policy making and daily life.

Roach, attracted to the dialogue metaphor, has rightly pointed to a number of instances where there has been interaction between the courts and legislatures on *Charter* issues – in such areas as police powers, the criminal trial process, prisoner voting rights, tobacco advertising, and gay and lesbian rights.[116] He attributes much of this dialogue to the structure of the *Charter,* particularly sections 1 and 33. He emphasizes that there are no corresponding sections in the US Bill of Rights. As a result, he maintains that Americans have much more to fear from judicial activism than do Canadians. Thus, "dialogue between the court and the legislature under modern (but not American) bills of rights is based on 'active citizenship' because it is about whether elected governments will use their powers to limit or override rights as declared by the court."[117]

Weinrib draws an even more pronounced distinction between Canada and the United States: "In sharp and deliberate contrast to the US Bill of Rights, the Charter is unequivocal in departing from the values of a stable, hierarchical, paternalistic and patriarchal society."[118] She then goes on to provide a list of some aspects of the *Charter* that are the basis for such contrasts. The *Charter* "guarantees freedom of conscience in addition to freedom of religion; does not entrench property rights; guarantees equality before and under the law, as well as equal protection and equal benefit of the law; prohibits state discrimination based on features of personal and community identity; permits affirmative action for disadvantaged groups; and requires that interpretation respect gender equality as well as multiculturalism."[119]

Yet, the accuracy of characterizing the role of the courts in constitutionalized rights review as a mere participant in dialogue has been strongly challenged. First, it has been stated that the empirical assertions of the 1997 study of legislative sequels, just discussed, are flawed. Shortcomings of the study include using nullification as the sole indicator of judicial blunting of democratic will, biased case selection, improper inclusion of lower-court decisions in the data set, the treatment of groups of cases that produced a single legislative sequel as evidence of multiple sequels, and the claim that most sequels involved only minor legislative amendments.[120]

Second, it is contended that some of the results of the study do not support the dialogue metaphor; indeed, they are evidence against it. Seventeen percent of the "legislative sequels" occurred *before* an appellate court proceeded to decide the constitutional question even in the face of the legislative change.

The court, in those circumstances, had the option of declaring the case moot (because of the legislative action) or of declining to hear it. In such circumstances these decisions are not evidence of dialogue. Rather, they demonstrate the courts' assertion that judicial pronouncements are the only source of constitutional meaning.[121]

Third, curial review, whatever the outcomes, can cause distortions in policy making and implementation. This warping occurs as legislators select policies that may be less effective but which more readily conform to standards set by courts for constitutional requirements. On the one hand, distortions of policy occur when legislators draft statutes to conform with judicial pronouncements and those pronouncements conflict with parliamentarians' understanding of what the Constitution requires. From this vantage, "legislative sequels" are not evidence of dialogue but indications of elected officials coping with interference by courts in the policy-making process. On the other hand, warping can occur when a legislature acts within a range of policies it believes is available to it, thinking in error that the policy it would prefer is outside the available range of options that the courts would tolerate.[122] In other words, "to assume that only judges can resolve Charter conflicts is not healthy for the polity, because it diminishes political responsibility to pursue important policy goals and may lead to the unnecessary use of non-ambitious or ineffective means to pursue these objectives."[123]

Fourth, the dialogue metaphor cloaks a claim for judicial supremacy in interpreting constitutional norms.[124] That assertion of judicial supremacy is hard to reconcile with a depiction of a process of working out constitutional values among equals. The rights in the *Charter* may indeed be fundamental. The problem is in equating the pronouncements of courts with those rights. For true dialogue to occur, legislatures would need to be recognized as legitimate interpreters of the Constitution and they would need to be able to assert that understanding independently of the judges. Yet section 33, "the notwithstanding clause," which allows legislatures to override court decisions, has become a dead letter. In a period in which court pronouncements on the Constitution are seen as supreme and in which politicians are highly mistrusted, section 33 has become "the forbidden fruit of Canadian politics."[125] So long as courts are the arbiters, the more accurate metaphor may be not one of dialogue but of a huge assembly of citizens being lectured to by a handful of unelected, unrepresentative, and unaccountable commanders.

Those who support the dialogue metaphor have rushed to defend it and the 1997 study that has been subject to the criticism just described.[126] Whatever may be its shortcomings, "dialogue" is a constructive way to approach the relationship between courts and legislatures. Yet, the preoccupation remains with rights as if they inevitably should be the focus of law making. Roach, for example, urges the courts to be even more activist, given the legislatures' opportunities to respond through "dialogue."[127]

However, "dialogue" assumes vigour on the part of legislatures in responding to the decisions of courts. But representative politics is in disarray; confidence levels in government are at a low; the fortunes of legislators are sagging. The judges, riding the crest of high public approval, can speak clearly and forcefully. The legislative response may, mostly, be weak and feckless.

The Court Party?

Another charge against *Charter* litigation and related developments has gone much farther than complaining of a lack of dialogue. It is contended that there has developed an elite preoccupied with having the courts enforce the *Charter* in the widest possible terms. This cadre, made up of a loose alliance of several subgroups, has been labelled the "Court Party."[128] Morton and Knopff allege that the Court Party threatens representative democracy because of its elitist, rights-oriented ways that seek to transfer so much power from parliaments to the courts, from democratic processes of debate, negotiation, and compromise to inflexible rights claiming.

What is more, the Court Party is supported by the state. The support is financial, providing funds to promote any number of causes related to rights claiming, from official languages minorities to equality-seeking groups (of many variations). The state also advances *Charter* goals through governmental offices, most prominently departments of justice, peopled with individuals sympathetic to the Court Party's agenda.

The result is the urging of a new constitutionalism. The classic understanding of the functions of a constitution was that it was to control the exercise of governmental power. The Court Party seeks a constitutionalism that imposes "Charter values." Thus, the goal is not so much to limit the coercive powers of the state; rather, this new constitutionalism guides the state, requiring it to act when it has not acted, and requiring it to act in certain ways when it does act – all to reflect and implement values the Court Party has deemed worthy.[129]

For Morton and Knopff, the Court Party and its fulminations pose a fundamental threat to representative politics. Liberal democracy rests on the premise of majority rule while recognizing that a majority at any time is made up of coalitions of minorities operating in a pluralistic society. There is the potential that opponents on one set of issues may become supporters on other questions. Thus, participants in political debates need to meet each other on common ground as fellow citizens. In representative democracy, there is dialogue, even if of a fractious, boisterous variety.

Litigation, courts, and entrenched rights change all that. "Dialogue" is a wildly inaccurate description of the process. Instead, what occurs is that the debate and compromise of representative politics are replaced by a context of win-lose outcomes in which all sorts of issues are placed beyond legitimate debate and in which winning partisans claim permanent victory: "As the morality of rights displaces the morality of consent, the politics of coercion

replaces the politics of persuasion. The result is to embitter politics and decrease the inclination of political opponents to treat each other as fellow citizens."[130] Morton and Knopff offer a number of examples of what they regard
as "the politics of coercion." For instance, they point to the fact that in 1988
only 24 percent of the Canadian population indicated that abortion should be
legal under any circumstances, whereas 60 percent said it should be legal under certain circumstances (14 percent indicated that it should be illegal under
any circumstances).[131] Yet, they show how abortion rights activists, using the
courts and a political process shadowed by rights talk, enshrined a position of
unregulated access to abortion that clearly did not reflect the opinion of the
majority.[132]

Nevertheless, Morton and Knopff's condemnation of the Court Party approaches the hysterical. Strident words and phrases are peppered throughout
their concluding chapter on the Court Party and the sorry outcomes its machinations are alleged to be producing. Here are some examples from just one
page: "extremists," "combat," "closed and intolerant" "constitutional trumps."[133]
Such strong accusations raise all sorts of questions.

Their description of "members" of the Court Party leaves one wondering
just who is included. For example, they point to law schools as recruitment
centres for "The Party." It is true that some of the greatest celebrants of the
Charter are in these faculties, particularly at the University of Toronto.[134] But
there are also many in law schools who have severe doubts about the enterprise. Some are ideologically opposed.[135] Others accept the *Charter* but worry
about the effects on underlying issues and about the long-term prospects for
responding to them.[136] Still others voice their concerns about the *Charter* as
part of more general doubts about using litigation to address complex social,
economic, and political issues.[137]

Beyond law schools, several of the most distinguished observers of courts in
Morton and Knopff's calling, political science, are among the skeptics of the
judicialization of rights.[138] The media may have fallen into line as it sees the
newsworthiness of rights battles. But many prominent journalists are doubt-
ers of the *Charter* enterprise.[139] Morton and Knopff point to civil liberties associations as another source of "Party" members. It is these groups that have
played a role in some *Charter* litigation, particularly in the criminal area. Yet,
the long-time head of the most prominent of these groups, the Canadian Civil
Liberties Association, has issued strong warnings about relying on the *Charter*
to protect civil liberties and about "possible usurpations by the judiciary."[140]

More generally, Morton and Knopff anxiously wring their hands about the
fate of representative politics: "The Charter Revolution is ... deeply and fundamentally undemocratic ... in ... eroding the habits and temperament of representative democracy. The growth of courtroom rights talk undermines perhaps
the fundamental prerequisite of decent liberal democratic politics: the willingness to engage those with whom one disagrees in the ongoing attempt to

combine diverse interests into temporarily viable governing majorities."[141] Their concerns about the fate of representative politics are well founded. Representative politics is in a sorry state – a matter that I pursue in the next chapter. Yet, what we will also see is that this dishevelment is not unique to Canada.

Generally, politics, legislators, and parliaments in many industrialized nations have suffered a marked decline in popularity over the last decades. Many of these societies do not use courts to resolve fundamental questions to the extent that Canada and the United States do. Thus, the reason for the turning from representative politics cannot be attributed just to the courts. What is more, there are other factors in Canada besides an expansive judicial role that have contributed to the sagging fortunes of representative politics. The failure to reach fundamental constitutional accords, the ascendance of markets, and the forces of globalization are surely among them – matters I discuss in subsequent chapters.

The "Wing of Rights"

Whatever the hyperbole and inaccuracies of Morton and Knopff's charges, they raise important questions. Our notions of what should be determined by politics has shifted. Our conception of individuals and their relationship to each other and to the state has been transformed. Perhaps what is wrong with the dialogue metaphor is not that it claims too much but too little. "Dialogue" scripts legislatures as respondents to court pronouncements, with rights and their implications dominating the order paper. What may have taken place is fundamental change in the concept of citizens, their participation in government, and the issues being addressed. The courtroom now vies with the polling booth as the essential place for public participation.

An eloquent but disturbing account of this move to the courts in the United States, as a reaction to the decline of representative politics, is Michael Schudson's *The Good Citizen: A History of American Civic Life*.[142] As the title suggests, the book recounts the different understandings of what has constituted desirable roles for individuals in public life at different periods of the republic. The colonial period was associated with a citizenship founded on social hierarchy; the nineteenth century emphasized mass political participation; the Progressive Era's ideal was the informed citizen. What is most relevant for our purposes is Schudson's assertion that the latest era is that of the "rights-regarding citizen" permeating all spheres: "the 'political' carried on the wing of rights, has now diffused into everyday life."[143] In this depiction, decline in voting, lack of trust in government, and dissatisfaction with popular politics are indicators not of the unravelling of public life but, rather, of its transformation: "rights and rights-consciousness have become the continuous incitements to citizenship in our time."[144] The "wings of rights" has fundamentally altered the sense of the "good citizen."

Schudson's book is important for many reasons. He asserts that what has been called the "long civic generation" probably never existed in America and that every era has had its skeptics warning about the dissipation of public life. He forcefully reminds us that the conception of citizenship did not include women, blacks, and other minorities not so long ago. Rights have clearly had a role in creating space for the excluded to take their place in public life. Even as he insists on this new characterization of citizenship he underscores that the transformation to rights-regarding is not itself the answer to democracy's discontents.

Yet, he promotes the centrality of rights and of courts as the vehicle for their recognition: "rights-consciousness places the courtroom along-side the polling place in the practice of public life."[145] As he does this he engages in an exercise linked to the themes of this book. He asks, what effects has this turning to rights produced on citizenship and a sense of community? And he examines seven measures: voter turnout, trust in government, social capital, quality of public discourse, disparity between rich and poor, access of least advantaged groups to political power, and the reach of state-guaranteed rights. He concludes that "there is clear decline on one measure" (voter turnout), "clear progress on two others" (access of least advantaged groups to political power and reach of state-guaranteed rights), "a mixed verdict on three" (social capital, quality of public discourse, disparity between rich and poor), and "one measure is ... far too faulty a concept to use" (trust).[146]

There is much to be said for using these measures and for Schudson's analysis. Yet, he is surely wrong about some of the conclusions he reaches, at least for the United States. Just the rise in the income of the top 1 percent since 1997 was estimated (in 1999) to exceed substantially the total income of the bottom 20 percent of the income earned by individuals. Wealth is distributed even more unequally than income. In 1999 it was more concentrated among the top 1 percent and top 20 percent than at any time since the Depression.[147] How do these figures add up to a "mixed verdict" on the (growing) disparity between rich and poor?

Moreover, Schudson is curiously uninterested in other obvious manifestations of public life and of commitment to community in his society. Where does he take account of the state of urban cores? Of education? Of the levels of crime? Of the number of people in prison? Of the imposition of the death penalty? Of availability of basic health care? Of welfare entitlements? Of access to basic housing? He is right to salute the growth of state-guaranteed rights and their contribution to human dignity. But he seems minimally interested in the ways that other democracies of a similar tradition have secured these and other advances without being awash in rights talk, without making the "commons a barren place."[148]

What of Canada and the "wing of rights"? That the commons will become a barren place may be the greatest concern. Those skeptical of the *Charter* worry that the entrenchment of rights with an enhanced role for the judiciary will make society much more individualistic and much more hostile toward government. As courts become more important, representative politics will continue to wane.[149] As a result there will be much less commitment to the public good as manifested in policies on health care, education, urban renewal, basic income entitlement, and social programs to prevent crime. It is not that rights of minorities and the disadvantaged should be excluded; it is that these protections – and other policy goals listed above – could have been accomplished through an evolving popular politics. Yet, such a possibility has now been foreclosed through the dominance of courts and the obsession with rights.[150] There may be dialogue, but the talk will be incessantly about a multitude of rights; common goods will be shunted to the sidelines.[151]

What is the evidence thus far? As in the United States, crime, including that of violence, mostly fell during the 1990s. Nevertheless, as with America, we have experienced the paradoxical effect of imprisoning more people as crime declines. True, rates of incarceration have not reached sky-high limits as they have in the United States. Moreover, except for the occasional outburst, there has been no sustained call for a return to the death penalty.[152] Yet, between 1980-81 and 1994-95, there was a 50 percent increase in the population of Canada's prisons.[153] Roach is someone inclined to view rights favourably.[154] Nevertheless, he allows that "victims' rights emerged ... as the new means to legitimate crime control, including its very shaky assumption that the criminal law controlled crime ... Victims' rights supported the tendency in an age of fiscal restraint and disillusionment to criminalize politics."[155]

What is more, politics in Canada have generally taken a right turn during the same period that we have turned to rights. Government budgets have been drastically cut, and there have been few social program initiatives in the last decade or so. Ontario, the most populous province, twice elected in the 1990s a very conservative regime that pledged to shrink government. Many of these measures were implemented in health care, education, and worker protection programs. In the fall of 2003, that government was turned out by the voters. It remained to be seen what policies would be implemented by Dalton McGuinty and the Liberals in the months ahead.[156] Meanwhile, support for the social democratic party at the national level and in many provinces has waned.[157] At the same time, the disparity between rich and poor in wealth and income, though not as great as in the United States, has increased over the last fifteen years.[158]

There may be other explanations for governments becoming more conservative. In the previous decades, governments of every stripe had accumulated huge public debts, making austerity toward social programs almost inevitable in the 1990s. Nevertheless, many countries of Western Europe have faced debts and deficits without disavowing the programs themselves.[159]

Moreover, disparity in incomes and wealth in most countries of Europe has not increased to the same extent as in Canada (to say nothing of the United States).[160] There are enough negative indications to put in issue proponents' claims that the *Charter* and the courts would bring about a new era in progressive politics. There are enough worrisome signs to suggest that the very notion of using politics to forge common agreement may be in jeopardy. These are issues to which I will return in Part 3.

Weinrib opposes root and branch Morton and Knopff's charges of the Court Party and its machinations. For Weinrib, the *Charter* ushered in the "activist constitution," "a world in which we live our lives as free, equal, rights-holding citizens, not merely occasional voters."[161] She charges that "the Canadian critics of judicial activism are social conservatives resisting a judiciary they perceive to be impermissibly liberal."[162] She is right to some degree about that. Morton and Knopff's examples of judicial excess do often target claims made about disadvantage. It cannot be a surprise that many of those who have been excluded historically from representative politics would come to view rights claiming as empowering. However, even as Weinrib insists that the battle line be drawn between social liberals and conservatives, she leaves a lot out.

If we become preoccupied with rights, however recognized, we are in danger of losing sight of other ways of viewing the world. Rights are important; if they are recognized through "dialogue," so much the better. But great public institutions and programs that allow citizens to fulfil themselves and lead lives in economic dignity are critical as well. Even some proponents of the "rights revolution" acknowledge that "when you engage in rights talk, you are committed to a certain kind of individualism ... rights talk has [difficulty] in focussing [on] the social and economic inequality that accompanies the competitive individualism of market society."[163] Others who are more skeptical of the "revolution" suggest that rights can undermine the common welfare otherwise forged through the tough process of negotiation and compromise: "When we use the language of rights, and make the strongest possible claims, the space for political compromise diminishes. It is easier to compromise when interests compete; we are adept at trading. Rights are foundational and non-negotiable."[164]

Weinrib charges that "the critique of judicial activism in Canada ... is the expression of deep anguish by the stakeholders of a world view in demise."[165] But which "world view in demise"? The one that promoted a temperate politics to produce an internationally recognized record for respect for human rights, universal health care, and a commitment to achieving excellent public education and basic income entitlements? If it is that one, some of us plead guilty to such "expression of deep anguish." From this vantage, the "wing of rights" as the essence of the "good citizen" is excessive on the one hand, and impoverished on the other. Meanwhile, we do know that, as the power of courts has increased, representative politics is more and more in disarray. Such dishevelment may not be blamed on the judges. Nonetheless, courts and rights talk, powerful on their own, become more so as confidence in representative politics plummets. That sorry state is a matter I turn to in the next chapter.

Conclusion

Holmes cautioned decades ago that "all rights tend to declare themselves absolute to their logical extreme."[166] That sentiment reflects worries about a cacophony of claims that will not be a route to empowerment. To the contrary, the fear is that such assertions will abet a swell of fractiousness, creating expectations for law that it cannot meet. Such societal dust-ups can blunt initiatives in tackling the very serious problems besetting common conditions. The hope that politics can be about "measured care for our fellow humans" will grow ever more distant.[167]

Those who advocate an activist role for judges complain about "court bashing" on the part of those who are unhappy with this enlarged role.[168] Some of this upset is justified; critics have often been wide of the mark and sometimes quite personal in their attacks on judges. Yet, such outbursts were a predictable reaction to the extravagance of a rights talk that compared the *Charter* to Louis Pasteur's discoveries, urged litigating the values of a nation, and asserted that judges are the "custodians of the *Charter*." What more needed to be said? The future of the country hinged upon entrenched rights: "as the *Charter* evolves so evolves Canada."[169]

True, things have settled down somewhat in legal circles. Now there is much attention to "dialogue" between courts and legislatures. Exploring such potential is a welcome sign. Yet, the focus remains on rights at a time of disarray in representative politics. The myth of rights at a time of such dishevelment pulls people farther from a commitment to governmental institutions and the common welfare. The "good citizen" may not yet be exclusively rights-regarding, but she is being drawn away from an identity linked to "good government."

3 Representative Politics in Disarray

Popular politics is in trouble. There is failing faith in the ability of legislators to tackle the problems faced by twenty-first-century Canada. Such disillusionment with the political process is not unique to this society. Decline in support for legislators and public institutions can be documented throughout Western societies and beyond. But Canada has its very own brand of discontentment. That souring attitude toward the political process – offset by a newfound love for courts and a celebration of the market as the great distributor of goods and services – is a combination that could spell disaster for public goods and institutions.

This chapter will document that transformation of Canadian politics over the last two decades. A number of developments are associated with this change, including the constitutional crises, the unstable position of Quebec in Confederation, and the rise of the right in politics. Such change has led to the "critical citizen," a term coined to refer to the deeply questioning attitudes toward government that have developed in many countries.

That citizens should be watchful of their political leaders and frequently skeptical of their policies is a good thing. Citizens dismissing politics and viewing government as the enemy bodes ill for the commonality essential to a good society. The consequences of turning from representative politics are vividly illustrated by discussing child poverty in this society. Despite their promises, governments have failed to attend to the plight of poor kids in Canada. Critical citizens, for all their supposed powers to direct politicians where they need to go, mostly stood by as the numbers of destitute children increased markedly during the 1990s.

At the same time, as representative politics became disordered, courts, for some purposes, and markets, for others, were offered as alternatives for providing answers to all manner of complex questions. For most people, courts and markets do not respond to many important issues, especially those involving public goods. The suggestion that they do is myth making. But this myth of exit from representative politics to courts and markets has gained a powerful hold.

A Comparative Perspective

Documenting the Decline

Who has confidence in politics, legislators, and public institutions? Hardly anybody anywhere, it would appear. It is not democracy itself that is imperilled. There is a lot of survey evidence demonstrating broad support for democracy as better than any other form of government.[1]

Probably most people would still challenge the accuracy of Zolo's assertion that "it is the democratic encyclopaedia as a whole that seems designed for obsolescence, along with its most basic paradigms: participation, representation, competitive pluralism."[2] Still, there is much discontent with the political process. Disillusionment with representative politics has spread like a contagion over the last two decades, infecting almost all of Western society and then some.

As with many public issues, the United States seems to be the extreme case, in part because polls over an extensive period have produced systematic evidence. Between the late 1950s and mid-1990s, the evidence of declining faith in popular politics is dramatic.[3] In the late 1950s, when Americans were asked about how often they trusted the government to do what is right, three-quarters of them responded "most of the time" or "just about always."

From that point on, public confidence steadily declined. By 1998, only 39 percent of Americans believed that government could be trusted to do the right thing. In 1964, 29 percent of the American public agreed that "government is pretty much run by a few big interests looking out for themselves." By 1984, that figure had become 55 percent; by 1998, 63 percent. In the 1960s, only about one-third of people asked agreed that "most elected officials don't care what people like me think"; in 1998, nearly two-thirds concurred with that statement. Such decline also applies to specific political institutions. In 1966, 42 percent of those asked expressed "a great deal" of confidence in the executive branch; in 1997, 12 percent did so. A similar statement about confidence in Congress was supported by 42 percent in 1966, but by a mere 11 percent in 1997.[4]

Not only do people not have confidence in representative politics, they do not even vote for the politicians. Since 1960, on average, more than 45 percent of eligible Americans have failed to vote. In off-year congressional elections, the average number of nonvoters has exceeded 50 percent. Higher voter turnout in the 2004 presidential elections appeared anomalous; in 1994 Republicans and their "Contract with America" won a majority in both houses of Congress on the basis of a turnout of only 39 percent.[5]

In 1966, the tragedy of the Vietnam War was being paraded before the public by the media and activists; race riots erupted in many of the largest cities. Yet, only about a third of Americans believed that "the people running the country don't really care what happens to you." In 1997, in the midst of a long period of peace and prosperity, about 57 percent concurred with that statement. After the horrors of 11 September 2001, measures of trust in government did rise substantially.[6] It is unclear whether these gains will hold over the long run.[7] In any event, such approval ratings may be associated only with a limited role for government in national defence and security and not with issues of domestic policy, generally.[8]

America may be the extreme case of failing faith in politics, but it is by no means alone. Such decline can also be seen in Western Europe and Japan. To take but one further example, Britain's long-standing respect for elites has changed to skepticism. In 1985, 48 percent of those interviewed expressed "quite a lot of confidence" in the House of Commons; by 1995 about 24 percent did so.[9]

The Significance of This Failing Faith

That widespread decline in confidence can be documented is unquestionable. But what does such lessening of trust in government mean? Are the implications all bad? Are there some positive effects as well?

One reaction to this clear decline is to minimize its relevance and, in any event, to see it as a manifestation of positive change. There are three variations of this response.[10] First, such skepticism can be taken as a sign of democracy's health. More questioning has been a precursor of new interests, feminism, environmentalism, and so forth, forcing their way onto the public agenda. From this perspective, the issue is not the decline in faith in politics. Rather, the challenge is to explain why support was so high in the late 1950s and 1960s, when so many were often excluded from the political process.

Second, it is suggested that the decline in confidence is a sign not so much that political participation is on the wane but that it has been transformed. Its channels now are such things as grassroots activism, membership in organizations fostering particular causes, and the advancement of rights – in the legislatures, the streets, and the courts. Pippa Norris, in her book *Democratic Phoenix: Reinventing Political Activism*, put this contention forcefully: "If the opportunities for political expression and mobilization have fragmented and multiplied over the years, like a swollen river flooding through different tributaries, democratic engagement may have adapted and evolved in accordance with the new structure of opportunities, rather than simply atrophying."[11]

Third, it is asserted that the fundamental task of government is to give the people what they need. To the extent the electorate is happy with what it gets, so much the better. In the end, though, sound and appropriate policies are the best measure of governmental performance. Confidence levels are secondary provided that the public continues to comply with the law by paying taxes and so forth.

Nevertheless, many worry about the long-term effects of such continuing erosion of confidence in government. A primary attribute of democracy is that the collective judgment of citizens is a singular criterion of performance. Thus, diminishing public confidence over the long run is important evidence that the performance of government has declined.[12] In this depiction there are two overarching explanations for that deterioration.[13]

First is the declining *capacity* of politicians and their agents to respond to citizens' interests. Globalization has been singled out as an explanation for this diminished ability. Globalization "creates a growing incongruence between the scope of territorial units and the issues raised by interdependence, reducing the output effectiveness of democratic nation-states."[14] Second is the declining *fidelity* of politicians and their agents regarding citizens' interests. There are many aspects to such erosion, including failure of political leadership, wrong judgments on the part of voters, and deterioration of civic infrastructure and of social capital, thus weakening the ways in which citizens' interests are articulated and combined.

I return to the far-ranging phenomenon of the "critical citizen" later in this chapter and discuss its significance for industrialized societies in general, and for Canada in particular. Something fundamental is happening to representative politics that is not unique to any one country, including this one. Whether such change spells disaster or is the harbinger of transformation, perhaps to even better democracy, is the vital question. First, let's examine our own discontent.

Canada's Political Dishevelment

The Declining Confidence
Canada has a relatively long series of political trust measures. Such evidence confirms an increasing discontent with the performance of the political system. This dissatisfaction may not be expressed as dramatically as in the United States, but it is clearly apparent; "ratings of specific political parties and individual leaders and of confidence in major institutions of Canadian politics and government have fallen over the last two decades."[15] Over the last decades, few federal or provincial leaders have been able to sustain high approval ratings for more than a short period, even when they have secured substantial election victories.[16]

Public opinion polls over the last decades tell the disheartening story.[17] In 1968, 45 percent of respondents agreed with the statement, "the government doesn't care much what people like me think"; by 1993, 67 percent concurred. In 1979, 30 percent of those interviewed felt a "great deal" of confidence in political parties; by 1999, 11 percent did so. In 1986, 51 percent said they were satisfied with their system of government; by 1992, 34 percent said so.[18] In 1980, 57 percent of interviewees believed politicians to be competent; by 1990, 33 percent did so. In 1980, 63 percent of interviewees believed politicians to be principled; by 1990, 28 percent did so.[19] By the spring of 2002, it looked like a new low had been reached: 69 percent of respondents to a poll believed that federal and provincial political systems are corrupt.[20]

Beyond statistical evidence, other sources, such as academic analyses, editorial commentary, and media stories, indicate an electorate deeply skeptical of possibilities for the political process. The mood places the idea of a Canadian society in suspension. Those who enter politics do so at their peril. The supposition is that office seekers must be running for no good reason. Jeffrey Simpson expressed this sentiment well, if extravagantly: "So corrosive is this mood that those who risk public life will be largely those who cannot think of anything better to do and who, elected, will earn more money than in any other job they might ever have."[21] A pervasive theme in academic commentary is that "divided and fragmented power is a fundamental barrier to the hard choices that must be made if the country is to respond to the policy challenges – domestic and international – that it faces."[22]

What's Happened to Canadian Politics?

How did we get to this point? Cause and effect are tricky matters in assessing many societal issues. Interviewees are rarely asked the reasons for their opinions. Collective views are hard to pin down to any one cause. Those views and their many possible causes interact in the ebb and flow of day-to-day Canadian life. That said, a number of developments over the last two decades can be documented that would appear to be related to the failing faith in the political process and its dismal prospects. Each of these developments cast doubt on the ability of politicians to adequately represent their constituents in solving complex problems or, in some instances, preventing the problems in the first place.

The Constitutional Crises

The Meech Lake and Charlottetown accords stand as a low point in attempts to reconfigure the constitutional makeup of the country. Whatever the achievements of the 1982 Constitution, it was clear that it had not responded to francophones' demand that the government of Quebec be given the status and power to be the representative of their aspirations. Quebec had refused to be a signatory to it, charging that last minute negotiations among other parties had betrayed its interests. Indeed, the *Charter of Rights and Freedoms* had compromised Quebec's powers – for example, in regulating access to English-language schools and restricting access to government services by migrants from other provinces.

The Meech Lake Accord responded to these aspirations but in a limited way. Quebec was acknowledged to be a "distinct society," but this was offset by a preceding clause involving a linguistic duality extending throughout Canada and was further qualified by a provision insisting that the federal government's "powers, rights or privileges" cannot be diminished.[23]

After initial indications that it would pass, agreement for the accord in the provinces unravelled, most prominently in Manitoba and Newfoundland. Its failure sent waves through the country, and Brian Mulroney's Conservative government reeled for about a year in dislocation. During the summer of 1991, the country girded itself for yet another attempt, this time coordinated by Joe Clark, federal minister for constitutional affairs. Quebec was officially absent from these talks until the last stages, as it displayed a high degree of solidarity in its reaction to the rebuff of Meech.[24]

As these events unfolded, leading to the fall of the Charlottetown Accord, yet another force became a critical constitutional player. The Aboriginal peoples had long pressed a number of issues, from land claims and treaties to self-government to sovereignty, demands by no means limited to Quebec.[25] Yet, in that province, Aboriginal assertions clashed with Quebec's own claims for autonomy from the rest of Canada. There were critical questions concerning the fate of Amerindian land claims should Quebec separate, since those claims were also tied to the First Peoples' relationship with the federal government.

The Charlottetown Accord failed, and explanations abound for its rejection.[26] One thing is certain: issues surrounding Quebec, its claim to be a distinct society, and its claim to be sovereign did not disappear with the rejection of that accord. The same can be said for Aboriginal issues, particularly the claim to recognition of the right of self-government, including its relationship to claims made by Quebec. Beyond these issues, the double failure of the two accords cast a long shadow on the capabilities of the political process to forge the necessary compromises that would garner popular support to reconfigure the makeup of the country and to hold it together.

Quebec: In or Out?

The push toward independence for Quebec continued after the debacle of the Meech Lake and Charlottetown accords. Quebec nationalists threatened to continue to hold referenda until the necessary votes were obtained to declare independence. In 1995 a referendum was held in which federalist forces won by only a few thousand votes.[27] In the aftermath of the defeat of the 1995 referendum, Premier Parizeau promised that "the battle for a country is not over, and it will not be over until we have one."[28] In April 1996, 61 percent of Quebeckers thought that their province would separate from Canada within two years; 40 percent of those interviewed in the rest of the country agreed.[29]

Meanwhile, Quebec's agitation and the federal government's attempt to address it became a lightning rod for the Reform Party. An important factor in its success was its opposition to concessions to Quebec. Thus, federal governments became caught between a rock and a hard place. On the one hand, they struggled to blunt nationalist forces in Quebec. On the other, they had to fend off charges that in so doing they were preferring Quebec to the other provinces, particularly those in the west. Resentment with this preoccupation with

Quebec nationalism spread to the general public. Polls taken after the failed accords and after the 1995 referendum confirmed this. A majority of voters outside Quebec were concerned about the possibility of Quebec's separation, but they wanted political leaders to attend to other issues.[30]

The situation in Quebec continued to cause turmoil into the early 2000s.[31] True, by 2001 support for independence among Quebeckers had dropped significantly for a number of reasons, many of which were associated with the government of the Parti Québécois.[32] Yet, separatist leaders continued to point to the European Union model as the one to follow on the road to the province's independence.[33] In 1998 the Supreme Court ruled on a reference put to it by the federal government that Quebec does not have a unilateral right to secede; however, the rest of Canada cannot block Quebec if a clear majority in the province voted "yes" on a clear question asking if Quebec should secede. If such a clear majority were to be secured, the Court indicated, the terms of separation would have to be negotiated.[34] But how? At what cost? And what would happen to the rest of Canada?[35]

The First Nations
There is no serious challenge to the tale of misery. Death for Aboriginals comes mostly because of poisoning, accidents, and violence, with an incidence for these three times that of Canadians as a whole. By the 1980s grim statistics were gaining prominence. Aboriginals in federal prisons doubled between 1977 and 1987; while they are only 3 percent of the population, they constitute 10 percent of inmates of federal prisons. A 1985 study by the Department of Indian and Northern Affairs revealed that 38 percent of reserve housing did not have running water, indoor toilets and/or a bath or shower, and 47 percent failed to comply with basic standards of physical conditions. The official unemployment level was two-and-a-half times the overall rate. In 1981, 36 percent of the Canadian population had some form of postsecondary education; only 19 percent of Natives achieved this level.[36] Similar statistics would haunt Aboriginals into the 1990s and the 2000s.

Yet, documenting the suffering and the wrongs – critical as that is – is one thing. Redressing the tragedies is, sadly, another. There were calls for reforms to specific institutional arrangements, such as fiscal policy, education policy, health care, child welfare, policing, criminal justice, resource management, economic development, and changes in political responsibilities toward the First Peoples and the dominant culture's perception of responsibility.[37] Native peoples pushed very hard for recognition of the "inherent right of self-government."

As part of a many-faceted deal in the Charlottetown Accord, such right – undefined and only briefly described – was incorporated.[38] There was much talk of empowerment, autonomy, and control. These are noble and essential aspirations for people who have been so marginalized and ill-treated. At the same time, little was heard about illiteracy, life expectancy, infant mortality rates, substance abuse, and the other blights that plague the First Peoples. The hope was that self-government would untap and harness the wills and abilities of the people themselves to expel these demons.[39] The fear, largely unspoken, was that self-government would be a black hole endlessly absorbing fractious debates about forms and procedures – perhaps mostly among the people themselves – while the list of woes would advance, conscripting ever more victims in its miserable cause.

At critical points, courts would have been plunged into this. The agreement stipulated a five-year period during which the respective parties were to negotiate over the meaning and implementation of self-government.[40] In addition, there appeared to be some contemplation that a specialized tribunal would make some of these decisions. What is clear is that after five years, courts would have been called on to make myriad decisions at a fundamental and structural level concerning Aboriginal governments "as one of three orders"[41] to which the *Charter* applied.[42] Meanwhile, there were charges among some Native women that their *Charter* entitlements were not sufficiently protected.[43] With virtually no guidance, the judges would have made decisions about "languages, cultures, economics, identities, institutions and traditions"[44] and, subject to any framework to be found in a subsequently negotiated accord, about "federal and provincial governments ... providing Aboriginal peoples with fiscal or other resources, such as land, to assist those governments to govern their own affairs."[45]

Charlottetown was rejected for many reasons, some of which had little to do with the arrangements for self-government. Nevertheless, there is much evidence that the First Peoples themselves were divided along several lines, including that of gender, and, in the end, a large proportion did not support the accord.[46] One thing is certain: the rejection of the accord was accompanied by deep dissatisfaction with popular politics, including among Indians.

In the 1990s, concern about the plight of the First Peoples continued, but with few concrete responses. The Royal Commission on Aboriginal Peoples worked for five years and, in 1996, produced a five-volume, 3,500-page report.[47] The thrust of the report's recommendations was the implementation of self-government for Indians with an enlarged land base, assured external funding, and an Aboriginal House of First Peoples. The hoped-for result would be strengthened Aboriginal cultures, marked declines in the indicators of social breakdown, more employment, and higher incomes. Thus, the report would massively transform the position of Aboriginal peoples and Canadian society based on nation-to-nation federalism brought about through substantial expenditures. Yet, the report has been largely ignored.[48]

As the twenty-first century dawned, the angst over the condition of Canada's Indians continued. In the fall of 2001, the *Globe and Mail* ran a series of articles entitled "Canada's Apartheid."[49] Yet, answers to what actions should be taken and how to create the political will to respond seem not to be emerging. I return to these difficult issues and their implications for courts, politics, and markets in Chapter 5.

Increased Diversity

There has always been diversity in Canadian society and in claims to recognition based on difference. Assertions by Aboriginals, Quebec, and the various regions are prominent examples. However, in the last two decades, any number of other groups have insisted on legal and political recognition of their particular identities.

The traditional claims of difference have not been displaced. They now exist alongside a host of more complex cleavages with which they interact in complicated ways. Claims based on gender, sexual preference, religious practice, ethnicity, age, and disability are some examples of identities working their way through the social fabric: "social diversity echoes through many spheres of life, sustaining greater variety in lifestyles, music, food, communications, entertainment, and other cultural activities."[50] Claims based on difference and reactions to them wrestle with each other in a wide range of institutions; "these movements have generated a new 'politics of difference' and have vigorously forced themselves into the political process, challenging the dominant frame of reference through which economic and social problems have been viewed, and sparking intense debates about diversity, rights, and social integration."[51]

Just one example of the increase in diversity in the last decades is presented by a cursory look at immigration patterns and policies toward multiculturalism.[52] In 1957, 91.4 percent of immigrants to Canada came from Britain and Europe. Between 1980 and 1989, only 27 percent came from Europe (46 percent came from Asia; 20 percent came from other countries in the Americas; and 5 percent came from Africa).[53] In 1961 non-whites represented just 3 percent of Toronto's population. At the start of the 1990s, that figure had grown to 30 percent; at the end of the 1990s, non-whites were in the majority.[54] At the same time, only about 7 percent of Canada's immigrants settle outside major metropolitan centres.[55] The proportion of visible minority residents in St. John's was, in fact, lower in 2000 than that of Toronto's 3 percent in 1961.[56]

Canadians are both positive about immigration and wary of it. In 1999, 60 percent agreed that cultural diversity enhances Canadian identity. Nevertheless, only 14 percent wanted more immigration; 43 percent agreed with the current levels; and 41 percent wanted levels reduced.[57] As immigration patterns worked to make the society much more racially and ethnically diverse, the federal government, since the 1970s, has officially adopted a multiculturalism policy. In addition, the multicultural character of the society was given explicit recognition in section 27 of the *Charter*. It has been argued that state recognition of multiculturalism encourages inter-group rivalries. That policy is but one example of diversity gone so far that recognition of difference is purchased at the price of commonality: "if what we have in common is diversity, do we really have anything in common at all?"[58]

Such fears are exaggerated. Much of the official policy of multiculturalism has been directed to encouraging the integration of newcomers into an established society – one more sensitive to various cultural and ethnic ways.[59] Yet, there are troubling signs. Canada's most recent immigrants are, on the whole, well educated but are losing ground in earning power.[60] At the same time, claims of difference emanating from a range of identities have contributed to the difficulties of forging agreement on a variety of political and social issues.[61] Here is the angst: "increasingly, immigrants are moving into established sub-communities and ... are maintaining as much connection to their homelands as to Canada ... We live side by side but not together."[62]

Changing Political Alignment and the Rise of the New Right

The 1990s witnessed conspicuous realignment among political parties. These shifts were a product of many factors, including the volatility of the electorate, Quebec nationalists establishing a beachhead in Parliament, the decline of the social democrats, and, significantly, the rise of the new right.

The Liberals won the 1993 federal election after a long period of rule by the Progressive Conservatives. This switch in government by the two major historical parties was accompanied by fundamental change.[63] In 1993 these two parties won the smallest proportion of the popular vote in history. This while two insurgent parties, each with very different goals, garnered noticeable support. The Reform Party, a western-based right-wing and populist party won 19 percent of the national popular vote and fifty-two seats in the House of Commons. The party was also able to break out of its western regional base. Though it won only one seat in Ontario, it finished second in the popular vote in that province. The separatist Bloc Québécois won the largest number of votes in Quebec, taking fifty-four seats. As a result, a party whose goal was the dismemberment of Canada became the official opposition. The Progressive Conservative Party was pummelled, winning only two seats. Its viability to even continue as a party remained in jeopardy throughout the 1990s. On the left, the NDP suffered major losses and was reduced to nine seats.

The successes of the Reform Party and the Bloc Québécois ended the unstable coalition of "soft" Quebec nationalists, alienated westerners, and proponents of fiscal conservatism who had elected the Progressive Conservatives in 1984 and 1988. The losses suffered by the NDP signified the waning power of social democrats to form governments or even prominent opposition parties. In the federal elections of the 1970s and 1980s, the NDP had averaged just under 18 percent of the popular vote; in the federal elections of the 1990s, it averaged just over 9 percent.[64] The NDP did form some provincial governments during the 1990s.[65] Into the 2000s, its fortunes were uncertain.[66] Only the Liberals, who continued to retain power throughout the 1990s and into the 2000s, could approach the status of a national party trying to bridge regional and linguistic differences.

The rise of the new right may be of greatest significance in political realignment. That upsurge has been part of a larger phenomenon in established democracies. Although there are important national differences, the success of the new right has, in general, two characteristics.[67] First, most new right parties seek a radical transformation of the socioeconomic and cultural status quo. The most important targets have been the social welfare state and multicultural societies. Second, these parties build their strength through populist appeal resting on faith in ordinary people's common sense (as in Ontario's Common Sense Revolution in the 1990s); belief in simple solutions for even complex problems; and resentment that ordinary people, in spite of their innate wisdom and moral superiority, have been shut out of the political process. Thus, there are calls for the strengthening of direct democracy through mechanisms such as referenda, recalls, and the use of technology, most prominently the Internet, to allow for direct participation.

The Canadian version of the new right has found expression mostly in the Reform Party; its successor, the Alliance Party; and most recently, in the "new" Conservative Party.[68] Although not without its own internal troubles, the Reform-Alliance-Conservative amalgam has established itself as a potent political force nationally, helping to drag the other parties to the right of the spectrum. In addition, the old Progressive Conservative Party, in some provinces, has taken on a new right cast. It had notable success in Alberta and Ontario during the 1990s and into the 2000s. Some of the Reform-Alliance-Conservative positions are extreme given the tone of Canadian politics up to the recent decades. Nevertheless, comparisons with similar parties in other countries suggest that its "supporters are less radical than most of their European counterparts and Canada's new right is less 'religious' than its American counterpart."[69]

The rise of the new right has been linked to the declining confidence in representative politics documented at the beginning of this chapter.[70] In one way, the success of the new right refutes the idea that people are no longer interested in established politics. Yet, the new right is not content to take power and govern in conventional ways. Its appetite for direct democracy, however successful, and its animosity to government programs pose a challenge to representative politics as traditionally understood in this country. For the new right, the links between the "good citizen" and "good government" are strained in many ways.

The Concentration of Power
Power in government – at the federal level, at any rate – became increasingly

concentrated in recent decades. The extent of such concentration may be unique to Canada. This phenomenon is attributable to a number of factors, including the dominance of the Liberal Party, the heft of central agencies, and the increased power of the prime minister. Meanwhile, Parliament has become less effective because of a lack, at times, of a strong opposition, the public service has been diminished, and cabinet has been reduced to what is frequently little more than a sounding board for the prime minister. Power is being concentrated even as the positive influence of representative politics and its agencies, as a whole, is in decline.[71]

The Liberal Party governed for more than two-thirds of the twentieth century, only three times with a minority; "Liberals were arguably the most successful political party among twentieth century democracies."[72] Historically, the Liberals demonstrated a keen sense of brokering the demands of various interests and regions. They, more than the members of any other party, played to the country's sense of moderation even as the party manoeuvred for power.

Over the last decades, power to govern has become more and more concentrated in the central agencies. Such agencies include the Privy Council Office, the Department of Finance, the Treasury Board, and the Prime Minister's Office. Increasingly, they have become the focus for government.[73]

Their expanded stature has largely been at the expense of other government ministries. That stature, in turn, has increasingly been employed in the service of the prime minister: "power in the federal government has shifted away from line ministers and their departments toward the centre, and also, within the centre itself, power has shifted to the prime minister and his senior advisers at both the political and public service levels."[74] Concerns about national unity, the encompassing demands of globalization, and the demands to reduce the levels of influence of the public service, in terms of line ministries, are among the factors driving this shift.[75] These alterations have even swept up the most senior officials in the ministries into the demands of these core agencies and their support of the prime minister.[76]

In many respects the centralization of power has been most manifested in the altered role of the prime minister. The prime minister has always exercised a great deal of power at the federal level. And this has increased over the last decades. More specifically, the increased influence of the central agencies put at the service of the prime minister and the dominance of the Liberal Party during the 1990s may have made Jean Chrétien the most powerful prime minister in Canadian history. Such power only adds to the woes of representative politics since it has come about largely without popular consultation and consent.[77]

The power of the prime minister is manifested in many ways, not the least of which is the appointment process. With few constraints, he selects a raft of individuals who shape the governmental process itself. Such appointments include cabinet members, the deputy ministers, the Governor General, the Chief Justice of the Supreme Court and all other justices, the chief of the general staff, and the Auditor General. Moreover, hundreds of appointments to other agencies are formally made by the cabinet but can ultimately be determined by the prime minister. In all this, merit can be shoved to the sidelines.[78]

Such centralization of power may be a distinguishing characteristic of Canadian government, since the prime minister wields more power than the US president and many leaders in other parliamentary systems. As the democratic apparatus has been weakened, the people have increasingly shrugged at this development as another manifestation of the unravelling of representative politics. The danger remains that there will be further enfeeblement of the basics needed to hold the society together; "a sullen and disengaged citizenry is no friend of democracy, because at the very least these attitudes allow governments to grow insensitive and arrogant, and to fail to steer the country in directions that maximize the well-being and solidarity of its citizens."[79] In 2004 Paul Martin, after becoming prime minister, vowed to take democratic reform seriously on a number of fronts, including the matter of concentration of power in his office: "the command-and-control systems of central authority in Ottawa have pushed the views of citizens and communities to the side."[80] Would Martin truly loosen the prime minister's hold on power?

Markets in a New Light – Debts, Deficits, Privatization, and Deregulation
A different attitude toward the market swept over Canadian society in the last decades.[81] So considerable has been this change that I discuss its many features, separately, in the next chapter. Here I highlight the turn toward the market driven by debts and deficits. Much of that reaction looked to privatization and deregulation. The debt and deficit, and reactions to them, had a marked effect on Canadian politics, particularly in the 1990s. The turning to market forces became intermeshed with reactions to Canadian governments' deplorable fiscal situation. Reaction to the burgeoning debt and deficits became a conspicuous force in politics.[82]

By the 1990s the need to address governments' strapped finances became obvious to many across the political spectrum. Those of a more pragmatic cast were less worried about the debt and deficits in themselves than they were about the drag they were having on the economy and the capacity of government to finance its programs. Nevertheless, eliminating debts and deficits became a rallying cry of right-wing forces, which pointed to them as the consequences of big and intrusive government run amok.

Such reactions had a number of consequences, including curtailing of government programs generally, raising payroll taxes to sustain the viability of the

Canada Pension Plan, and a tightening of the employment insurance scheme.[83] There were several experiments with balanced budget legislation despite warnings of fiscal and policy distortions that could ensue.[84] In sum, Canada had the most restrictive fiscal policies among all the countries in the Organisation for Economic Co-operation and Development (OECD) by the mid-1990s.

Still another reaction to debts and deficits was a push for privatization and deregulation in the public sector.[85] Historically, public enterprises played an important role in economic development, especially in areas such as transportation, energy, and communications.[86] But by the 1980s, governments, faced with growing debts and deficits, created a wave of privatization to relieve themselves of the financial burden of subsidies to state enterprises and to create a source of cash from their sale. As a result, a number of major public entities – including Air Canada, Teleglobe, Petro-Canada, the Canadian Development Corporation, and Canadian National Railways – were sold off. This shedding of Crown corporations and related organizations was not without limits or complications. Some attempts foundered, including those initiatives where governments paid insufficient attention to the challenges posed by integrated public- and private-sector infrastructure.[87] Privatization, even where successful, often led to more regulation and not the anticipated deregulation.[88] Nevertheless, by the mid-1990s, the overall direction was clear both for continued efforts at privatization and for a curtailment of government initiatives in the face of claims by the private sector to perform the task.[89]

By the 2000s the fiscal prospects for Canadian governments looked brighter. Fiscal restraint on the part of the federal and most provincial governments produced a combined federal and provincial surplus of $30 billion in 2001. In that year, the ratio of federal government debt to GDP had shrunk, to 49 percent (from about 70 percent in 1995).[90] Yet, it was apparent as the 2000s dawned, that attitudes toward the role of government in the economy had significantly shifted.

In 1995 a survey of four hundred business leaders concluded that "corporate executives once saw government as a helpful partner in the building of the national economy. But today, corporate Canada embraces the radical free market view that government is no longer the solution but the problem itself."[91] If government can always be characterized as a problem for market forces, a very different attitude has taken hold: "Regulation is seen as an inherently limiting and constraining policy instrument in relation to private sector economic behavior. This neo-classical economic thinking is based on the idea of the 'free' market economy ... so that government action of almost any kind is cast as interventionist and restrictive."[92]

True, the efficacy of regulatory responses ought to be carefully scrutinized.[93] The danger is that the possibility of using regulation to respond to the deficiencies of the market regarding the protection of the environment, safe work situations, discrimination, the social safety net, and so forth is being put in doubt. The scope of activity for representative politics and its administrative agents had, again, been curtailed.

The Ascendance of Courts – As the Public Cheers Them On

The shift to the courts was addressed in detail in the previous chapter. That turning to the judges is in marked contrast to what was happening to representative politics as it suffered a dramatic decline in public confidence and its capacity to govern on issues of constitutional reordering, the plight of the First Peoples, and so forth. What is more, as the role of courts expanded dramatically, public confidence in them seems not to have been compromised. There is little historical data on the public's perception of the judiciary in Canada.[94] However, since the introduction of the *Charter,* pollsters have been more attentive to issues related to the courts and their approval ratings by the public. Thus, over time, we are developing a sense of the level of public support for the judiciary.

A survey taken in 1999 provided information on a number of issues about the courts and compared those attitudes with reactions coming from a survey taken in 1987.[95] There are high levels of awareness of the *Charter* and it enjoys much support. In 1999, 87.3 percent of those interviewed had heard of the *Charter* (in 1987, 83.9 percent had).[96] Of those who had heard of the *Charter,* 82.2 percent thought that, in general, it was "a good thing" (in 1987, 82.6 percent thought so).[97] These results pertaining to both knowledge and approval are consistent across the country and for all party affiliations, including those without a partisan preference.[98] Concerning the final say on the constitutionality of a law, roughly 60 percent in both 1987 and 1999 preferred that the courts make the final determination (about 30 percent preferred the legislature, and about 10 percent did not know).[99]

Awareness of the Supreme Court itself and approval of it is also high and strong when compared with survey results in other countries. Nevertheless, only about 43 percent of Canadians disagreed that the right of the Court "to decide certain controversial issues should be reduced."[100] This figure is lower than that in several other countries, including the United States, where about 53 percent disagreed.[101] Moreover, a poll taken in 2001 indicated that 69 percent of the respondents think that Canada's Supreme Court is prone to partisan politics some or most of the time (78 percent of respondents in the United States agreed with that statement).[102] Nevertheless, that same poll revealed 91 percent of Canadians had a great deal or a fair amount of respect for the judiciary in general in this country. The comparable figure for the Supreme Court was 88 percent (85 percent among Americans for the US Supreme Court).

Things might change. The percentage of Canadians prepared to have the Supreme Court's power curtailed could increase as more and more controversial decisions are made. A poll taken shortly after the Ontario and BC courts' decisions regarding gay and lesbian marriages revealed that 71 percent of respondents agreed that "it should be up to Parliament and provincial legislators, not the courts, to make laws in Canada." However, 77 percent of respondents agreed that "courts are within their right to issue decisions, that are based on constitutional grounds, that become legally binding."[103]

What is at present clear is that the courts' role expanded considerably during the last several decades and that growing influence was accompanied by very high approval rates for judges. Conversely, confidence levels in representative politics, the courts' main competition in the exercise of power, have fallen markedly. Not only are politicians losing the public approval but that support now has other places to go: judges, markets, and cyberspace are calling. As an alternate venue, the courts get a particularly high rating.

Enter the "Critical Citizen"

Earlier in this chapter, I indicated that the decline in confidence in representative politics was a widespread phenomenon in industrialized countries. This turning from representative politics and the reactions such spurning has produced have led some to suggest that the notion of what constitutes the citizen has been altered. Whatever that fundamental construct of democracy now means, for many it has the modifier "critical" firmly attached to it. A number of analyses have been offered to explain this failing faith in politics and its important repercussions. A brief canvassing of some major explanations will provide a useful context before we look at the Canadian "critical citizen."

A Further Comparative Perspective

In accounting for disaffection with politics in industrialized countries, five factors are prominent.[104] These factors and their consequences are producing "disenchanted democrats" who view their relationship to the state and each other as "critical citizens":[105]

- *Democracy itself no longer the issue* – Fighting Hitler or opposing totalitarian Russia confronted people with a stark choice. The fall of Communism has made people complacent about the freedoms that are enjoyed through representative politics. Yet, that state of mind may change in the aftermath of 11 September 2001 and the increased threat of terrorism.[106]
- *Representative politics linked to the nation-state* – As the nation-state loses significance, the influence of institutions of representative politics can also wane. This decreased significance can be brought about in two ways. On the one hand, demands for more homogeneous regional entities create pressures to dismember large countries. The worry that "homogeneous nations not only attract authoritarian leaders but also tend to become less tolerant within and more aggressive without"[107] can be shoved aside in the push for a homeland. On the other, there are threats posed by internationalization. Any issue that is removed from a nation-state is taken away from the decision-

making power of representative politics in that state. The ability of representative politics to respond to a variety of issues can be diminished.

- *Creeping authoritarianism* – Opinion polls have come to have a major role in decision making by the executive: "some governments trust focus groups more than parliaments."[108] This while seemingly nonpolitical institutions have become more acceptable in performing a range of functions; "there is consequently much support for independent central banks and for increasing the decision-making role of the judiciary."[109]
- *Public apathy* – Democratic theorists often assume that people are active in asserting their political interests. Such activism was at one time easily triggered when basic civil and political rights were at stake. Such rights largely secured, most people have become tired of politics, seeing it as little more than a game.
- *The erosion of civil society* – Civil society, an important basis for political participation and engagement, has been eroded. Conflicts have been transformed into individual competitions. Churches, neighbourhoods, schools, clubs, and so forth have declined in influence.

Taking stock of these five factors and their implications leads to two very different accounts of where democracies and representative politics are heading.[110] The first is pessimistic and, generally, is reflected in these pages. The erosion of support for core institutions of representative government may gradually undermine faith in democratic values. If there is little trust in parliaments, parties, and politicians, over time there may be disillusionment with the idea of democracy itself. Thus, the long-term stability of even established industrialized societies could be imperilled.

The second account is more optimistic. This second version needs to be fully acknowledged. In this depiction, the "critical citizen" will not be disengaged. Instead, he will experience politics differently and participate in other than traditional ways; "too much blind trust by citizens and misplaced confidence in leaders for good or ill, can be as problematic for democracy as too little."[111] Civil society has not been eroded so much as transformed.[112] In this account, older forms of representative democracy have declined, but there is an increase in new forms of self-expression and political participation, such as in social movements and by taking direct action.[113]

Nonetheless, a leading American commentator on such matters warns of the implications of a turning away from representative politics as traditionally conceived. Although his comments are focused on the United States, their possible relevance for this society should be pondered. Putnam suggests that Americans "remain ... reasonably well-informed spectators of public affairs, but many fewer ... actually partake in the game."[114] It may be that "because of the dysfunctional ugliness of contemporary politics and the absences of large, compelling projects, [Americans] have redirected [their] energies away from conventional politics into less formal, more voluntary, more effective channels."[115] Yet, the consequences for representative politics are depressing: "today's cynical views ... undermine the public confidence necessary to motivate and sustain political involvement."[116]

The Canadian Critical Citizen, Rights, and the Myth of Exit

In 1992 a leading Canadian journalist described some of the main characteristics of the Canadian version of "disenchanted democrats":[117] "a generation of rights-hungry but responsibility wary citizens for whom the old totems of Canadian federalism – federal-provincial negotiations, inter-governmental compromise, French-English accommodation – mean next to nothing."[118] Harsh. But quite possibly accurate, and perhaps even more so over ten years later. The sources of difference, of identity, of claims – of defiance against commonality as reflected in representative politics – seem only to be increasing. To a leading political scientist, these challenges assert that "the values and identities formerly associated with the centre are simply another set of personal choices, the product of one among many possible backgrounds, with no special claim on the allegiance of others."[119]

It may still be that Canadians retain a set of values premised on a sense of shared community in which they are actively involved. Extensive work by the Canadian Policy Research Networks (CPRN) suggests that they do.[120] The CPRN study indicates that Canadians possess a social morality based on a common set of shared norms (compared with American social morality, which is linked to legalism and religion). Moreover, Canadians share a sense of community; they reject gross inequalities between people (Americans pursue a more assertive individuality that tolerates more inequality). The vital question is whether these values can find expression through representative politics at a time of such sagging confidence in legislatures and their agencies.

Critical citizens are out in full force, decrying the shameful state of representative politics and looking for alternative spaces and institutions in which to assert themselves. Some urge a turning to the market. The potential of that institution to effectively and equitably provide public goods is taken up in the next chapter. Some, especially younger ones, believe cyberspace holds endless possibilities, including the building of new forms of direct democracy. The alleged wonders of the Internet are explored below, in Chapter 6.

Yet others have been drawn to the promise of rights, more particularly judicialized rights. Rights claiming vies with marking a ballot as a core act of citizenship: "Democracy relies on a full slate of rights which can be claimed by citizens, and an effective allocation of resources to groups who can benefit from rights. The process of claiming rights is as fundamental to democratic institutions as is the act of voting."[121] Indeed, if there is a problem with rights, it is not that we are relying too much on them but that there are too few available for judicial enforcement.[122]

That response may demonstrate the potential of rights and their fundamental role in new understandings of democracy. Or, it may manifest a refusal to cede a reasonable role to representative politics, the administrative state, and the market in forging public policy and in creating the good citizen.[123] It is also part of the myth of exit. Rights and courts are portrayed as alternatives that can be resorted to as people turn away from the sorry state of representative politics. Yet, in actuality, rights often do not live up to their promise, while the potential of representative politics grows weaker.

What does the critical citizen mean to accomplish through rights claiming? Cause and effect raise difficult issues in almost any area, not the least being the impact of law. I discussed these issues, in relation to the impact of litigation, in Chapter 2. At the least it can be said that the coming of rights has been accompanied by a better understanding of the need to take account of a whole range of interests often left out of traditional decision-making processes, including minorities of all sorts – linguistic, ethnic, racial, the disabled, and of sexual orientation, to name a few.

Drawing distinctions between different types of claims is useful in assessing where rights and the critical citizen may be taking us as a society. Critical citizens may have in common their clear distaste for representative politics and their high regard for courts. Yet, confidence levels, whether high or low, in society's institutions are only general indicators. On specific issues different citizens may support a variety of positions. The differences can be magnified by the dynamics of litigation, with its win-lose outcomes, and the values of the judiciary that have historically been focused on individualism, property, and negative liberty.

Thus, it is useful to consider the differences between issues involving, on the one hand, claims based mainly on cultural injustice and, on the other, claims for redistribution premised on economic injustice.[124] These two kinds of claims would also seek different kinds of remedies. The first would require transforming social norms so that there is a change in patterns of recognition and representation. The second would require some form of political-economic restructuring, such as redistributing income, reorganizing division of labour, or subjecting some aspects of market forces to democratic forms of decision making.[125]

The evidence indicates that claims that are more recognition oriented than distributive in nature have done better in the last decades.[126] Such success is consistent with the ascendance of market forces (hostile to distributive claims), with the individualized orientation of courts, and with "critical citizens" asserting "voice" against political institutions over which judges now have an increased supervisory capacity. Fudge emphasizes the explanatory power of the distinction between these two kinds of claims.[127] She illustrates her analysis with several examples; here I will focus on her discussion of the efforts of gays and lesbians to free themselves from discrimination.

In a series of cases beginning with *Canada (Attorney General) v. Mossop* in 1993 and concluding with *M. v. H.* in 1999, the Supreme Court condemned discrimination against homosexuals as a violation of their right to equality under the *Charter*.[128] These decisions prompted various legislative reactions designed to further protect the rights of gays and lesbians.[129] In 2002 and 2003 the courts of Quebec, British Columbia, and Ontario moved to legalize gay and lesbian marriages.[130]

In recognizing the claims to protect sexual orientation, the courts were, mostly, not leading the way but, instead, joining the current of history. During the 1980s and 1990s, public opinion polls indicated growing tolerance for homosexuals. What is more, legislatures and human rights agencies in many provinces had increasingly during that period taken steps to redress discrimination based on sexual orientation.[131] But how the rights of gays and lesbians were recognized by the courts emphasizes the distinction between recognition and distribution claims.

In *M. v. H.*, the Supreme Court recognized same-sex couples for the purpose of spousal support under the Ontario *Family Law Act*.[132] The Court declared the offending section of the act that defined spouse for the purposes of support to be of no force or effect. The Court's decision in *Egan v. Canada*, reached in 1995, had taken quite a different approach.[133] There the Court agreed that the exclusion of same-sex couples from access to social benefits in the form of old age pensions constituted a violation of equality rights but upheld the violation as a limitation justified under section 1 of the *Charter*.

This focus on litigation, particularly recognition claiming, has had an impact on the dynamics of the gay and lesbian movement that skeptics would predict. Above I discuss the ideas of those who doubt the efficacy of using litigation to bring about social change. One of the most prominent skeptics asserts that courts produce the "fly-paper" phenomenon. Litigation is a "lure" that entices groups and organizations to use it. As a result, groups exhaust scarce resources that could have been better spent in the electoral, legislative, and administrative processes making democracy live up to its ideals.[134]

Smith, in her study of the politics of sexual orientation, reached conclusions that support these more general assertions. She found that Equality for Gays and Lesbians Everywhere (EGALE) focused on *Charter*-based rights and winning legal victories at the expense of grassroots mobilization, class inequalities, and alternative models of family life.[135] Predictably, rights talk loomed large, with the effect that it pulled "lesbian and gay rights organizations towards an assumed lesbian and gay identity [while focusing] on the achievement of legal change as a primary goal."[136]

Smith's points are reinforced by court decisions concerning the legalization of gay and lesbian marriages.[137] Gays and lesbians should be able to marry; it is their basic human right. At the same time, it was clear, by 2004, that these judgments, as well as the pending reference to the Supreme Court of Canada on these issues, were testing legislators' capacity to address this issue and the public's ability to accept such rapid change.[138] What is more, it is not clear how many gays and lesbians actually wish to marry.[139] Long denied access to marriage, gays and lesbians have arranged their sexual and intimate lives in a variety of ways. As a result, many gays and lesbians are skeptical about embracing an institution they view as having been created for straights by straights.[140]

People understandably want their rights – whether they choose to exercise them or not. The majority in society must fully recognize this. However, the questions that might be asked within the gay and lesbian community are these: Do you wish to have the right to marry immediately even if public acceptance of gays and lesbians is set back? Or are you willing to defer the right to marry for a few years to permit tolerance for your community to increase further?

Lesbian and gay issues may indeed illustrate "dialogue" between courts and legislatures.[141] But this "conversation" also underscores the power of a rights focus to shove other considerations to the sidelines. It is "talk" that can allow little space for deliberations about how best to foster public support for progressive change. What is more, it is "dialogue" in which recognition claims are often, rightly, established, but where issues of distribution are increasingly muffled.

Citizens in Waiting and in Want – The Disgrace of Child Poverty

For all the ballyhoo about the critical citizen, it is not clear where these more questioning attitudes are taking us as a society. Individuals may be less deferential to authority and more inclined to question their political representatives on all fronts, but where is all this skepticism leading? This is a question that is explored throughout the book, particularly in the examination of the developments in specific areas of social policy in Part 3.

One group that has lost out in the midst of all this transformation is poor children. A large, urgent project for societies is to eradicate poverty among the young. Canadian politicians in the late 1980s declared war on destitution among youth. The enemy was to be vanquished by the year 2000. But the battle cry of the legislators was hollow. Critical citizens did not use their powers to demand that governments honour their commitments to conquer poverty among children. Shocking numbers of kids in this country remain citizens in waiting and in want.

How can a society countenance the raising of poor children? Whatever the currency of arguments about individuals' responsibility for their circumstances, such positions have little force when it comes to kids. Being born into poverty cannot be construed as the fault of that child; "it is the lottery of birth."[142] There are powerful philosophical arguments that "it is fundamental to shared concepts of progress and civilisation that an accident of birth should not be allowed to circumscribe the quality of life."[143]

Beyond any philosophical arguments, the effects produced by raising poor children suggest that it makes no economic sense for societies to tolerate the impoverishment of kids. There is one positive element in the life course of poor children in Canada: a higher proportion of them experience intergenerational mobility than poor children in many other societies; fewer Canadian kids stay poor throughout their life compared with children in some other countries.[144] Nevertheless, those who grow up in poverty are likely to be a greater drain on a society's resources on a number of fronts: they are prone to developing more learning difficulties, to dropping out of school, to resorting to the use of drugs, to committing crimes, to being out of work, to becoming pregnant at too early an age, and to living lives that perpetuate poverty, with the need to draw on the social welfare system.[145]

The arguments against child poverty are overwhelming. Their power gained sufficient force in Canada so as to lead, in 1989, to an all-party resolution in Parliament committing the government to eradicate child poverty by 2000. It seemed that, again, this society was demonstrating its historical capacity for compassion and clear-mindedness in terms of the most effective way to spend its policy dollars: rescuing kids from poverty was the right thing to do, and it was the smart thing to do in terms of overall savings by minimizing dependency on social programs. In 1989 Canada's child poverty rate was 15.3 percent. The battle cry was to drive it relentlessly to zero over the next ten years.

The resolution of Parliament was not accompanied by any specific plans for how the goal would be achieved. Nevertheless, for a while this great project seemed to be headed for success. But the economy was not to cooperate. By the early 1990s a severe recession had set in and governments were wrestling with huge deficits and staggering debts. Social programs came under the axe. By the mid-1990s the Chrétien government cut $7 billion in transfer payments, while giving the provinces more latitude with the funds that they did receive. Health and education were priorities; kids living in poverty were not.[146] By 1999 child poverty had *risen* to 20.5 percent; at least a 33 percent *increase* since the 1989 declaration to eliminate the situation by 2000. As the 2000s dawned and the economic situation improved, the escalating rate fell somewhat only to rise again; the target of ending child poverty by 2000 had become a cruel joke played on poor kids.[147]

The disgrace of child poverty in Canada is underscored through international comparisons. The number of our children who are poor is shocking. The comparatively low rates of destitute kids in some other countries demonstrate that such figures are far from inevitable, especially in wealthy societies such as ours. A recent report of UNICEF compared rates of child poverty in twenty-three countries of the OECD. It assessed both the countries' absolute (the percentage of children living in households with incomes below the US official poverty line converted into national currencies) and relative (households with income below 50 percent of the national median) rates of poverty. The latter is "today the most commonly used definition in the industrialized world."[148] In absolute poverty rates, Canada placed seventh,[149] but in relative poverty rates, Canada was seventeenth.[150]

The alleviation of poverty is not an easy matter, but it can be done. Canada's deplorable record on poor youth is in marked contrast with its successful efforts to reduce poverty among older adults over the last decades, discussed in Chapter 8. A firm commitment to use public resources to respond to the plight of kids seems a necessary precondition.[151]

If ever there were a project to be taken up by the "critical citizen" to compel governments to honour their commitments, this is surely one of them; "child poverty ... confronts the industrialized world with a test both of its ideals and its capacity to resolve many of its most intractable social problems."[152] Yet, except for a few committed groups and the occasional media story, the public registers its distress over child poverty and then mostly turns away.[153] The notion of the "critical citizen" may have some force in reshaping representative politics. Or, it may mostly be about underscoring the hapless state of governments in contemporary democracies, including our own – mostly about vociferous complaining, not constructive engagement. One thing is clear. However our society is being reordered, poor kids have been largely left out: for them, 1989 was "the year of the false promise."[154]

Conclusion

These days it is hard to find a celebrant of politics. In 1987 John Kenneth Galbraith answered the question about what distinguished Canada on the world stage by singling out legislatures and their agencies: "The greatest Canadian achievement has been in the conduct and purposes of government."[155] Today that characterization would be greeted by many with, at the least, puzzlement and, most likely, a great deal of derision. Would most of us still shrink from Henry Adams's characterization of politics as "the systematic organization of hatreds"?[156] Probably. But few would rouse themselves to a valiant defence of an institution that was once so central and which is now in such disarray.

When almost 70 percent of those asked indicate that government is corrupt, politicians, legislatures, and public servants are in big trouble.[157] They are in even greater difficulty when their dismal state is compared with markets and courts. These two other major institutions for public decision making are riding high both in terms of critical tasks being assigned to them and in approval ratings. Think of the implications for shifts in power, whatever the results produced, when only 11 percent have a great deal of confidence in political parties[158] and 91 percent have a great deal or a fair amount of respect for the judiciary.[159]

I explored, in the last chapter, how exaggerated notions of rights may pull people farther from a commitment to government and to the common welfare. In the next chapter, I turn to the market, the institution which now abounds in forging the "new" economy and in daily life. Although starting from very different perspectives, those clamouring for rights and those celebrating laissez-faire have become frequent, uneasy allies. One cry unites them – before they go their separate ways: Choice, Choice, and more Choice!

4 Chasing Choice: The Market Abounding

There never was a time when the Canadian economy was not dominated by the market. Nevertheless, historically, there was a large role for the government in nation building that resulted in its strong influence in the economy.[1] Successive governments all used public enterprises, subsidies, infrastructure and industrial policy, and weak competition laws to pursue various social, cultural, and economic policies.[2]

By the final quarter of the last century, pressure began to build to alter the relationship of Canadians with the market. The arrival of globalization, the need to wrestle with debts and deficits, the rise of right-wing parties, the promises of technology, and the influence of the United States, whose love affair with the idea of laissez-faire has intensified even more during recent years, were all factors that moved this society to become more market oriented. Such change clearly had effects in traditional areas of economics such as production, manufacturing, trade, and labour relations. But the influence of the reorientation did not stop there. The language of the market spilled over into day-to-day life: "efficiency," "productivity," "enterprise," "growth," and "marketability," however loosely used, became the new watchwords. And "choice." And more choice.

Canadians were repeatedly told that strictures placed on them by governments, unions, education, churches, and social norms had to be obliterated so that they could be free to determine their own destiny. The reality about how much choice how many people actually have, in this society, is very much a question. But the idea of choice, the illusion, the striving after, the demanding of it, came to pervade day-to-day life.[3] And with the clamouring for choice came the insistence for means to exercise choice. The claiming of rights took on a whole new force. Rights would permit choice, insulating the rights bearer from all those forces, especially governmental, that had restricted freedom all these years.

Thus, those demanding a greater sphere for the market and those seeking an expanded role for rights entered into an uneasy and at times contradictory alliance. Yet an effective one. The myth of exit took hold. Courts and their vaunted capacity to protect rights and enhance freedom took on a new aura even as laissez-faire exulted "choice" as the new watchword. Representative politics suffered. Woe unto the politician or public official who paid insufficient homage to the market, to rights, and to choice.

The Turn to the Market

The Transformed Economy

During the 1980s and 1990s, a number of factors contributed to significant changes in the Canadian economy.[4] The effects produced were complicated. Governments continued to exercise influence over industrial policy in matters such as technological change, education, and various legal issues (e.g., competition, securities).[5] Some of the strategies that were advocated to make the economy more competitive, more productive, more technologically driven and so on were not nearly as effective as advocates hoped. But the direction was clear: the Canadian economy became much more market oriented.

Changes in this society interacted with transformations around the globe as the "new economy" emerged. It was both defined by and defined as a "new world order"; "new patterns of state-civil society relations"; and a "new techno-economic paradigm" that replaced the postwar *Pax Americana* and Bretton Woods institutions, the interventionist welfare state, and the Fordist paradigm of mass manufacturing.[6] The foregoing is a stark rendering of the shifts. The unfolding of the new economy was, in fact, a complex tale.[7] Nevertheless, there was no doubt that significant changes were shifting power to the market, expanding its role in this society.

Internationalization

During the 1980s and 1990s, Canada was affected by certain rapid shifts in the global economy. Trade liberalization under the General Agreement on Tariff and Trade (GATT), and the development of trading alliances in Europe, Asia, and North America, most notably NAFTA, opened up borders to the forces of global trade and competition. Communications and transportation linked markets – and societies – so closely that these connections proclaimed the "death of distance."[8] Such forces make for economic competition among various countries. Trade in manufactured goods can reflect the costs of wages, social security, and health and safety. A society that permits its workers to be paid less in wages and benefits can be more competitive, at least in the short term. Thus, many traditional sectors of economies were challenged, from automobiles to machine tools, from household appliances to electronics. The role of the state was put in issue, a matter returned to below.

The economies of many countries were pressured by globalization. The Canadian economy was especially affected. Canada has always been a trading nation. It has depended on imports in its manufacturing industries more than other industrialized nations and that dependence only increased during the 1980s. It also seeks to export much of its natural resources. This dependence on natural resources to spur the economy has declined. Nevertheless, as of 1995 exports by Canadian resource industries still comprised more than one half of the country's exports, compared with one-third in both the United States and the European Community.[9] Our economy is, therefore, particularly sensitive to changes in international commodity prices. The effects of these shifts are especially felt in regions most dependent on resource-based industries. The apparent dictates of international competitiveness were brought to bear on a variety of aspects of Canadian industrial policy: framework issues, infrastructure, research and development, education and training, and labour market programs such as unemployment benefits.[10]

Another major external factor having important consequences for Canada is its dependence on the United States: no other OECD country relies so heavily on a single market.[11] Moreover, this reliance increased in the final decades of the last century. During the 1970s, there were some efforts on the part of the Canadian government to diversify trading relationships. Yet, despite these overtures, the proportion of exports bound for the United States rose from two-thirds in the mid-1970s to more than 80 percent by 1994.[12]

Such reliance on the American economy was a major contributing factor in the move to forging free trade agreements, particularly NAFTA, with the United States. The hope was that these agreements would stave off protectionist manoeuvres in America that could be damaging to trade and thus wreak havoc with our economy. The implications of free trade, especially with the United States, are far-reaching for the Canadian economy and society as a whole; "free trade" became a lightning rod for many hopes and fears in Canada.[13]

Because Canada is the smallest of the G7 countries, its policy decisions and economic performance have little impact beyond its borders. As international trade economists would have it, Canada is a small, open, price-taking economy. This country is strongly tied to a global economy over which it exercises little influence. The combination of the internationalization of trade and the growing dependency on the American economy with the fear of that nation's protectionist tendencies and the competitiveness of global forces shoved Canadians to embrace the market during the 1980s and 1990s.

Technological Change

As much as it was the nation's goal to have a market-dominated economy, the aim was even more so to have that economy driven by high technology. During the 1980s and 1990s, new technologies produced substantial changes in the production and delivery of many goods and services. In many sectors the basis of the market is changing from one of "mass" with standardized products to one with products tailored to specification. Workers increasingly need greater skills, but fewer people are required to produce a product or service. Thus, the strategy became one of producing a highly skilled workforce that would spur the Canadian economy through technology and that would meet the threat of low wage but minimal skills economies competing in global trade.

Governments and businesses trumpeted this positioning.[14] However, making it happen remains a challenge into the 2000s. The level of skills and the amount and quality of education of many workers in Canada remain inadequate. Moreover, statistics suggest that the Canadian economy is not nearly as technologically oriented as advocates for this strategy might suggest. Through the 1980s and 1990s, many in the United States were concerned about what they believed was the United States' hesitancy in embracing technology. However accurate those worries were, during this period, high-technology manufacturing represented a more weighty component of the economy of the United States than Canada in the areas of employment, exports, and the proportion of establishments by major industrial groups.[15]

Nevertheless, the idea of technology and its ability to drive the economy flourished. High technology came to be seen as the guarantee of prosperity. New information systems, robotics, computer-aided design, and manufacturing and communications – particularly the Internet – would be the way to ensure individuals' and society's wealth.[16] What was needed was a robust market to unleash these forces of economic betterment.

Productivity Trends

During the 1980s, the slowdown in productivity growth in both Canada and the United States increased fears that economic leadership in the future would be elsewhere in the world, even though, in the same period, productivity growth rates had slowed down, generally, in industrialized nations. Between 1960 and 1973, the average rate of growth among OECD countries ranged between 3.5 and 4.0 percent; between 1973 and 1993, it was below 2.0 percent.[17] As a result, "productivity" became one of the loudest of the battle cries during the 1980s and 1990s. At the core, this attentiveness to productivity was well-founded. Over the long haul, productivity is a vital factor in the competitiveness of companies in global trade, the economic and political power of nations, and the well-being of individual citizens.

After the recession of the mid-1990s, productivity growth became more rapid than it had been for some years. Optimists insisted that the restructuring of the Canadian economy was taking hold. Those who were less sanguine suggested that such increases were only bursts that typically occur after a recession ends, with the prospects for long-term increases still dim.[18] What is more, taming deficits and keeping interest rates and inflation low are macroeconomic factors that create an environment for competitiveness but are not by themselves sufficient to create prosperity. Instead, it is asserted that microeconomic fundamentals that produce distinctiveness are key to international competitiveness. The lacklustre state of those fundamentals has led to stern admonitions: "Only by migrating from a replication economy to an innovation-driven economy will Canada prosper in the 21st century."[19]

The debate over productivity and where it is headed continued into the 2000s. Market champions celebrated the forces of "creative destruction." Any setbacks were part and parcel of building the road to betterment. All the while, ordinary folk tried to cope with the consequences as best they could.

Organized Labour

One way that workers have attempted to protect themselves from the hardships of the market is to organize through unions. Collective bargaining was used to achieve better wages, working conditions, and benefits. Of course, that bargaining and the concessions that it won imposed costs in terms of the goods or services being produced by the employer. Thus, the economic restructuring that took place in the 1980s and 1990s put pressure on unions. This pressure sometimes resulted in reductions in benefits and protections that were negotiated during what seemed to be more secure economic times. In other instances, new firms sought to blunt unions altogether, particularly in the service sector, which has always been more difficult to organize.

Nevertheless, unions in Canada fared relatively well during the 1980s and 1990s, at least compared with the fate of organized workers in the United States and despite the increasing economic integration between the two countries. In the 1950s unions had organized nearly the same proportion of workers in each country; thereafter, there was noticeable divergence. Canadian unions expanded to include close to 40 percent of the workforce by the mid-1980s. There was a small decline, to 36.2 percent, by 1990; the figure then stabilized into the mid-1990s. In contrast, in the 1960s, American unions began a decline that quickened in the 1980s. By the mid-1990s only 15 percent of the workforce was organized.[20] Moreover, Canadian unions were more powerful than their American counterparts in ability to protect their members' interests against employer pressure for "concessionary bargaining," including wage freezes and rollbacks.

Whether this divergence and the relative strength of Canadian unions will persist remains to be seen in the face of intensifying economic integration between the two countries and the general mobility of capital. Some predict a "lagged convergence." The pressures for greater flexibility and efficiency will eventually erode the power of Canadian unions, bringing them much closer to the shrunken role of their American counterparts. Others point to factors, such as their greater organizational capacity and less restrictive legislation, which could help maintain a comparatively greater role for Canadian unions.[21]

Employment, Incomes, and Inequality

Whatever the success of unions in protecting the conditions of workers, the "creative destruction" of the final decades of the last century took its toll on many employees and their families. Canadian society bore higher levels of unemployment; employment with less security, including short-term, part-time, and contract work; and an intensified sense of economic insecurity.

During the 1990s, the standard of living of Canadians declined substantially. The dollar, which was at 87 cents (to the US dollar) in 1991, declined to sixty-five cents by the mid-1990s. It remained in that range in the first years of the 2000s but showed improvement in 2004. In international terms this decline was a pay cut in excess of 20 percent for all Canadians. The country's purchasing power parity (PPP) fell two places in eight years (from 1990 to 1998).[22]

For many working people, incomes stagnated. Wages enjoyed real growth in the immediate decades after the Second World War. But, from the late 1970s, earnings for the average worker were at a standstill. Increases in the incomes of families were usually attributable to additional members, often women, going to work outside the home.[23] At the same time, there was a relative loss of middle-wage jobs and a comparative increase in jobs paying very low or very high wages. Contrary to popular myth, this shift in jobs did not occur primarily between sectors – laid-off steelworkers pouring coffee in doughnut shops. Instead, the movement was mostly within sectors: the pattern of wage polarization was common to most industries and occupations. This growing disparity in wealth and income had many negative effects. One of the most devastating was the increase in child poverty that intensified in the 1990s.[24]

However, governments did continue to play a role in income maintenance. That support continued to stabilize the level of income inequality during this period. Without such intervention, that inequality would have been much greater. I return to governments' role in social policy during these decades later in this chapter. Nonetheless, the picture that emerged during the 1980s and 1990s for a large segment of the population was grim. Larger numbers of young people increasingly found it hard to get work at all. Unskilled and older workers and women and ethnic minorities were likely to be unemployed longer, not as likely to find another job, or, if they did find one, likely to bear a decrease in wages.[25] For these people there seemed to be more "destruction" than "creativity."

Is the "Efficient Society" a "Cult"?

Market forces now dominate the Canadian economy. But the influence of the market extends far beyond commercial and individual transactions. The market is no longer just a means of exchange for bargains big and small. It is something to analyze, discuss, and admire. Some read the financial pages as eagerly as others do the sports section. The performance of the stock market is an event, with participants, analysts, and spectators intent on keeping score of the hits and misses. The language of the market has entered into everyday life, shaping thought and behaviour. The forging and implementation of policy in governmental and other institutions is driven by market concepts, however loosely used. There is "more public talk about efficiency, accountability, and choice, and less and less about equity and justice."[26]

Individualism and choice are central as the idea of the market suffuses not only into Canada's economic life but into its social, political, and personal lives as well. In the early 1990s, Lawrence Friedman wrote a book on American society entitled *The Republic of Choice*. He contended that "the concept of choice, the desire for choice and the experience of choice" have come to pervade modern life not only in the United States but in Western society generally.[27] This demand for choice is accompanied by veneration of individualism, whatever the reality of people's lives: "the culture of individualism does not depend on whether people are free to choose ... it is enough that they believe they are."[28] Friedman extols the obvious benefits that choice and individualism can bestow, particularly on the population at large, when people truly are able to choose. Yet, he also issues a warning about choice and individualism marginalizing other values: "Modern individualism ... carried to extremes can destroy the ethical basis on which a plural society rests. Even at its best, it requires a delicate balance. That balance, alas, is not easily achieved or easily kept."[29]

Why is there this insistent talk of choice? And choice not just as a means to ends, whatever they may be, but as an inherent value? One reason may be the affluence of our society, regardless of how those riches are distributed.[30] If the market is producing wealth that makes us comfortable and secure, and choice is central to the working of the market, then choice, however it is exercised and for whatever purposes, must be good. Even many of those whose working lives have been thrown into turmoil and who have wages at a standstill have embraced choice. For if they have choice and they make good decisions, maybe their lives will be better.[31] And even economic pawns can celebrate choice by selecting from hundreds of television channels and multiple percentages of milk fat (skim, 1 percent, 2 percent, and homogenized; light, table, coffee, cereal, and whipping cream).

The way that society is now organized also fosters the culture of choice. We have long been a consumer society, glorifying material pleasures while stimulating wants through advertising.[32] Now not only can those demands be spurred, but technology boasts that they can be satisfied in ways specifically chosen by the individual: "We can design a car, or a computer, or a course, or a house, through the World Wide Web. Digital technology and private markets are multiplying the choices consumers have and giving them the autonomy to customize what they want."[33]

Deference to authority, once a Canadian hallmark, is in notable decline. We have seen that distrust of political leaders is at a high.[34] But this skepticism has spread to others who exercise authority, including religious and union leaders and medical and educational authorities. In this atmosphere there is a grow-ing unwillingness to follow the dictates of those exercising power. Instead, individuals choosing for themselves become the new watchwords: "the asser-tion of the right to choice is the voice citizens raise against authority that they increasingly distrust."[35]

This exulting of choice spills all over the place. For Stein, this rambunctious celebration has sinister implications for public policy. She is particularly con-cerned with the way that demands for "choice" have been joined to cries for "efficiency." She worries about how these assertions have come to target issues of common concern, especially those addressed by the government. It is not that considerations of efficiency are not important. Debates about efficiency can focus our attention on how to best use scarce funds to achieve a variety of goals. Resources are finite, and critical choices need to be made about the delivery of public services that often are in competition for these assets. Rather, it is the way that efficiency has come to be prized in and of itself: "Effi-ciency, or cost-effectiveness, has become an end in itself, a value more impor-tant than others. But elevating efficiency, turning it into an end, misuses language, and this has profound consequences for the way we as citizens con-ceive of public life."[36] So concerned is Stein about this misplaced veneration that she entitled her Massey Lectures and her subsequent book *The Cult of Efficiency,* for "when we define efficiency as an end, divorced from its larger purpose, it becomes nothing less than a cult."[37]

Even when there is an attempt to use efficiency correctly as the most cost-effective way to achieve goals, such efforts are often warped because there are no sustained conversations about what constitutes effectiveness in the par-ticular setting. Instead, there is frequently an obsession with costs and their reduction, and "when the public discussion of efficiency focuses only on costs, the cult becomes even stronger."[38] Much of the "cult" is directed against gov-ernment. The public sector is seen as the preserve of waste and irrationality, shielded as it is from the discipline of competitive markets and the demands of productive efficiency. The solution to the wasteful state is the efficiency of the market. Its mechanism will deliver goods as citizens freely strive after their own self-interest as citizen consumers.

Stein is intent on demonstrating how the obsession with efficiency regard-ing the delivery and consumption of public goods is misplaced. The state creates these markets to stimulate competition among providers of public goods and services. That competition is to result in the efficient delivery of such goods and services. But public markets often do not operate in the manner envisaged by their architects. Stein particularly focuses on the failings of pub-lic markets in education and health care. I return to a detailed discussion of education in Chapter 7.

More generally, Stein is dismayed by the way in which those who should know better have embraced efficiency as the new watchword in the forging and implementing of public policy. One of her targets is Joseph Heath and his book *The Efficient Society*.[39] As the title suggests, Heath is only too eager to celebrate efficiency in this society: it is a criterion we use to decide what is good and bad, guiding us in our choices and in how we attain them. Not surprisingly, therefore, efficiency has rightly come to prominence in our society. It is now of such importance that "it is the central value in Canadian society. It has largely displaced religion, ethnicity, and language as a source of public loyalty ... we have seen the future, and it is ... efficient."[40] Such assertions very much illustrate what Stein so strongly opposes. After quoting them, she retorts:[41] "We no longer, as we did even three decades ago, proclaim the justice of our society, or its equity, or its excellence. The dogma is simple: efficiency grows out of competition that markets bring, and accountability comes through the survival of the fittest in the market. For the high priests of efficiency, the conversation ends here. There is nothing more to talk about."[42]

Such a sharp response may be too harsh when it comes to Heath. He may exalt efficiency. Yet, he does so at least in part to defend a resilient role for government in providing public goods and in engaging in some measure of redistribution of wealth and income. Such a role for government is scarcely antagonistic to the thrust of Stein's arguments. Heath is far from a celebrant of laissez-faire. He is explicit that a main threat to the enviable balance that Canada has achieved in the private and public spheres is the political right and its pushing of market mechanisms.[43]

Still, Stein's warnings are not to be ignored. Whatever the usefulness of efficiency, its employment should be limited to means rather than to ends. The goals we are seeking to achieve must surely be informed by other values that we prize, such as justice, fairness, and equity, as complex as the working out of those may be. Stein's admonitions are not directed against market mechanisms, which are fully necessary for generating the wealth that is a precondition for the good society. But she opposes the market triumphant, with its demands for efficiency that stifle debate and push other goals aside.

Markets, Politics, Courts

Politics and the Globalization of Markets

The Impact of Globalization on Individual Societies

Whatever the controversies within societies over the role of governments and public goods, the part played by the state in the welfare of citizens, it is said, is bound to shrink as the forces of globalization take hold. Those forces will narrow the scope of governments, constraining what they can do, including the provision of social welfare programs. Thus, the triumph of the market within our society and the pressures of globalization from without spell the end of public goods as we have come to know them.

Globalization is a much-used term that can convey a variety of meanings depending on who is using it and in what context. At its most general it is the integration of various elements – economics, technology, politics, the environment, and so forth – of different societies. Take two examples: the communications revolution and fundamental entitlements. The Internet and the World Wide Web interactively link all who are connected, whether they are in Arnprior or Bangalore. The demand for human rights has taken on a universal character, with various advocacy groups participating in a global community. Yet, for some, globalization is essentially a code word for American imperialism – cultural, economic, political, and otherwise. The United States, under the rubric of internationalization, is exporting its way of life and its iconography, from McDonald's to CNN news, from Tom Cruise to blue jeans. In this depiction, the Internet, dominated as it is by the United States, is a vehicle for American popular culture, infusing it into offices and homes around the world. In a similar vein, those who see globalization dominated by the United States view international human rights as driven by courts and the judiciary and dedicated to the confinement of the state.

A meaning often accorded to globalization focuses on the international development of trade. Increasingly, the economies of various countries are being integrated into a single market through trade, finance, production, and a host of international obligations and institutions. The production and application of knowledge drives this market globalization. In the past the most advanced economies evolved from dependence on natural resources to the processing of these resources and the development of industry. Now, the "advanced economies ... lead because of their capacity to innovate, to create, and to draw on and expand existing knowledge ... [as] an infinitely renewable resource, only loosely related to geographical space."[44]

Market liberalism has been enshrined in this new world order. The politics and law of individual countries chase globalization as it gallops ahead. Opponents of market globalization assert that it constrains individual states, confining the capacity of governments in numerous ways, including the provision of public goods. For some, the very idea of the modern state is being put in question, at least as an instrument of progress, however that term may be understood. This warning by Richard Gwyn, a leading Canadian journalist, is typical: "In order to compete successfully with a South Korea ... our wages, social systems, and taxation schedules cannot be too different from those of South Korea. Many government policies are being decided now by the urgent need ... to create a market economy as efficient as those with which Canadian businesses are now competing directly."[45]

The state is weakened as borders no longer limit various economic, social, and other developments: goods, services, ideas, culture, and, alas, terrorism move freely without regard to the limits of particular countries. Much of this enhanced mobility produces much pressure to restructure domestic economies, altering types and methods of work for many people. Critics point to a variety of developments to underscore their concerns about the impact of globalization on individual societies:

- *Migration of capital* – Capital is able to move to countries that provide the greatest opportunity for investment and profit; the nation-state is immobile. This mobility of capital has many ramifications. Exit may be the response to higher minimum wage provisions, stricter environmental regulation, and strong occupational health and safety laws. Organized labour is weakened (less mobile); many businesses are strengthened (more mobile). Generally, there are strong competitive pressures to narrow policy differences that raise the costs of production in one country above those prevailing in trading partners.
- *Strength of global markets* – National markets are weaker than global ones; individual countries have less freedom to employ traditional instruments of fiscal policy to promote economic growth and respond to recessions. Governments are pushed to act, on the assumption that economic integration requires policy convergence on a variety of matters. There is a competitiveness agenda: policies should be promoted that will foster adjustment and adaptation to the new world order and that will support an increasing openness to international markets.
- *Rise of transnational institutions* – The terms of transnational treaties and their implementation by associated institutions can directly limit policy instruments of individual states. The World Trade Organization (WTO) and its authority to regulate an array of issues can penetrate into domestic jurisdictions.[46] At the same time, many transnational institutions are insulated from the citizens of the affected societies. Such lack of transparency has set off a wave of protests (for instance, in Seattle in 1999; Prague, 2000; Quebec, 2001) by various groups concerned about the power wielded by these institutions, the ramifications for individual states, and a variety of domestic policies, including labour rights.[47]

The Hollow State?
Despite all the fears expressed above, the powerless state is far from a foregone conclusion: "constraints facing governments are not impenetrable walls ... states still enjoy important degrees of freedom in charting their course."[48] Many of those who urge a robust role for government do not accept that its atrophy by the forces of globalization is inevitable.[49] What is more, a leading critic of an expansive state in Canada has presented persuasive evidence that, at least thus far, individual countries have a lot of room to chart their own course on a variety of fronts. Watson rails against the excess of the state in Canada both historically and at present.[50] Yet, he contends that it is by no means inevitable that globalization will lead to more limited government. Even in the face of

pressures for increased trade and economic integration, there is significant diversity in societies in taxation and public spending; capital is much less mobile than is widely contended, and borders still matter when it comes to trading.[51]

Those who contend that globalization will bring about the hollowing of the state often highlight rates of taxation and of public spending. They contend that globalization will depress tax rates and public spending in those societies where they have been higher. Such declines will be necessary to compete with countries that keep taxes and public spending low. Depressed rates of taxation and of public spending must inevitably shrink the state and its capacity to provide public goods. Watson arrives at quite an opposite conclusion.

He surveyed figures for levels of taxation and of public spending for Europe and for Canada and the United States. He points to the fact that, despite the continuing integration of these economies, taxes rose in every one of nineteen industrialized nations over twenty-five years (to 1998). Nevertheless, tax rates differed considerably within the OECD, across Europe, and among the American states. Tax rates became more similar for some of the most important European economies over fifteen years (to 1998). But the spread is still much like it was in the 1950s and 1960s, when there were prominent trade and investment barriers.[52] More specifically, there is a substantial variation in corporate tax rates. Watson points to a review of the twenty-four OECD countries that documented a wide divergence; as a proportion of GDP, corporate tax revenues ranged between 0.9 percent (Iceland) to 8.2 percent (Luxembourg; Canada's was 2.5 percent).[53] The author of that study asserted that "the divergences across countries are large no matter which alternative measure is chosen ... the prospects [for harmonization of corporate taxes] are not good."[54]

In Canada and the United States, there is also evidence of continuing divergence over taxes and public spending. In the mid-1960s Canada and the United States had essentially the same tax rate. Since then, Canadian taxes have constituted a higher percentage of GDP than those of America. Generally, that figure increased in Canada during the thirty-year period from the mid-1960s to the mid-1990s.[55] Public spending in the United States rose from about one-quarter of the GDP in the 1950s to over one-third in the 1990s. In Canada during about the same period, public spending increased from one-quarter to one-half of the GDP.[56]

Whatever the differences between Canada and the United States, generally, societies that trade the most have the largest government budgets as a proportion of GDP. They have the most capacity to deliver public goods if their governments so choose:[57] "the post-industrial states that trade the most have the largest budgets as a proportion of their gross national product. The most open economies – those most heavily engaged in the global economy – have the largest opportunity to provide public goods to their citizens."[58]

Watson also contends that capital is far less mobile than is supposed. Those supporting the "globalization equals hollow state" argument contend that the threat of capital leaving a society forces states to adopt policies agreeable to holders of wealth so that they will not exit. If capital does not migrate as easily as supposed, the "globalization equals hollow state" argument loses force. Statistics suggest that, in fact, capital largely stays in the country of origin. In the late 1980s there was strong evidence of citizens investing in their own country: 98 percent of the equity capital held by Americans was in US firms; for Swedes the equivalent figure was 100 percent; for Italians it was 91 percent; for Japanese, 86.7 percent; for the British, 78.5 percent; and for Germans, 75.4 percent. Despite these figures, it could be that the domestic firms in which these citizens held so much stock could invest in the economies of other countries. Again, that kind of migration of capital also does not occur as frequently as is supposed. In 1994 US foreign investment was only $130.8 billion; only 1.9 percent of its GDP of $6.7 trillion.[59]

One explanation that has been offered for capital staying at home is known as asymmetric information. Foreign investors have less information about an economy than do domestic investors. Therefore, they fare less well and, as a result, tend to invest in their own markets. During the approach to the Mexican devaluation of its currency in December 1994, domestic investors shifted large amounts of funds into foreign currencies, but most foreign investors liquidated their holdings only in February 1995, after large losses had been suffered. Even in an economy as open as that of the United States, foreign subsidiaries report considerably lower rates of return than domestic firms, even after controlling for industry, length of existence, and other relevant factors.[60]

Finally, Watson contends that borders still matter in trade. The exchange of goods and services, a central component of globalization, may not be occurring to nearly the extent that is widely assumed.[61] Canadian economists as esteemed as Thomas Courchene emphasize that "Canada is progressively less and less a single national economy and more and more a series of ... cross-border economies."[62] But such conclusions are premised on the *volume* of trade between the two countries.[63]

In contrast, a study of Canada-US trade up to 1998 confirms the importance of borders, even one as open as the one shared by these two countries.[64] That study found that, on average, trade among Canadian provinces was twenty times greater than would be expected if only economic size and distance between jurisdictions (state, provinces) mattered: "even the relatively innocuous Canada-US border continues to have a decisive effect on continental trade patterns."[65] The study is dated, particularly in light of the developments under NAFTA. Trade between Canada and the United States increased substantially during the 1990s and into the 2000s. Nevertheless, as Watson comments: "Cut east-west trade in half – or double north-south trade – and Canadians will still be trading with each other ten times more than they would if the border didn't matter."[66] Statistics on trade among countries of the European Union also support the contention that borders still matter. For example, trade between France and Germany represents only about 3 percent of each country's GDP. A comparable figure for Ontario and Quebec ranges between 6 and 9 percent of the GDP.[67]

There may be several explanations as to why borders continue to matter in the face of major efforts to liberalize trade. Differences in legal systems can raise the cost and risk of engaging in commerce outside the home jurisdiction. Meanwhile, nationals may enjoy the benefits of institutional comity: laws that permit individuals and firms that conduct business in one province to enjoy a favoured status in other provinces. In addition, there may be cultural differences. Tastes may differ in ways that outsiders do not understand: Canadian Tire, a household brand in this country, was a flop in the United States. In sum, "globalization may have to create a truly impressive levelling of the institutional and regulatory differences across countries before flows of trade, labour, and capital will be as sensitive to differences in their returns across countries as they currently are within countries."[68]

Global Trade and the Protection of the Environment
Increasingly, there is an international focus on environmental issues, particularly on the impact of trade agreements on the environment.[69] The nub of concern is that trade agreements will require the dilution of national standards because such regulation is seen as impeding the free flow of goods.[70] In addition to other consequences, the demands of free trade will negate domestic legal efforts at ecological protection. The environmental laws of any particular nation will be blunted both within and outside its borders. When free trade and domestic laws to protect the environment clash, the former will limit and confine the latter. Thus, free trade will be a severe constraint on the impact of law in protecting the ecology.[71]

Yet Vogel claims that the growth of trade and the protection of the environment are not doomed to be at odds.[72] He argues that the enhancement of trade and agreements to facilitate it do not undercut regulatory standards but can actually strengthen them. He asserts that the liberalization of trade "has, on balance, contributed to strengthening national regulatory policies, especially for traded goods and ... for domestic production standards as well."[73]

Environmentalists worry about a race to the bottom – the "Delaware effect." States in America can charter corporations and are required to recognize each other's ability to do so. There has been some loosening of standards by those states seeking to attract companies. Delaware is seen as creating conditions in the interests of management. There are fears that the Delaware effect will induce countries to dilute environmental requirements in order to facilitate trade.

In fact, there has been a race to the top. The "California effect" refers to the role that wealthy green jurisdictions, such as California, can play in promoting strict regulatory standards and compliance with them. Within the American economy, California has driven many American environmental regulations upward.

According to the Delaware effect, stringent standards produce competitive disadvantage. That may be the result in other areas, for instance, labour standards. But compliance with stricter environmental standards has not been so costly as to force jurisdictions to dilute these standards to maintain domestic entities' competitive position.

There have been examples to the contrary: for instance, in the United States the automobile emission standards of the 1977 Clean Air Amendments were modified as a response to the automobile industry's competitive difficulties; in the early 1980s automobile safety requirements were delayed for similar reasons.[74] However, overall, wealthy nations such as Germany and the United States stipulating stricter standards means that their trading partners are forced to comply with them to retain their export markets. In turn, nongovernmental organizations (NGOs) in the exporting country can claim similar requirements for products in the domestic market.

Vogel's position has caused much debate. He is given credit for asserting the conditions under which trade liberalization and environmental protection will work together: nations with a strong impact on the world economy need to support strict environmental standards and there must be effective international institutions that promote the acceptance among other nations of these higher strictures. He is taken to task for ignoring the crucial question of how to transform influential trading nations which do not have strong ecological protections. He refers to Japan as indifferent to leading the greening of Asia, without suggesting how this position might be altered.[75] He has also been criticized for presenting insufficient data to establish his contentions, particularly the relationship of increasing trade and environmental protection in less developed countries.[76] Finally, there are questions concerning causation. It is alleged that the California effect is not produced by trade liberalization but, rather, "as a result of the affirmative regulatory activity characteristic of a higher degree of structural integration than that found in most free trade agreements ... As international institutions acquire more active rule-making powers, it is that affirmative authority, not the constraints imposed by trade liberalization, that has the capacity to offset the deregulatory effects of trade liberalization."[77]

Vogel may not be as deterministic as some critics would suggest. He concludes by underscoring that the influence of free trade on domestic efforts to regulate safeguarding of the environment is not preordained.[78] The power of trade to enhance regulation on behalf of the environment hinges on the acknowledgment by wealthy nations that trade can be a positive influence on their willingness to see these effects materialize: "To date, increased economic integration has, on balance, contributed to strengthening national regulatory policies, especially for traded goods and – in the case of the EU and, to a lesser extent NAFTA – for domestic production standards as well. Whether or not it continues to do so depends on the preferences of the world's richest and most powerful nation states."[79]

A study of the pulp and paper industry in several countries, including Canada, indicates that domestic standards have neither converged at the top nor at the bottom. Rather, the unique political and institutional context within each country has produced a range of impacts on intergovernmental competition. That said, the upward pressures on standards for pulp and paper effluent regulation have mostly prevailed.[80]

The conditions under which trade and efforts to safeguard the environment can be mutually reinforcing pose problems but these can be solved. At the same time, the quest for such solutions will be "one of the great themes of economic integration in the 21st century."[81]

Conclusions

Watson, Vogel, and others present evidence that the forces of globalization are not nearly as potent as they are often represented to be. Moreover, whatever their power, these forces need not be as antagonistic to an activist state, as is often suggested.[82] Even in the near future things could change, yet again. That said, the hollow state is not inevitable, and certainly not because of globalization.

David Cameron and Janice Gross Stein agree that globalization is having profound effects on societies. However, they strongly resist the notion that any particular consequences are inevitable. In that light, they make four observations:

- There are many uncertainties in the pace and trajectory of globalization.
- Some of the threads of globalization may thicken more quickly than others; some may even diminish. It is unlikely that the revolution in information technologies will be reversed but economic integration could be.
- The nation-state remains the primary provider of social justice and is uniquely accountable to its citizens for their governance; however, it does face powerful challenges to its core mandates.
- The state has strategic choices to make about the role it will play. These choices will differ depending on the pace and intensity of globalization, its specific impacts on a particular state, on the state's institutional capacity, on the quality of political leadership, and the resilience of that society.[83]

Yet, the language of globalization and its foretold consequences are everywhere. Legislatures, courtrooms, the media, offices, and homes are full of talk about this new world order; "this language has been far more important than markets themselves in changing the face of the state and the way it delivers public goods."[84] Whatever the reality, the image of globalization and of world-wide markets fuels doubts about the capacity of representative politics to tackle an array of contemporary issues.

Politics and Social Policy as the Market Exerts Its Influence

If the market is gaining ascendancy, domestically and internationally, there should be impacts on social policy. Governments could become more austere in their spending both to curtail deficits and to lower taxes to permit the economy to respond to the dictates of competitiveness. Those favouring an activist state are quick to predict dire consequences for a variety of governmental programs. The warnings of nationalist Maude Barlow, uttered in the context of increasing economic integration between the United States and Canada, are typical: "It is not possible to harmonize the economic systems of the continent and allow our social and environmental infrastructures to remain intact ... with cutbacks in social services, education, and welfare, we are witnessing nothing short of the Americanization of our social programs."[85] In 2004 a book written by a Canadian law professor and the subsequent movie gained notoriety.[86] *The Corporation* depicts the goal of this business entity as "the pathological pursuit of profit and power."[87] It rails against its wrongdoing, including the capacity of corporations to warp the electoral and political processes.

What did happen to Canada's social policy during the last two decades as the forces of globalization and economic integration took hold? Banting answers this question by comparing alterations in the welfare state in Canada and the United States during the 1980s and up to the mid-1990s.[88] Historically, welfare programs in Canada have been more generous than in America in three ways. First, they were more comprehensive: they provided significant support for a broader range of the population. Second, they provided greater transfers to the poor; universality in health care was a notable exception, and Canada had the stronger tradition of income security by targeting benefits to the poor through income supplements, refundable tax credits, and social assistance. Third, they had a greater redistributive impact: the combination of more comprehensive coverage and more strongly targeted programs reduced the levels of poverty and inequality in Canada more effectively than has been achieved in the United States.[89]

These differences should not be exaggerated, especially compared with other OECD countries. In 1990 in OECD countries of Western Europe, public spending on social programs was about 25 percent of the GDP (at the low end of the range was the United Kingdom, at 22.3 percent; at the high end, Sweden spent 33.1 percent). In Canada the comparable figure was 18.8 percent; in the United States it was 14.6 percent.[90] Thus, while Canada has outspent the United

States on these programs, our financial commitments to the welfare state have been lagging behind those of Western European societies. Nonetheless, as Banting observes, "especially for the poor and for marginal social groups, the differences between Canadian and American social programs are important."[91]

Was there divergence or convergence in the social programs of Canada and the United States during the 1980s and 1990s? In responding to the question, Banting examined health care and a number of income security programs – pensions, employment insurance, child benefits, and social assistance. The answer is complicated. The broadest trend was toward incremental divergence. The differences between the two countries grew in health care, in the balance between universal and selective income transfers, in publicly funded pensions, and in the redistributive aspects of these programs. Such divergence has mainly occurred not because of enlargement of these programs in Canada but, rather, because of their contraction in the United States during the Reagan-Bush years.[92] In the case of social assistance, the strong divergence of the 1980s as a result of reduced support in America decreased in the mid-1990s because of cutbacks by the federal government and some of the provinces in Canada.[93]

In contrast, there was strong convergence in two areas: child benefits and employment insurance.[94] Banting contends that the convergence in child benefits programs has predominantly been a reflection of parallel domestic trends and not of economic integration. The changes in this sector have involved a slow process, fuelled by a common ideological debate on poverty and the interaction between tax and transfer systems. That debate goes back to the 1960s and had as its source proposals for a negative income tax.[95]

The convergence in employment insurance programs may be more attributable to economic integration, but that is not the entire explanation.[96] For example, in the 1991 changes to these programs, the special benefits for fishermen, a source of tension with the United States over trade policy, were retained. In addition, regional differences, which some have argued would be undermined by economic integration with the United States, in fact, grew larger. Economic integration with the United States did play a role in promoting changes to this program. More generally, the changes were a result of reassessments of labour markets, income support, and training programs; such reassessments were occurring in most OECD nations.

Banting sums up his analysis of social policies in Canada and the United States and the relevance of economic integration as follows: "The pattern in many sectors is incremental divergence, and it is arguable that the Canadian and American welfare states are as different in the mid-1990s as they were in the late 1970s. Moreover, where convergence has taken place, it is difficult to establish a simple link to economic integration between the two countries."[97] He ends by underscoring the continuing relevance of the state and its politics even as pressures from worldwide markets may increase: "Despite a pervasive globalization of economic life, the nation-state retains important degrees of freedom in charting its course, and politics within the nation-state retains social importance."[98]

Nevertheless, Banting elsewhere points to worrying signs. We may still be charting our own course in social programs compared with the Americans, but that does not mean that those programs are not under stress. Government spending in the 1990s became focused on eliminating debts and deficits. As a result, at the federal level, program expenditures as a proportion of the GDP fell to levels not seen since the late 1940s:[99] "program spending reductions in Canada were uniquely deep; only three other OECD countries experienced a similarly large shrinkage in the relative importance of government spending during the 1990s, even though several experienced budget deficits that were equally large if not larger."[100]

Thomas Courchene is one of our most brilliant thinkers on economic policy. He is confident that the effects of global forces are so strong that the Canadian economy will be forced to become sufficiently competitive. He is less confident about the future of our other programs. He fears that "as we fall in line competitively with the Americans, our social policy will drift south as well."[101] He proposes the following mission statement for Canada: "Design a sustainable, socially inclusive and internationally competitive infrastructure that ensures equal opportunity for all Canadians to develop, to enhance and to employ in Canada their skills and human capital, thereby enabling them to become full citizens in the information-era Canadian and global societies."[102]

An admirable prescription. But are our politics up to the task? Will our new-found focus on courts and on rights permit us to do so? Does the myth of exit already have too powerful a hold?

The Courts, Rights, and Laissez-Faire
Before the transformations of the 1980s and 1990s, courts had a limited role in Canadian society. That role was largely dominated by conservative values: celebration of an unfettered market and self-regarding behaviour with minimum state involvement in social policies. That dominance was apparent in the structure of civil litigation, with its saluting of active parties, the passive judge, and a costs regime that rewarded winning litigants by making losers pay costs.[103]

There are many examples of judicial opposition to claims that challenged traditional values and the social and economic arrangements they fostered. That animosity was apparent in cases questioning the role of women in this society.[104] Movements to improve conditions of workers, such as claims for compensation and for the right to organize collectively, were hobbled by the judiciary. So, too, were attempts to curb discriminatory behaviour.[105] Ultimately, these and other interests to protect ordinary people were given recognition through legislation and agencies of the administrative state. These bodies could be scrutinized through judicial review of administrative action to ensure they were not operating outside their limits. That review, largely of the courts' creation, was often used to blunt the effectiveness of the agencies.[106] The driving premises of tort litigation (the type of lawsuit most generally concerned with compensation) were individualism and individual responsibility based on fault.[107] Of the judicial record up to 1980, Arthurs contended that the courts had failed to address "the revolution of rising expectations in the twentieth [century]."[108]

On the left, some predicted that immediate and dire consequences would result from the courts' role under the *Charter*. Among other assertions they claimed that the *Charter* would be used to enhance the interests of the powerful, such as large corporations, that had the resources to litigate and the incentives to resist regulation. The courts' "hidden ideology of the state as inhibiting rather than promoting human rights" and of "negative freedom" ignored "the possibility that government action might facilitate individual freedom ... of the less powerful in society who depend upon government to provide and protect their rights and freedoms."[109]

The Supreme Court has rendered some judgments that reflect conservative values in areas as diverse as criminal process and market regulation. For instance, the Court was severely criticized for its initial decisions on "rape shield" laws. These judgments struck down legislation that attempted to protect the history of victims' intimate lives from disclosure during proceedings in sexual assault trials.[110] One of the most criticized decisions of the Court struck down parts of legislation regulating tobacco advertising, on the grounds that the act offended free speech.[111] Even enthusiastic defenders of an aggressive role for the courts had difficulty with a judgment that was complicit in the peddling of toxins.[112]

Yet, the Court's record in the final decades of the last century and into this one is much more complicated than the dark predictions of the left. The judiciary is more diverse; there have been greater strides taken to appoint more women and minorities. Judges are now more sensitive to the enhanced and complex role that courts play in the forging and implementing of policy. They are more attuned to the positive role that government plays in supporting people in their daily lives.

Many of the Supreme Court's decisions recognize, even urge, a positive role for the state and are sympathetic to the difficult choices its agents must make in carrying out programs.[113] The Court has demonstrated genuine concern for the disadvantaged. Its concern over Aboriginals has been displayed very prominently.[114] On the record of the last decades, it is hard to paint the Supreme Court as a celebrant of market liberalism. Indeed, conservative critics are adamant in depicting the Court as going too far, too often, in indulging rights claimants.[115]

However, as I have discussed, most of the decisions involving disadvantaged groups, when supportive of them, have involved symbolic victories. The basic socioeconomic order has not been disturbed. In the case of gay and lesbian rights, the courts joined the current of history that had been for some time moving in directions favouring homosexuals.[116] One of the prime consequences of the victims' rights movement is that criminal law, in an age of fiscal restraint, has been a means of controlling crime rather than an instrument to get at its root causes.[117] The Aboriginal peoples have secured some major court victories. Yet, the seeking of rights has become an entanglement taking them farther from their goals. Rights and the insistence on nation-to-nation status are deflecting attention away from the increasing numbers of Native people who are leaving the hideous life that is often led on reserves and migrating to the cities in search of something better. I discuss this in more detail in Chapter 5.

Meanwhile, rights advocates and free marketeers are uneasily allied. True, they often decry each other's goals and busy themselves depicting one another in negative ways. But they are united in preaching that government cannot be trusted. They both spin the myth of exit. The free marketeers tend to paint government as wasteful and meddling. Rights advocates incline to accusations of oppression and exclusion. But both sets of charges repeatedly flash the message, Government is bad! Government is bad! Those holding "rights-regarding citizen" and the "citizen as consumer" viewpoints may often want different things, but they are, in many ways, fundamentally compatible. They can both be devout worshippers in the Temple of Choice. Arthurs and Kreklewich describe their view of this market/rights culture: "By subordinating the decisions of elected parliaments to judicial review, the Charter has helped to weaken confidence in electoral politics. By reinforcing the notion of ... rights-bearing individuals, it has helped to delegitimate ... communitarian [ideas]. By making all legislation and administrative action subject to open-ended judicial review, it has provided a tactical weapon for anti-state and anti-interventionist litigants."[118]

Conclusion

The Canadian state may have been battered during the 1980s and 1990s, but it is far from hollowed. The market/globalization and courts/rights may be magnets drawing people away from representative politics, but their allure is not irresistible.

Globalization need not lead inexorably to the atrophying of the state. The nations that trade the most have the largest government budgets as a proportion of their GDP. There is room for societies to make strategic choices about the role of governments in the lives of citizens. Borders still matter in trade; capital may not be nearly as mobile as extravagant depictions of globalization suggest; economic growth and increased trade and protection of the environment are not inevitably opposed.

In the midst of all these transformations and volatility there must be a firm resolve that representative politics does have a vital role to play in people's lives. If pursuit of efficiency becomes a cult, we will be in danger of believing myths about globalization inexorably leading to the hollow state. Good health care, education, a clean environment, and a decent social welfare net do not just happen; they are mostly brought about through deliberate decisions and wise use of public resources. Having these public goods – including at an improved level – is still possible. At the same time, their fate has probably never been more in question.

PART 3

Some Examples of a Changing Canada

5 Aboriginals: Two Row Wampum, Second Thoughts, and Citizens Plus

Of all the issues facing Canadian society, the plight of Aboriginals may be the most intractable. Successive governments have tried a number of strategies to address the demands of the First Peoples. The result has been a legacy of failure. Many Aboriginals now live in conditions that rival those in Third World societies. There is a small middle class emerging in some urban areas. Sadly, many of the Aboriginals who have received an education and secured a place in mainstream society have had to do so by defying the traditional way of life sought to be protected by many of the demands for nationhood status.

There are three main positions on the Aboriginal question. On the one hand are the advocates of assimilation: both the First Peoples and the rest of the country would be better served by Aboriginals being treated no differently than other individuals; the First Peoples should simply be integrated into mainstream society. On the other is the claim that First Peoples are nations; the governments of Canada must respond to their demands by honouring treaties, constitutional rights, and other legal entitlements. The third, in the middle of the other two positions, sees the First Peoples as "citizens plus": Aboriginals need to take their place in Canadian society as citizens of this country; their historical mistreatment and the horrible conditions of life of many Natives entitle them to programs of support so that they may attain full participation in this society.

These three positions clearly illustrate the changing roles of markets, courts, and representative politics – a theme developed throughout this book. The first position is strongly influenced by considerations of the market. A competitive and globalized society awaits. Aboriginals must relinquish claims for special treatment; abandon unrealistic dreams of a separate, land-based economy; and take their place in mainstream society by obtaining the necessary training and education. The second is driven by the hope that courts and governments will declare and enforce a plethora of rights that will ensure Aboriginals' claims to nation status and to special treatment. The third looks to representative politics to work out understandings of the good citizen, an understanding that makes room for Aboriginals while recognizing that history and their way of life makes them "citizens plus." Where will these three, often irreconcilable, positions take us in the initial decades of the twenty-first century? What do they tell us about the push for the market, the ascendancy of courts and rights, and the turning away from representative politics discussed throughout this book?

Rights, Groups, and Horizontal Societies

There is much talk of a global village. It is an image that is at once evocative and inaccurate. Few, at least in industrialized nations, live in quaint rural settings. The village way of life lies in the remote past for most individuals in modern societies. Yet, that image summons up convergences between nations and cultures even as they remain dramatically different. Are there common characteristics of a world society that pervade day-to-day life of people in Japan and in Norway, in India and in Canada?

Lawrence Friedman maintains that there are.[1] He identifies four such characteristics. The first is change and the rapidity at which it is taking place – "compared to older, traditional societies, we live in a period where change is constant, unremitting, and the pace of change seems to be accelerating."[2] The second is popular culture: "primarily a culture of leisure and entertainment[,] it is soccer, movies, and rock and roll," and dependent on television and movies for its proliferation and prominence.[3] The third is celebrity culture. Like popular culture, this fame phenomenon is heavily dependent on television, which makes the distant, famous, rich, and powerful seem accessible and all too human. The celebrity culture produces many outcomes, not the least of which is the public-opinion state, "a polity where spin doctors are constantly taking the public pulse. Image, short-term popularity, and communication skills become of sublime importance to politics."[4] The fourth is technology and ubiquitous information gathering, which creates the expectation of privacy: "people worry about, and debate, ways to protect and preserve zones of intimacy and seclusion in a world with satellite eyes."[5]

For Friedman, these four characteristics add up to the "horizontal society" that is coming to replace, yes, "the vertical society." In a vertical society, one's position is more or less fixed in a hierarchical structure; in a horizontal society, the ties on individuals are loosened so that more movement is possible. The shift from vertical to horizontal is bumpy and is occurring at different rates in different countries. The United States leads, but the phenomenon is global. The vertical authority of priests and fathers yields to the horizontal influences of nationalist tribes, identity groups, and celebrities. The engine driving such transformation is "an ideology of individual wants, desires, and fulfillments, an ideology of choice."[6] Yet, such individualism leads to a push toward group identities, tribalism, and ethnic differences as individuals experience choice (or at least the belief in choice) about their identities that leads them to seek some wider affiliation. At one level, individuals in a horizontal society are shaped by a common global culture; at another, they want to link themselves with some group identity and to have that association play a more prominent part in their lives.

Horizontal society and its outcomes are apparent in Canadian society. The rapidity of change and popular culture – the need to be entertained and mesmerized by TV, the worship of celebrities, and angst about privacy – find expression here. Meanwhile, expressive individualism, driven by choice and more choice (or at least the belief in it), grows ever stronger.

And then, as Friedman emphasizes, there is group identity. As in other societies, the disadvantaged have affiliated themselves by identifying with groups that have been the basis for the exclusion: gays and lesbians, people with disabilities, feminists, and so forth. These claims are most prominent on behalf of two groups whose fate is tied closely to the founding of the country: the French in Quebec and Aboriginals. The French in Quebec were a conquered people. Yet, their laws, religion, and language were protected as far back as 1774 by British imperial acts. Quebec entered Confederation only on condition that these protections would be incorporated. From then on, a significant segment of Canadian history has been about working through claims of the French in Quebec, as a group, to be treated as a distinct society.

The claims of Aboriginals in many countries around the globe are an important manifestation of the horizontal society as Native peoples protest their subordination. Certain treaty rights of Aboriginals in Canada were recognized by an imperial proclamation of 1763. It is claimed that such recognition included their status as separate nations, and their communal rights to be different and to be treated separately in some fundamental ways. But the First Peoples were excluded from the constitutional and political order of 1867. They were neither treated as citizens, equal to all other citizens, nor were they accorded some special, independent status. Instead, they were suspended in a state of wardship under the *Indian Act*.[7] They were exempted from certain obligations, such as paying taxes, but forbidden basic entitlements, including the right to vote. This wardship was associated with a number of grievances, such as the legacy of emotional and sexual abuse in residential schools to which Native children were sent to be educated in the ways of the white man and of Christian civilization.

Aboriginals laboured in this state of wardship up to the last quarter of the twentieth century. There were some improvements, such as finally being given the right to vote. By the 1970s, the rights movement was under way on a number of fronts. The First Peoples succeeded in having section 25 of the *Charter* not "abrogate or derogate" from any "treaty or other rights" and in having section 35 of the *Constitution Act, 1982* declare that "the existing aboriginal and treaty rights of the aboriginal peoples of Canada are hereby recognized and affirmed." What did all that mean? The next twenty years were spent wrestling with the question of what rights Aboriginals were to have, as a group, beyond their rights as citizens. Were they to be accorded no additional recognition? Treated as separate nations – a third order of government, in addition to the federal and provincial levels? Or were they to be "citizens plus" – and if so, what did the "plus" consist of?

The Aboriginal Dilemma

Squalor into the Twenty-First Century

There is no serious challenge to the tale of misery as we begin a new century. The following is but a sample of statistics that chronicle the desperation. Registered Indians are more than three times as likely as the rest of the population to die accidentally or violently. Alcohol-related deaths and drug-induced suicides are eight times higher than for the rest of the country. The rate of HIV is three times higher in Aboriginal women than other Canadian women. Native people are six times more likely than other Canadians to be in prison. In 1997, 50 percent of Aboriginal children lived in poverty.[8]

There are exceptions; a small middle class is developing among Native people. There are instances of entrepreneurial successes; for instance, the recent opening of diamond mines in the Northwest Territories.[9] These positive results need to be highlighted, and the ways in which progress has been achieved examined. Yet, whether on reserves or in urban areas, the day-to-day lot of many Aboriginals is a swirl of drugs, alcohol, violence, broken families, malnutrition, welfare, and confrontations with the police and the justice system. In western Canada, single-origin Aboriginals (those identifying themselves in the census as having only Aboriginal ethnicity) are five times more likely than non-Aboriginals to live in poor neighbourhoods.[10] The lack of academic success in schools is appalling. Winnipeg is an extreme case in terms of the percentage of Aboriginals living in poor neighbourhoods. Nevertheless, 66 percent of all Aboriginals in poor neighbourhoods and 55 percent of all Aboriginals in that city lack a high school diploma. Even worse is the record for Aboriginals in Manitoba living on reserves: 72 percent of those between the ages of fifteen and forty-nine do not have this basic qualification (compared with 39 percent of the non-Aboriginal population).[11] Some schools on reserves are so bad that parents voluntarily have their children bussed to a local public school.[12]

What is worse is that all this deprivation is occurring despite the fact that enormous amounts of public money are being spent on addressing Aboriginal issues. By 2001 the federal government's budget for such issues was $7 billion.[13] The December 2001 budget alone contained $185 million dedicated to addressing fetal alcohol syndrome and other early childhood problems affecting Aboriginals.[14] It has been estimated that if the money spent every year by the federal government were simply divided by the number of status Indians, every man, woman, and child would receive more than $10,000, a sum sufficient to support families above the poverty line.[15] Yet, unemployment is as high as 90 percent on some reserves, and standards of health, education, and incomes are well below those of many developing nations.[16]

How can this be? Whatever the long-term explanations are, fiscal mismanagement of the reserves is one immediate cause of so much money yielding such miserable results. In 1998 the Department of Indian Affairs estimated that it would have to put in place "remedial management plans" for 20 to 25 percent of Indian bands: "15 of 43 First Nations in Alberta [were] on a remedial fiscal plan, after audits showed their deficits exceeded 8 percent of total revenues." In April 1999 the Auditor General's annual report criticized the federal government for not exercising adequate control over the billions of dollars it provides each year to Aboriginals: "The department is not taking adequate steps to ensure that allegations of wrongdoing, including complaints and disputes related to funding arrangements, are appropriately resolved." Here are two examples of such mismanagement. The Gitxsan Health Authority, representing Aboriginals in central British Columbia, lost $300,000 of "surplus" funds in the Calgary stock market. A Saulteaux Indian band in Saskatchewan – with eight hundred members – spent $600,000 on travel in one year; the chief alone spent $176,000. The total amount spent exceeded the travel budget of the entire Saskatchewan cabinet.[17]

Meanwhile, millions of dollars are being spent on legal costs as the court cases involving Aboriginal claims increase. As of December 2001 over one thousand claims had the potential to become lawsuits against the federal government. Yet, since 1973, fewer than eight claims a year have been resolved. In 2001 Robert Nault, the minister of Indian Affairs and Northern Development, asked for over $11 million just to manage the litigation inventory. Not surprisingly, "within the government, there is a deep frustration that existing federal policies and decades of wrangling over the nature and extent of aboriginal rights have achieved little."[18]

In 2003 the federal government introduced the *First Nations Governance Act,* intended to amend the *Indian Act.*[19] Supporters of the legislation emphasized that the bill would give the reserves more control in electing leaders and managing finances. At the same time, it mandated more accountability. Its provisions required the development of rules on conflict of interest, tendering contracts, auditing band councils, and public disclosure of information.[20] The proposed act created a furor. Many First Nations leaders charged that it would undermine Aboriginals' right to govern themselves; the bill was fatally flawed because it sought to reinvigorate the despised *Indian Act.*[21] An opportunity for both more power for the First Peoples and more accountability for that power faded as accusations of intimidation and silencing were hurled by and at those holding a position on the bill.[22]

Canada and the First Peoples: A Troubled Past

The dominant policy toward Aboriginals up to the 1970s was assimilation. On the one hand, they were kept on reserves and treated as wards of the federal government. On the other, that separate existence was meant to hold them in a state that could prepare them for full integration into the white man's society. It was as if the reserve were a kind of training school tutoring Natives to meet the expectations of the dominant culture. They were an administered people, likened to children in need of constant guidance and supervision. In 1887 John A. Macdonald declared that "the great aim of our civilization has been to do away with the tribal system and assimilate the Indian people in all respects with the inhabitants of the Dominion, as speedily as they are fit for the change."[23] More than fifty years later, the minister responsible for Indian Affairs was asserting much the same position: "The ultimate goal of our Indian policy is the integration of the Indians into the general life and economy of the country."[24] Yet, throughout history, Natives defied efforts to extinguish their identity. They managed to persist against great odds and concerted efforts to vanquish their very existence.

The subjugation by the dominant society was the source of many wrongs: "as wards of the state, in a little more than a century aboriginal people were deprived of their traditional means of livelihood, their culture and language was wiped out, and their communities became socially dysfunctional."[25] Status Indians, with few exceptions, could not vote until 1960. From 1927 to 1951, soliciting money from an Indian to pursue legal claims without the approval of the Superintendent General of Indian Affairs was a crime, punishable by a jail term. There were forced resettlements. Many of these ill-conceived initiatives were hopelessly botched, bringing untold suffering to those involved.[26] Aboriginal customs, such as the potlatch on the West Coast and the Sun Dance on the Prairies, were banned.

Residential schools were vehicles for assimilation. Children were "educated" by being punished for speaking Indian languages and rewarded for internalizing antipathy toward their own cultures. Physical and sexual abuse at some schools was rampant. The message was constant; "from birth to death most Indians have been caught in a situation where they have had to listen to one unvarying and unceasing message – that they are unacceptable as they are and that to become worthwhile as individuals they must change in the particular manner advocated by their current tutelage agents."[27]

There were sporadic cross-currents even in the dominant society. The Hawthorn Report of the mid-1960s was a study for the federal government of the conditions of status Indians.[28] That report coined the phrase "citizens plus." It recommended that Native people be treated as full citizens; much of their suffering had resulted from their mistreatment as wards. The "plus" referred to entitlements based on treaties and needs because of wrongs suffered at the hands of Canadian society. Thus, Indian distinctiveness was to be preserved even as Native people came to be citizens of this country. Native communities would be maintained and supported even as migration to the cities and embracing of the dominant culture would be recognized as a valid choice for increasing numbers of Aboriginals.

Nevertheless, the strongest effort at assimilation followed shortly after the Hawthorn Report. The White Paper of 1969 recommended shock treatment.[29] The *Indian Act* would be abolished, the Indian Affairs Branch would be dismantled, and treaties were to "be equitably ended":[30] Indians were to be speedily assimilated. Most of these vast changes were to be implemented in five years. Pierre Trudeau was directly involved in the framing of the policies. He asserted that it was "inconceivable ... that ... one section of the society [could] have a treaty with the other section of the society. We must be all be equal under the laws and we must not sign treaties amongst ourselves."[31]

Instead, the White Paper had a catalytic effect on Native people. Aboriginals were galvanized and successfully lobbied, in massive opposition, for its defeat. The vanquishing of the White Paper brought an era to its close; the policies of successive governments since Confederation had been repudiated. Assimilation as an official option was abandoned. Aboriginals were no longer the audience but actors shaping their own destiny. They had moved to centre stage. What for Trudeau was "inconceivable" was happening. The People would assert themselves as nations. Treaties would be claimed to be a primary means for the First Nations and Canadian society to coexist. Assimilation went dormant but it was not dead. It would be roused in a much harsher form at the dawning of the new century.

From People to Nations: By Rights Possessed

In 1975 the Dene made a declaration that startled many: "We the Dene of the Northwest Territories insist on the right to be regarded by ourselves and the world as a nation."[32] By the 1990s the notions of Aboriginal peoples as nations, having inherent rights that are constitutionally guaranteed, whose relationships with this country should be worked out through treaties, had permeated the way in which Aboriginals were viewed in this society. How did this sea change in status come about? How did we move from an official policy that urged assimilation with all due speed to one pushed to view the People as a "third order of government."

Four factors explain this massive transformation. All are linked to law and to rights. The conversion from "People" to "nations" provides a dramatic instance of the use of law to transform the categorization of social, political, and economic issues. It also raises insistent questions about the consequences produced by a discourse of rights. To what extent do rights forge solutions to the underlying issues? To what extent do they prevent the forging and implementing of effective responses?

The first factor was horizontal society. Friedman's claim is that a hallmark of the late twentieth century is its move away from "vertical" authority to more choice and to more individualism.[33] Rights, propelling expressive individualism, give rise to claims for legal protection. This individualism expresses itself in many ways; an important one is through chosen identities with groups, or "nations." Native people had important claims to some form of recognition as a group. Those claims in Canada formed part of an international movement questioning all manner of authority and pressing for special recognition for various groups; conspicuous in these movements were demands of Aboriginal peoples from places as far-flung as British Columbia and New Zealand.[34]

Second was constitutionalism. The repatriation of the Constitution and the battles over the provision in the *Charter* afforded an opportunity for Native peoples to voice their claims as constitutional entitlements within a "nation to nation" discourse. Section 35(1) of the Constitution declares that "the existing aboriginal and treaty rights of the aboriginal peoples of Canada are hereby recognized and affirmed."[35] The chosen term was "Aboriginal," defined to include Indians, the Inuit, and Metis; the term thus embraced Native peoples with some very different traditions and problems. What were these "Aboriginal rights"?

Two other aspects of this constitutionalism were related to the conversion to nation status. The first were a series of four constitutional conferences in the 1980s in which Aboriginal issues loomed large and "which contributed to the emerging definition of Canada as a multinational polity that now coexists uneasily with the historic federal-provincial division of who we are."[36] The second were the failed Meech Lake and Charlottetown accords. These agreements were primarily designed to accommodate Quebec and its place within Confederation. Meech Lake was unacceptable to many Native people because they viewed it as inadequately addressing their needs. The Charlottetown Accord had a number of provisions addressing the First Peoples. Fundamentally, it would have constitutionally entrenched a third order of government based on inherent rights of Aboriginals; the First Peoples would have been removed from the power of federal and provincial governments to the extent that they assumed jurisdiction over themselves.[37] The Canadian people also rejected that accord. But its provisions for Aboriginals were kept very much alive by the First Peoples.

The third factor in this massive transformation in the status of Aboriginals was the 1996 Royal Commission on Aboriginal Peoples (RCAP).[38] Indeed, RCAP's objective was sea change in the position of Native peoples in this country. Rights and constitutionalism would back that revolution; it would be insulated from the vagaries of representative politics. An entirely new relationship was to be forged between Aboriginals and Canadian society, with almost every institution making a contribution.[39] There would be a royal proclamation that would acknowledge past injustices, recognize the inherent right of Aboriginal nations to self-government, and establish the principles of the new relationship and its institutional components. The transformation would take decades to complete. The arduous process would involve legislation, treaty commissions, an Aboriginal land and treaties tribunal, an Aboriginal nations recognition act, and an Aboriginal peoples review commission to monitor progress.

This transformation would yield sixty to eighty self-governing Aboriginal nations with an enlarged land base, assured external funding, strengthened cultures, marked declines in social breakdown, more employment, and higher incomes for Native people. Urban centres would need to be more responsive to Aboriginal culture; there would be Aboriginal control and administration of some basic urban services. An Aboriginal House of First Peoples representing the Aboriginal nations would safeguard Aboriginal issues.

There were five main justifications for this huge undertaking:

1   The tragedy of the status quo;
2   The need of society to redress injustices;
3   The substantial expenditures would pay for themselves as healthy nations arose;
4   This vision of the future emanated from the most thorough investigation ever undertaken in Canada of the situation of the Aboriginal peoples and their relationship to Canadian society;
5   The inherent right to self-government had to be buttressed by sufficient resources, including a land base.

The commission and its report have become a signal influence in the way that Native people's place in this society is discussed: "for years to come, [RCAP] will inform public debate, academic research, and Aboriginal claims ... the Commission's existence and its legacy will transform the political and intellectual context of future discussions on Aboriginal/non-Aboriginal relations in Canada."[40] How, exactly, RCAP has transformed the debate is a question I return to below.

The fourth factor in the transformation was the courts and academic activists. In the last decades of the twentieth century, the courts became responsive to Aboriginal claims. Through a series of cases, the Supreme Court responded, under section 35 of the Constitution, to claims of self-government based on treaty rights and premised on various common law obligations. The principles generated by the Supreme Court up to the close of the 1990s have been summarized as follows:

1   Section 35 rights are exercised by individuals, families, and groups but held by broader collectivities, showing continuity from pre-contact societies ...

2   Aboriginal law, together with the common law, must be taken into account in determining the nature of rights, as well as such matters as entitlements to rights ...
3   There are several types of rights protected and affirmed under section 35 ... [These include specific entitlements to certain practices, such as harvesting, spiritual customs, and the education of youth. Aboriginal title is also included. Aboriginal title has been defined as the capacity to determine the use of title-based lands for any purpose consistent with the continuing relationship of the people concerned to that land]
4   The federal Crown is uniquely empowered by section 91(24) to regulate section 35 rights, subject to fiduciary obligations and tests relating to valid infringement ...
5   [Generally, the Crown is bound by] fiduciary obligations to Aboriginal peoples ...[41]

Pushing the courts was a body of academic literature, mostly authored by law professors.[42] Those writings are filled with the language of rights and entitlements of Aboriginals. Among their ambitions, they seek to have expansive interpretations given to section 35 of the Constitution regarding self-government and to establish treaties as a main vehicle for forging the relationship between Native peoples and the rest of Canadian society. These writings confidently assume that the conferring of rights will somehow bring about betterment: "The contemporary role of legal scholarship in fleshing out Aboriginal rights and in general seeking to put law at the service of Aboriginal aspirations can scarcely be exaggerated."[43]

Legal academic writing is replete with hope for using litigation to forge a new existence for the First Peoples. A huge problem is the "Anglo-Canadian legal imagination," which has generated a "set of principles" that "maintain a hierarchical relationship between native peoples and the Canadian state."[44] Yet, courts are "an institution native people trust,"[45] law can be a "powerful source of potential social transformation,"[46] and, together, they can produce "moments of transformative possibility."[47] A prime vehicle for such a turnabout is the *Charter,* which is "an interpretive prism ... the refraction which it provides will protect the rights and freedoms of the aboriginal peoples of Canada."[48] Accordingly, "it is now time for the common law's treatment of Aboriginal peoples to be judged by stories indigenous to this continent."[49]

Courts and legal academics have entered into a mutually reinforcing push to address the Aboriginal dilemma through a series of rights, from claims of Aboriginal title, to protecting traditional use of the land and activities such as hunting and fishing. A general comment about the role of judges and activists in the growth of rights, in the United States, seems apposite in this context: "court majorities with an expansive view of the judicial role, and their academic admirers, propelled each other, like railway men on a handcar, along the line that led to the land of rights."[50]

Yet, Roach contends that an accurate analysis of Aboriginal cases would suggest that, at least more recently, "the Court has given governments [latitude] to limit Aboriginal and treaty rights in favour of a broad range of interests, including the economic and other interests of the non-Aboriginal majority."[51] He might have gone on to suggest that the cases addressing Aboriginal issues demonstrate, again, that courts are more inclined to recognize rights premised on recognition than those with distributional consequences.[52]

Rotman, deflecting accusations of judicial activism, insists that the controversial *Marshall* decision[53] is "at its roots, an affirmation of the status quo."[54] Roach asserts that "public and media hysteria about the Supreme Court's so-called embrace of Aboriginal rights is based on deliberate distortions or wilful ignorance of what the cases actually say."[55] Perhaps. Yet, advocates, especially legal academics, might also ask themselves if they have contributed to this "hysteria" by making claims about rights, generally, and those of Aboriginals, in particular, that likely can never be met.

This body of work focused on Native rights has shown little interest in the details of how this new order would work, how the daily life of ordinary Aboriginals would be improved, or how a relationship of mutuality with the majority society, whose financial support would be vital, would be maintained. That work "displays minimal interest in Canadian citizenship, or in the more general question of what kind of overall Canadian community will coexist with Aboriginal self-government. What holds us together – why we should feel obligations to each other – is not on its agenda."[56] Instead, it is often baldly asserted that "constitutional recognition of indigenous difference also gives rise to corresponding state obligations to establish the fiscal, social, and institutional arrangements necessary to promote Aboriginal and treaty rights"[57]

Without a Nation? Aboriginals in Cities
Substantial numbers of Native people have moved to urban centres over the last several decades. This migration has several important implications. First, Aboriginals in cities tend to fare better in quality of life indicators than they do on the reserves. This is not to say that there are not problems for Native people in the cities; but as harsh as they are, they are exceeded by the squalor on many reserves. Second, moving to the cities is associated with intermarriage and with loss of identity as an Aboriginal person. If these trends continue over the next decades, the "Aboriginal dilemma" may fade as Native people blend into the majority society. Such a loss of Aboriginal identity, culture, and nations would carry with it its own tragic implications.

Third, even now, the fact that so many Aboriginals reside in cities means that the "nation to nation" (treaty, land-based, third order of government) solutions urged by RCAP and legal academic activists and buttressed by the courts is of questionable applicability to many Native people. Whether the recommendations of RCAP are at all viable is another question. The point here is that the applicability of such solutions to a large number of intended beneficiaries is problematic.

The Growing Shift to the Cities

The movement of Native people to urban centres over the last decades has been considerable and is growing. Reserves are declining in their importance in the daily lives of many Native people. In 1951 only about 7 percent lived in urban areas. By 2001 about 50 percent did.[58] These are arresting statistics. If these trends continue over the next decades, the very existence of reserves will be imperilled and, conversely, the real possibility of incremental assimilation will loom large.

The urbanization of Aboriginals is, in large part, a western phenomenon. Aboriginals account for about 3 percent of the Canadian population, and this number is growing, as the birth rate among Aboriginals is higher than that of the general population. At the same time, they represent up to 7 percent of the population in some western cities. Urban Aboriginals, on the whole, form a much younger segment of the population. About only one-fifth of the non-Aboriginal population in western cities is under fifteen years old. For Aboriginals, the figure is closer to one-third.[59]

Urban Aboriginals and Quality of Life

Life for urban Aboriginals is, in some critical ways, much better than the one led on reserves. Nevertheless, Aboriginals in cities do markedly less well and suffer from many more problems than the rest of the populace. What is more, there can be a severe loss of identity (an issue I pursue below).

The list of favourable indicators of city life, compared with the existence on reserves, is a long one. The projected growth of jobs is better. Incomes are substantially higher, levels of education are superior, and unemployment rates are lower, while the chance of a full-time job is increased. As a result, the percentage of social assistance recipients is much lower. Indians living in cities have the highest life expectancy among Aboriginals. Indicators of social breakdown are lower for Aboriginal urban dwellers: rates of family violence, suicide, sexual abuse, rape, and alcohol and drug addiction are much higher for Aboriginals living on reserves.[60]

Aboriginals in cities may in many ways experience a better life than their counterparts living on reserves. Yet, urban existence remains fraught with peril for far too many Aboriginals. The rate of welfare dependence by urban Aboriginals is still between two and a half and three times higher than that of the general population.[61] Particularly in western Canada, they live disproportionately in poor neighbourhoods.[62] Life for Natives in the cities can be one of a ghetto existence with the terrorism of youth gangs, substance abuse, and episodes of violence the daily lot. Tension is often high between the police and Aboriginals, particularly in some cities in the western provinces; "in recent years, [Saskatoon] has come close to a racial explosion after allegations of rampant police abuse and police complaints that they cannot cope alone with a crime-ridden native community."[63] A study of urban Aboriginals in the western provinces, comparing them with their non-Aboriginal counterparts, compiled this discouraging list:[64]

- Aboriginal families are over twice as likely to be lone parent families and more likely to experience domestic violence.
- Aboriginal people are more likely to have lower levels of education.
- Aboriginal people typically have lower labour force participation rates and higher unemployment rates.
- Aboriginal people frequently have lower income levels.
- Aboriginal people tend to have higher rates of homelessness and greater housing needs.
- Aboriginal people are over-represented in the criminal justice system, both as victims and as offenders.
- Aboriginal people generally have poorer health.

If the trend of migration to urban centres continues, these problems may only intensify. If this is so, there will be more and more pressure to find resources to grapple with such problems. Will government funds be diverted away from the reserves and directed to programs in cities targeted to assist Native people?

Loss of Identity, and Intermarriage

There is noticeable slippage between the numbers of those who acknowledge an Aboriginal ancestry and those claiming an Aboriginal identity. An important factor in this slippage is the extent of intermarriage that has been taking place over the last decades between Natives and non-Natives. This loss of identity and substantial rates of intermarriage are more prominent among Aboriginals living in cites; these factors, therefore, are associated with the increasing trend to live off reserve.

In 1996 RCAP reported 1,100,000 people in Canada had Aboriginal ancestry. Yet, over a third did not identify themselves as Aboriginals (720,000 identifying; 375,000 not identifying). This failure to identify is associated with urban existence. In five of eleven metropolitan areas having a relatively large number of Aboriginal residents, less than half of those with Aboriginal ancestry declared an Aboriginal identity. Identity figures were notably higher in the western provinces, especially Saskatchewan, than elsewhere. In Regina and Saskatoon over 80 percent of those with Aboriginal ancestry declared an

Aboriginal identity. The point is that a considerable number of Aboriginal people, mostly in cities, no longer think of themselves as being Aboriginal.[65]

Native people have, for some time, been intermarrying at significant rates. Exact figures are difficult to ascertain. It has been estimated that about 50 percent of status Indians married nonstatus individuals between 1965 and 1985. Another study, in 1992, suggested an overall rate of 34 percent for intermarriage by status Indians; for Native people on reserves, the percentage is at 25 percent and for Native people off reserves it is as high as 62 percent. It is useful to compare intermarriage rates among African-Americans, another group that has had a difficult relationship with the dominant society. By 1993 intermarriage rates for blacks in the United States were rising but were still only at about 12 percent.[66]

Intermarriage can have the consequences of weakening the connections of language and traditions.[67] Children produced by these marriages will have Aboriginal ancestry; whether they and their descendants will identify themselves as Aboriginals is another matter. Cross-cultural adoption can also result in loss of Native identity and is opposed by many Aboriginal leaders.[68]

It is no surprise that life off the reserve is more closely associated with intermarriage and loss of Aboriginal identity. The consequences of such dilution can be tragic. But whatever the outcomes, they are not addressed by ignoring them; "the reality for Aboriginal, as for non-Aboriginal peoples, is the interdependent, cosmopolitan reality in which all of humanity now lives, albeit the pace and degree of our incorporation varies."[69] What is more, if the rate of migration to the cities and of intermarriage continues at about the same level, these issues will intensify over the next decades. Over the next fifty years will a dwindling percent elect to live only among their own on reserves?

"Nation to Nation" in the Cities?

As indicated above, RCAP's solution to the problems of the First Peoples was to entrench self-government in Aboriginal nations. These nations, with separate land bases, would constitute a third order of government, entering into treaties with the federal and provincial authorities as appropriate to reflect their respective needs. RCAP's recommendations are analyzed below. Here I look at the issue of how there could ever be Aboriginal self-government in the midst of cities. Answering that question begins with observing the emphasis RCAP placed on the First Peoples being accorded nation status with a separate land base.

Urban Aboriginals, regardless of their large and increasing numbers, have an awkward fit with such a perspective: "[They] are not the hope of the future. That status is reserved for their kinfolk on a land base."[70] RCAP did advance recommendations designed to make urban policies more sensitive to the needs of Aboriginals. Those recommendations included guaranteed representation on various urban commissions and the establishment of Aboriginal affairs committees. In addition, there could be "community of interest arrangements": associations responsible for the provision of functions such as health, education, and child welfare.

But RCAP's focus was on nations with land bases. Other Aboriginal issues were a distraction: "the lesser importance to the Commission of 'Aboriginal groups without any form of land base' was systematic not accidental."[71] RCAP, commenting in an earlier publication on Aboriginals without land, asserted that their situation "poses a range of complex problems that cannot be dealt with here."[72] A noted columnist, commenting on RCAP's report, observed that the "recommendations for urban Aboriginals ... [were] distressingly thin."[73] When the RCAP co-chairs appeared before the Standing Senate Committee on Aboriginal Peoples to discuss the commission's report, they "focussed almost entirely on Aboriginal nations, government-to-government relations, and the proposed third order of Aboriginal nation-governments."[74]

Could urban Aboriginals achieve self-government? Possibly. It may depend on the meaning of self-government in the context of life in cities. A study by the National Association of (Aboriginal) Friendship Centres and the Law Commission of Canada suggests that there could be three main variations.[75] The first would involve "nation specific approaches."[76] This variation would rest on a "land-based conception of nationality, tied to a non-territorial extension of governance to national citizens where they are in fact located and present in sufficient numbers to permit governance arrangements to apply."[77] The second would focus on urban communal governance.[78] This would involve "all urban Aboriginal residents, without regard to status, treaty, specific nationality or other criteria, in the formation of a common authority for governance over whatever institutions or jurisdictions may be capable of being negotiated, delegated, or successfully asserted as a matter of right."[79] The third would use territory within an urban setting.[80] This "territoriality" might be the "federal enclaves or reserves with urban settings, or ... the concentration of at least a portion of the Aboriginal community in urban neighbourhoods as local majorities."[81]

These three variations raise all sorts of questions about how they would actually be implemented. For example, the first variation assumes that nations have reorganized themselves and have been recognized so as to be in a position to assert their authority over urban Aboriginals. RCAP contemplated that that reorganization and recognition could take as long as twenty-five years. That length of time is surely too long a delay in addressing urban issues. The second, in providing all urban Aboriginals with the same programs, seems to fly in the face of the separate nations concept central to claims of self-government. The third, however well intended, raises the spectre of apartheid; that is, it causes concerns that concentrating Aboriginals in specific areas within cities would accentuate rather than reduce the lack of integration of First Peoples in urban settings.

The study was clearly supportive of the concept of self-government in cities. It also recognized that there are formidable obstacles to its realization: "the priority assigned to common cultural, historical community features, together with the need to illustrate at least rough continuity with pre-established Aboriginal societies, provides some clear indication of the difficulties facing any ... assertion of an inherent right."[82]

In addition, proposals for self-governance in cities are met with strong opposition from sectors in both the dominant and Aboriginal societies. Opponents in the dominant society tend to the view Aboriginals that live in cities as "voluntary immigrants."[83] In this depiction, Aboriginals who choose to come to cities are in no different relationship to the wider institutional and political governance of urban Canada than any immigrant racial or ethnic minority. Indeed, some Aboriginals on reserves view city living as "un-Aboriginal."[84] Urban areas are seen as magnets drawing individuals away from reserves, accelerating assimilation, and diluting assertions of self-government. Aboriginals who move to cities are viewed as complicit in the erosion of traditional ways of life. Urban areas and migrant Aboriginals are not to be aided by recognizing self-government in the cities. Meanwhile, leading analyses of the plight of the First Peoples scarcely mention issues around Natives in cities. Macklem, a leading advocate of Aboriginal rights, has written an eloquent and challenging brief for the First Peoples in his book *Indigenous Difference and the Constitution of Canada*.[85] Yet, that book never once specifically addresses the problems of urban Aboriginals.[86]

The continuing debates about self-government are doing little for the plight of urban Aboriginals. There are many problems in achieving effective responses to these conditions. A major difficulty has been that, until recently at least, no level of government has been willing to acknowledge responsibility for Aboriginals living in cities, whether in terms of self-government or otherwise. Historically, the federal government took the position that its authority was over on-reserve Indians. It largely ignored Aboriginal people living off reserves. The provincial response was that all Aboriginals were the primary responsibility of the federal government. Thus, few provincial policies are specifically directed at improving conditions for the First Peoples. Individual municipalities were often left to respond to the needs of urban Aboriginals and frequently lacked the resources – and the will – to do so.[87]

Recently, the federal government has become more responsive. In its reply, in 1998, to the RCAP report, the government specifically acknowledged the problems of urban Aboriginals and that it should have policies to address those conditions.[88] But tangible support for programs remains meagre. The main way the federal government underwrites the transition to urban settings is through Native Friendship Centres, to the extent of about $13.4 million a year. It spends over $256 million on immigrant settlement and integration. On a per capita basis, this works out to $34 for the former and $247 for the latter.[89] The point here is not to take issue with expenditures to assist recent immigrants in settling in this country; it is to question whether support for Aboriginals in facing a new life in the city should be less than that amount. In fairness, the 2003 federal budget did provide for $17 million over two years for cost-shared pilot projects to explore new ways to better meet the needs of urban Aboriginals; the results remain to be seen.[90]

There have been some initiatives, particularly in western cities, by the three levels of government. A recent study examined programs for Aboriginals in six major western cities.[91] The study investigated programs in twenty fields, including education, training, youth, and corrections.[92] Enhanced programming does exist in most of the fields. In the majority of the fields, at least two levels of government have programming activity, sometimes combined with efforts of Aboriginal or nonprofit organizations. However, there was a notable lack of activity in the fields of income support, suicide prevention, and human rights.[93]

Beyond documenting the existence of programs and pointing to gaps in services, the study raised a number of evaluative questions. For example, it had concerns about the lack of coordination among the levels of government that might be leading to duplication of efforts in some fields and inadequate services in others.[94] It also urged that assessments of the effectiveness of the programs be undertaken. Among the questions it urged be answered was this critical one: Is enhanced programming for Aboriginals more, less, or as effective as programming for the general population (from which Aboriginals could benefit) in attaining articulated goals?[95]

Citizens Plus?

As the twenty-first century begins, three main positions on the Aboriginal dilemma are on offer as responses to the plight of the First People. The first, typified by the recommendations of RCAP, scripts the First Peoples as rights-bearing, land-based nations that will negotiate with Canada to bring about a separate, third order of government. The second urges assimilation; the 1969 White Paper has returned in an even harsher form. The sooner the First Peoples are treated the same as all other members of society, the better for everyone. The third, Citizens Plus, recognizes the special status of Aboriginals while situating them firmly in Canadian society. Do these positions, alone or in combination, offer a way forward? Is there a way forward?

RCAP and the Embrace of Two Row Wampum

An image referred to frequently and more favourably by those advocating "nation to nation" treatment for Aboriginals is that of two row wampum: "The two-row wampum, which signifies 'One River, Two Vessels,' committed the newcomers to travel in their vessel and not attempt to interfere with our voyage ... This is how the First Nations still understand our relationship with Canadians."[96]

There have been a number of efforts to make the relationship between the First Peoples and Canada conform to this image. The most prominent attempt in the last decades has been RCAP. However well intended, its recommendations display "antipathy toward majoritarian democratic politics and consistent espousal of a regime of rights coupled with monitoring and enforcement mechanisms distanced from government and from the ebb and flow of public opinion."[97] What is more, that nation-to-nation constitutional vision clashed with its other analyses of the necessity of interdependence of a number of concrete policies.

The report's main focus was the ultimate formation of Aboriginal nations (sixty to eighty). These nations would have treaties with Canada; their status would be constitutionally entrenched as a third order of government, with as many areas of jurisdiction as possible. These would be the primary community for individuals belonging to them; the governments of the various nations would control who would belong. The nation would be the appropriate unit for determining representation in an Aboriginal parliament and, ultimately, in a House of First Peoples.

Participation of Aboriginals affiliated with these nations in the institutions of the larger society was another matter. Such participation was largely ignored. There was no discussion of whether these Aboriginals would vote in provincial elections. There was no discussion of whether they would vote in federal constituencies for members of the House of Commons. The participation of individuals in federal and provincial elections who belong to neither a nation nor a people was not discussed. In sum, RCAP had little interest in direct linkages of individual Aboriginals with federal or provincial governments. Instead, "the nation ... [was] to be the intermediary between the nation-based Aboriginal and the two other orders of government."[98]

There are enormous difficulties with these recommendations. Whether they could ever be implemented, at what cost, and over what period are crucial questions. Even if they were somehow implemented, they carry with them the risk of eroding, not strengthening, Aboriginal communities. The separation recommended by RCAP could so distance Aboriginals from Canadian society as to undercut the necessary support to address the many problems that beset them. Cairns points to this risk and asks a vital question: "The Commission's gamble is that a constitutionalized treaty relationship between nations is a substitute for ... a community of citizens ... Can a nation-to-nation relationship, even given the proposed infrastructure of treaties, tribunals, enforcement mechanisms, and rights, generate the necessary civic empathy to sustain the long-term commitment that is required?"[99]

A substantial part of the difficulties grappling with the RCAP recommendations must be attributed to the inadequate response of the federal government. It took more than a year for the government to issue a reply – *Gathering Strength: Canada's Aboriginal Action Plan*.[100] Cairns has called that reply "an embarrassment."[101] It basically ignored RCAP's constitutional vision; nor was there any response to many of the hundreds of specific proposals: "the general direction of *Gathering Strength* is a litany of support for good causes rhetorically described."[102] To add insult to injury, the government did not send RCAP's report to committees of either the House of Commons or the Senate; nor did RCAP receive funding to publish many of the research studies that it had sponsored.

What reaction there was to the report in the media was mostly critical. It was characterized as well-intentioned but misdirected: "a report that 'blue skies' everything ... it sets forth minimalist positions ... that have little, if any, chance of being adopted."[103] The fear expressed was that the "blue skying" deflected attention away from the hard task of reconciling the claims of the First Peoples with life in Canadian society in the twenty-first century: "the commissions produced not a roadmap for action into which aboriginal and non-aboriginal Canadians could buy, but a document that may make a real reconciliation between aboriginal and non-aboriginal Canadians more difficult."[104]

Second Thoughts: Assimilation Renewed
The defeat of the White Paper witnessed the end of assimilation as official policy. Yet, over the last decades it has continued to have its supporters. At the beginning of the new century, it has emerged anew in a form that is even harsher and more aggressive.

The Nielsen Task Force was appointed in 1985 by the Mulroney government to eliminate waste and duplication in government. Native programs came under its review. The task force's conclusions were unsympathetic to a separate way of life for the First Peoples.[105] Reserves were dismissed as places where Aboriginals "live in virtual quarantine in communities which have no real economic base and ... a disintegrating social and cultural fabric."[106] There was no room for cultural distinctiveness. The task force's position on Aboriginal rights unwittingly demonstrated why advocates view them as so fundamental: "rights [prevented] absorption into society."[107]

By the 1990s, near assimilation was being advocated by the Reform Party. That party urged acceptance of the fundamental norm of constitutional equality of all citizens. Any dilution because of treaty and Aboriginal rights was to be minimized. Preston Manning, the former leader of the Reform Party, alleged that "special status in federal law [for Aboriginals] has been an unmitigated disaster."[108] Others took a similar position. A former deputy minister of British Columbia asserted that "a new native policy must be built on the ... integration for natives within the mainstream of Canadian society, thus enhancing a sense of self-reliance ... such a policy must be formulated and implemented absent any sense of collective guilt over what may have happened in times past."[109]

In 2000 Tom Flanagan's *First Nations? Second Thoughts* pushed assimilation even more stridently.[110] Flanagan's book is a denunciation of what he sees as the orthodoxy determining Aboriginal policy. The results are that a small elite of activists, politicians, and entrepreneurs are enriched while conditions for most First Peoples get worse. Flanagan has many targets. He is furious with RCAP. Referring to its recommendations, he warns: "Canada will be redefined as a multinational state embracing an archipelago of aboriginal nations that own a third of Canada's land mass, are immune from federal and provincial taxation, are supported by transfer payments from citizens who do pay taxes, are able to opt out of federal and provincial legislation, and engage in 'nation to nation' diplomacy with whatever is left of Canada."[111]

Flanagan has a long list of grievances attributable to the present Aboriginal policy. At base, he contends that there are three "grave problems" with such orthodoxy:

- It is at variance with liberal democracy because it makes race the constitutive factor of the political order. It would establish Aboriginal nations as privileged political communities with membership defined by race and passed on through descent.
- It wrongly encourages Aboriginal people to see others – so-called Euro-canadians – as having caused their misfortune and, therefore, as holding the key to their improvement. Most Aboriginal advocates define "doing better" as succeeding not by their own efforts, but by getting something from the oppressors.
- It encourages Aboriginal people to withdraw into themselves, into their own "First Nations," under their own "self-governments," on their own "Aboriginal economies." Yet this is the wrong direction if the goal is widespread individual independence and prosperity for Aboriginal people.[112]

Such assertions may be the "contemporary version of the imperialist world view which formerly provided sustenance ... for the ... European empires."[113] But they cannot be dismissed; they may enjoy a good measure of popular support.

A recent book on popular culture and attitudes in this country contends that Canadians are sympathetic to the plight of the First Peoples but wary of anything that smacks of special status.[114] The smaller number of Canadians open to special status tend to be younger, better educated, and concentrated in Ontario, a province that has relatively few Aboriginals.[115] In a 1998 poll, 61 percent of those asked agreed that Aboriginals were "too dependent on government" and 49 percent agreed that Aboriginals "would be better off if they just joined mainstream Canadian society."[116] By November 2002 a report of a poll indicated that 59 percent of respondents wanted Natives to be treated "just like any other Canadian" (up from 50 percent in 1987).[117] In a poll reported on in February 2003 regarding increases in social spending, only 1 percent of those asked wanted additional expenditures on Aboriginal affairs.[118] The book concludes its discussion of Aboriginal issues with a laudatory reference to Pierre Trudeau and the 1969 White Paper: "Perhaps Trudeau ... was simply ahead of his time."[119]

Citizens Plus?

Can obligations arising from treaties, the Constitution, and the rulings of courts bind together Aboriginals and non-Aboriginals? This is the question Cairns asks in his book *Citizens Plus: Aboriginal Peoples and the Canadian State.*[120] He asserts there must be coexistence but one that includes "some element of common belonging and allegiance to a single polity by Aboriginal and non-Aboriginal peoples if it is to flourish."[121] A single, flourishing polity is a worthy goal. How is it to be accomplished?

Cairns makes four main points about the fundamental importance of a shared sense of citizenship between Aboriginals and other Canadians:[122]

1   Whatever the assertions of some Aboriginal advocates, independence for the First Peoples is not a realistic option. Regardless of how advanced a form of self-government Aboriginals may obtain, they will always remain a part of Canada, "locked in an inescapable interdependence."[123]
2   If Aboriginals and non-Aboriginals see each other as strangers instead of fellow citizens, they will become indifferent to each other. Such indifference will be harder on the First Peoples. Even if self-government is fully realized, they will need to rely on services and transfers funded by other taxpayers. Such services and transfers are "more likely to be met if they are seen to belong to the Canadian community, for which citizenship is the obvious symbol."[124]
3   The assertion that Aboriginals should relate to Canada as members of nations that are separate from Canada fails to do justice to the complexity of "Aboriginality."[125] Aboriginals should be encouraged to view federal and provincial as legitimate governments, in addition to their own, of their communities. Aboriginals should participate in these governments as voters, candidates, and parliamentarians.
4   The benefits to be gained from self-government are more limited for Aboriginals living in urban areas. Urban Aboriginals are marginalized by the "nation to nation" paradigm. They would be better served by focusing on the rights of citizenship.[126]

Cairns's rallying cry is "citizens plus." He has returned to the basics of the Hawthorn Report of the 1960s, with which he was involved as a researcher.[127] That report coined the phrase "citizens plus." For Cairns those words recognize Aboriginals' difference. They simultaneously emphasize that a sustainable relationship between Aboriginals and the dominant society must be grounded on common citizenship: "neither our togetherness nor our separateness can be escaped from."[128] Yet, more divisive alternatives shunted the position of Citizens Plus aside in the last quarter of the twentieth century. The polarities of the assimilationist insistence on the absolute equality of all citizens, on the one hand, and the nation-to-nation demands of parallelism, on the other, suppressed the middle path represented by Citizens Plus.

Cairns's book has been widely praised as "influential"[129] and "truly important,"[130] as containing "generosity of ... vision,"[131] and as right in asserting "that no one is really well served when the political rhetoric is more about sovereignty than it is about poverty, education, and housing."[132] Yet, in this age of extremes, its temperateness was bound to draw fire. Three main criticisms have been levied against it: Cairns is too hard on advocates of Aboriginal difference; he distorts the concepts of nation-to-nation and self-government; and the concept of Citizens Plus is too vague to be a basis for addressing issues involving First Peoples.

Concerning the first criticism, it is not surprising that Cairns's search for a middle ground would be unacceptable to many Aboriginal activists. Patricia Monture-Angus, a prominent advocate, flatly rejects Cairns's approach: "There is significant potential for ... 'citizens plus' ... to fundamentally denigrate these constitutional affirmations ... returning to a defensive, reactive, and rhetorical position, such as 'citizens plus,' must be rejected."[133] Former Ontario premier Bob Rae suggests that the present difficulties arise more from governments' unwillingness to act than from the deficiencies in positions taken by those espousing the cause of the First Peoples: "There are still too many in government unwilling to address what must be done ... Cairns spends too much time analyzing and criticizing the academic and political literature on Aboriginal sovereignty."[134]

The second criticism focuses on Cairns's questioning of concepts central to the autonomy of Aboriginals, such as nation-to-nation and self-government. Cairns insists that the concept of self-government, including in the failed Charlottetown Accord, lacks precision. Rae responds that Cairns's criticisms reveal weaknesses in his own analysis: "Self-government negotiations cannot be centrally described, because their meaning and conclusion will depend so much on time and circumstance ... the failure of ... governments to engage in serious discussions about these issues is not because of the 'woolliness' of the concept ... while Cairns talks around the problem he does not address it as centrally as it needs to be addressed."[135]

Kymlicka suggests the Cairns describes the "nation to nation" paradigm as promoting maximum autonomy for Aboriginals and maximum cultural differences. In contrast, Kymlicka insists that consent is central to that paradigm: "relations between aboriginals and Canada must be reformulated on the basis of *consent* rather than force ... endorsing this idea of consensual relations is perfectly consistent with recognizing the complex interdependencies of aboriginal and non-aboriginal Canadians."[136]

The third criticism alleges that the concept of Citizens Plus is too vague to be the basis for addressing issues involving the First Peoples. It points to the fact that the Hawthorn Report also does not set out what the components of Citizens Plus would be but instead insists they would emerge from further debates and discussion. Flanagan observes that "thirty five years later, the future has arrived; but [he is] still not spelling out what 'citizens plus' will mean in practice."[137] He then suggests that a major practical result of implementing Citizens Plus will be increasing transfers of public funds to First Peoples governments and groups that will not benefit ordinary Aboriginals: "The aboriginal elite will do well for itself by managing the cash flow of government programs and enterprises, but most people will remain mired in poverty and misery."[138]

Conclusion

Their history is filled with tragedy. Contemporary life for many is horrific. So much has been tried – leaving a legacy of failure. In this age of law, it is understandable that Aboriginal people would turn to rights and to the courts. But such activism has largely been another valiant effort gone wrong. Meanwhile, the champions of laissez-faire urge their tried-and-true response: No special treatment. Let market forces prevail. Peoples: equip yourself to compete in a globalizing world or suffer the consequences.

Whatever the criticism of Citizens Plus, it is a middle path in the excruciating task of coming to grips with the Aboriginal dilemma. In Cairns's hands, Citizens Plus raises "the tough questions that are necessary for good governance, despite the sensitivities of these issues."[139] Cairns's position urges that two things happen so that good public policy can be forged. Governments need to recognize that the question of the rights of Aboriginal people is still not resolved and must be faced. Aboriginal leaders must engage their fellow citizens and governments on a practical basis. With patience, fortitude, and trust, good public policy in this area could be achieved.

But this is an age of polarities. Two row wampum, on the one hand, and assimilation, on the other, are fiercely opposed visions of the way issues involving First Peoples should be addressed. Citizens Plus is a hopeful middle path. Yet, it may be that none of these three visions will be realized in any coherent way. Fractiousness and litigation may predominate amid a drifting sense of frustration even as Aboriginals shift to the cities and their identities fade.

6 Citizens in Cyberspace: The Internet and Canadian Democracy

Telegraphs of any kind are wholly unnecessary.
– *The British Admiralty, 1816*

Television will never be a serious competitor for radio because people must sit and keep their eyes glued on a screen; the average American family hasn't time for it.
– New York Times, *1939*

There is no reason for any individual to have a computer in their homes.
– *Ken Olsen, chair of Digital Equipment Corporation, 1977* [1]

As the foregoing illustrate, predictions, perhaps especially about technology, and even by the very knowledgeable, can be stupendously wrong. A chapter on the Internet and Canadian democratic institutions will do well to keep the prospect of such errors in mind. Yet, pondering the effects of the Internet is difficult to resist. Perhaps no technology has burst forth with such hoopla as the one that allows us to voyage through cyberspace at the click of a mouse. Its growth over the last decade has been phenomenal. Its use, within and across societies, is stunningly uneven – the digital divide – even as thousands become wired daily. It is owned by no one; its commercial applications abound and are coming to dominate it. It has endless possibilities for direct political engagement – the new Athens; mostly it is buttressing a twenty-first-century embodiment of citizenship – the entertained shopper.

Prophecy is a tricky business. But here is an attempt. Hand-wringers: relax. Yes, the Net does have some bad stuff on it – pornography, messages of hate, terrorist communications; the last became of particular concern after the horrors of 11 September 2001. Political activists: don't get your hopes up. Yes, there have been campaigns facilitated via cyberspace. Yes, the poor and the excluded can link up with each other round the world. Nonetheless, those who are wired are, by and large, not preoccupied with either white supremacy or global improvement of health care.

There's money to be made through the Internet. Corporations have moved in, and the market is everywhere in the real – and virtual – worlds. And courts and rights, whose growing influence in so many areas has been illustrated in this book, are playing a subsidiary role in the unfolding of the virtual.

The three Cs will triumph: Consuming Citizens in Cyberspace. The Internet is unlikely to contribute to the renovation of Canadian democracy. Rather, it may be a part of the further dishevelment of representative politics. Again, the myth of exit is at play. A citizenry, dissatisfied with the sorry state of representative politics, can leave it behind. Cyberspace – with its promise of disintermediation (the reduction or elimination of agents) and direct democracy – beckons. As we shall see, the reality is different. But myth making rarely concerns itself with the complexities and hard work that necessarily accompany the tough job of tackling real life; in this case, making democracy live up to its ideals.

The Internet: A Brief Tour

A Little History
There's lots more to come. But the phenomenon that's the Net has gone from pinprick to global everywhere in less than twenty years. From the start, Americans have dominated for better and for worse.

The Internet is a gift from the American military. The American Defense Department's Advanced Research Projects Agency (ARPA) sponsored a project to connect computers across that country. The result was ARPANET. Up to the early 1980s, the main users of that system were large research universities.[2]

The Internet grew rapidly during the 1980s. However, it was the development of hypertext, browsers, and servers, leading to the World Wide Web in 1991, that transformed the use of the Net. Mosaic, the multimedia Web browser, arrived in 1993 and the development of search tools came shortly thereafter. Travel through cyberspace became the stuff of daily life. The opposite of "real" was no longer "unreal" but "virtual." In comparison with other major communication innovations, the Internet reached fifty million people worldwide at a staggering pace; it took the telephone seventy-four years; the radio thirty-eight years; television thirteen years. The Web did it in only four years. Traffic on the Internet doubles every one hundred days.[3] Arnprior and Bangalore are worlds away and a click away.

But the use of the Internet is not uniform, either within or across societies. That brings us to the "digital divide."[4]

Who's Wired?

Industrialized Nations

So popular is the Internet that one might think that its use is extensive throughout developed nations. Not so. There is a digital divide both within these societies and between them. By a number of measures, the United States leads. This is for several reasons. America developed the Net, it has by far the most websites, English is overwhelmingly the language of choice in cyberspace, and the United States employs a rate structure – unmetered access – that encourages plentiful use. Canada is also at the forefront in "connectedness."[5] According to 1997 figures, Canada has the most networks per million of population, with the United States and Australia not far behind.[6] In the case of broadband connections, access that is high speed and dedicated, Korea leads, but Canada and the United States are number two and three, respectively.[7]

It is a different story for the rest of the OECD nations. Central and southern European countries as well as Japan may be falling behind. A reliable measure of the extent of the Internet in any country is the number of hosts, the computers on which websites and other information are stored. Between September 1999 and March 2000, the United States added 25.1 Internet hosts for every thousand people. During the same period Britain added 5.5; Japan, 4.1; Germany, 3; and France, 2.7.[8] The 1997 statistics cited above on networks per million people reveal a similar pattern in the gap between OECD countries. As indicated, Canada (192), the United States (114), and Australia (110) lead. Other rich nations were far behind: France (37), Britain (24), Germany (22), and Japan (15).[9]

Within societies that are wired there is a wide discrepancy based on a number of factors, including socioeconomic status, education, race, age, able-bodiedness, and geographical location. For rich countries, a rough guide is that, for every $10,000 increase in household income, the number of homes owning a computer rises by seven percentage points.[10] A 1999 report in the United States documents that use of the Net has been increasing in all demographic groups. However, individuals with college degrees were eight times more likely to have a PC and sixteen times more likely to have Internet access at home than those with only elementary school education. White children were more likely to have access than black or Hispanic kids; the urban and affluent citizens were more likely to be connected than poor rural individuals; and more able-bodied people than people with disabilities were wired.[11]

In the end, money, or lack of it, accounts for much of the digital divide. In 1993 in the United States, middle-class and affluent households (annual income of $50,000 or more) accounted for 46 percent of all computer owners. By 1998 that figure had risen to 54 percent. The poorest households (income below $10,000) had slipped from 4 to 3 percent during that same period.[12] Further, being unwired is more a result than a cause of underlying problems:

lack of education, money, and other resources. It makes no sense to connect someone who does not have the skills and the confidence to exploit the opportunities in cyberspace: "access to all the books in the Library of Congress is of little use if you cannot read."[13]

The Third World

If there is a digital divide between and within rich countries, there may be a chasm between them and the Third World. Rich nations account for only 15 percent of the earth's population but for 90 percent of world spending on information technology and 80 percent of the world's Internet users. A computer in Bangladesh costs eight years' pay.[14]

The Internet depends on technology that is much less accessible and much more expensive in developing nations than in industrialized countries. Take telephone lines still relied on by many Net users for access. There are more such lines in Manhattan than in the whole of sub-Saharan Africa. Calls from Senegal to Zambia are routed through London. More than half of the connected computers in the world are in the United States. Less than ten countries in Africa are directly connected to the Net.[15] On that continent, only about 0.1 percent of the population uses Internet services. What access there is is very unevenly distributed: South Africa accounts for 90 percent of the growth.[16]

What is more, in many developing nations there is cultural and governmental resistance to cyberspace. In 1996 the Chinese government banned access to hundreds of websites so as to eliminate "cultural rubbish."[17] The Burmese government outlawed the unauthorized use of a computer with networking capability. The Iranian government centralized access to the Internet through the Ministry of Post and Telecommunications, which effectively bans sites of the Mujahedeen, the B'ahai religion, and other opposition groups.[18]

Still, the developing world is increasing the use of the Internet at a fast pace. In 2002 it was predicted that the number of Web users in Latin America, the Caribbean, and east and central Europe would quadruple from 7.6 million to 25.6 million. Even in lagging Africa there are signs of activity; AT&T has solicited investors for Africa for various projects.[19] In any event, the many challenges faced by Third World nations must be at the forefront of any Internet developments: "People face far more important challenges than the lack of internet access, namely lack of access to water, food, medical treatment and education. For them, the digital divide is a symptom, rather than the cause, of wider inequality."[20]

So Many Ways to Communicate – and Be Entertained

The Internet's digital divide is an important factor to be reckoned with. Nonetheless, there is a communications revolution that is sweeping the globe. The Net is but one component of this transformation. The mobile phone, fax, and new applications of television and radio are others. Each of these has an important role in this sweeping change. The convergence among them is even more critical. Two points need to be made: one is about different uses of technology; the other is about the communications revolution, and consumption and entertainment.

Technology is used differently in various countries. The digital divide among rich nations runs two ways. It is true that the United States and Canada lead in the use of the Net and that many OECD countries lag in their employment of it. Mobile phone use, though, is much higher in Europe than it is in the United States. The penetration of mobile phones is 50 percent more in Europe than in the United States. Around the world, the number of mobile phones exceeds Internet connections.[21] In the spring of 2000, 76 percent of Swedes had mobile phones, the highest rate in the world. The point here is that the mobile phone can give access to the Internet. Thus, in time – possibly quite a short time – convergence may occur between the phone and the Net that will suddenly give many in Europe access to cyberspace, and with a flexibility not possessed by many Americans.[22] So the figures on who's wired in various countries could change quickly for several reasons, among them the power of converging technologies.[23]

The second point is about entertainment. Cairncross is direct concerning the commercial dominance of the Internet that will lead to "consumer" as the greatest role for individuals: "Companies will make more use of the Internet ... Consumers will be the main beneficiaries of the revolution ... for consumers everywhere, electronic commerce will eventually bring empowerment: to search, to bargain, to specify; to have what they want, when and where they want it."[24] The communications revolution will bestow many benefits on consumers, from greater access to improved health care to greater access to improved education. In this way, the Internet, converging with other technologies, will have a truly democratizing impact. Like the other communications revolutions before it, this one will make products and services accessible to the many that were before available only to the few. Falling costs of ocean freight and air transport revolutionized, from diet to travel, the lives of ordinary people. The communications revolution will make all manner of activity that was previously confined by geography available worldwide and to common folk.

Yet, what this sea change may do most is pacify individuals even further, underscoring their role as inert consumers of corporate America. A considerable portion of many people's lives can be characterized that way in the real world. In any given evening, half the people in the United States and Europe are watching television. After work, the consumption of TV takes up more waking time than anything else for the average person.[25] Yes, television informs. But mostly it entertains, titillates, and lures. In America, "scream television," with audiences hooting and participants yelling, convinces people that they are engaging the issues of the day by shouting insults at each other.

High-quality newspapers can provide a much more reflective way to digest and react to society's developments. But newspaper readership has been falling for some time.[26] In America, in 1948, daily newspaper circulation was 1.3 per household. By 1998 that rate had fallen by 57 percent despite the fact that the number of years of education, usually positively correlated with such reading, had risen substantially during the same time.[27] Even the circulation of supermarket tabloids – the *Star,* the *National Enquirer,* and so forth – is down. That might be an indicator that people are tiring of warped sensationalism being passed off as reporting. But another explanation is that mainstream media, especially TV, are aping the tabs, "invading [their] territory with gossipy entertainment channels and endless chat shows that blur the distinction between speculation and news."[28]

The communications revolution is unlikely to stem this rush to entertainment as consumption. In many ways it will make it worse. The Net is an alternative to the old media, allowing for interactive communication in pervasive and highly specialized forms. In 1998 there were about ninety thousand public e-mail lists, thirty thousand Usenet discussion groups,[29] and twenty-three thousand Internet relay chat channels.[30] Skeptics suggest that what is critical is that the Internet is not a departure from mass entertainment but is instead "a deepening of the social experience sired by television."[31]

There are dreams of a "new Athens" in cyberspace where "netizens" will be enlivened by a new democracy. I'll come to such hopes in a moment. What's driving the Internet is not political engagement or a renovated sense of community. Corporate America and the websites it controls are coming to dominate the Net.[32] Millions of sites have been created. Yet, 83 percent of Internet users go to no more than ten domain names each week.[33]

The top 1 percent of sites account for more than half the traffic on the Web, with the top 0.1 percent capturing more than 30 percent. These sites, aided by popular search engines such as Google, are portals that bring consumers in and direct their interests.[34] The gatekeeping capacities of these top sites are heavily weighted to corporate America: "AOL, Yahoo!, Microsoft sites, Lycos, Excite@home – ... attract huge number of users and then draw their attention to other, smaller sites."[35] Some of these sites openly sell the top slots of search results to the highest bidder.[36] Unwanted junk e-mail, spam, continues to proliferate despite efforts to control it.[37]

Meanwhile, producers of WebTV are trying to harness the Net. Cyberspace is to be consumed as but another form of television and just as passively taken in: "Perhaps all it takes to enjoy everything the Internet has to offer is a more familiar setting. Since you already have a television, a cozy place to watch, and you already know how to use a remote, you're all set. So just kick back, relax."[38]

The real and virtual worlds are rapidly intermingling. Driving the mix is mass media and mass marketing: "a dominant screen culture, which over time becomes the familiar reference point of everyday life."[39] All the while, there are hopes that changing television channels and roaming the World Wide Web somehow produce a revitalized citizenry.

Public/Private Control

In important ways, no one controls the Internet. The Net grew out of public funding and academic research. Its protocols can be used by anyone. There is no central gatekeeper for access to it; there is no membership requirement. No one owns it: "not a single line of computer code which underpins the net is proprietary; and nobody who contributed to its development has ever made a cent from intellectual property rights in it."[40] This lack of control can be a cause for concern. Prominent among any worries, especially since the horrors of 11 September, are the uses terrorists might make of the Internet.[41]

Such freewheeling origins of the Net have led to claims that cyberspace is beyond the law, immune from regulation. Consider cyber-activist John Barlow's Declaration of the Independence of Cyberspace: "Governments of the Industrial World, you weary giants of flesh and steel ... you of the past leave us alone ... you have no sovereignty where we gather ... you have no moral right to rule us nor do you possess any methods of enforcement we have true reason to fear ... governments derive their just powers from the consent of the governed. You have neither solicited nor received ours ... cyberspace does not lie within your borders."[42] These assertions are wrong. Nonetheless, in combination with the forces of deregulation, they have led governments to adopt a more hands-off approach to the Internet than to other forms of communication.[43]

There are problems with accountability for words and actions in cyberspace. The Net's global and often anonymous character can challenge those seeking to enforce legal rights and obligations. A prosecutor trying to track down child pornographers using anonymous retailers to distribute their materials, a court attempting to provide redress to a libelled person when the defamation was perpetrated online in another, remote country, and a state striving to protect consumers that cannot determine the owner of a website that distributes fraudulent material are but three examples of the difficulties of legal enforcement.[44]

Nevertheless, the World Wide Web is not a lawless land.[45] The law may apply and have effects that vary in important ways.[46] Yet, in the first instance, "real" law extends to activities online. Illegal gambling is no less so just because it takes place in cyberspace. Trafficking in child prostitutes is not immunized because it is done on the Web. A sales transaction on the Net attracts applicable taxes. It's true that the virtual world may give rise to complications, such as determining jurisdiction of courts and problems with giving effect to judgments.[47] These complexities may require special responses, for example, particular legislative provisions and international action.[48] But similar issues can arise in the real world as well.

The Internet is increasingly subject to regulation.[49] To date, there has been a significant role for self-regulation in two important areas: developing technical standards and administering the system of domain names. Three main bodies oversee these and related issues: the Internet Engineering Task Force (IETF), the World Wide Web Consortium (W3C), and the Internet Corporation for Assigned Names and Numbers (ICANN). There have been controversies, particularly over ICANN and the coordination of numeric addresses and the management of the domain-name system.[50] Nonetheless, these organizations, which have a heavy American presence, have so far succeeded in governing some of the most important issues involved in the running of the Net,[51] and there is potential for more international cooperation.[52]

Beyond self-regulation, governmental agencies have intervened on issues concerning the functioning of the Net, for example, in rates structures and their effects on use. Governments have used competition laws to challenge objectionable behaviour, especially by the corporate giants. A much publicized example has been the US Department of Justice's litigation against Microsoft and that company's domination of operating systems to force the use of its other products.[53]

What is more, some governmental agencies have used their regulatory powers to bolster policies that enhance the development of the Net. As indicated, Canada is a leader in broadband access. An important factor in this growth is Canadian regulators requiring the "unbundl[ing] [of] the local loop," that is, forcing carriers to give other companies access to the wires running into homes.[54] Indeed, regulatory intervention by many governments, including in Canada, has mostly focused on paving a way for development of the Internet by the private sector through market-driven, competitive activities.[55] Part of that stance are programs designed to facilitate access for individuals and communities that otherwise might not be connected. Canadian federal and provincial governments have provided funds to develop "smart communities," wired in various ways, for a number of purposes, and to facilitate access for individuals who face barriers to usage of the Net.[56]

Governmental agencies have been much less enthusiastic about applying regulatory activities associated with more traditional forms of broadcasting – radio and television – to the Net. An example of this is the decision by the Canadian Radio-television and Telecommunications Commission (CRTC) not to regulate content on the Internet, including the amount of Canadian material, as well as French-language usage, hate speech, and pornography.[57] These are matters about which the commission has, for some time, asserted its authority in television and radio. More fundamentally, the government in Canada, along with many others, has shown almost no interest in establishing a public system on the Net, akin to the CBC and its role in radio and television. There could be many practical difficulties in implementing such a proposal. That said, what stops such overtures cold is the overwhelming idea that private, competitive forces are to drive the growth of cyberspace. Pleas for substantial and systematic governmental presence through developments such as a "public.net"[58] and for "public entrepreneurship" backed by a "charter of information rights"[59] have gathered little support.

The Internet and a Changing Canada

Social, political, and economic phenomena interact with each other. A development in one area influences and is influenced by transformation in others. These complicated relationships can make the assessment of outcomes produced by any one change difficult.[60] These complexities are intensified by different philosophical viewpoints that may be applied as assessments. To take but one example, free marketers and political progressives are likely to approach the ascertainment of outcomes produced by minimum wage laws quite differently. There is also the prospect of unintended consequences, especially when technology is involved.[61]

The Internet and Canadian democratic institutions are interacting with each other in complicated ways. Canadian society increasingly scorns representative politics, turns distributional issues over to the market, and venerates individual choice in the courts and on the street. This celebration of choice, assertion of individualism, and cynicism toward legislatures makes for receptive ground to propagate myths about the wonders of the Net, whatever its actual impact.

One of the claims made on behalf of the virtual is that it fosters disintermediation. No longer will netizens and cyberconsumers be encumbered by the need to rely on third parties and institutions, whether to speak their voice, organize, educate themselves, or shop. When it comes to commercial transactions, such simplification between supplier and purchaser may make for a more efficient and, therefore, more prosperous economy in many areas.[62] Those who participate in such arrangements need to be aware of the hazards – think about all those day traders and their deflated dot.com holdings.[63] But the arguments that parties should have the option of bypassing intermediaries are powerful.

Different considerations pertain to the unfolding of democracy, an exercise that involves a great deal more than individual economic circumstances. But, here too, there are powerful forces of disintermediation at work. Take the print media. Too progressive? Too conservative? Too general? Not enough sports? Enter "The Daily Me" – "a communications package that is personally designed, with each component fully chosen in advance."[64] Increasingly, the Net is allowing individuals to exercise more control over the news and information to which they are exposed and the environments in which they function. Fears about the negative effects of such compartmentalization may be exaggerated.[65] Yet, this is the paradox: even as cyberspace seems so open and diverse, any number of forces are at work, from limited corporate portals to filtering technology, that could shut out differing views, limit perspectives, and restrain challenging opinions.

This is not to laud newspapers as they now exist. The largest of them are dominated by narrow interests (too corporate for some, too progressive for others). The newsstands are also full of special-interest publications catering to an array of interests not likely to intersect with any frequency. The worry is that disintermediation in cyberspace and beyond will exacerbate the waning will to engage in deliberative engagements of how our democracy should make its way: "there are endless newsgroups, email lists, and other online information sources dedicated to the most specific interests, but you'd be hard pressed to find a Random Interests group, let alone one committed to the General Common Good."[66]

A major assertion about the effects of cyberspace is that it has set off a "control revolution." At the heart of this change is an assertion about the shift in power from institutions to individuals. The governing of information, experience, and resources is moving away from large organizations and toward individuals. The click of a mouse empowers the user to learn, to transact, to organize, to select (to shop, to be entertained ...). Thus, the forces of disintermediation are shoving aside large institutions and powerful professionals – governments, corporations, unions, doctors, accountants, and lawyers. What is more, this massive shift has intrinsic characteristics that will lead to a renewed politics because "new technologies and, in particular, the Internet are inherently democratic."[67] As the "inherent democracy" unfolds, there will be choice, choice, and more choice: "you will be able to obtain governance at least as well customized to meet your personal needs and tastes as blue jeans."[68]

Corporate America, beaming its message everywhere, including to Canada, is only too glad to use the babble of personal control, individual will, and the celebration of choice to hype its products for cyberspace. Microsoft's ads inquire, "Where do you want to go today?" Netscape has TV ads that assert, "The world according to you." AT&T tells consumers they are at the centre of the world of new options and mobility: "Have you ever installed a phone on your wrist? You will." Lotus has a ditty that boasts, "I am superman and I can do anything."[69]

Such claims about the "control revolution," whatever the reality of ordinary people's lives, are finding adherents in a changing Canada. A society grown tired of conventional politics, that is awash in rights, and that more and more relies on markets to sort and distribute sees the Internet as a mirror reflecting, and a force spurring on, these changes. Canada and the United States, societies with these characteristics, are among the leaders in the race to be wired.

Yet, as Shapiro argues, the "control revolution" may not be so much about giving common folk more real power over their lives as it is about the illusion of control. It may be about convincing them that market forces and restrained government, particularly involving health, education, and social welfare, should dominate in both the real and virtual worlds: "the control revolution represents the merger of the communications revolution and the free-market revolution."[70] In making this point, he reminds us of what Jean-Jacques Rousseau observed: "There is no more perfect form of subjection than the one that preserves the appearance of freedom."[71]

Cyberspace and Canadian Democracy

> In the electronic republic, it will no longer be the press but the public that functions as the nation's powerful "fourth estate," alongside the executive, the legislative, and the judiciary.[72]

> With ... the Internet ... the identifiable and stabilizing body politic and its buttresses in civil society become unmoored, the relation between deliberation and decision making is unhinged, and the very concept of the political is appropriated and put to work to service media conglomerates and accumulated economic interests rather than the interests of citizens.[73]

These two quotes assert starkly different positions on the effects of the Internet and other electronic forms of communication. The coming of cyberspace has brought with it all manner of characterizations of the effects that will ensue, particularly on democratic institutions. Such descriptions are based on less than ten years of experience, with the Internet developing in societies that are otherwise in flux. The previous section underscored the point about general volatility in Canada. Accurate depictions of complex developments are hard enough; they are the more so when major components of such changes are gyrating. Thus, even a more or less accurate analysis of the effects of the Internet on Canadian democratic institutions today can be moved off the mark as the Internet veers in a different direction tomorrow.

That said, much of the commentary appearing at the end of the 1990s and into the 2000s was more skeptical about the transformative possibilities of the Net in terms of politics and democratic institutions than was the utopian prophesying of the early 1990s. There are still those who believe that cyberspace will usher in a new age of citizen empowerment. Many of those who have carefully examined the evidence to date on actual Internet usage are more dubious. Increasingly, they are concluding that the virtual will not alter the real world of politics. Rather, the real world will come to bound the virtual, harnessing it to serve established interests. At the same time, the myths about freedom, unfettered choice, and the bypassing of established institutions that are associated with cyberspace fit well with forces in the real world determined to curtail the scope of government.

Many of the studies and projections focusing on the effects of the Internet on democracy are based on the American experience. Their application to other societies, including Canada, must to some extent be based on conjecture. Available evidence regarding Canada will be analyzed. In any event, the structure, content, and use of the Net is so dominated by America that experience in the United States has clear relevance for other nations and their democratic institutions.

This section first looks at the effects of the Internet on the day-to-day workings of established institutions: government and its agencies; the courts and legislatures; and political parties. The Net is helping government organizations be much more responsive to the needs of citizens and there is potential to enhance this role even more. The next section looks at legislatures, parties, politicians, lobbyists, and courts, and how they are part of the communications revolution. These players are making extensive use of the Net for traditional purposes: organizing, fundraising, communication with members, and so forth.

The section then turns to an examination of political organizing and the Net. Here the focus is on forms of political behaviour that go beyond established methods and institutions. It is in this context that one might expect the vaunted freewheeling ways of cyberspace to come to the aid of new/challenging/ marginalized interests, helping their voices to be heard and providing a vehicle for organizing and building. Yet, the evidence is largely unsupportive of such claims. Some political activism, of groups with resources, has been assisted by the coordinating and linking power of cyberspace. However, beyond its assistance of such activists' efforts, there is little evidence that cyberspace has ushered in a new form of politics or rejuvenated democracies in any way. Few citizens participate in political discussions or community building online. Participants in Usenet groups are unrepresentative of the general public; many postings are brief, unresponsive to alternative views, and frequently contain negative, personal remarks. The few Canadian websites that purport to enhance democracy clearly do not do so. Efforts at community building online have mostly been unsuccessful. With some exceptions, attempts that have had positive results have had little connection with political activism.

These (non) developments should not be surprising. Throughout the twentieth century and even before, ambitious claims of the transformative possibilities for democracy were made for each new development in the media. The radio receiver went beyond the literacy barrier and offered mass communications, reaching millions simultaneously. Television permitted the viewer to see the events; it overcame the limited powers of newsprint or radio to convey and allowed individuals to become eyewitnesses to events of the day as they unfolded. Cable and satellite expanded the viewing options and offered live, unedited access to political developments and policy making in courts, in legislatures, and by special commissions. But predictions that these developments would "revolutionize everything we're doing today"[74] were off the mark. Of course, important modifications occurred and the other media do not have the interactive potential of the Internet. In each instance, though, technological developments were corralled by "existing media players to continue their role in ... society and politics."[75]

Yet, hopes remain high for the Internet and its potential to bring about widespread engagement with public policy issues. Such optimism is often conditioned by illusions about the extent of educational and deliberative uses of cyberspace. The Net can be used for such purposes, but the extent to which it is being so employed on a meaningful basis for any particular purpose is an important factual issue.

The report of the Roundtable on Governing in an Information Age was published in 1999.[76] The roundtable (also known as the Changing Maps Roundtable) was composed of senior Canadian government officials, private-sector executives, and leading academics. The roundtable had many purposes, but an important one was to provide recommendations for inspiring more confidence in government at a time when dissatisfaction with the public sphere was at a high – when there was a "crisis in governance."[77] It urged the development of the "information infrastructure ... to foster public dialogue and learning across boundaries."[78] It provided this list of initiatives:

- varieties of "electronic town meetings";
- ongoing discussion groups around particular issues (as in Internet newsgroups);
- parliamentary and government websites in which citizens can participate; and
- websites allowing groups and individual citizens to prepare their own online "programming," contributing their perceptions to the broader learning process.[79]

These are inspirational recommendations. Can their objectives be realized? The roundtable recognized that there are difficulties in ensuring such initiatives develop in ways that would produce the desired outcomes. Indeed, the evidence presented in the next sections suggests that the chances of them succeeding are not great.

Established Institutions

Government and Its Agencies

There are important reasons why the public sector should be eager to embrace cyberspace. Open and accessible governments are hallmarks of democracy; dictatorships are rarely models of communication. The Internet should foster international cooperation if only because countries fear loss of their sovereignty. It is even possible that the Net could foster peace through better communications and understanding among various cultures

On a more day-to-day level, the Internet could help governments be more responsive and accountable by aiding in the more efficient delivery of goods and services.[80] If these goals are achieved, they might boost the standing of democratic institutions. Licensing, welfare, procurement, crime prevention, health care, and education are just some of the areas where being online could lead to better service for citizens. At present, governments lag behind the private sector in many uses of the Net. Increasingly, though, they are taking steps to be a presence in cyberspace. Deloitte Research conducted a survey of governments' use of the Internet in Canada, the United Kingdom, the United States, Australia, and New Zealand. In 2000, 12 percent of citizens on average in these countries used the Net as their primary means of accessing public services. That figure was expected to rise to about 34 percent by 2002.[81] Canada may already be a leader. The 2000 figure for our country was 40 percent.[82]

Moving governments online to serve the needs of all citizens faces considerable challenges. In many instances, individuals have no choice but to deal with governments for particular goods and services. Governments and their agencies can be thick bureaucracies: unaccustomed to thinking of citizens as consumers; not driven by market forces; and organized into vertically structured "silos" not prone to cooperate in providing integrated services across a number of areas. There are more legitimate reasons for public agencies to be slow in embracing cyberspace. Individuals have to be able to go online. Access, even in the United States and Canada, is far from universal, particularly among the poor, ill-educated, and elderly, groups that have many needs for government assistance. In addition, governments need to invest heavily in their computer systems to upgrade them for integrated online services. Finally, privacy concerns loom large. Governments collect much personal, even intimate, information about their citizens. The Internet heightens concerns about the capacity of public officials to collect, organize, and disseminate such data.[83]

The Net's potential to save costs and provide more efficient and even higher quality services are powerful incentives moving the public sphere along. Thus, many governments, particularly in Canada and in New Zealand, have engaged in business process re-engineering (BPR), redesigning the fundamental ways in which they interact with citizens. Manitoba is pursuing a "single window to government" system, following an across-the-system assessment of how technology and staff capabilities could reduce administrative complications.[84] Ontario is working toward an information technology system for the province. That system will permit a variety of integrated applications; for example, an automated Ministry of Community and Social Services' social assistance network is to be used by caseworkers.[85]

An obvious area where government can be more responsive by being online interactively is routine form-filling tasks, many of which otherwise require individuals to line up to be served. Such services on the Net can be available twenty-four hours a day and there is no need for queues. North Dakota accepts fishing licence applications online; ServiceArizona enables people to renew motor vehicle registration and to replace a lost driver's licence. Online processing can save governments substantial amounts of money. One transaction costs ServiceArizona $1.60; the same transaction done over the counter in that state costs $6.60.[86] Governments have a number of ways in which to encourage use of online services. On its home page the Government of British Columbia prompts visitors to indicate what forms and payments they would like to be able to submit electronically; they are also asked to indicate what other services would be "faster, easier and cheaper ... to do online."[87]

There is also great potential for more complex transactions. A number of governments are actively involved in using the Internet for more efficient and better delivery of health care.[88] Britain is experimenting with NHS Direct, a telephone and Internet helpline begun in 1998. Staffed by nurses, it is accessible and less expensive than when a patient sees a doctor, and much less costly than if the patient is admitted to a hospital emergency room.[89] South Auckland Health is experimenting with several facets of patient information management systems to avoid more "adverse events" in the treatment of patients. The hospital envisages the day when each bed will have its own terminal, replacing the ubiquitous chart, and staff will carry hand-held terminals to receive and record information about patients.[90]

The American Army Medical Department is experimenting with a mobile operating room brought to the injured. A surgeon, far away, can operate by using a three-dimensional monitor and a control that manipulates forceps, scalpels, and so forth.[91] In time, such procedures could be particularly useful for civilians in remote areas, especially for countries, like ours, with vast areas and dispersed populations. In Canada, the task force on broadband access has recently urged that extensive efforts and resources be deployed to use the Internet to develop better health care for Canadians. It documents successful efforts to use the Net for diagnosis and treatment in distant parts of the country.[92]

The potential of municipal governments to engage citizens through the Internet is particularly promising. Municipalities are important providers of transit, utilities, and community programs, and they supply infrastructure that supports the economy. Industry Canada's Smart Communities initiative, costing $60 million, is funding twelve communities' development of various technological applications, including several model regional websites.[93]

A recent study of municipalities in western Canada (with populations greater than 1,000) and their use of the Internet suggests that employing the Net in conjunction with urban government is spreading rapidly. Almost 80 percent had an online presence, while another 16 percent intended to establish a Web presence within two years. Municipalities go online primarily to provide information to the public and to promote economic development. Only 22 percent of the municipalities cited citizen demand as a reason for establishing the site.[94]

While websites are widely used by western municipalities, their functions are limited. They are largely information based, with little in the way of online services or other interactive features. Larger municipalities are beginning to develop a limited number of e-services, but currently few e-services exist. While there are some survey features, most websites do not provide for citizen interaction.[95]

The Economist, as usual, comes to the point: "Prosaically, most e-government projects [aim] to reduce costs and make tax revenues go further."[96] That may be true. And, if along the way, ordinary citizens are delivered better services, more efficiently, that is surely a good result for democracy. True, people are being exhorted to be shoppers all over the place, to allow themselves to be passively entertained. I've discussed some of that already in this chapter and I'll be discussing more. But there is nothing wrong with the idea, itself, that transactions should reflect the legitimate needs of consumers. Cyberspace seems to be effectively delivering that message to public services.

Legislatures, Parties, Politicians, and Lobbyists

Direct Democracy?

> [Technology is] forging a new Athenian age of democracy.[97]
> – *Al Gore*

> A mass cannot govern.[98]
> – *Walter Lippman*

One of the most far-reaching claims about the transformative effects of the Net is that it will pave the way for the direct participation of citizens in government – the "New Athens." Such unencumbered engagement will be a dramatic illustration of the disintermediation for which cyberspace is a vital catalyst. In the electronic democracy, citizens are to exercise a whole new kind of power: "Wireless organizers, wireless networks, and community super-computing collectives all have one thing in common: *they enable people to act together in new ways and in situations where collective action was not possible before.*"[99] In this depiction, the representative model where elected officials are to use their judgment, expertise, and time to govern on behalf of citizens will be sidelined. Another instance of decisions not being made "by me, for me" will be eliminated. Citizen governors, by direct vote and other means, will determine outcomes of the exercise of state power, from questions about taxation to distribution of resources, from issues of protection of rights to who should get parole.

Isn't this far-fetched? Those toying with these ideas point to the general dissatisfaction spreading in democracies to assert that fundamental changes may be needed to the way we govern ourselves. They look to indicators such as low voter turnout, especially in the United States,[100] on the one hand, and the increase in referenda in recent years, on the other, to argue that citizens are ready for drastic modifications to the way democratic institutions wield power.[101] Such ideas are also being promoted in Canada.[102]

As with many other aspects of the Internet, things in the realm of electronic democracy could change rapidly.[103] However, thus far, there is little movement toward the "New Athens." Even many enthusiastic fans of the Net, who otherwise see major changes occurring, take a pass on the prospect of voters making binding decisions at the click of a mouse ("armchair voting every night [will] ... remain a dream").[104] Those who see a downside to the "control revolution" being fomented in cyberspace take particular aim at the negatives of direct democracy. Representative democracy, as it exists thus far in the twenty-first century, may be faulty. But it at least aims for a set of desirable characteristics for those who aspire to represent us: willingness to debate and deliberate; expertise; independence; a concern for civil liberties. Shapiro discusses these attributes. He then returns us to the perils of disintermediation in the media, combined with similar forces intent on altering democracy: "Push-button politics could be particularly hazardous when combined with excessive personalization of experience and ... of the news industry ... we [should not] try to steer politics from such a warped perspective."[105]

Use by Political Players
There are lots of uses of the Internet by politicians, legislatures, and other parties. Websites – some of which are interactive – e-mail, and even some chat rooms are increasingly being employed by elected officials and political parties to communicate with voters. There have been some notable successes on the Net. Jesse Ventura, former wrestler and actor and governor of Minnesota, is said to have raised a third of his campaign funds over the Net and used cyberspace effectively to recruit and mobilize supporters.[106]

Nevertheless, there is little evidence that the Internet itself has been responsible for sustained alterations in politics, either in policies or decision-making processes. There are several reasons for this. Two of the most important are the commercialization of cyberspace and the effectiveness of dominant players asserting themselves.

The growing influence of corporate America on the Net means that the use of cyberspace for political engagement is more likely to be limited to the committed few while most users of the Net choose to be entertained and to shop. A search of articles in major US newspapers from May 1994 to April 1998 averaged more than 1,000 articles *per month* that mentioned the "Internet" or "World Wide Web" or "Information Super/Highway." But a mere 398 articles in total (less than 1 percent) also contained words with the roots "politic" or "democratic" within 100 words of the three terms just listed.[107] Yahoo's home page in 1996 contained no advertisements. By 1999 it offered not only advertisements but hotlinks for a whole list of "in-house" or partnered goods and services.[108] In 2000 the advertising revenue on the Web was projected at $5 billion:[109] "the Information Highway is increasingly here to advertise and to sell products and services, not to improve the democratic quality of American politics and civic life."[110]

Even when e-mail is used for communications with legislators and their officials it is not necessarily effective. Comparatively few individuals and advertisers can generate a large volume of messages, many of which are not relevant to a legislator's agenda; indeed, at times there are so many messages that even politicians with resources may not be able to manage them. As a result, in the United States, many members of Congress and the Senate, in 2001, were actively discouraging e-mail messages; an increasing number were no longer accepting e-mail through public addresses.[111]

The commercialization of the Web assists established players in maintaining dominance in cyberspace. Minor parties and other groups can use the Web to attract more attention than they receive from the mass media. Nevertheless, the Republican and Democratic parties and their candidates have superior resources to dominate politics on the Web. In 1994 the preponderant number of political party sites belonged to minor parties. By 1996, as the Republican Party geared up for its convention, major party sites formed 59.2 percent of 477 direct links to party home pages listed on Yahoo. In 1998 the proportion for the two major parties rose to 70 percent; that same figure applied in 1999.[112]

It does not appear that the use of cyberspace by the dominant parties has had an important impact on people's attitudes.[113] In the 2004 presidential campaign, there was some evidence of success in using the Internet to stir protest movements within the Democrats and to raise money.[114] Yet, the main effect of the assertion by major players of a presence on the Internet appears to have been to help neutralize the influence of the interests of minor parties and other fringe groups.[115]

The effect of cyberspace on politics in other industrialized countries has been even less than that in America. Given the digital divide, even among developed countries, this is not surprising. That has not stopped some from engaging in wishful thinking. One article claims: "the Internet as a people's democracy has redefined not only British but also European economic, social, and political empowerment."[116] This is hyperbole. The evidence offered for that statement consists of conventional and limited uses: the major parties, witnessing the spread of the Net, used it for campaign purposes in the 1997 elections; of a population of fifty million, one million were online for part of election night and, when the *Financial Times* set up an election website with interactive capacities, twelve people responded. That article concludes: "This then is teledemocracy in the style of the Greek polis."[117] Which style? The one that kept women and slaves (the majority) from participating and voting?

More accurate is a set of observations made in a collection of papers on the influence of the Internet on Great Britain. The editors conclude that the Net is still a "significant minority medium,"[118] rather than a mass medium, and established players are in the "driving seat":[119] "instead of a move to a form of leaner, mediated direct democracy the shift appears to be toward a less politicized management of popular demand."[120] A study of Australian parliamentary democracy and the effects of the Internet concludes that cyberspace has mostly played a modest, conventional role in the politics of that country.[121] A somewhat optimistic account asserts that "the restructured opportunities for information and communication available via digital politics will potentially have positive consequences for civic society, altering the balance of relevant resources and slightly levelling the playing field."[122] Nevertheless, that analysis acknowledges that "digital politics functions mainly to engage the engaged."[123]

Lobbyists and Activists

It is no surprise that lobbyists are adept users of cyberspace. Generally, they have the resources to experiment with any new forms of communication. Getting a message across by any legal means is their stock-in-trade. What about public interest organizations? The efficiencies and costs saving of the Net should be a boon to grassroots organizing and the mobilization of opinion on an array of issues.

Prominent examples of such activity may be an indication of even further developments. Think of the international campaigns against some of the policies of the World Trade Organization[124] or of the protests against the war in Iraq.[125] One analysis, assessing the use of cyberspace to lobby against the Multilateral Agreement on Investment (MAI) concludes, more generally, that "activists have carved out an ethereal, non-territorial space, circulating in and around the traditional spaces inhabited by states."[126]

Web Networks is Canada's national nonprofit Internet service provider. Its Web pages reflect commitment to progressive social change. Citizens for Local Democracy, C4LD, was a community group that effectively used the Net to fight – unsuccessfully – the Harris government's amalgamation of the six cities of Metro Toronto.[127] An American site, E The People, permits users to set up their own online petition on a variety of subjects, including the right to scavenge in dumpsters.[128] Moreover, there is some evidence that Internet use is associated with increased participation in voluntary organizations and politics.[129] Responding to such possibilities, the Government of Canada is promoting the use of the Internet among such entities.[130]

Again, resources are an important factor in the deployment of the Net by activists. Those organizations with substantial resources are the ones that make the most effective use of cyberspace. A 1997 survey of interest groups in the United States revealed that 85 percent of groups with annual budgets over $5 million had a website. For those with budgets of from $1 million to $5 million, only 56 percent had one, and the figure dropped to 50 percent for those with budgets of less than $1 million.

Moreover, the websites themselves differed greatly. The groups with greater resources tended to have sites with more content, an attractive layout, with more extensive technical innovations (such as interactive elements and multimedia features), and specialized information databases. Thus, traditional and well-established interest groups have used the Internet for disseminating information, maintaining contact with their members and recruiting new ones, and for mobilizing opinion.[131] But, even groups with resources have met with mixed results in their use of the Net for political purposes. The efforts against the proposed release of Lotus Marketplace were successful; those against the adoption of the clipper chip were not: "the impact of political uses of the Net, even on matters concerning politics that affects the Net, has been mixed."[132] And, as indicated, members of the US Senate and of Congress are decreasingly inclined to communicate by e-mail, whether with activists or otherwise.[133]

Courts
Courts, especially in the United States, have begun to use the Internet. Their stance is that they are not interested in public opinion, at least on any specific issue they are charged with deciding. Thus, as might be expected, their use of cyberspace has been quite conservative. Courts in various countries, including Canada, are experimenting online to better process cases, for example, by permitting service and filing of documents by e-mail. But judges themselves are cautious in their employment of the Net.[134]

The US Supreme Court's opinions are available online and are accessible through e-mail subscription. The Court does not permit either audio or video broadcast of its hearings. The Canadian Supreme Court and other courts in this country have gone farther in this area: they permit television coverage of some of their hearings.

Several Canadian courts have their own website. In the United States, Cornell University's Legal Information Institute maintains an extensive site for the Supreme Court. Other law schools maintain sites for various circuit courts (of appeal). However, the general public rarely visit these sites. In 1997 the site for the Supreme Court at Cornell ranked only in the top fifty thousand sites visited. Some of the circuit courts did not even rank in the top one hundred thousand.[135] There is little interactivity on these sites; courts do not seem to wish to encourage public contact, much less lobbying, on specific questions before them.[136]

Politics, Community, and the Net

Democratic Deliberations in Cyberspace?
Whatever their reaction to the evidence that the Internet is not making a great difference on established politics, advocates of the transformative potential of cyberspace might urge that we examine aspects of the virtual world that are genuinely different from the real one. True revolutionaries want to avoid entrenched institutions, with their bedraggled ways of governing, as much as possible. It is the use of those elements of the Net that have no parallel in the real world that will be a catalyst for significant changes to democracies. Thus, those who are optimistic about transformative possibilities online pose this question about the relation of the Internet to democracy: "[Are there] new forms of power configuration between communicating individuals?"[137]

One of the hopes for these visionaries is the capacity of the Net to allow freewheeling discussion by like-minded netizens at any time and no matter where any of them are. Such exchanges can take place through e-mail and listservs. They can also take place with simultaneous communication among the members of chat rooms. For optimists, discussions online can approach an ideal of communitarian democracy in which mutuality and egalitarianism are underscored. Netizens enjoy equal powers to receive and send messages and to access vast quantities of data: "information technologies genuinely offer the chance to empower people ... who for one reason or another have become either effectively disenfranchised or merely disenchanted."[138] In short, a new form of engagement has arrived: "whether politics involves resolution of differences among competing interests, unitary processes for building consensus, or some combination of the two, the Internet provides the means for realizing democratic participation in the policy-making process."[139]

But how do individuals actually use the Internet for political engagement and public affairs? For those wanting to see cyberspace as the catalyst for a new form of democracy, the answer is not encouraging. The evidence reinforces a major theme of this chapter: a growing trend toward commercial and consumptive use. Margolis and Resnick conducted online surveys of the politics and civic life of Internet users in 1994 and again in 1999.[140] In 1994 the user population was highly educated, wealthy, and disproportionately youthful, white, and male. Users spent a median of six hours weekly using e-mail or reading bulletin boards, newsgroups, or mailing lists. Moreover, respondents reported above-average rates of political participation, for example, communication with public officials. Yet, even then, respondents used the Internet more for entertainment or for gathering information for work-related purposes than for expressing their views on any subject, including those relating to public affairs. At the same time there was very little employment of the Internet for commercial transactions.

By 1999 the users of the Internet still were better educated and more afflu-ent and politically active than the population in general, but the gap was narrowing. As with those responding in 1994, cyberspace was used mostly for purposes other than participating in political activities. In stark contrast to the earlier findings, more than two-thirds of Internet users had carried out a commercial transaction online. Most did not use newsgroups or mailing lists to obtain information. Rather, they used a search engine to go to the relevant Web pages. The news they obtained about political matters was usually about the latest developments rather than an analysis of public affairs.

But what of those who employ elements of the Internet particularly suited to foster political engagement? What does that use look like? To answer these questions, Davis did a content analysis, in 1997, of three Usenet groups de-voted to political issues.[141] His findings suggest that Usenets are not employed in ways that are ushering in a new form of wide-ranging political engagement. Instead, discussions are dominated by relatively few subscribers, of like-minded opinion and unrepresentative of other users (let alone the general public), who actively discourage open inquiry and exchanges of differing views. Davis summarizes his findings: "Those who participate in Usenet, particularly those who post, are a small and atypical minority ... there is little incentive for oth-ers, 'lurkers,' who are less vocal, to participate in the discussion ... posters ... dominate like-minded groups by controlling the agenda, setting the standards for participation, and, in some cases, even attempting to drive off others who differ with them."[142]

One earlier study did characterize the use of online forums as facilitating interaction, in the sense that half of the messages coded induced one or more replies or were, themselves, replies to previous postings.[143] More recent stud-ies, including of chat rooms and websites and their uses, are much more con-sistent with the conclusions reached by Davis.[144]

Websites as a Catalyst for Democracy: A Canadian Study

One element of politics, community, and the Net that has been examined systematically in Canada is that of websites purporting to enhance democracy in some fashion. Between October 2000 and January 2001, Hanselmann con-ducted a search of Canadian and other websites that were possibly relevant to electronic democracy.[145] Political party websites were excluded on the grounds of partisanship; other overtly partisan websites, such as those for election cam-paigns, were also not included in the study. In other words, the study was responding to the assertion that the Internet's democratic potential can be achieved only through unbiased, unfiltered information and interactivity. As a result, twenty-five Canadian, ten American, four British, and one Australian websites were analyzed.[146]

These websites were examined for three main features. The first, citizen information, assessed whether, for example, the site contained information on politics and government. The second, citizen-government interaction and citizen dialogue, focused on, for instance, whether the site supplied contact information for elected officials. The third, policy making, scrutinized whether, for example, the site provided for moderated discussion forums with elected officials as participants.[147]

Some of the non-Canadian websites that were analyzed fared well.[148] The Canadian websites did poorly on all three counts. They also failed in terms of bilingualism: only one included text in both English and French.[149] The study concluded that "Canadian electronically enhanced democracy efforts are falling short of the promises made on their behalf. Citizens must check different websites to obtain background information on Canadian politics and government, to learn about policy issues, to engage in a discussion of those issues, and to contact public officials ... Citizens [may] lose interest in participating as they will find the effort to be excessive."[150]

Wired Communities

Those who contend that cyberspace will improve democratic institutions point also to the way it can support a sense of community. A developed sense of community in the real and virtual worlds will support its members and facilitate a shared sense of needs and how they might be responded to, from health care and education to babysitting and tips on woodworking. Such sharing may lead to organizing and activism that strives to make democratic institutions, at all levels of government, responsive to various issues affecting a community. This desire for connection with those who are similarly situated has led to a multitude of virtual communities, some of which run separate networks, such as, in the United States, Cleveland Free-Net and Seattle Community Network.[151] Some municipalities in America run networks designed to encourage citizens to use the Net for community and self-help purposes. One municipally related network that appears to have been successful is Phoenix at Your Fingertips. The workstations that have been the most successful are those in community, career, and senior centres, since users come to these places with specific tasks to be accomplished and use cyberspace to assist them.[152]

The use of the Internet to support communities is one area where Canada has been active. These activities have also been examined to some extent. The federal government and some of the provinces have policies that support communities' access to the Internet. One of the federal government's six cyberspace priorities has been support of the development of Smart Communities, communities where municipal governments are connected to local residents and businesses through information technology.[153] ("Smart Communities ... empower their residents, institutions, and region as a whole."[154]) There is particular concern in official policy that remote areas and the First Peoples be part of the Smart Communities program and related initiatives, and there have been some experiments to achieve these goals, with mixed results.[155] One involves Rankin Inlet, in Nunavut, one thousand kilometres from the nearest sizable community.[156] Launched in 1996, Igalaaq, which means "window" in Inuktitut, continues to be successful. This community net links Rankin Inlet to the world even as one of its goals is to "preserve Inuit culture."[157] Moreover, there has been at least one experiment with a connected community supported by private initiatives. A study of Netville suggested positive results:[158] "when the Internet is not treated as its own unique social system, we find that computer-mediated communication supports the growth of social networks, social capital and community well-being."[159]

Critics suggest that government policy is directed more at getting individuals wired than at supporting use of the Internet to foster a sense of community and the activism that might ensue. Besides Smart Communities, Industry Canada has a program called Community Access Program (CAP). Whether unfairly or not, it has been characterized as "a seed program, designed to kickstart public demand for commercial services in areas not yet served by ISPs [Internet service providers]."[160] More generally, community nets have not become the catalyst for political organizing that visionaries had hoped for. At least to date, they have not been able to generate content that focuses the attention of Canadian society on issues of community, cyberspace, and democratic institutions.[161] Meanwhile, the World Wide Web permits almost all community nets to go onto the Internet. Often this transition changes the very nature of the service: "the people running [the community net] are encouraged to stop looking inward at their local community and to begin looking outward, a change in focus that often has these [sites] morphing into promotional chambers of commerce."[162]

Conclusion

This chapter concludes as it began: by acknowledging that any predictions about the Internet are subject to change without notice. To assert that the Internet is prone to rapid alterations is to be guilty of making an understatement. What is more, the volatile Internet is interacting with shifting forces in a Canadian society that is experiencing massive transformation. That said, here is a stab at some conclusions.

The Internet's greatest contribution to democracy will not be in societies that already know the luxury of political freedom. Rather, it may be of greatest assistance to those who must struggle to have democracy take hold in their country. The Internet and its spreading of knowledge is a forceful engine for wealth production, and wealth can facilitate the rise of democracy. The spreading of knowledge is also a powerful tool against tyrants. The Net may be a formidable weapon deployed against oppression in societies where ordinary means of public dissent are stifled.[163]

What about the Internet and Canadian democracy? We need to know much more about the effects of the Internet on this society. There is a lot of ballyhoo about cyberspace but little systematic study of the outcomes it is producing. Nevertheless, the information that is available on Canada and other countries, especially the United States, suggests that the Internet is not a catalyst for fundamental democratic change. While theories of the Net leading to disintermediation and direct democracy, with frightening implications, have not been proven true, neither have lesser claims about the benign nature of the effects of cyperspace been confirmed. On the whole, potential for more widespread involvement, lobbying, and interaction with politicians and government officials has not been realized.

Yet, myths about the Internet continue. Representative politics in this and other industrialized nations is in big trouble. The last decades have witnessed continuous and rapid decline in citizens' confidence in politicians and political and administrative institutions. Failing faith gives rise to beliefs that the difficult work of making representative politics respond to the common good can be avoided: the myth of exit. Fables about the transformative capacity of the Net for democracy entice citizens away from the hard labour of making representative politics strive for its ideals.

The Internet is not the only supposed means of exit from representative politics and its foibles. Some do leave for cyberspace. Others take to the courts through rights claiming and a belief (never mind the reality) that judges can do what legislators cannot or will not accomplish. Still others quick march to the market, as not only the necessary engine of wealth creation but as the great sorter and distributor of goods and services, including those that were long thought to be held in common – education and health care among them.

Thus is the way paved for the further disarray of representative politics. Recently, *The Economist* painted a picture of what the world may be like not so far from now for those fortunate few who are profiting from the new order.[164] These patrician gypsies with their "fuck-you money" will roam around the world seeking the best tax havens, climate, and cultural variations suited to their well-heeled needs.[165] Compliant governments will be at the ready, seeking to respond to the whims of these rich vagabonds. An exaggeration? Perhaps – consider the source. Yet, the prospects for representative politics, the means by which ordinary people have secured public goods for themselves and their children – health care, education, a safety net, and so forth – seem bleak. Nor is the future brightened by fables of empowerment by rights, of the liberating forces of the market, and of the transformative capacities of cyberspace.

7 The Youngest Citizens and Education as a Public Good?

Education is of prime importance to society. Schools prepare children to take their place as citizens and to live their own lives productively and fully. The public classroom has been the common meeting place over the generations for the rich diversity of this society. But, now, education is on trial in Canada. Scarcely a month goes by without some media report on the inadequacies of our schools. Testing, discipline problems, special education, funding for religious schools, and minority language issues, to name but a few topics, are all occasions for exposing the failures of the system.

Schools are independent in many ways. At the same time, public schools are funded by government, and their administration and curricula are subject to a degree of governmental control. As the tales of woe about education are repeated, they come to be seen as part of the malaise besetting government and representative politics at the turn of the twenty-first century. A prime response to the foibles of representative politics regarding education is to turn away from these weaknesses, to search for other means of redress. And, as with so many other areas, that search has come to focus on the power of markets and the lure of rights.

Markets have been turned to to control the costs of public education. An important aspect of this strategy, particularly in Ontario, has been to raise tuition fees at universities so that consumer-students bear a greater proportion of the cost of their education. This fee increase raises critical issues about access. At the primary and secondary levels, the market is being invoked to create competition, among public, private, and charter schools. Such competition, it is claimed, will improve standards for all participants. The evidence, at best, is mixed; meanwhile, confidence in public schools is undermined.

Rights have also come to play a key role in the transformation of education. In other areas that have been discussed, litigation and courts have been a prime source for the rights that have been created. A similar story has unfolded over some educational issues, particularly minority-language rights. On other issues, such as funding for religious schools and the placement of students with special needs, the courts have been, on the whole, quite deferential toward the difficult choices that elected officials and their agents have made.

Nevertheless, in the area of education, rights claiming beyond the courtroom continues apace. In the case of funding of religious schools, rights talk and market forces entered into a very effective alliance in Ontario under the banner of choice. Such lobbying efforts led to the underwriting of fees for all private schools, not just religious ones. Education in Ontario as a public good was weakened. The market was assigned tasks for which it is ill-suited. The moral force of rights was diluted. With the election of the Liberal government in 2003, these forces were turned back. For how long?

The Importance of Education

Education serves many purposes, including the fostering of democracy and rights, achieving individual aspirations, and buttressing the economic competitiveness of societies through a well-trained labour force. In some nations, it also underwrites certain communitarian values; in Canada, minority languages and religions, particularly Roman Catholicism, have been so privileged. In short, schools play a central role in advanced societies: "they are means by which people ... strive for civic virtue, economic wealth, social integration, and cultural survival ... public schools also express conceptions of human needs, make statements of moral principles, and convey visions of individual and collective development."[1]

Education and Its Purposes

The civic purposes of education have long been recognized. These, of course, are ideals: there have always been obstacles to the attainment of the goals. Problems of uneven quality, including differences between rural and urban schools and between affluent and poor neighbourhoods, have been a mainstay. Whatever the reality, there is much faith in the capacity of education to instil fidelity to open societies, to resist the horrors of terrorism.[2] Education can serve darker societal purposes as well; dictators and thugs are well schooled in the power of propaganda. Nevertheless, Western democratic nations have long had faith that knowledge and debate will lead people, especially the young, to embrace freedom and open societies: "the existence of a high-quality national education system ... is the key to a democracy where legitimacy lies with the citizen."[3] What is more, education, enshrined as a democratic right, enables citizens to exercise many of the fundamental entitlements that open societies confer: "If citizens have no education ... it becomes far more difficult to exercise the right to free speech and political assembly ... Public education has been widely recognized as a positive substantive right because it implicates other rights."[4]

The importance of education in allowing each individual to achieve his or her aspirations has also long been recognized. By the early twentieth century, the great educational philosopher John Dewey was espousing an educational system that developed the full potential of every learner: "A common error is the assumption that there is one set body of subject matter and skills to be presented to the young [person] ... whose failure to meet the material supplied is attributed to his own incapacity or willfulness, not to failure of the educator to understand what needs are stirring him."[5] In the latter decades of the last century, such emphasis on the importance of individual development as a prime function of education came to be associated in this country with what Manzer has called "ethical liberalism": "Education should be person-regarding ... programs and methods should be designed to fit the progression of human physical, intellectual, and emotional development, which can vary greatly among individual learners."[6]

More recently, the role of schools as agents of global competitiveness has come to the forefront. A vital factor in the location of production and services is the skill of employees. Thus, a "better-educated workforce is the best investment post-industrial societies [can] make to enhance their capacity to compete in a knowledge-intensive global economy."[7] Schools play a critical role in preparing individuals to take their part in the highly skilled, flexible workforce necessary for Canada to have an advanced technological economy. In this conception, students should be provided a uniform education, the results of which should be capable of being judged objectively: "Desired outcomes can be defined and their achievement measured by standardized testing. Legitimacy is ascribed accordingly to the enforcement of a common curriculum."[8]

Minority Languages and Religion

The purposes of education have largely focused on the individual and his or her place in society. In some countries, education has been seen to serve communitarian goals as well. Some of these ends have been dark; in the last century, Communist regimes directed schools to exult the collective and undermine the individual. Yet, many societies have underwritten more benign communitarian goals in education. In Canada, religion, most prominently Catholicism, and minority-language rights – English in Quebec and French outside Quebec – have been viewed in some parts of society as communitarian aspects integral to a child's education: "communitarians who were minority-language protectionists, especially francophones who were also Roman Catholics, rejected the ... assumption that a political community must have one standard language of public communication, the official language should be the language of the majority, and, hence, the language of the majority had to be the language of instruction in public schools."[9] Such insistence on the primacy of certain communitarian elements in a child's education was met with resistance. These claims clashed with a model of education that saw schools as a common meeting place where development of the individual was paramount and where the diverse elements of this society were respected but where none were privileged.

Historically, in Canada, tensions between these two basic visions of the role of education led to a range of results in the provinces. In British Columbia and in Manitoba, few concessions were made for support of religion or minority-language rights in education. In British Columbia, there was little public debate over such issues; in Manitoba, they caused a firestorm. In the Maritime provinces, concessions were made by permitting, in some city districts, separate schools for Roman Catholic children, and by granting linguistic and religious autonomy to school boards in Acadian communities. In Ontario, Saskatchewan, and Alberta, certain legal recognitions and funding were accorded to separate schools for Roman Catholic or Protestant minorities, depending on the province, and limited to elementary schools in Ontario and Saskatchewan. In Quebec, there were substantial divisions between the English Protestant and the French Roman Catholic communities. In Newfoundland, prior to Confederation, denominational schools were supported by the state but controlled by the churches.[10]

Clashes among the Purposes – and the Threat of Choice

These several purposes of education have not always been harmoniously expressed. Contrary to the hopes of those who believed in one public school system, the insistence that education recognize certain collective goals did not abate as the twentieth century progressed. Advocates of minority-language rights and of funding for religious schools continued to press for greater recognition on a number of fronts in the various provinces. Some of this advocacy was quite successful. In Ontario in the early 1980s, the Roman Catholic Church secured expanded funding for its high schools.[11]

Aside from debates on the extent of recognition of collective purposes, there were tensions among the more individual purposes. As the pressure to compete in a knowledge-based, competitive economy took hold during the 1980s, charges were laid against what was seen to be the loose standards of ethical liberalism and its emphasis on students learning in their own way. Those advocating that the primary goal of education was to equip students for global competitiveness demanded that the schools produce a well-trained workforce by means of a uniform, exacting, testable curriculum. At the same time, they decried the permissiveness of ethical liberalism: "education must strive for 'excellence' in the context of a global economy in which standards are determined, not by personal needs for self-fulfillment ... but by the educational ... outcomes of Canada's major national competitors."[12]

Thus, conflicts among the goals of education have been a mainstay. By the 1990s, a combination of factors intensified these debates and equipped combatants with new strategies. The rise of rights, the disenchantment with public schools as one manifestation of representative politics gone awry, and the lure of market forces at the end of the last century combined to provide new armaments. Any number of viewpoints marshalled their demands by repeatedly invoking the magic word: choice. Some efforts were successful. We will come to the diverse demands seeking to advance their agendas under the banner of choice in a moment. First, we need to explore the problems that beset public education in recent decades and the miserable tale of failing faith in public schools.

Public Education and Its Discontents

Things look bad for public education. The system is seen to be suffering from a multitude of failings: "an unrelenting assault on the content, processes, and outcomes of schooling in Canada has elevated school reform to a major movement for all levels and for all populations."[13]

At the outset of this discussion of these discontents, it is important to emphasize that there remains significant popular support for the public school system. Parents may insist on heightened accountability, tougher standards, and greater discipline, but there is still support for meeting these demands within the public educational system. Moreover, the public still sees that system as playing a critical role as a building block, as an instrument of social cohesion. Canadians still value diversity, accessibility, and accommodation for special needs in their schools. There are enormous difficulties in giving these values expression in specific programs. Nonetheless, support for social cohesion in schools remains high. For example, there is much concern over educational opportunities for the economically disadvantaged: "there is strong support for early childhood development programs, which are intended to level the playing field so all kids are ready to learn when they arrive in Grade 1 ... seven out of ten Canadians think children from low-income families don't have the same chance for a post-secondary education as those from upper-income backgrounds."[14]

What is more, amid the many statistics that raise concerns about public education, there is evidence that, comparatively, the Canadian system is doing well, at least by some measures. This country has the highest rate of postsecondary participation within the OECD; Canada has the highest proportion of eighteen- to twenty-year-olds enrolled in colleges and universities and the biggest percentage of twenty-five- to sixty-four-year-olds with college diplomas or university degrees.[15] Further, in some recent comparative tests, Canadian students have performed quite successfully. In one instance, reported in late 2001, students in OECD countries were examined for reading and for science and math skills. Out of thirty-two nations, our students placed second in reading and fifth in science and math skills.[16]

It has also been recently demonstrated that Canadian schools do a good job educating most students to a reasonable level. In a study of several nations that compared the gap between students who fared poorly and those who did very well, Canada ranked fourth (Britain was seventh; the United States was eighteenth).[17] Commenting on these results, Churchill, a comparative education expert at the University of Toronto, said, "We have been deluged in Ontario ... by alarmist stories pushed by politicians ... suggesting that we are in a terrible situation. In fact, we've never been in a terrible situation."[18]

Still, anxieties about our public schools are evident: "Public schools have been savaged by stinging criticism in the past two decades. A new emphasis on what students know and what skills they have so that they can ... 'better meet the challenges of the post-industrial economy,' infuses public talk about education."[19] In 1986 the Angus Reid Group began asking Canadians to name priority issues. Education was not cited by even 10 percent of those polled until 1996. By 2000 it was being named by 29 percent, second only to health care as a national priority.[20] Meanwhile, faith in the system has weakened. In 1989, 62 percent of respondents in a poll indicated that they had a great deal or quite a lot of confidence in the school system. By 1993 confidence had fallen to 44 percent; in English Canada it had fallen to 25 percent.[21] In the 1990s two-thirds of Canadians polled expressed fears that private schools were providing students with a much better education than was the public system. Only 38 percent agreed that high schools adequately prepared kids for the modern workforce; two out of three believed that high school graduates lacked essential reading and writing skills.[22]

The results of actual performance are mixed. Above I cited some positive indicators, such as percentages of the population attending postsecondary institutions and performances on tests taken by students in OECD countries.[23] But there are decidedly negative signs as well.[24] A high proportion of students (and adults) cannot name Canada's first prime minister or identify major events from our past.[25] Results from an intensive round of math and science testing in the mid-1990s are not encouraging. More than half a million students from grades four to twelve in forty-one countries participated in three rounds of testing in these two subjects. Canadian students ranked only tenth – ahead of those in the United States but behind those of several countries of Western Europe and Asia.[26] In 2000 and again in 2002, more than 25 percent of grade ten students in Ontario failed a standardized literacy test.[27] More than one-third of Canadian youth do not have the skills required for many entry-level jobs. In some international tests for literacy, Canadian students have ranked only in the middle ranges, trailing many European and Asian countries.[28]

There may be a variety of viewpoints of what constitutes a first-class education. Nevertheless, it is now almost a truism that public schools are not providing the quality of education that they need to to equip our youngest citizens with the skills necessary to meet the challenges of this society and of a global marketplace. An obvious part of the problem is resources. In late 2002, funding in Ontario remained at 1998 levels despite inflation and growth in the number of students.[29] Injecting more money into the system is not sufficient in and of itself. Resources must be spent wisely with due regard to what makes the best public schools such successes.[30] In any event, such inadequacies in the system serve no agenda: "not [that] of economic liberals who want to fit knowledge and skills to the global economy, not of political liberals who believe passionately that the existence of a high-quality education is the most important building block of a civic democracy, and not of radical individualists who look at the whole child and want an education that is tailored to individual needs."[31]

Part of the problem is not just the mixed evidence concerning the quality of education in the public schools but also a set of rising expectations of what these institutions should be capable of delivering. In a 1988 poll, 60 percent of the respondents described the education received by young people as either excellent or good; a similar proportion judged the quality of education as higher than that obtained by the parents of these youths. In 1999 a worrisome 82 percent of parents expressed concern over the quality of education their children were receiving. In short, "consumers of education felt that the status quo no longer sufficed; they expected far more from the education system than ever before and were unconvinced it could deliver."[32]

For some these enhanced ambitions for schools focus on the institutional arrangements. It is claimed that such arrangements are outmoded and are ill-suited to serve the needs of postindustrial societies. In this depiction, the current public school system is a product of the industrial age. It is a "one best system" that is a factory model: "the organization – if not the content – of public education was standardized, homogenized, and delivered as a mass-market public [model]."[33] Such a model is incompatible with globalizing economies, which emphasize innovation and which assume flexible arrangements rather than rigid, top-down hierarchies. This model fits poorly with the expressive individualism and skepticism of government that is now so prevalent.

Ironically, much of the force of reform has been focused on a device that is oriented to command and control, to "one best system" techniques: testing. Whatever the irony, the move to testing as a prime means of quality assurance has swept through education in this country and many others over the last decade. Many educators accept the need for reliable assessments of scientific and mathematical skills and of literacy, especially as we shift to a knowledge-based economy. Yet, some argue that multiple-choice exams, the often-used method for standardized testing, measure the wrong kind of knowledge. Such tests can be easily scored and emphasize memorization, technical skills, recognition, and the capacity to find the right answers quickly. Nonetheless, they do not assess a student's capacity to reflect and to engage in actual problem solving: "they just measure a kind of lowest common denominator of facts and skills ... getting students to do well on them doesn't mean much in the real world."[34]

However trenchant the criticisms, testing enjoys much public support. In a poll done in 2000, 86 percent supported standardized testing for students;

the vast majority of those asked indicated that they felt strongly about the issue. Two journalists who assessed public opinion in the early 2000s on an array of current issues claimed that support for testing was "striking": "the time is well past when parents accepted as an article of faith that their children were on the receiving end of a good education and that teachers and schools were equipping them for the challenges of the future."[35]

By the 1990s the discontent with public education was intense and persistent. Something had to be done. The blandishments of the market and the lure of rights were at hand. But would the cures be worse than the disease?

Choice: Markets and Rights as Solutions

The combination of the market and rights poses challenges for public education on a number of fronts. In terms of markets, one response to the pervasive sense of failure of the public education system is a simple exit strategy: private schools promise the excellence not being delivered by public ones. For those who can afford the fees, a clear alternative is on offer. Another is turning university education over to market forces by deregulating tuition. The unleashing of fees is particularly controversial in medical and law schools. The market also is asserting its influence in ways underwritten by the public purse – through the cries for vouchers and for charter schools.

Rights advocacy has also made claims about both public and private schools. In one instance, rights claiming has focused on establishing constitutional entitlements for students with special needs within the public school system. In another, rights claiming focused on a constitutional right to funding of private religious schools. In yet another, litigation was directed at ensuring minority-language education (in French) outside Quebec. In Ontario, rights claiming and market advocates engineered a spectacular result under the banner of choice: the underwriting of tuition for all private schools whether religious or otherwise.

Markets: Exit, Pay as You Go, and Public Laissez-Faire

The influence of market forces on education during the recent decades was manifested in several ways. More families simply exited the public system: more students attended private primary and secondary schools; their families, through individual choice, were embracing a market model of education. Tuition fees for many university programs in a number of provinces were deregulated. Essentially, each university was allowed to set tuition for at least some programs. Market celebrants exalted choice and competition. Social justice advocates decried lack of access and the further crumbling of the civic pact. There was dabbling with vouchers and charter schools: the complexities of public markets came calling on primary and secondary education in Canada. The results of such experiments are mixed and in some ways unexpected, surprising both skeptics and advocates.

Exit

Private schools have many attractions. They can respond to calls for specializations, whether religious, cultural, pedagogical, or for an enhanced curriculum, and some assist students who are wobbly in meeting academic standards, even helping them to gain entrance to some universities. Usually, classes are smaller – so often an advantage whatever the curriculum. They can engage in "cream skimming": unlike the public school system, they need not take all who wish to attend. They can select students whom they judge will most successfully respond to their program. These schools have become increasingly aggressive at marketing themselves. One example: in the fall of 2002 the *Globe and Mail* published an entire supplement devoted to the whys and wherefores of these enterprises.[36]

But they cost. Public primary and secondary education is usually free to parents and students; taxes pay for this education. Private schools bring with them a hefty price tag – anywhere from a relatively small fee for some religious schools that receive other funding to something like $20,000 a year (not including room and board) at academically exclusive schools.

As of the early 2000s, the numbers in private schools were small as a percentage of the overall population of students. But they were increasing. In 1987-88, 4.6 percent of students attended private schools. By 1998-99, 5.6 percent did so. These small but growing figures for private schools do not include students attending separate (usually Roman Catholic) schools, which many Canadians would consider have an important private aspect to them – their religious focus.[37] In Ontario enrolment in private schools is proportionately small: in 1999, 2.1 million kids attended public schools; there were only 103,000 in private schools. Yet, numbers have increased markedly. Between 1995 and 1999, the numbers in private schools grew by 40,000 to 103,000; over a 60 percent increase.[38]

It is not only the affluent who send their children to private schools. Twenty-nine percent of those attending such institutions in Canada come from families with annual incomes of less than $50,000. What is more, those with higher incomes and education tend to register greater support for public funding of education.[39] It remains the case that 26 percent of students attending private school come from families with annual incomes greater than $100,000. In Ontario that figure is even higher: 37 percent come from families with incomes of $100,000 or more.

Where private education is going in Canada remains to be seen. But its potential to grow and mount a real challenge to the public model is surely on the horizon. That potential in Ontario was increased by the education tax credit, a development I discuss later in this chapter.

Pay as You Go

The story of rising tuition in universities, particularly in professional programs, is a tale of the unravelling of a pact that held for many decades. Government funding for universities was comparatively high, and tuition was kept low. In turn, students who had the benefit of the lower tuition would repay society, at least in part, through taxes. In a progressive system of taxation, those who earned more would pay more.

So much has changed. It is difficult to pick a starting point for the breakdown. Certainly, government funding of universities declined for several years in the last part of the twentieth century. In 1980-81 the total share of university revenue from government grants and contracts was about 74 percent. By 1999-2000 the comparable figure had decreased to about 55 percent.[40]

The decline in government spending had the potential to lead to two results. Either universities could face the lessening of quality that would be the result of lack of resources over time or they could replace the lost dollars by some combination of two other means: fundraising and tuition increases. Many universities, basing their approach on whatever evidence, decided that the first option was not on.[41] Thus, experiments with the second proceeded apace in the 1990s and into the 2000s.

In 2000, Ontario passed legislation permitting private, for-profit universities.[42] So far, no private universities have been founded that truly challenge the public ones. But the concept of universities as public institutions has been disturbed. The government of the day declared a victory for "innovative and flexible choices."[43] Critics worried that the legislation diverted "attention away from the need for investing in our public institutions."[44]

About the same time, public universities were turning to fundraising and increasing tuition to bolster their revenues. In addition to being a source of income, these initiatives did something else: they unleashed the forces of competition and the market among the universities. Now any university's claim to excellence could be tested in terms of its capacity to secure resources from fundraising (back a winner) and from higher tuition set at what the market would bear (you get what you pay for: Mercedes programs, Mercedes fees; Wal-Mart programs, Wal-Mart fees). Of course, life is more complicated. Even the most aggressive universities blunted unbridled market forces by, for example, enriching bursaries so at least some students of modest means could still have access to the programs. Nevertheless, the change was unmistakable: the market had come to the academy.

There were aggressive fundraising efforts, some of which were quite successful. But even for the most ambitious universities, fundraising was the more restricted route. This was partly because none of the Canadian universities has endowments anything like their great counterparts in the United States. Even very successful fundraising campaigns contributed only single-digit percentages to the overall budgets of Canadian universities.[45] This could change over the long haul for some universities if endowments grow appreciably.

In the shorter term, increases in tuition were primarily looked to to make up the shortfall in declining public grants. Approaches to tuition increases varied among the provinces. Some, such as Ontario, allowed tuition fees, especially in professional programs, to rise markedly and to vary considerably among the universities. These increases in Ontario were frozen by the Liberal government in 2003.[46] Others, such as Quebec, maintained relatively low fees in almost all programs, limiting increases, at least for residents of the province, more to amounts that kept pace with inflation.[47]

For the provinces experiencing substantial tuition increases, few programs were spared. Hikes for undergraduate programs were kept comparatively modest in the name of access and because of the lesser oomph that an undergraduate degree brings to earning power. Nonetheless, nationally, even the fees for these programs doubled between 1991 and 2001 – an increase about six times that of inflation. Into the 2000s those increases seemed to be easing.[48]

The professional programs were the ones that experienced especially sharp increases in their price tags. They were the ones – particularly law and medicine – where the debates about the effects of such raises in fees were the loudest. The case for increases for tuition fees for professional schools, beyond increases in other programs, rests on two arguments. First, graduates of these schools will earn comparatively large amounts of money. Thus, higher tuition fees should be looked at as an investment to secure the opportunity to earn more. Second, it is inequitable for the public, most of whom have modest earnings, to underwrite extensively the cost of programs whose graduates will have high incomes and who can, therefore, afford a price tag that more closely approximates the cost of such programs.

Those who oppose such increases, or at least the extent of them, raise three issues.[49] First is a concern about access. As tuition fees rise, the programs will become less accessible to those from families of modest means, even given enhanced bursary programs. Second, there are worries about responding to the needs of low-income patients and clients. Students of more modest means who meet the criteria for admission should be in the programs because they have an understanding of the effects of low incomes on the client population. For instance, in primary health care, social and personal issues often have as big an impact on health problems as physical complaints. The expectation is that students of more modest means will be more likely to practise among those of more modest means. Third, there are concerns about the large debt load students will need to assume to pay for the hefty tuition. The fear is that students will choose more lucrative specializations regardless of interest or need, in order to more easily pay off the debts. In addition, there are fears that more professionals will become even less inclined to support government programs. The prevailing attitude among them will be that, if less taxes went to support their professional programs and they had to pay more tuition, then they have a lessened obligation to support a system of progressive tax in which they pay more to support public programs.

It is too soon to say what the actual effects will be. There were early indications that tuition increases in medical schools in Ontario were associated with problems of access. Between 1997 and 2000, the percentage of Ontario medical students who reported annual family incomes of less than $40,000 fell from 23 percent to 15 percent.[50]

Such concerns may not have materialized in law schools. The Faculty of Law at the University of Toronto is leading the charge on raising tuition.[51] In the early 2000s annual tuition was $14,000 and scheduled to go to $22,000. In 1999-2000 the annual tuition was $8,000. That year, in response to a survey, 17.8 percent of students reported that they came from families with an income of $60,000; 13.9 percent came from families earning between $60,000 and $90,000; about 30 percent came from families earning more than $90,000; and 37.8 percent did not fill out the survey. These proportions remained the same over the next three years even though annual tuition rose to $14,000. Part of the explanation may be attributable to increased financial aid: in 2001, 13 percent of first-year students received complete relief from paying tuition (as opposed to 3 percent in 1999); 64 percent received some relief (as opposed to 53 percent in 1999).[52]

What the scenario will look like over time, especially if fees reach the $22,000 mark, remains to be seen. Since other laws schools, as of 2003, had no plans to raise tuition to anything close to the University of Toronto rates, there could be any number of developments. All sorts of talented students could flock to the University of Toronto, convinced it is worth the price tag. Or, if financial aid falls behind, more students of lower income may need to beg off. In any event, a certain percentage may conclude that, whatever the worth of that faculty, a very good legal education can be obtained at other law schools at a considerably lower price. Legal education as a market commodity has come to Canada.

Public Laissez-Faire: Vouchers and Charter Schools

There is extensive support for choice in education. As indicated above, support for public schools remains high, but for a system in which a range of needs is responded to: "[the] strong preference is to inject greater differentiation and greater choice into the public system itself: performing arts schools, computer programs, middle immersion, special needs, and so on."[53] Moreover, whatever the forces that urge a standardized, testable curriculum to maximize competitiveness of the workforce in the global economy, there remain strong philosophical currents, led by ethical liberalism, that "affirm the legitimacy of educational pluralism and seek to institutionalize in Canadian public life the diversity of beliefs and cultures that nurture individual development in a multidenominational, multilingual, and multicultural society."[54]

Still, questions remain about the boundaries of choice in a resilient public school system. Some choose to exit the public system altogether. Others, increasingly, are pressing to expand the boundaries of choice within the public system itself. Two such challenges to these boundaries are vouchers and charter schools. Although they differ in important ways, both represent market forces and their claims to be able to reinvigorate education through competition and choice. In their full-blown expression, vouchers and charter schools would go beyond being part of the desirable flexibility in the public school system; they would challenge its very foundations.

Vouchers and charter schools are both attempts to create public markets in education. The idea behind a public market is to have the state move away from direct provision of certain goods and services. Instead, it funds others who then provide those goods and services. The goal is to separate suppliers from buyers: competition and, thus, efficiency, and, thus, quality will result. However, vouchers and charter schools attempt to achieve these goals in different ways.

Vouchers in education involve public funding to permit citizens to choose among different schools (suppliers of education) where there need be no commitment to universal access. Goods (education) will be better and more efficiently supplied because inefficient providers (schools) will be forced out of the market. In contrast, charter schools work within a framework of universal access. They are meant to respond to market forces, in terms of the exercise of choice on the part of students and parents. Public funding is provided to charter schools on condition that they work within a framework of rules that stipulate certain goals, including access and equity. Because of these differences, it is useful to examine vouchers and charter schools separately and then comment on their implications for public education.

Proponents of vouchers advance various arguments. Those who emphasize the utility of the market and the dangers of blunting its effectiveness emphasize the monopolistic abuses that occur when the state is nearly the sole supplier of primary and secondary education. Others, more focused on politics, argue that quality in education is being destroyed by various groups – bureaucrats, unions, teachers – that are determined to advance their own self-interest regardless of the consequences. Still others decry the inequality of public education. Those living in disadvantaged neighbourhoods must go to low-quality schools. Thus, public education in such areas is helping perpetuate disadvantage, not alleviating it. In sum, "a monopoly that is captured by special interests, and is responsive – if it is responsive at all – to those best able to voice their interests, is unlikely to provide quality and equal access to public education."[55]

What is needed, therefore, is the creation of a market for public education. Parents should be given vouchers to spend at a private school of their choice. Parents and students will become consumers, educators will be suppliers, and governments will be the regulators of the market but not the direct provider of the goods. Competition will result. The excellent schools will flourish; the poor ones will be forced out.

To date, vouchers have been used mostly in the United States. These programs were given a boost in 2002 when the US Supreme Court ruled that there was no constitutional objection to them based on the fact that vouchers were often used at religious schools.[56] Advocates, including President Bush Jr., compared the decision to *Brown v. Board of Education* in terms of its significance: "The Supreme Court in 1954 declared that our nation cannot have two education systems ... [in 2002] the court declared that our nation will not accept one education system for those who can afford to send their children to a school of their choice and for those who can't. And that's just as historic."[57] Critics shot back that the real issue facing public schools is lack of funding, a problem that vouchers exacerbate: "What is holding the public schools back ... is not lack of competitive drive but the resources to succeed. Voucher programs ... siphon off public dollars, leaving struggling urban systems with less money for skilled teachers, textbooks and computers. They also skim off some of the best performing students and the most informed and involved parents."[58]

The exchange just quoted illustrates a strong ideological clash. But what effects have these programs actually had? Where vouchers have been implemented, what has been the result? In short, it appears that they can result in more equity but no more efficiency. To understand why, we can examine a well-known voucher experiment, the Milwaukee program.[59] The goal of that program was to provide better educational opportunities for the children of poor families, many of whom were African-Americans. It was targeted: only families with incomes to 175 percent of the poverty line or lower were eligible; current students in private schools were ineligible; and students to be given vouchers had to be randomly selected so that schools could not "cream-skim," selecting only the best students.[60]

Generally, costs were not reduced. What is more, it is questionable whether vouchers improved the quality of the education: some students did do significantly better but many others did no better at all. Thus, in terms of both measures of efficiency – cost and effectiveness – it is unproven whether students do markedly better than those who remain in the public schools.

The vouchers did result in more equitable access. They permitted students from low-income families to leave the public schools and enter the school of their choice. The program used (restricted) market forces to create greater equity of access. These effects were dependent on the program being targeted. When vouchers are given to everyone, their effect is to decrease equity since those already in private schools make the greatest use of them.

Restricting vouchers to low-income families can raise very real problems. Students who remain behind lose some of their most articulate speakers for urging whatever improvement is possible. Yet, should students who are prepared to leave in an attempt to improve their education not be permitted to do so? What are the implications of using a lottery to prevent "cream skimming" for those who would leave but who do not "win" the lottery? Moreover, targeted vouchers are a form of means testing; students holding them could become stigmatized.[61]

Finally, what of the parents who are dissatisfied with public schools but whose income is insufficient to send their children to private schools and yet too high to qualify them for vouchers? Such families can become resentful and be amenable to arguments that voucher programs should be universal and, therefore, accessible to them. Such advocacy, mixed with rights claiming and the invoking of choice, in Ontario led to an untargeted voucher program and, predictably, fears that there would be a lack of equity. I discuss that program later in this chapter.

Trebilcock and colleagues conducted an extensive review of the use of vouchers in a number of areas.[62] They came to a decidedly mixed verdict. These authors are scarcely hostile to the notion of injecting market forces into issues of public policy. Yet, they conclude: "The claim that invoking the discipline of market driven exit vouchers offers an escape from the messy and unprincipled compromises of politics and frailties of voice as a disciplining mechanism is largely an illusion."

What of charter schools? These institutions are independent schools that still are part of the public school system. The hallmark of these schools is that they are accountable for results but are given much flexibility in meeting set standards. They are "tight as to ends but loose as to means."[63] The first charter school was instituted in 1991 in Minnesota. As of 2001 there were over 1,700 such schools in the United States. Alberta has had legislation permitting charter schools since 1994. That law allowed for fifteen such schools; as of 2001, twelve existed.[64]

These schools are another response, along with vouchers, to the dissatisfaction with the public school system. They usually are promoted by those who wish to provide a different kind of education than is publicly available. In Alberta, for instance, two charter schools focus on gifted children, another targets children whose first language is not English, one is designed to assist "at risk" teens, and so on.

What have been the outcomes of charter schools? They have had very good "consumer" approval track records: surveys record consistently high levels of satisfaction on the part of parents, and 70 percent of these schools report that they have waiting lists.[65] Nevertheless, the available evidence indicates that these schools, on the whole, are not any more effective than public institutions.

Some charter schools in Los Angeles seem to have been able to considerably improve performance of students. Others, in different states, are yielding very mixed results.[66] In Alberta results on standardized provincial tests indicate that students at these schools are achieving at least at the level of children in public schools in that province. Nonetheless, there is no generally applicable evidence that would indicate that students at these schools are performing consistently better than those in public schools: "charter schools ... are scoring high on process and low on results."[67]

What about equity? Here the results are complicated. Because charter schools have discretion to reject students not suitable for their targeted programs, some engage in "cream skimming," whether for ability, being able bodied, or some other reason. At the same time, one of the strongest benefits of these schools is that they build a sense of community that may promote a sense of belonging, particularly among disadvantaged peoples.[68] The argument is that the work involved in organizing, launching, and running a charter school increases civic engagement in the furtherance of a public good: "market imperatives reinforce community building."[69]

These same market imperatives may encourage niche schools appealing to more homogeneous groups with similar values. An evaluation of charter schools in Arizona, where 25 percent of all these institutions are located, found a widespread pattern of racial segregation.[70] The worry is that charter schools will result in more differentiation in the name of community rather than in tolerance and inclusiveness. Charter schools may, therefore, embody a sense of community that flies in the face of a civic ideal of education where children and parents from diverse backgrounds come together with educators to create schooling as a public good.

The greatest danger posed by both vouchers and charter schools may be that they play into the myth of exit, a theme that runs throughout this book. This is the risk of people abandoning representative politics and its capacity to deliver public goods. Some parents do literally exit by sending their children to private institutions. Many others who rely on public programs, including education, can be seen as leaving what is scripted as a disintegrating system by turning to vouchers and charter schools. Persistent inequalities in finance and the rates of child poverty are important causes of low student performance. Groups that in the past may have supported a strong state and its efforts to address these issues are now turning to proposals aimed at radically decentralizing education. In the United States there is growing support among Latinos and African-Americans for vouchers.[71] Such withdrawal of support for traditional public schools and increased support for alternatives fit with the idea that autonomy and choice should dominate postindustrial social organization.

Thus, it is claimed that there is the need to "inject market forces ... into what many perceive as an over-regulated, over-centralized public education monopoly with strong allegiance to the status quo and no institutional imperative to improve student performance."[72] True, voucher programs and charter schools, especially in this country, at present educate relatively small numbers of children. But the idea of exit from the traditional public system is a powerful magnet drawing support away from reform of that system and toward the idea that parents and children should seek decentralized alternatives. Is the ideal that "only in a larger public square can the ... causes of inequality be addressed"[73] fading?

The Promise of Rights:
Minority Languages and Accommodation of Special Needs

Rights claiming is spreading throughout society. It is not a surprise that such advocacy is especially prominent in education. The demand for rights facilitates the many choices now seen to be central to accommodating diversity and to wrest control from the top-down "one best" factory model. The story of rights in education has many aspects. Here I will discuss two prominent ones: minority languages and the accommodation of children with special needs. The important issue of the "right" to funding for religious schools is taken up below.

These stories of minority languages and of accommodation of children with special needs demonstrate the necessity of rights and their capacity to protect minorities and to shelter the disadvantaged. They also reflect the mostly careful, balanced approach the courts have tried to chart in the face of many competing, legitimate claims in education. They also indicate the absolutist tendencies that rights claiming can exhibit. A right once formulated tends to be pressed to its logical extreme. "Moderation," "compromise," and "settlement" become suspect words as the many implications of the right are pushed forward. Even advocates of any particular right can divide among themselves as different versions of the claim emerge. Rights talk fits uncomfortably with the vision of schools as a common meeting ground where those of different backgrounds and various needs forge a common, public education.

Minority-Language Rights

Language is central to our identity. It is a critical means by which we express ourselves and identify with others who speak the same tongue. Recognition of two official languages has been a crucial building block of this society – and the cause of endless division. Our two official languages are now constitutionally protected. Language issues raise classic questions about the extent to which minority aspirations should be protected at the expense of the majority. Critical questions arise, not about whether such rights should and will be recognized but, rather, about the extent of recognition and the various costs of doing so.

Developments up to the Charter

The history of French, as the minority language outside Quebec, is long and complicated.[74] By the 1980s there was some basic recognition of the importance of education in nurturing the French language of the francophone minority outside Quebec. The provision of some form of French-language programs was mandatory in six provinces (Quebec was the reverse case, with English the minority language). In most provinces, though, both English- and French-speaking parents were free to choose which programs they enrolled their children in. If schools did provide French first-language programming, it was often in conjunction with immersion programs (to instruct English-speaking students in French), sometimes with the two streams even sharing classes.[75]

Language rights were central to Trudeau's vision of an entrenched charter.[76] Thus, demands by advocacy groups that the right to minority-language education be enshrined fell on receptive ears. After much negotiation, the result was section 23 of the *Charter*. That section provides the right, where numbers warrant, to instruction in the minority language and to the facilities for such instruction, both paid out of public funds. These rights belong to parents meeting two qualifications: (1) they must be Canadian citizens and (2) (a) they must have learned French first and still understand it (or, in Quebec, English); (b) the parent's primary school instruction must have been in English or French in Canada; or (c) the parent must have or must have had children in English or French primary or secondary schools in Canada.

Mahé v. Alberta

After the *Charter* came into force in 1982 and until the Supreme Court's decision in *Mahé v. Alberta*[77] in 1990, there were a series of developments in various provinces.[78] The most prominent were in Ontario. In 1984 the Court of Appeal ruled that Ontario's legislation violated section 23 of the *Charter* by imposing a standard numerical requirement across the province for the provision of French-language education, granting too much discretion to school boards, and not providing for some degree of management and control over French-language programs and facilities.[79] In response, legislation was enacted that guaranteed, by 1988, proportional representation for francophones on any school board that offered French-language instruction. These representatives were given authority over the operation of minority-language programs and schools but not over budgetary matters. Francophone school boards (with public and Catholic sections) for the Metro Toronto and Ottawa-Carleton regions were also created. The developments in the other provinces, both legislative and judicial, tended to interpret section 23 less generously than that accorded it in Ontario.[80] The crucial issue that developed was the extent to which section 23 guaranteed a right to manage and control the programs and facilities providing OMLE (official minority-language education).

In *Mahé* the Supreme Court gave a ringing endorsement of section 23, including the possibility that it could require management and control of OMLE programs and facilities. The Court also unanimously ruled that the rights guaranteed by section 23 needed to be viewed with a "sliding scale" in mind – with instruction at one end and management and control at the other – that was dependent on "where the numbers warrant." The position on the scale, for various school boards, would be determined by factors such as the actual and potential demand for services, pedagogical considerations, costs, and the differences between rural and urban areas.[81]

The Aftermath of Mahé – Too Much of a Good Thing?
The decision was reported on the front pages of newspapers across the country. Francophone groups intensified efforts to develop francophone management models and to pursue their implementation. By 1997 all provinces except Quebec had some system of OMLE governance. Most provinces made access to such instruction mandatory for section 23 eligible children and gave some discretion in admitting other qualified students. Funding formulas provided for more equitable funding for francophone schools. Enrolments in such programs increased or, at least, remained the same even in the face of declines in the number of children eligible under section 23 and continued declines in the proportion of francophones in the population.[82]

In the late 1990s and into the 2000s, advocates of OMLE continued their intense efforts to expand programs and to secure control over them. This advocacy has created tensions within the movement itself. The creation of a public and Catholic francophone board for southern Alberta in 2000-1 resulted from a dispute between francophones in Calgary who wanted to remain with the public and Catholic school boards and those who wanted a francophone authority established to run francophone schools in Calgary. Those parents who wished to stay within the existing boards argued that these boards had more resources on a number of fronts. Those who wanted a separate school board argued that a new board was necessary to help stem assimilation, that francophones could not rely on the goodwill of majority-controlled boards and independent management, and that control had been sanctioned by the Supreme Court. They threatened litigation. It was finally decided that a Catholic francophone authority for southern Alberta would operate the Catholic French-language school.[83]

Meanwhile, some courts have applied the sliding scale standards of *Mahé* in demanding ways. In 2000 the Supreme Court itself held that the government of Prince Edward Island had to provide for an OMLE facility in the town of Summerside.[84] The PEI government argued that a school with under one hundred students would not be able to offer the pedagogical advantages of a larger school and that OMLE was provided in a larger school in a town twenty-eight kilometres from Summerside. Nonetheless, the Court held that the OMLE facility in Summerside was necessary to preserve and promote the francophone community in that town. In that same year, a judge in Nova Scotia issued a mandatory injunction ordering that francophone schools be made more homogeneous.[85] Such actions were to include preventing interaction of English- and

French-speaking students during the school day despite the fact that a number of both French-speaking and English-speaking students and their parents feared the spectre of segregation.[86] In 2003 the Supreme Court of Canada upheld the trial judge's holding that he had extensive powers under the *Charter* to supervise the implementation of the Court's order. The majority expressed few reservations about the actual effects that may be produced by such well-intentioned but intrusive orders.[87]

Support by the federal government for an ambitious interpretation of section 23 rights continues. Many of the court cases seeking an expansive interpretation of section 23 have actually been funded by the federal government through the Court Challenges program. Up to March 1999, about $2.5 million had been spent funding section 23 cases and interventions.[88] Furthermore, the government has contributed meaningful amounts to the implementation of many OMLE programs in the various provinces.[89] The commissioner of official languages continues to advocate for a number of policies designed to enhance OMLE, including programs to bolster the French-language skills of children eligible under section 23 but who, in fact, could not function in an OMLE because of their lack of knowledge of French.[90]

At this point, we want to contemplate the old adage "too much of a good thing." It is a good thing that the need for French-language education outside Quebec be recognized as a right in substantial ways. But at some point, other factors may legitimately bound the ways in which the right is recognized. Polls of public opinion do demonstrate support for French-language education, at least for instruction. In Alberta, resistance to minority-language rights has been intense. Nevertheless, in 1998 almost 95 percent of Albertans indicated that, where there are sufficient numbers of children, there should be the right of instruction in French. Other polls have indicated less support throughout English Canada. Moreover, that support decreases once the prospect of large increases in taxes to pay for such instruction is raised as a condition.[91]

To the extent that any negative public reaction arises from hostility to francophones, those opinions need to be blunted as part of protection of minority rights. Insofar as they express reasonable concerns about use of scarce resources for a number of legitimate interests and rights, they need to be taken into account. Instruction in the French language is important. But, as we discuss in a moment, so are accommodating special needs. So are providing for sound teacher-student ratios, excellent texts and materials, and environments conducive to learning.

Divisions within the francophone community also suggest that pressing separate language instruction to its logical extreme may not be sound policy for anyone: "in a number of provinces the Francophone community [has been] split over the need for homogeneous French schools and Francophone governance."[92] For example, the government of Manitoba has argued that its decision not to give francophone school boards exclusive authority over relevant programs and schools was based on its conclusion that many francophones want to participate in French-language education through regular school boards. Debates continue on the need for homogeneous francophone schools within the francophone community in Nova Scotia.

Rights protecting minorities is a proud accomplishment for democracy; rights paving over legitimate differences is not. Riddell has taken a close look at these issues. He observes that "over time Francophone proponents of French schools and school governance have used judicial decisions and rights discourse ... to persuade others in the Francophone community of the value of French schools and governance." So far so good. But then he continues: "and to trump those in the community who continue to disagree."[93] Not so admirable.

Accommodating Special Needs – Together or Apart?

Are students with special needs better educated separately from the main school system? The answer is not an easy one and can depend on many factors. If such students are educated separately, their similar, special needs may be responded to in specialized ways in facilities designed to maximize the effectiveness of instruction in a supportive environment. Yet, separate education runs the risk of segregating these students, setting them apart from the mainstream, and minimizing their chances of ever being integrated into society. If integrated into the main system, students with special needs can take advantage of the entire range of resources available. As educators and other students make reasonable accommodations for those with special needs, they begin a process that the entire society needs to undertake so that those with special needs live full lives and make maximum contributions whether at work, at home, or at leisure. However, inclusive education may not be able to adequately respond to the special needs, and in a system that is strained for resources, there may be resentment on all sides. In such an atmosphere few interests are well served.

Nevertheless, many advocates of the disabled came to see the integration of students with special needs as a goal in and of itself. That advocacy, operating in an atmosphere of strained resources and a multitude of demands, has often produced disappointing results. One expert surveying the terrain has described inclusive education as an "enterprise ... characterized by ambiguity and inconsistency accented by simplistic and naïve declarations of how to achieve the goal."[94]

In February 2003 there was a front-page headline about litigation over the alleged mistreatment by school authorities of a boy with hearing and learning problems.[95] The parents are suing for damages and are challenging certain provisions of the *Education Act* concerning special education. The complaints are serious and, if proven, could have severe implications for the education system.

What is of note for our purposes is that the mere filing of the lawsuit attracted such media attention. At that point not only had the allegations not been proven, but the school authorities had not even had a chance to respond. But such is the volatile, litigious atmosphere in which special needs and other issues are being played out.[96]

Responding to Special Needs – and the Move to Inclusion
Historically, those with special needs were educated in separate institutions. While special needs can embrace a wide variety of situations, including the intellectually gifted, most issues revolved around those students with some form of disability. By the early 1900s segregated classrooms were a feature of public schools in larger urban areas. Up to the 1960s, special schools and segregated classes in regular schools were the main way that students with special needs were educated.

From the 1960s onward, the movement for inclusive education gained momentum. While there are different understandings of the term, a basic definition is that "students with disabilities will attend the school or classroom that they would attend if they were not disabled. Services are brought to the child rather than the child being removed in order to access services."[97] In the 1960s the larger social and civil rights movement for recognition prompted many parents and educators to advocate for inclusive education. The notion that students with disabilities should be educated separately from their peers was increasingly rejected. The segregationist aspect, seen to have parallels with the oppression of black children in the United States, cast a long shadow over separate facilities for the disabled.

By the early 1980s, law, advocacy, and pedagogical innovation had created a force for fundamental change in the way students with disabilities were to be educated. In the United States, federal legislation had been passed in the late 1970s designed to address special education.[98] In 1980, following on an official study, the Ontario government passed the *Education Amendment Act,* the first legislation specifically addressing special education in Canada.[99] At the same time, budgetary constraints were becoming a force in this area. For some, inclusion became a cost-cutting device. Children with special needs would be moved into regular classrooms, with the expenses associated with separate facilities being curtailed. Whether the main system was given adequate resources and personnel to support children with special needs was another question: "integration was interpreted by many as a license to close segregated classes without providing the necessary skills and resources to regular classrooms."[100]

Whatever the implications for quality of education, the push for inclusion continued into the 1990s. Some of the strongest proponents for inclusion were advocacy groups. In 1987 the Canadian Association for Community Living (CACL) established a task force to identify issues for people with mental disabilities. Integrated education was rated a top priority. As a result

CACL founded the Integration Action Group, designed to support parents in achieving integrated education for their children.[101] With the introduction of the *Charter,* proponents believed that the answer was at hand: inclusive education would be enshrined as a right.[102]

Eaton: The Supreme Court Struggles with Special Needs
The 1980s and 1990s saw a stream of cases being taken to the courts on behalf of students with disabilities.[103] *Eaton* was clearly the most important.[104] Advocates of inclusion secured a dramatic victory in the Ontario Court of Appeal and, in their view, suffered a staggering blow in the Supreme Court. The case brought to the fore the dilemma of special education in a system already struggling to respond to a multitude of demands.

Emily Eaton was an eleven-year-old grade four student who used a wheelchair, could not speak, and needed full assistance for personal care. After Emily spent three years in a regular class, her teachers concluded that she was becoming increasingly isolated both intellectually and socially. They determined that she should be educated in a special class. Her parents were unhappy with this decision and appealed it to the board and then the district level. Unsuccessful, they then launched a court case alleging that the decision violated section 15 of the *Charter* and Emily's equality rights.

The Eatons secured a dramatic victory in the Court of Appeal. Speaking on behalf of the Court, Justice Arbour (subsequently appointed to the Supreme Court) ruled that a placement in an educational setting made without the consent of the parents violates a child's right to equality under section 15 of the *Charter*. Justice Arbour held that Emily had a constitutional right to attend school with fully able children despite the school board's judgment that it was in her best interests to attend a segregated facility.[105]

In 1997 the Supreme Court of Canada reached a very different decision. The Court started from the proposition that the placement of a child should be determined by what would be in the best interests of that child – the wishes of the parents are not necessarily determinative. The Court was careful to underscore the importance that integration can play. But it rejected the claim accepted by the Court of Appeal that a placement in a special class could not occur against the wishes of the child's parents. Thus, there was no violation of Emily's right to equality in placing her in a special class since there was objective evidence that her needs were not being met in a regular one.[106] Instead, in placing her in the special class, school authorities made a difficult decision but one that was in her best interests.

The Problem Is Not Rights but Resources
Many advocates on behalf of disabled children were dismayed by the decision. They suggested that the decision would create a backlash against disabled

children and that school boards were using it as a justification for not doing more.[107] To the extent that such charges were accurate, advocates might contemplate what exactly such litigation had accomplished.[108]

Had this lawsuit provided yet more evidence of how turning to courts illustrates the "fly-paper" phenomenon? This image captures the way litigation can siphon off resources and be turned against those who invoke it. Various groups hope that lawsuits will provoke responses from bureaucracies and from legislatures and will blunt wrong-headed majorities. Instead, turning to courts frequently exhausts scarce resources that might have been better used in advancing issues in the electoral, legislative, and administrative processes.[109]

In Ontario, there was some legislative response seeking to clarify decision making about children with special needs in the education system.[110] However, the pressing issue is one of adequate resources to support schools and teachers in responding to children with special needs, especially concerning inclusion.[111] In 2002 an auditor appointed by the Ontario government to take control of the budget deficits of some school boards criticized the Ottawa board for spending money on busing children with special needs to separate classes.[112] Whatever the validity of such criticisms, demands for such resources must compete with other legitimate claims at a time of constraint:[113] "unless ... supports for teachers and students with special needs increase, it may be that inclusion will become a nonissue or one that falters badly in the face of educational realities."[114] Is representative politics up to the task of providing for these vulnerable children?

Markets, Rights, Vouchers, and Religion: Ontario Subsidizes Private Education (and the Affluent)

It's an Ontario story. It started out as an argument about religious equality, about the rights of all parents to send their children to religious schools with the same amount of financial support from the state. It then expanded to a claim that all parents should have a right to choose private education for their children with financial support from the state. Concepts of equality and choice were accorded a misplaced emphasis; the idea of the public school as the common meeting place for young citizens faded even more.

Catholics in Ontario have a constitutional right, because of section 93 of the *Constitution Act, 1867,* to have their separate schools funded by public dollars. The exact nature of the right might have been debatable but, in any event, funding was available to Catholic schools throughout the twentieth century. There were constant grumblings from other religious groups which, understandably, felt themselves disadvantaged. The right of Catholics or those of any other religion to educate their children was never at issue. The extent of the state's obligation to fund these separate schools (especially while not financially supporting educational institutions of other religions) was.

In the last two decades of the last century, the movement to extend funding to other religious schools gained momentum for at least two reasons. First, in the age of rights, funding for Catholic schools, and a denial of it to other religious educational institutions, seemed a clear example of discrimination and an affront to equality. Second, after a number of political twists, funding to Catholic schools was extended by the government to all grade and high school years in the early 1980s, thus widening the gap between these schools and other institutions providing religious-based education and underscoring the privileged position of Catholics.[115]

Predictably, the issue of funding to Catholic schools went to the Supreme Court in the 1980s[116] and the 1990s.[117] Although the Court was sympathetic to the equality arguments, it wisely held that a bad situation should not be worsened. The constitutional obligation under section 93 to fund Catholic schools in Ontario was necessary to bring about Confederation: "section 93 is the product of an historical compromise which was a crucial step along the road leading to Confederation."[118] Yet, a pact made long ago on the difficult road to nationhood was not to be the basis for grounding an obligation to fund religious schools generally.

Nonetheless, "rights talk" does not just happen in the courts. Advocates decided that which could not be brought about through litigation could be realized through other means. One of these was to accuse Ontario of violating international human rights. In 1996 a Jewish parent, with two children in private school, appealed to the United Nations Human Rights Committee. He argued that the Ontario government funding Catholic schools violated the International Covenant on Civil and Political Rights to which Canada is a signatory. In 1999 the committee found that the right "under article 26 of the Covenant to equal and effective protection against discrimination" had been infringed. The committee further found that the government "is under the obligation to provide an effective remedy, that will eliminate [that] discrimination."[119]

The reaction to the UN committee decision was unseemly tactics of avoidance and stonewalling by public officials. The federal government, as the signatory to the covenant, was required to respond. It passed the buck to Ontario: "within Canada, decisions regarding education are ultimately for the provinces to resolve in accordance with their constitutional authority."[120] Meanwhile, the Ontario government "remained adamant that it found no reason to change its policy on funding denominational schools."[121] Even those steadfastly opposed to funding of religious schools acknowledged the force of the UN committee's ruling and were dismayed by the governments' responses.[122] That reaction was understandable. Advocates of funding for private schools had been handed a powerful symbolic weapon: the status quo – financial support for only Catholic schools – was staining Ontario's (and Canada's) reputation in the international community.

And there was more. Free marketeers – exalting private schools generally – soon realized that they could take particular arguments on behalf of denominational schools and join them to more wide-ranging claims about choice in education. The laissez-faire advocates' solution? A voucher that could be used at any private school, whether religious or not. The tax system could be used to provide subsidies for parents to send children to any qualified private school. The lacklustre public system would finally be subject to a stiff dose of badly needed competition. In one fell swoop denominational schools would have their funding; other private schools would have public support to enhance their market position. Choice would be venerated.

In another era the movement pushing a voucher might have been turned aside. The momentum could have been stalled by widespread acceptance of public schools as central, with support for Catholic educational institutions seen as a mistake: an error of constitutional proportions but wrong nonetheless. Such a position would have applauded Alan Borovy's statement. Borovy is general counsel of the Canadian Civil Liberties Association. During the debate over the tax credit/voucher, he urged that "it's better to treat the Catholic arrangement as a regrettable historical anomaly rather than a precedent."[123] In that other era, the movement might have been toward a constitutional amendment that would have dislodged Catholicism from its privileged position. That modification would have been backed by public approval that all private schools of any nature should pay for themselves. That would have been a position not easily attained but one arising from a worthy view of the nature of education and its role in society.[124]

But the developments around the tax credit took place in the age of choice and of rights. Thus, the momentum became unstoppable. The result was the Equity in Education Tax Credit.[125] The legislation, phased in over five years, gave a credit against tax levied by Ontario of 50 percent of tuition paid, to a maximum of $3,500 per child; that is, on $7,000 worth of tuition. The credit, subject to a few restrictions (for example, private schools being required to meet the same standards for instruction time as the public school system), was available to any parents sending their children to any private school, whether or not it is religiously based.

Market celebrants in Ontario and beyond were ecstatic.[126] The *Wall Street Journal,* saluting the voucher, proclaimed that the "plan has been hailed as revolutionary by education reformers world-wide ... 'far more radical than anything yet seen in the United States.'"[127] Advocates for religious groups were quick to assure that the voucher was a required step in the right direction for addressing the inequality arising from the funding of Catholic schools. The credit's availability to "socially elite private schools" was largely sidestepped by rights advocates: "the two groupings should be justified on different grounds and should not stand or fall together."[128]

Public school supporters were appalled at the prospect of the credit.[129] Yet, the credit was supported by important factors. First, there was broad support for funding those who send their children to private schools. A poll taken in 2001, during the extensive public debate over the voucher, showed that 60 percent of Canadians (54 percent of Ontarians) backed tax relief for those sending their children to private schools, whether religious or otherwise.[130] In the circumstances, it is difficult to make the case that the voucher was a stealth operation foisted on an unsuspecting and nonconsenting public. Second, Ontario's move to fund other religious schools and private schools was not unique. Several other provinces have provided such funding in a variety of ways for some time.[131] That fact does not lessen the controversy over the wisdom of doing so. However, in the face of these circumstances, it is impossible to characterize what Ontario did as an aberrant breaking of the nation's commitment to fund only public schools. Third, statistics suggest that many more families with comparatively low incomes send their children to private or religious schools than is often supposed. Nationally, 29 percent attending these schools come from families with annual incomes of less than $50,000.[132] Thus, it is difficult to characterize the credit's use for nonreligious institutions as exclusively underwriting "socially elite private schools."[133]

That said, the credit may have serious negative consequences for the public education system. It was initiated in Canada's most populous province at a time of unrivalled skepticism toward public schools and public goods generally. It was introduced by a government sending strong messages about its lack of faith in the public system and its high expectations of what the private one can do. The credit was put in place while new standards of effectiveness were ushered in for public schools, even as private schools were exempted from any such testing until grade nine: "governments are now prepared to use public money to subsidize parents to remove their children from the curriculum that they have imposed in the public schools and that they insist is more effective."[134]

Further, the greatest proportion of high-income earners whose kids attend private schools is in Ontario (according to 1999 reports, 37 percent come from families with annual incomes over $100,000).[135] What is more, Ontario has many of the country's most exclusive private educational institutions (Upper Canada College, Bishop Strachan, Toronto French School, to name just a few). The result is that many affluent, influential families were having their detachment from the public system underwritten by the government.

The popular support for these measures by many of those who will likely ever use only the public system is, nonetheless, applauded by private school advocates. Such support can be seen as further evidence of the myth of exit. The idea that representative politics and its discontents can simply be left behind leads people to support an initiative of which they will probably never take advantage. Yet such support is consistent with a rebellion against government gone wrong, with deep skepticism toward the capacity of representative politics to deliver good public goods.

If the tax credit had to be, it could have been brought about in a substantially different way. It could have been confined to religious schools. It could have been targeted toward those of modest means. Its use could have been tied to schools subject to the same standards of heightened effectiveness and testing as the public schools. But no such qualifications were put in place. This could have occurred if there had been a capacity to take a nuanced approach to the problems with the public school system and a willingness to contemplate a variety of solutions, including some reasonable role for private and religious schools. But the bandwagon of rights allied with the cheering for the market drowned out such subtleties. The result was a broadside against public education.

When the Ontario Liberal government was elected in 2003, the tax credit was repealed.[136] Its abolition is some evidence of the capacity of representative politics to turn back from the wrong path. Its ending can also be viewed as one of several manoeuvres by a cash-starved administration. In any event, those advocating the underwriting of private education had been stopped – for the moment. What would be their next strategy?

Conclusion

Mordechai Rozanski, then the president of the University of Guelph, recommended in his December 2002 report to the Ontario government that substantial funds be injected into the public school system. What is more, the *Globe and Mail,* scarcely an apologist for big government, applauded that recommendation: "The public system ... must be protected; it remains the key to social progress and mobility."[137]

So there is hope that the cause of public education as a public good can be renewed. But for that to happen, public education itself must remain central. All the while it must be accountable, it must be responsive to a variety of needs, and it must be competitive with the best school systems internationally. This is a tall order, and one that will be filled only by providing the system with sufficient resources and popular and political support to do the job well.

The real danger is that there will develop a widespread belief that the task is just not doable. Instead, the idea may take hold that a variety of market mechanisms and rights claims are the only hope to bring unruly and under performing public institutions to heel. Such is not the case. These mechanisms and claims have a role, but it is wrong to think that they can be a substitute for the system that "remains the key to social progress and mobility." Sound advice? In this age of rights and this time of markets, will we have the wisdom to take it?

8 Ever More Citizens Who Are Senior: An Ageing Canada

Our society growing old is a topic that is receiving a great deal of attention of late. The United Nations designated 1999 the International Year of Older Persons. The United Nation's Second World Assembly on Ageing was held in May 2002. Several human rights agencies and other institutions in Canada have published reports on issues involving older adults. In the spring and summer of 2002, newspapers, reacting to results of the census and other developments, carried headlines such as, "Canada facing an age crunch" and "Little in the national fabric will remain untouched as 2001 census shows what could be in store for a greying population."[1] The Law Commission of Canada has an extensive project on "generational justice," a large component of which focuses on older adults.[2]

This attention should not be a surprise. Large numbers of people are growing old as the baby boomers age. Except for the few who die young, we will all experience growing old. Seniors suffer discrimination and insensitivity. Yet, they also benefit from public programs that are a significant cost to the public purse.

An ageing Canada tells us a lot about courts and rights, politics, and markets and how their changing roles influence and are influenced by a society in transition. Courts, by and large, are not the problem. The Supreme Court has taken a balanced approach, one that is alive to the larger context, to issues involving seniors. Rights have been extremely important in exposing discrimination and insensitivity to older adults. But the extravagance of rights claiming for the aged is also on display, especially the ignoring of the important ways that older adults benefit from the regulatory state. The market has thus far largely not been responsive to the special needs of seniors. Yet, in one area, free enterprise is marshalling its forces to dismantle another public program: a retirement for senior citizens that has some measure of economic dignity supported by governmental pensions.

Many More of Us Are Getting Older – and We Have Issues

An Ageing Canada

We live in a time of rapid change. Technological developments, globalization, volatile markets, and the threat of terrorism are just some of the factors contributing to substantial transformations to our society. Demographic change is yet another way our society is being altered. Because of altered immigration patterns and other factors, we are a much more diverse society than we were only decades ago. Still another way we are being transformed demographically is the increasing number of older adults in Canada.

Older adults are the fastest growing segment of the population in this country. In 2001 approximately 3.92 million Canadians were sixty-five or older. That figure is more than two-thirds what it was in 1981; yet during the same period, the overall population increased by only one-quarter. The proportion of seniors has gone from one in twenty in 1921 to one in eight in 2001; by 2041 it will be one in four. The fastest growth in seniors is occurring among oldest Canadians. In 2001 over 430,000 individuals in our society were eighty-five years or older: more than twice as many as in 1981 and more than twenty times as many as in 1921.[3]

When we speak of older adults we usually are referring to people who are sixty-five or older. Being "sixty-five or over" is one important aspect that people in this group share. Yet, seniors are diverse in terms of socioeconomic status, gender, race, and so forth. The boundaries between those who are old and those who are not are increasingly blurred. Of course, diversity is not unique to seniors. Canadian society is becoming increasingly varied. Other groups of people who may suffer discrimination, such as gays and lesbians or visible minorities, are also diverse in terms of socioeconomic status, gender, race, and so forth.

However, there may be aspects of diversity among older adults that require special attention. Old is something we become. For many other groups that suffer discrimination, the characteristics that are burdened are fixed; for example, race, sexual orientation, and many forms of disability. Moreover, no one starts out old. Ageing is a process that *everyone*, except those who die prematurely, will experience.

What is more, the very characteristic that is the focus of attention – age – is itself varied. Someone who is sixty-five may be considered old. Someone who is ninety-five is surely old. Yet, those thirty years can give rise to a great deal of difference. Take the image of seniors as suffering from diminished mental capacity. For "young seniors," this is an extremely negative stereotype. At age sixty-five, only one in fifty is cognitively impaired. At age eighty-five, one in three is experiencing these failings.[4] Activity limitations affect only about one-fifth of seniors aged sixty-five to seventy-four. Over half of adults over age eighty-five are so affected.[5] Older women outnumber older men: 60 percent of seniors aged seventy-five to eighty-four are women; 70 percent aged eighty-five or older are women.[6]

Because of the differences within the ageing process, it may be useful to think of at least three stages of ageing, while recognizing that the boundaries for these stages are fluid: "young" older adults – sixty-five to seventy-four; "mid-range" older adults – seventy-five to eighty-four; and "old" older adults – eighty-five and older. These three stages should never be employed mechanically: "eighty-five" as a dividing line may be just as arbitrary as "sixty-five." Nevertheless, these stages can be useful in highlighting the differences that can occur within the ageing process: "these three groups have three distinct lifestyles. The young seniors are still healthy and spend a lot of time and money traveling. The mid-seniors are still at home but health problems are rendering them less mobile. Many senior seniors are in nursing homes."[7]

At base there is a need to come to grips with the various ways society views and acts on its images of older adults. Seniors are frequently the subject of stereotypical but contradictory images. Consider two prominent but colliding views. On the one hand, they are seen as healthy, living lives of carefree luxury – at least compared with much of the rest of the population – and caring little about the needs of society, particularly the issues affecting younger generations. On the other, older adults are thought to be a growing burden on the social welfare and health systems and on their families and communities.

In fact, older adults are a group of individuals who are diverse and who may possibly grow even more so in the coming years. These many differences caution against lumping together a whole segment of the population just because its individuals are "old." As one study has colourfully put it, sometimes "heterogeneity swamps generation."[8] For example, seniors have on average lower levels of education than other adults. This situation will change. In the future, some seniors will be better educated because of the higher attainments now being achieved among younger adults and, possibly, because of increased educational opportunities for some older adults. The changes among seniors are part of rapid transformations in the population as a whole, all of which need to be carefully taken into account as Canada confronts the many issues presented by the twenty-first century.

Laws, Policies, and Older Adults

General Discussion

Issues relating to older adults can arise in two ways. First, age can be explicitly addressed in legislation or in a policy, including in terms of triggering benefits, imposing burdens, and regulating various schemes. For example, sixty-five is the triggering age for receiving Old Age Security (OAS) and the Guaranteed Income Supplement (GIS) benefits; for the latter, certain financial eligibility requirements must also be met.[9] In terms of burdens, some provinces impose additional licence testing once a driver attains a certain age.[10] In terms of regulating various schemes, sixty-nine is the triggering age for terminating contributions to RRSPs.[11]

Second, law and policies may be silent about the relevance of age, but their applications can have particular consequences, including negative effects, for older adults. Consider the abuse of seniors. Many experts who have examined these issues believe that laws are adequate to respond to such mistreatment. They also believe that there is a need for greater sensitivity on the part of law enforcement officials, courts, and others to the needs of seniors who may have been abused.[12]

On the one hand, there is a need to identify the legitimate circumstances where age can be used as a "marker," either alone or in conjunction with other appropriate factors, for various laws, policies, and their applications. For instance, age is used as an important factor in the operation of life and automobile insurance for the setting of premiums. Using age in a way consistent with sound actuarial practices may be permissible and, in some instances, there may be no effective alternative to doing so. Moreover, in some instances, such as the design of products and the provision of services in both the private and public sectors, age, not currently taken into account, could be factored in, so as to assist older adults to live fuller, more independent lives.

On the other hand, it is vital to identify circumstances where age should not be used to differentiate for entitlements, responsibilities, and so forth. Such concerns are heightened when there are other bases for making the distinction, such as need or ability, that are attuned to the individual lives of older persons. Many experts who have examined the relevant issues are opposed to broadly applicable laws or policies requiring mandatory retirement based on a fixed age such as sixty-five. They argue other criteria, most prominently ability, should be used to assess any person's fitness to continue in a particular position.[13] I return to issues relevant to mandatory retirement below.

Two other issues are very important. Both deal with the effects of using age as a marker. The first concerns the effects on other generations, especially regarding benefits conferred on older adults. The most particular focus is on public pensions. There are fears that these programs will become a drain on public resources paid for, in large part, by younger generations who may never enjoy the benefits. The issues around public pensions are returned to below.

The second concerns the way that "age" intersects with other characteristics such as race, gender, and socioeconomic status. Here, particular attention is focused on the way that age may add to other burdens. A disabled person may face many challenges in daily life. An older disabled person may be challenged even more.[14] The difficult life of most Aboriginals can become even harder as they grow older. At the same time, seniors of high socioeconomic status can lead lives that depend little on the web of social programs and benefits critical to the lives of other older adults. The interaction of law, policy, and the needs of many seniors is illustrated by the following discussion of health care and social services.

Health Care and Social Services
Many older adults, especially the "young" older adults, enjoy healthy lives. In 1997, more than three-quarters of seniors living at home viewed their health as good to excellent; only 6 percent reported their health as poor.[15] Nevertheless, as they age, people do tend to develop health problems that can cause them to increase their use of health and social services. The great majority of seniors use prescription or over-the-counter medication. In 1997, 84 percent of seniors reported taking some medication in a two-day period and 56 percent reported taking two or more medication. Seniors are far more likely to be hospitalized than other age groups and stays tend to be longer.[16]

This growing dependency on the health care system gives rise to a number of issues that reflect two opposing considerations: older adults have increasing requirements that need to be met, yet, there are concerns about the costs of responding to these needs at a time of reassessment of our health care system. The tension between these two considerations can be played out in several ways.

First, there are issues about the ability of the health care system to respond to the individual needs and wishes of older adults. That response can give rise to questions of access: policies and their application may be denying some seniors access to a full range of treatment, based on their age rather than based on the need for the treatment and the benefits that could be attained. There also might be issues involving the subjecting of seniors with grave health problems to treatment when they have made it clear that they do not want active intervention in those circumstances. Generally, there should be a greater sensitivity on the part of health care professionals to the needs of seniors and to their treatment. Medical and nursing faculties and other institutions of health care education should consider developing more programs and training in the care of older adults.[17]

Second, there is a need to scrutinize policies that are, on their face, neutral but which may create a disproportionate burden for older adults in their application. Consider the issue of allocating resources to different kinds of care. There may be valid reasons to allocate more resources to acute care than chronic care. On the face of it, the decision appears equitable: it is an assessment that those who require acute care have a greater need. However, because older adults often have greater requirements than the rest of the population for chronic care, a decision to put more resources into acute care may have a disproportionately negative impact on seniors.[18]

This discussion is not urging a rush to judgment on this or the many other complex issues concerning the delivery of health care. Rather, it emphasizes that the needs of older adults should be fully taken into account, including through a careful assessment of the actual effects of laws and policies on the lives of seniors.

Third, there is a greater need for community and social services resources. Such resources can provide support for an array of activities, from housework and transportation to health-related services and group activities. We want to support older adults in their striving to live healthy and independent lives. For older adults with serious health problems, adequate levels of community and social support can help to realize these goals. More particularly, the efforts to curtail length of hospital stays are intensifying. Such efforts may be misdirected in terms of overall health care unless those discharged from hospitals – the population, in general, and seniors, in particular – have access to appropriate levels of community and social services.[19]

Fourth, as the population ages and the percentage of seniors increases, the cost of health care and the implications of the issues just discussed need to be taken fully into account. Many factors create financial pressures on the system; increasing health care costs for older adults is only one of them. The reality of an ageing population and its needs, at a time of reassessment of our health care system, is an important factor that must be responded to by those addressing such issues.[20] Forging an appropriate response will be a continuing challenge into the new century.[21]

Is the Market Responding? Seniors and Negative Stereotypes

A growing response to problems, documented throughout this book, is to urge a turning to the market. If government and its laws and policies cannot deliver a solution, maybe free enterprise will.[22] How is the market doing in responding to the needs of older adults?

To date, not so well. Ageing baby boomers throughout the world, by virtue of their numbers and relative affluence, are creating new markets in rich countries. Yet, the commercial world has been mostly unresponsive: "business remains largely obsessed with youth. Many companies seem blind to the fact that their customers are greying ... few see the elderly as an exciting group to sell to."[23]

There have been notable exceptions.[24] The sale of Unilever's margarine was in decline until it launched its Proactive spread, which reduces cholesterol; the successful advertising campaign focused on happy consumers – mostly over age fifty – attesting to their lower levels. When NTT Do Co Mo, a Japanese telecom company, identified the older population as a promising market, it launched a new, well-selling mobile phone. Raku-Raku (easy-easy) has a panel with larger buttons and easier-to-read figures.

What seems to be critical to a product's success is that it not only be well designed to respond to older adults' needs but that it also be marketed through positive images: "rejuvenated patients cycling with their grandchildren or practicing *tai chi* are far more effective than the stereotypes of a frail arthritis sufferer."[25] Moreover, products and services, designed and marketed for seniors, should try to benefit everyone. RATP, the Paris public-transport network, responded to older adult users' complaints with a simplified and more readable map that was meant to coexist with the original layout. The new version was so popular with all users that the original was discontinued.

Such initiatives involving design and marketing are the exception. Most advertising campaigns seem to have ignored the obvious: consumers are greying.[26] The situation could change rapidly.[27] Thus far, though, the market is "lumping all people over the age of 60 into a grey basket of frailty, tweed and stinginess."[28]

There is one area where free enterprisers have busied themselves: retirement. They want to get rid of it and sharply curtail publicly funded pensions. Publicly funded pensions, assaults on them, and responses to these attacks, returned to below, will take us back to a discussion of public goods and to a concept for civic betterment that is much talked about these days: social cohesion.

Law Can Be Hard on Older People – but It's Good to Them, Too

Law's interaction with social forces is a complicated story. Making statements about the effects of law is a chancy business.[29] That said, there are two thrusts to comments on the impact that law and related policies have on the lives of older citizens.

The first, promoted especially by rights activists, focuses on charges of discrimination against seniors. The private sector is criticized for its prejudiced behaviour. But, as is often the case, government is also castigated. Legislatures and their agents are responsible for an array of laws and policies that result in discriminatory treatment of the aged.

It is not that the charges are without foundation. There are numerous instances of prejudice against seniors. Such behaviour and attitudes do need to be rooted out. But the problem with rights claiming, in this and many other contexts, is that it becomes unqualified. Its advocates focus on the rights holders and their needs, with little regard for the larger context. Rights claiming, in its extravagant form, becomes myopic to the larger implications. The vindication of the right – however extremely put – is all that is important.

The second focuses on the way that law and the regulatory state provide a network of support for older citizens, including heath care, social services, and education. A critical element of support is the system of pensions that law has erected over the last several decades. That system, a mix of public and private elements, has been a big success story in terms of representative politics' capacity to tackle important social issues. Canada now has one of the lowest rates of poverty for seniors among OECD nations. There is more work to be done. Older single women remain at risk of being poor. Nevertheless, the pension system is an example of the capacity that legislatures and their agents still retain to tackle important social issues.

But the pension system and the idea of retirement is under attack. The free marketeers would have us believe that there is no need for retirement in a knowledge-based economy. There being no need for retirement, public pensions should be viewed as just another drain on the public purse that should be sharply curtailed. To engage such lovers of laissez-faire, we need to ask some questions. Is retirement a public good? What is intergenerational justice? Are we socially cohesive? I respond to these queries later in this chapter.

Human Rights: So Necessary – but Not Enough

There Are Infringements

There is a need for all levels of government to assess laws, policies, and their applications concerning older adults to ensure that they are not based on stereotypes of seniors and that they do, in fact, respond to their requirements. Indeed, the Ontario Human Rights Commission in its report on older adults asserts that "all levels of government [should] evaluate laws, policies and programs to ensure that they do not contain age-based assumptions and stereotypes and that they reflect the needs of older persons."[30]

But how should such assessment occur? What standards should be used to evaluate laws and policies as diverse as those dealing with pensions, mandatory retirement, health care, and drivers' licences, to name but a few, that have direct consequences for the lives of older adults? What are the criteria for taking account of not only the situation at present but also the changing conditions for all generations in a society in transition? What are the benchmarks for an array of laws and policies that must avoid burdening older adults while other laws and policies use age as a marker to benefit seniors?

Those who see us increasingly as rights bearers scrutinize laws and policies to ensure that the rights of older adults are not violated. Such scrutiny focuses on discriminatory behaviour and, at the least, insensitive treatment of seniors. This approach is especially vigilant about any ways that age as a marker imposes burdens on older adults. Some laws and policies may explicitly refer to age in a manner that creates a burden for seniors. Other laws and policies may not explicitly refer to age but they are applied in different ways for various age groups in a manner that creates burdens for older adults. Any burdening of seniors may be the foundation of a claim of discriminatory treatment based on age – ageism.

According to the Ontario Human Rights Commission, there are two types of ageism, or "behaviour that [has] a negative effect on older persons. The first involves the social construction of age, including incorrect assumptions and stereotypes about older persons. Another form of ageism involves a tendency to structure society based on assumptions that everyone is young, thereby failing to respond appropriately to the needs of older persons."[31]

The foregoing is an excellent, concise definition of ageism. It isolates two types of negative behaviour that can have deleterious consequences for seniors; such behaviour must be avoided in the making and applying of laws and policies. Yet, the two types of ageism may collide: responding to one type may lay the grounds for charges that the other is being committed.

Those enacting laws and formulating policies that attempt to address the needs of seniors may leave themselves open to the charge of relying on negative stereotypes of seniors; in not acting, they may be accused of not taking the needs of seniors into account. Consider laws that particularly aim to protect seniors against abuse. On the one hand, they seem to be sensitive to concerns that older adults not suffer mistreatment. Not to enact them may leave legislators open to charges that they are not responding appropriately to the needs of older persons. On the other, they may be characterized as premised on negative stereotypes of seniors that suggest that, because a person is old, he or she for that reason alone is more likely to be frail in some way that justifies protective measures. Such laws may then be faulted as premised on incorrect assumptions and stereotypes about older persons.

The point here is not to in any way invalidate the definition. We need to be dedicated to rooting out ageism in all its forms. Yet, such resolve should recognize the complexities of responding to many issues that affect older adults. We need to strive for laws and policies that address appropriately the requirements of older adults but which are not premised on negative stereotypes. This is an essential task, but a difficult one.

Whatever the complexities of defining ageism and applying it, the rights approach is vigilant about the identification of laws, policies, and their applications that may burden older adults. Age as a marker used explicitly or otherwise to impose burdens is closely scrutinized. Thus, laws and policies on issues as diverse as mandatory retirement, drivers' licences, qualifications for employment insurance benefits and training programs, and health care have all been subject to searching criticism on the grounds that they burden older adults on account of their age and are therefore discriminatory.

Do policies requiring mandatory retirement violate the human rights of seniors? Some provinces and the federal government have abolished mandatory retirement for employment within their jurisdictions.[32] Nevertheless, in some provinces – Ontario for example – mandatory retirement is still permitted, despite a number of initiatives to end it.[33] Usually there is no law requiring someone to retire; rather, the law, often a human rights code, permits employers to choose to require their employees to retire at sixty-five or some other age. This ability of employers to force retirement comes about by limiting the protection against discrimination based on age, in the case of employment, to exclude people over a certain age, usually sixty-five.

Where mandatory retirement has been abolished, it appears that few people choose to continue to work past what was formerly the mandated retirement age, usually sixty-five.[34] In the future, more older adults may choose to work longer as various changes to the working environment take place, such as more flex-time and part-time positions. In any event, those opposed to mandatory retirement emphasize that the choice to work or not is important to the sense of freedom and dignity of older adults.

The Supreme Court, in *McKinney v. University of Guelph,*[35] held that mandatory retirement does not violate the *Charter,* including on the grounds that the activities of universities were not sufficiently governmental in nature to be subject to scrutiny under the *Charter.* Nevertheless, for rights activists, mandatory retirement is ageism writ large. On the face of it, mandatory retirement is discriminatory behaviour; making a decision about a person's employment solely on the basis of his or her age rather than capacity to perform the job would appear to be a clear example of unequal, burdensome treatment.[36]

What is more, mandatory retirement may have a disproportionate impact on some people. Women may have more interruptions in work outside the home because of child rearing and other responsibilities; in addition, they often earn less than men when they do work outside the home. This shorter period of work with lower wages can have negative consequences, which are worsened by mandatory retirement; examples include lower amounts of savings and lesser pensions from CPP or QPP because of lower contributions for a shorter time. Recent immigrants may face similar problems. From the time of their arrival in Canada to a date at which they are mandatorily retired, they may have only a relatively short amount of time to build a pension.[37]

Defenders of mandatory retirement have pointed to a number of reasons that they claim justify the policy, including the

- need to facilitate planning in terms of an entity's workforce;
- desirability of promoting job opportunities for younger workers;
- need to ensure that older workers leave their jobs in a dignified way;
- requirement to control costs arising from poor job performance and otherwise.[38]

Rights advocates reject such rationales. They insist that basic fairness and respect for the individual require that older workers be evaluated on their merits and not be ejected from their jobs because they have reached a certain age. Moreover, advocates assert that

- many older adults require the income from continued employment;
- labour shortages, at least in some areas, result in the need to draw upon the pool of older workers to fill the demand;
- women and minorities, because of more limited opportunities for employment, may particularly need to work to an older age; and

- international trends favour the abolition of mandatory retirement – it has been eliminated in many other countries, including the United States, New Zealand, and Australia.[39]

Advocates assert that, where mandatory retirement has been abolished, there have not been any negative consequences that would justify its retention in jurisdictions where it still exists. They insist that the right of older workers to choose to continue to work or not, and not to be forced out of a job just because of age must be paramount. Yet, the extent to which abolishing mandatory retirement addresses the many issues older workers face in a rapidly changing job market remains a question – one which I return to in the next section.

Can Rights Blind?

The compelling strength of the human rights approach is that it focuses on the individual. It underscores the need for autonomy, freedom, dignity, and choice: values that too often are ignored in responding to issues touching the lives of individual seniors. We have seen, at many places in this book, how "Choice!" has become the rallying cry both for free marketeers and for rights advocates in widely varying contexts. The demand for choice on behalf of common folk is everywhere; the reality of choice in their lives is another matter. There are, of course, circumstances where there are legitimate claims to be made for more choice. One such area is in the lives of seniors: "Choice tends to be limited by age much more than is really necessary, either through negative expectations or just poor planning. The revolution in longevity puts choice high up the list of priorities."[40]

This rights advocacy points to the burdens that may be imposed on older adults, especially by laws, policies, and their applications. We saw this in mandatory retirement and the examples in other areas referred to above. What is more, such analysis draws on the rapidly evolving understanding of human rights taking place in the legislatures, commissions, and courts over the last decades.

Yet, this approach has limits. First, there have been comparatively few formal complaints to the various human rights commissions and even fewer cases litigated in courts based on age discrimination.[41] There are a number of explanations for this sparse record, including the obvious one that some jurisdictions do not protect against age discrimination, particularly in employment, as fully as they should. Nevertheless, it would be a mistake to rest the case for a wide-ranging examination of issues affecting older adults solely on the basis of relatively few formalized complaints about human rights violations.

Second, this approach may not fully take account of the larger context in which the relevant issues are embedded. Focusing on burdens, as important as this is, may not fully assess all relevant aspects of the issues. For an example, let's return to mandatory retirement. The issue of whether older adults should be forced to retire is an important human rights issue. But that question is embedded in the larger context of work, training, and financial security for seniors.

Quite apart from mandatory retirement, older workers lose their positions for a number of reasons, such as closing of operations by employers and sectoral shifts in jobs. A variety of tools must be used, such as the benefits and programs of the employment insurance regime, to counter both the real and attitudinal barriers to retaining older people in the workforce. Without such efforts, abolishing mandatory retirement may appear to be a response to the needs of older workers while doing little to alter the underlying reality with which seniors cope as they attempt to continue in the workforce. The employment insurance regime may be satisfactory for middle-aged males, especially of middle income, but it is inadequate for older, visible minority women, particularly those with low-paying positions.[42]

What is more, abolishing mandatory retirement is no substitute for the need for an adequate system of public and private pensions. The notion that, because individuals have a right to work in old age, they can and should do so, with no or reduced need for pensions, is a myth that needs to be exploded. Yet, this is an idea that market gurus are spreading. They wring their hands at the fiscal burden of the pension system. The solution? People should continue to work: "fixed retirement ages for people in reasonable physical and mental condition may have been abolished to prevent the pensions burden on the working population from becoming unbearable."[43] I return below to a discussion of the central role of public pensions in the financial life of many seniors.

Or consider health care. There can be discrimination against seniors regarding access to a full range of medical services. For instance, Ontario's Court of Appeal held that the ministry's Assistance Devices Program could not restrict the provision of closed-circuit television magnifiers only to persons under the age of twenty-five. A seventy-one-year-old man had been refused this visual aid.[44] In another instance, the Ontario Human Rights Commission has started a complaint against the government and its contractor for using age-based criteria in the provision of certain assistive devices.[45]

Such denial of services based on age, when done on a discriminatory basis, needs to be rooted out. Again, however, the larger context is vital. Many older adults may be more concerned about having unwanted medical technology imposed on them in a way that prolongs life when there is no longer the possibility of any quality.[46] The health care community needs to be reassured that following the clear wishes of individuals concerning the cessation of treatment does not constitute discriminatory behaviour. Beyond the issues of the wishes of individual older adults concerning treatment are larger issues of rationing scarce medical resources. In specific situations there may be rational and defensible reasons for not aggressively treating seniors.[47] There has to be room for careful debate and discussion about these issues without charges of discrimination being hurled at those who would contemplate such questions.

Third, the human rights approach, with its focus on burdens, does not address the full range of issues affecting the lives of older adults. An excessive focus on rights can blind us to the various ways law interacts with the lives of seniors. To the point, society does not just burden seniors. It benefits them in important ways, very prominently through the pension system, backed by law that has been erected over the last several decades. We should be proud of the pension system and its capacity to better the lives of seniors. At the same time, its costs and the implications for other generations are important issues needing to be addressed. The human rights approach has comparatively little to say about the need to balance the claims of different groups. I return to a discussion of the pension system, below.

Here let's look at an example of the blinders that extravagant rights claiming can place on policy analysis. The Ontario Human Rights Commission in 2001 published a report on human rights and older adults.[48] There is much to admire in the report; its work is cited throughout this chapter. It documents the prevalence of ageist attitudes and discriminatory treatment in many areas, including employment, housing, health care, and elder abuse.[49] It makes a number of useful recommendations to respond to such prejudice. For example, it highlights the five principles on ageing developed by the National Framework on Aging, an initiative of the Ministers Responsible for Seniors throughout Canada.[50] These principles are dignity, independence, fairness, participation, and security. It recommends that these principles be integrated into the policies of both the public and private sector.[51]

Yet, the report illustrates how restricted rights analysis can be. A right is highlighted and deficiencies involving the right are documented. Indignation at the affronts then takes over. The solutions proposed are driven mostly by an unqualified vindication of the right, with little regard for the implications for other interests or even other rights. The report makes no real mention of the many ways society supports older adults, including through the pension system. Here are but two examples of the blinders.

First, the report does a good job in describing the difficulties many older adults have in accessing the health care system and related services. Yet, one of its "commitments" is to communicate with various medical organizations "to advise that unequal access to medical treatment and other health care services on the basis of age or disability may constitute discrimination."[52] This is a broadside.

Yes, there can be discrimination on the basis of age or disability and the denial of such services. Conversely, many older adults live in fear that medical treatment will be forced on them simply because it is available, at a point when there is no longer any quality of life. There can be defensible and humane reasons for not aggressively treating older adults in certain circumstances. Many believe that it would be inhumane to aggressively treat a patient for cancer who is otherwise suffering with advanced Alzheimers. Yes, we want to protect against discrimination. But we need nuanced discussions about what constitutes inappropriate care in these circumstances. The idea must not take hold that medical organizations need always treat older adults, even against a senior's will and even when to do so could painfully prolong the inevitable; otherwise, they will have violated a right.

Second, the report, in discussing access to medical services, takes up the issue of dental care. It mentions several organizations' insistence that the "cost associated with dental care [is] a significant barrier for older persons."[53] This is undoubtedly an accurate statement, at least for seniors of modest means. But what is critical and entirely omitted from the report is acknowledgment of the fact that it is a correct observation for all persons of modest means, most prominently children. Many are persuaded that the place to begin innovations leading to universal dental care is not at the aged end of the spectrum but with kids. They will probably cost less to start (maintaining young, healthy teeth is cheaper than fixing old, bad ones) and will have much greater long-term benefits. It can also be strongly contended that children, in modest circumstances not in any way of their making, have the greater moral claim.[54] But once the rights machine is cranked up, a claim must be completely satisfied. Other interests are sidelined; in this instance, they are not even mentioned.

The Law, the Policies It Backs, and Conquering Poverty among Seniors

Over the last decades the law has created a system of public and private pensions that has greatly improved the lives of older adults. That system provides an excellent example of the capacity that representative politics still has to forge and implement policies that respond to major social problem; in this case poverty among senior citizens.

The Supreme Court understands the importance of the policies that have been put in place. In the 1990s it turned back an attack by rights advocates that could have seriously undermined the pension system. Now, market celebrants are busy undermining support for the concept of retirement. We're knowledge workers. We can go until we drop. Retirement is an artifact of industrial societies; it should disappear along with so many other aspects of those societies. Why the need for public pensions?

Economic Dignity in the Autumn of Life

Older adults usually do have lower incomes than adults in other age groups. These lower incomes are offset to some extent by the lower expenses seniors often have: mortgages have been paid off, any children are financially independent, there may be no work-related expenses, and so forth. Thus, older adults may have larger disposable incomes.[55]

In any event, the financial situation of seniors has improved markedly in the recent past. The incomes of older adults have grown faster than that of other age groups in the last two decades. If inflation is taken into account, the average income of seniors rose 22 percent between 1981 and 1998; for those between the ages of sixteen and sixty-four during the same period, the increase was a mere 2 percent.[56] The increase for older adults is mostly attributable to developments in public pensions and the private retirement income system that have been put in place by the political and legal process over the last several decades.

Over the last two decades, the rate of low incomes among older adults has declined substantially. Much progress has been made toward the alleviation of poverty among senior citizens. In 1980, 21 percent of seniors had after-tax income below Statistics Canada's low income cut-off (LICO), or poverty line. By 1999, this figure was only 8 percent. Low-income rates among older adults in Canada are among the lowest of all OECD countries.[57] Nevertheless, poverty among older adults can still be a problem in this country. Unattached older adults, particularly women, are more likely to experience low income than those in families. This poverty is attributable to the fact that women have generally had less involvement in the labour force and, when involved, have had lower wages than men.[58]

As indicated, much of the improved financial situation of seniors is attributable to the maturing of the system of public and private pensions that operates at three levels. The system is mostly governed by federal legislation. It generally serves our society very well. The OECD rates the Canadian system highly on income adequacy, equity, and affordability.[59]

The first level of the system is the publicly funded Old Age Security (OAS). The OAS provides a basic pension (adjusted for inflation) to almost everyone over age sixty-five who has lived in Canada for a required length of time. For those who have high incomes, all or part of the OAS may be clawed back through the tax system.[60] Included in the OAS is the income-tested and therefore targeted Guaranteed Income Supplement (GIS).[61] The GIS provides extra money to OAS recipients who have little or no other income; about 35 percent of those receiving the OAS also receive the GIS in whole or in part.[62]

The second level of the pension system is the earnings-based Canada and Quebec pension plans (CPP/QPP). These plans provide a retirement pension, generally at age sixty-five, to those individuals who have contributed to the CPP or QPP. Seniors may choose to take the pension as early as age sixty or later than age sixty-five, with appropriate actuarially adjusted benefits.[63] Concerns were expressed in the 1990s that the CPP and QPP were becoming fiscally unviable. Governments have responded to these issues and the plans are now sound. Further adjustments to the age of entitlement may need to be made because of the growing numbers that are electing to take their benefits at age sixty.[64]

The third level comprises private plans: occupational or employer sponsored pension plans (RPPs), registered retirement savings plans (RRSPs), and deferred profit sharing plans (DPSPs). The federal government does provide tax assistance on savings in these plans up to specified limits and subject to certain constraints based on age. RRSPs are available to everyone with eligible income, although they tend to be used by those with higher incomes who have the means to make the contributions and to obtain the deduction.[65]

Yet, a large portion of contribution room in RRSPs remains unused; people are not contributing as much as they are allowed to. This unused contribution room, combined with high levels of personal debt for some segments of the population, has raised concerns that a portion of affluent Canadians may face a marked decline in their standard of living during retirement.[66] There are also concerns about the implications of any downturn in the stock market and, consequently, the viability of employer-sponsored pension plans.[67]

The pension system uses age as a marker in several ways. For instance, sixty-five generally is the triggering age for entitlement to the OAS, GIS, and CPP or QPP. Age is also used, in combination with need, as a criterion of eligibility for GIS, in whole or in part, and to determine entitlement and whether the clawback provisions of the tax system will apply to the OAS. The CPP and QPP depart from the rigidity of age sixty-five as the "magic" age of entitlement by allowing recipients to access lower payments at any time after sixty or to have higher payments by deferring the pension to sometime after sixty-five; the amount of such higher or lower payments is based on actuarial determinations.

The Supreme Court Understands the Issues

This book in several places has warned against over reliance on rights, particularly judicialized ones. In a democracy committed to the welfare of all citizens, we privilege courts and denigrate representative politics at our peril. But it is a mistake to cast the judges as power-hungry marauders. The *Charter* has given them a job; most courts are struggling to do a good one. An important instance of the Supreme Court steering through various extravagant depictions of the right to equality comes to us from the pension context.

Generally, the courts have approved of using age as a marker in the public pension system. For example, under the CPP and QPP, full benefits are paid to surviving spouses over age forty-five, partial benefits are paid to those between thirty-five and forty-five, and no benefits are paid to those under thirty-five. Such distinctions based on age were upheld by the Supreme Court of Canada in *Law v. Canada* as being justified within the overall scheme of the plans.[68]

Nancy Law was a thirty-year-old widow with no children. Hers was a sympathetic story: besides losing her husband, she had also lost their business.

Under the CPP, she was entitled to receive a survivor's pension from her husband's CPP only if she was older than forty-five, was disabled, or had children. She sued based on age discrimination under section 15 of the *Charter* and the right to equality.

The Court held that the scheme clearly denied a benefit on the basis of age but that that distinction was not one violating section 15. To rise to the level of a *Charter* violation, any distinction not only discriminates but does so in a way that is a "violation of human dignity." In this instance, the legislation did not "stereotype, exclude, or devalue adults under 45." Nor have adults under age forty-five "been consistently and routinely subjected to the sorts of discrimination faced by some of Canada's discrete and insular minorities." Rather, the government had used an "informed generalization," not a stereotype, to conclude that within the scheme of the CPP and QPP, young, able-bodied, and childless survivors did not require a pension.[69]

Rights enthusiasts were indignant at what they viewed as indifference to the plight of Ms. Law and an excessively cautious approach to what constitutes violations of section 15.[70] Yet, the Court's approach is an attractive one not only in terms of these pension issues but with regard to equality generally. It may be that the CPP and QPP scheme should be revisited on a number of fronts. However, its main purpose is to allow working people to provide for a minimum standard of financial security in their old age over and above the OAS and GIS. Any adjustments to that scheme for other purposes would need to be done bearing that central goal in mind and would involve a number of difficult trade-offs.

More generally, the approach in *Law* does allow the courts to engage in searching examinations of the implications of violations of equality, particularly concerning disadvantage. The approach also permits legislatures to make the many reasonable distinctions they need to in order to forge and implement myriad policies, including those designed to achieve some measure of equality for all citizens.

Arbitrariness Is Regrettable – but a Universal Pension Scheme Is Good

Using age as a marker in the CPP and QPP is justified, even though certain arbitrariness does result. A fifty-nine-year-old individual, dependent on the welfare schemes of a province, may have a lower income than a sixty-six-year-old in the same province who is in similar conditions. The difference may be attributable to the latter having reached the "magic" age of sixty-five and, therefore, being entitled to benefit from the federal OAS and GIS. Such arbitrariness may be a necessary by-product of the federal scheme: there has to be some clear point where the federal system of public pensions begins to confer benefits. Any efforts to address the arbitrariness should not result in lowering benefits that are otherwise attained through the federal system.

People do not become eligible for the GIS just because they turn sixty-five – age as a marker. They become eligible because they are sixty-five and of lower income – age as a marker combined with need. Because of the effects of the GIS and OAS in improving the standard of living for low-income adults, some have argued that it is arbitrariness of another kind to wait to confer such benefits until the "magic" age of sixty-five and, conversely, to withhold them for those who need them but who are not yet sixty-five. They make an important point about the rigidity of the public pension system and the way that age as a marker obscures the more important criterion of need. The general implication is to assert that need, not age or other criteria, should be used to create a coordinated system of income maintenance throughout a person's life.[71]

This suggestion has much force. It gives rise to a host of issues, however. How would the revamped OAS and GIS be coordinated with the provincial systems of welfare benefits? The predecessor programs of the OAS and GIS were initiated by the federal government in the 1950s to address the patchwork of provincial provisions for old age pensions. A strong federal presence in this regime is essential. Would the revamping of the system weaken that presence? Moreover, when it was initiated, the old age pension, as it was called at that time, started only at age seventy. The age limit was then lowered to sixty-five. However arbitrary sixty-five as a marker may seem, its use brought important benefits, at a younger age, to older adults.

Are Government Pensions a Public Good? What Is Intergenerational Justice? Are We Socially Cohesive?

The effectiveness of the pension system in alleviating poverty among seniors is clear and is a major achievement. But pensions are costly, and the cost of the public aspect has sparked predictable debates about the desirability of these specific governmental programs.

Senior OAS and GIS benefits and related minor programs constitute the largest federal income security expenditures. Total expenditures rose from $16.0 billion in 1980-81 to $23.7 billion in 1998-99 and were projected to reach $26.2 billion by 2003-4.[72] The relentless rise in the benefits during the 1990s was all the more striking in light of deep cuts to many other social programs during that same period.[73]

Those who support governmental pensions and the retirements they fund tend to characterize them as public goods. As such they should be assessed not just for their costs but for the benefits they bestow. Evaluations of pensions should not be driven by some extravagant notion of efficiency and, in any event, should take full account of the contribution to social justice these programs make.[74]

In contrast, those concerned with the cost of pensions tend to assess them based on claims of intergenerational justice. Discussions of intergenerational justice can encompass many issues, including the responsibilities of present generations to future ones to protect the environment. Often, though, the focus of concerns is the financial strain that older adults may be placing on a variety of programs, such as the pension system, health care, and social and community services.

In the end, the future of public pensions may be wrapped up in the fate of social cohesion. Social cohesion is a much-used term that has taken on a variety of meanings. It has received official status in many Western countries, at least at an abstract level.[75] Its basic thrust is to acknowledge market-driven economies while insisting on the value of "solidarity and mutual support" among citizens.[76] Although there are all sorts of questions about the role for governments in achieving social cohesion, there is an assumption that governments should be key participants. Even a modestly ambitious concept of social cohesion can embrace public pensions and retirement as an important means of demonstrating that there needs to be some modicum of economic dignity in the autumn of life for Canada's older citizens.

The idea that an ageing population can lead to negative fiscal consequences originated in the United States in both academic writing and political action. Some academic writings tended to extreme assertions, such as that the ageing population would cause such burdens on the health care system that all sorts of treatment should be rationed or even withheld from older adults. Political action on these issues has taken a variety of forms, including AGE (Americans for Generational Equity), a lobby group arguing for reforms to social policy characterized as privileging older adults at the expense of youth.[77]

Inflammatory positions aside, the intergenerational justice approach is an important vehicle for assessing valid concerns about the costs of programs benefiting older adults and the impact these costs and programs have on other generations. Such concerns may be part of general reservations about government support of social programs. Those who broadly favour such expenditures may also have more specific concerns. For example, they may applaud the system of public pensions and urge even more action to alleviate poverty among older adults. They may also be concerned about the increasing number of children in poverty, individuals at the other end of the age spectrum. Giving people some economic dignity at the end of their life is noble; rescuing a starving child from the trap of destitution may be nobler still.

The intergenerational justice approach presents a set of competing considerations and questions. On the one hand, programs that benefit older adults are largely paid for by younger generations. These payments are being made by fewer people and, in some cases, people with less money. As the population ages there will be comparatively fewer younger people to support these programs. In recent decades the youngest of these workers have either made less or, at best, made the same as their counterparts of twenty years ago.[78] Will these programs continue to be financially viable? Will younger people have paid for these programs, only to see them curtailed or even dismantled as they approach old age?; "already[,] young and middle-age people at work suspect that there will not be enough pension money to go round when they themselves reach traditional retirement age."[79]

Further, differences in economic status among seniors could become an important element in responding to issues affecting the lives of older adults, particularly those involving public benefits. Already, entitlement to the benefits of the public pension system is based not only on age but also on need. Older adults of higher economic status qualify for benefits in terms of age. But the amount of their incomes disqualifies them from receiving the GIS at all, and a portion of them may have all or part of the OAS clawed back. As more affluent people reach old age, they will realize that they are benefiting only partially or not at all from the public pension system. Increasingly, they may join the ranks of those questioning the system and its costs; "the sweeping of seniors into a single 'similar circumstance' category may be distinctly inappropriate. This further disadvantages seniors who are already disadvantaged, widening the polarization within this generation."[80]

On the other hand, older adults need to be given greater credit for their past and continuing contributions. Such contributions reciprocate for the benefits seniors receive. Up to old age, seniors work, honour family obligations, and create and implement programs in the public, private, and voluntary sectors that benefit the economy and society generally. Older adults continue to contribute by some participation in the workforce, and by supporting their children, families, friends, and neighbours. Seniors have high levels of charitable giving, engage in an impressive rate of volunteer activity, and support all public programs, not just the ones from which they benefit, by paying taxes.

What is more, we need to consider the overall costs to society of a variety of programs, not just those benefiting older adults. True, the costs of health care and pensions may increase as the population ages, but other costs, such as education, may decrease. There can be shifts within budgets to accommodate rising demands in some areas by taking account of falling demands in others: "population aging is not itself a 'crisis,' nor does it cause one; it is one aspect of a whole set of changes in our society."[81]

The intergenerational justice approach emphasizes the social policy context of the relevant issues. The implications of responding to a specific problem in a particular way are more fully assessed; attention is directed to more far-ranging consequences for society in general. Thus is paved the way for deep questioning of the concept of retirement.

Retirement and its funding lies at the core of discussions about the benefits and costs of our public pension system. The social history of retirement is long and involved. Suffice it to say here that an important aspect of it was to allow workers to leave the labour market as their physical capacity to do jobs diminished. This ending of labour was to be supported by a pension scheme that provided for some level of economic means in old age. Gradually, the pension scheme, supported by governments, expanded and came to apply to almost all older adults. But the world has changed. Ours is now a postindustrial society, with knowledge as its inexhaustible resource. In the era of globalizing markets and the growth of knowledge-based jobs requiring no physical labour, how do we view the idea of retirement?

Is retirement, as some have argued, an outmoded concept as we become a society of knowledge workers? Is retirement an artifact from fading industrial societies where labour was much more physical and workers wore out? If the answer to these questions tends to be "yes," the case for retirement and the role for the state in its funding through the public pension system and otherwise is seriously undermined. Take note of the following comments, in a Canadian bestseller on demographic shifts, about how our clinging to the concept of retirement has become little more than government discouraging people from working: "Retirement was a 19th century invention that is becoming outmoded ... it was invented in the 1880s by ... Bismarck to help quell revolutionary fervor. Now it has become a system in which the state pays people not to work, including quite a few who don't need the money and who would rather keep working."[82]

Some see the dark hand of "apocalyptic demography" in the attack on pensions. Those who are philosophically antagonistic to a strong public sector use the threat of an ageing population as a battering ram against a range of programs, including pensions: "population aging, because it is perceived as a threat, is used as a political weapon for attacking public social programs, for urging cutbacks in entitlements, and for promoting private-sector methods."[83] There is a point here. Saluters of the market are stark in their predictions that, as the population ages, the world will fully embrace knowledge work. Pensions will significantly decrease.[84] There will be little need for them among a population that celebrates this new labour: "by 2030 at the latest, the age at which full retirement benefits start will have risen to the mid-70s in all developed countries, and benefits for healthy pensioners will be substantially lower than they are today."[85]

In contrast, does the concept of retirement continue to embody our collective aspirations about old age? Do we hope that people in the later years of life, whether knowledge workers or otherwise, will be freed from the demands of employment, have some basic level of financial security, and know others and themselves through more than their identities as workers? If the answers to these questions tend to be "yes," then we see retirement as a public good, like education and health care. We believe that government, including through public pensions, should play an important role in maintaining its quality. As with so many other areas, comparisons are made between this nation and the United States: "The highly individualistic nature of the United States promotes an apocalyptic view of the nature of population aging: conflict ... against a backdrop of shrinking resources is seen as nearly inevitable ... in Canada, by contrast, aging tends to be a more social issue, with the government response embodying collectivist principles set forth in such policies as universal health insurance. Greater reliance on social solutions defuses the apocalyptic aura of aging."[86]

We shall see. Yes, there is a lot of talk about the need for social cohesion and how it is compatible, even essential, for an economically competitive society. Yet, achieving social cohesion costs. Public money needs to be spent wisely and accounted for rigorously. But it will need to be spent on the schools, the hospitals, the environment, and the social welfare programs that give people true opportunities. The test for social cohesion is not whether it is applauded as a concept. The test will be in its realization for ordinary people in their everyday lives, with government and public resources playing a vital role.[87] There is, of course, room for debate on how best to deploy those resources for the benefit of older adults and Canadian society generally.[88] A big challenge will be to preserve the economic dignity of older citizens over the next decade. Can even more be rescued from poverty?

Conclusion

Getting older is nothing new. It has forever been part of our common humanity. But now, more of us are ageing at a time of rapid transformation. The boomers, far removed from being babies, are demanding attention be paid to issues affecting seniors.

Older adults are concerned with their rights. As well they should be. There are many instances of infringements or at least insensitivity in the lives of seniors. They are enmeshed in stereotypes, and contradictory ones at that: they are living lives of comparative luxury and care little for the rest of society; they are a growing burden to families and communities, siphoning off scarce resources. Matters get worse when old age is added to other forms of disadvantage – disability, race, economic status, and so forth.

Even the market has been a laggard in responding to the needs of older citizens. Enterprise itself seems captive of distorted images of the ageing that prevent it from adequately responding to this growing market. Things could change quickly; the market can sometimes rapidly respond after an initial stalling. Right now, though, greying consumers are being treated as mostly frail and stingy.

Representative politics has been attentive to the economic needs of seniors. The system of pensions that has been put in place has lowered levels of destitution among older adults. We now have one of the lowest levels of poverty among the ageing of all OECD countries. This is an important achievement. It demonstrates that government is still capable of forging and implementing responses to widespread and serious social problems. It stands in marked contrast to all the hand-wringing over the incapacity of dishevelled politics to achieve the common good.

Our treatment of seniors over the next years will teach us a great deal about rights and benefits, choice and obligations. As a society we need to continue to support seniors according to need. The efforts of free marketeers to curb pensions and other public goods need to be blunted. At the same time, older adults and their advocates must realize that a good civic society cannot be achieved only through rights claiming. Perhaps it is appropriate to end on a note of reciprocity. May older adults continue to enjoy their economic safety net. May they use their time and energy to enrich other members of the society that expends significant resources to support them.

Conclusion: "The Dance of Adjustment"

A Changing Canada

Our society is different from that of only a couple of decades ago. Change is all about. So is the idea of change. Tradition, continuity, and custom are, mostly, suspect words. Institutions, whether religious or secular, are scarcely more than tolerated, and only so long as they respond to current demands.

Some things remain the same. The search for accommodation between Quebec and the rest of Canada and the rivalries among regions are ever-present issues. The plight of the First Peoples is a sobering constant. There are current variations to these intractables. At the present moment, "the distinct society" does seem more inclined to chart its course within Confederation. Whatever the permutations, these issues are with us and will be for a long time to come.

Nevertheless, our society, in many critical aspects, scarcely resembles the one of just a few decades earlier. Canada has become more diverse and tolerant of many kinds of difference. We are less deferential to authority and to hierarchy. Canadians have become deeply skeptical of government in their lives. We are much more open to the market producing and distributing all manner of things. Judges not so long ago were older, white, able-bodied, straight men. Now they are a group that increasingly reflects and celebrates difference as they enjoy high levels of confidence from a public that is otherwise suspicious of almost anyone who exercises power.

We have become more inclusive. The lives of women, of the disabled, of visible minorities, and other excluded groups enjoy a range of possibilities scarcely contemplated fifty years ago. A two-page story in a national newspaper in 2003 trumpeted "Canada's top 25 women lawyers – at the top of their game."[1] The notion that women should be an integral part of the legal profession, let alone at the highest echelons, would have been dismissed as girlish babble thirty years ago – about the time that many of the "25" were contemplating a career in law. More does need to be done to open up opportunities.

Yet, such work will go forward on a foundation of greater religious, racial, and sexual tolerance and on an insistence that this is a society open to all who would live in peace.

We are more outward looking, taking part in the momentous forces pushing globalization. The economy has become more responsive to international forces with competitiveness, productivity, and innovation the watchwords. The role of government in the market has become more circumscribed. Policies have been reconfigured on various fronts: infrastructure, research, education, labour market programs (such as unemployment benefits), and so forth. This society is becoming even more a part of an international one, whether in terms of human rights, alarms about the growing rates of obesity, the combating of AIDS, pop stars as cultural icons, or the horrors of terrorism. Cyberspace has spelled the "death of distance."[2] Arnprior and Bangalore are thousands of kilometres apart; they are linked by the click of a mouse. Once it was insisted that this country had "too much geography."[3] In virtual reality, Dartmouth and Coquitlam are in the same place, in the same time.

We are more rights oriented. If we need proof that ideas do matter to a society, the ascendance of rights is surely evidence. Rights consciousness can claim a good portion of the credit for the increasing inclusiveness and tolerance of the last decades. The ideal of rights is noble. The uncritical acceptance of rights claims is not. A lack of curiosity about the actual effects of rights, particularly those produced by litigation, is irresponsible when developing public policy. Rights' role in the combating of discrimination of excluded minorities should mostly be praised. The success of rights in bettering the lives of First Peoples is debatable. Rights claiming to underwrite the cost of nonreligious private education is shameful.

In the fall of 2003 *The Economist,* not an easy touch when it comes to this country, pronounced us "rather cool."[4] It had taken a fancy to what it saw as our social liberalism (it cited gay marriage and decriminalization of marijuana) and our governments' fiscal austerity. Canada, to be sure, has much to be complimented on. Yet, within a week of *The Economist* editorial, the Conference Board of Canada issued its report comparing this nation with twenty-three other leading industrial countries.[5] Canada ranked high in economic performance (third). However, its ratings on several health and social measures were below those of many other countries (ninth and tenth). We ranked even more poorly on environmental indicators (sixteenth).[6] Among the social measures for which Canada's ranking was weak was child poverty (twelfth). Our dismal record on poor kids was, again, on display.

There were those who were quick to bask in *The Economist*'s editorial.[7] After all, a sentinel of laissez-faire had bestowed its approval on the land. Will this be our fate in the new century: "cool" achieved by embracing a bounding rights culture allied with doses of market libertarianism?

Courts, Politics, and Markets in a Transforming Society

As Canadian society has changed, so too have three of its main institutions. In the society that was, representative politics played a central role. Even as that politics was of critical importance, it was diverse. True, liberalism was the prime ideology. But it was enriched and challenged by Toryism and social democracy. Liberalism's individualism was everywhere expressed – but within the community. Even Canada's "Conservatives" were "Progressive." Politics of the 1950s and 1960s enjoyed sufficient popular support to create great civic projects: universal health care, more public universities, the enhancement of the social safety net, efforts to protect the environment, and so forth. Politics was confident that it could respond to the challenges faced by the society through the "dance of adjustment."[8]

Economic competition was less robust than it should have been. Nevertheless, markets were assigned a central role in wealth creation. But they were not seen as central in the fashioning of responses to many important social issues. Courts were respected, but few regarded them as institutions that should forge and implement responses to public policy questions. Judges were to resolve civil disagreements that those in conflict could not settle themselves, enforce the criminal law, and be the referees of federal and provincial constitutional authority.

In the last decades, the roles of the three institutions changed dramatically. The big loser was representative politics. The public's lack of confidence in legislators and their agents increased noticeably. Indicators reflecting that decline were all too numerous. By 2002, 69 percent of respondents to a poll agreed with the assertion that government was corrupt.[9] There were any number of reasons for such deterioration, including the failed efforts at constitutional reform, the rise of the new right, the complexities of forging consensus because of all manner of diversity, and concentration of power in government, particularly at the federal level. Not so long ago, John Kenneth Galbraith claimed that "the greatest Canadian achievement has been in the conduct and purposes of government."[10] As the new century dawns, that assertion is greeted with mostly a mixture of puzzlement and derision.

At about the same time that the fortunes of representative politics were sagging, the role of markets took on greater importance. Markets expanded because of a number of factors, including globalization, the need to address public debts and deficits, the ideology of the right, technology (mostly the Internet), and various policies in the United States, Canada's biggest trading partner. Beyond such factors, the language of markets became woven into the larger society, influencing ways of thought, behaviour, and policy making. Ours had become "the efficient society"[11]; so much so that one of our leading public intellectuals warned that "the cult of efficiency" was coming to dominate public policy making.[12] Meanwhile, the clamouring for Choice was all about – whatever the reality of most people's lives.

The biggest winner in terms of changing roles was the courts. The *Charter* and the enhanced powers given to judges were central to the growth of curial influence. At the same time, law, generally, became more pervasive and other types of litigation, such as class actions, became important. Rights talk in the courts but also in the legislatures, the media, and the streets became pervasive. It was also often extravagant. It compared the *Charter* to Pasteur's discoveries, urged "litigating the values of a nation," and asserted that judges are the "custodians of the *Charter*." The future of the country hinged on entrenched rights: "as the *Charter* evolves so evolves Canada."[13]

The effects of rights talk and claiming, particularly in the courts, were another matter. The United States is the society with the longest and most intense experience with using courts and rights to address complex issues. There, progressives hoped that lawsuits would bring about change that could not be achieved through the political system. Examination of the evidence suggests such aspirations have largely been misplaced.[14] *Brown v. Board of Education*[15] and its judicial denunciation of "separate but equal" in education has been hailed in this country as a "moral supernova in civil liberties adjudication that ... almost single-handedly justifies [constitutionalized rights adjudication]."[16] *Brown v. Board of Education* was noble in its aspiration. The consequences of the trail of lawsuits and other developments thereafter is a different matter. Costly and prolonged litigation involving battles over desegregation, busing orders, and other judicial fiats embittered parents of all races, perpetuated a dysfunctional public school system, and, paradoxically, may have resulted in at least as much separation of black and white children as existed before the intense efforts at desegregation began.

Nonetheless, it was clear that people in Canada during the last decades were witnessing sea change in the judicial role. Generally, they liked what they saw. In 2001 a poll indicated that respondents were concerned about the partisanship of the judges. That said, 91 percent indicated that they had a great deal or fair amount of respect for the judiciary in this society.[17] A 91 percent confidence rating for courts as 69 percent believe government is corrupt reflects the dramatic polarities that had formed in the public's views of these two institutions.[18]

Good Government? Good Citizens?

In the summer and fall of 2003, several articles appeared in the *New York Times* about the newly established right of gays and lesbians to marry in Canada.[19] One of these articles focused on the fact that, while this new right was deeply controversial, debate about it was largely free of the rancour and bitterness that characterizes exchanges on so many topics in the republic. The journalist, surely mindful of his American audience, suggested that Canada is a country "where compromise, consensus and civility are the most cherished political values."[20] Good attributes, and quite probably in greater evidence here than in the United States. Do we have the collective wisdom to hold on to these fine characteristics, even increase their influence? Or will we see them dissipate as the new century unfolds?

There has been a resurgence in the concept of the citizen in recent years, including in Canada.[21] Such renewed "critical" interest is understandable as ideas about the citizen respond to the many changes in societies.[22] Much of the writing has been at a philosophical level as various theoretical understandings of the concept are advanced.[23] This book has focused on how our ideas about the citizen are being altered as the roles of representative politics, courts, and markets are changing so substantially over a comparatively brief period in this nation's history. A summing up here of the main points about such alterations and these changes may be helpful.

The founding words of this society were "peace, order, and good government." Individuals, as citizens, were involved in a complicated relationship with the state. Their individual and collective welfare was achieved not in isolation from government but, rather, as a part of it. The connections of individuals with their governments through representative politics now seem much more tentative. The explanation that Michael Schudson would give, at least based on his observations of American society, is that we have all become rights bearers as the defining element of the citizen: "rights-consciousness place[s] the courtroom along-side the polling place in the practice of public life."[24] Schudson's bold assertion characterizes what at least Americans have arrived at: "rights and rights-consciousness have become the continuous incitements to citizenship in our time."[25]

Our situation is nuanced. Many of those seeking an enlarged role for rights and courts correctly argue that we are less engulfed by them than are Americans. Their assertions are accurate in many ways. Judges and rights advocates can point to the dialogue between the judiciary and the legislatures about the best way to recognize both the promise of rights and their limits in forging the common good in a democracy. Such dialogue is to bolster the role for representative politics, in an age of rights, in making decisions about fundamental values in the life of the nation. Canada's record over the last decades in lowering the rate of poverty among older adults to one of the lowest among OECD countries is an important example of the force that representative politics retains in the quality of life of this society's citizens, including its seniors. This success in providing basic economic dignity to many older adults demonstrates that we retain a commitment to using "good government" to nurture fundamental aspects of the citizen. We are approaching the era where the essence of the citizen is rights-regarding, but we are not there yet.

The issues we face have not arisen, primarily, because we have the *Charter* and an enhanced role for judges. The issues that confront us arise because we have the *Charter*, more judicial power, and more rights talk even as the market has an expanded role in our lives and faith in representative politics' capacity to forge the common good has receded. The problem is with the myth of exit. The market, courts, and cyberspace are hailed as alternatives that can be turned to as the populace increasingly resiles from representative politics and the hard task of its rehabilitation.

Courts, markets, and the Internet have important roles in the making of the good citizen. Cyberspace exploits knowledge, the inexhaustible resource, with its infinite capacity, properly used, to better our individual and collective lives. Markets create wealth: a reward for individual striving and innovation and a precondition for the realization and distribution of the common goods that support citizens in fashioning their lives. Courts, buttressed by public trust, are bastions for fundamental freedoms. The problem is thinking that courts, markets, and cyberspace are alternatives for many of the tasks of representative politics.

Disturbing fables are being propagated about the Internet. The Internet's greatest political contribution may be to those who must struggle in countries to have democracy take hold. The Net may be a formidable weapon deployed against oppression in societies where ordinary means of public dissent are stifled.[26] The Internet bettering democracy in Canada will be a challenge. The information that is available about Canada and other countries, especially the United States, suggests that the Internet is not a catalyst for fundamental democratic change. In some ways, this lack of transformation is decidedly to the good. Prophecies that the Net will lead to disintermediation and direct democracy are frightening in their implications.

Lesser claims that could be benign in their results also do not seem to be materializing. On the whole, potential for more widespread involvement, lobbying, and interaction with politicians and government officials has not been realized. What is disturbing about the Internet are the myths about it. Failing faith in traditional politics gives rise to fanciful exit strategies as disenchanted democrats look about for alternatives. Whatever the reality, fables about the transformative potential of the Net on democracy can lure citizens farther from the difficult and painstaking task of rehabilitating representative politics.

The market, joined to forces of globalization, does not lead inevitably to the atrophying of the state. The nations that trade the most have the largest budgets as a proportion of their GDPs. There is room for societies to make strategic choices about the role of governments in the lives of citizens. Borders still matter in trade; capital may not be nearly as mobile as extravagant depictions of globalization would suggest; economic growth/increased trade and protection of the environment are not fated to be opposed.

Yet, if the pursuit of efficiency dominates, will we not be at risk of believing myths about globalization inexorably leading to the hollow state? Ensuring good health care, education, a clean environment, and a decent social welfare net requires deliberate decisions and wise use of public resources. Realizing these public goods, including at an improved level, is still possible if we reject market fables. The solution to the inadequacies of public education is not to underwrite exit to private schools and to engage in untempered rights claiming. The answer lies in adequate levels of funding by government and a careful working through of the problems by our political representatives, school officials, and the community in collaborative efforts. Yet, Janice Gross Stein warns, "We no longer, as we did even three decades ago, proclaim the justice of our society, or its equity, or its excellence. The dogma is simple: efficiency grows out of competition that markets bring, and accountability comes through the survival of the fittest in the market. For the high priests of efficiency, the conversation ends here. There is nothing more to talk about."[27]

The courts, the biggest winners in institutional fortunes, have not turned out to be the regressive force that the left predicted they would be because of their enlarged role under the *Charter*. Instead, the judiciary has become more diverse because of greater strides to appoint more women and minorities. Judges are now more sensitive to the complicated role of courts with regard to social policy.

Many of the Supreme Court's decisions recognize a positive role for the state and are sympathetic to the difficult choices its agents make in carrying out programs.[28] The Court has voiced concern for the disadvantaged. That concern has been clearly demonstrated with regard to Aboriginals.[29] Meanwhile, conservative critics charge that the Court is going too far, too often, in responding to activists' agendas.[30]

Problems do not arise just from the enhanced role played by courts in this society. The source of difficulties is primarily in rights talk and its extravagant expectations, in fables about the capacity of litigation to respond to a range of complex social, political, and economic issues at a time of disarray in representative politics. Most judicial decisions concerning disadvantaged groups, when supportive of them, have mostly involved symbolic victories. The basic socioeconomic order has not been disturbed. In the case of gay and lesbian rights, the courts joined the current of history that had been for some time moving in directions favouring homosexuals.[31] One of the prime consequences of the victims' rights movement, in an age of fiscal restraint, has been to underscore the criminal law as a means of controlling crime rather than expending resources to address its root causes.[32] The Aboriginal peoples have secured some major court decisions in their favour. Yet, the assertion of rights and the insistence on nation-to-nation status, however attainable, are deflecting attention away from the increasing numbers of Native people who are exiting the tragic existence that is often led on many reserves. Their migration to cities, as they seek something better, is giving rise to a different set of issues.

At the same time, rights advocates and free marketeers have become wary allies. This confederacy was prominently on display in attacks on public education over the funding of religious schools and the underwriting of various forms of private education.[33] They may often excoriate each other's ambitions. They may occupy themselves depicting one another in negative ways. Yet, rights abounding and the market triumphant can be a potent mix sealing the fate of more temperate responses to a variety of dilemmas. A Citizens Plus approach to the problems of the First Peoples can never be realized if the polarities of a rights-driven Two Row Wampum and the forces of market assimilation occupy the field of policy choice even as they unyieldingly oppose one another.

Free marketeers and rights advocates are as one in preaching that government cannot be trusted. The free marketeers tend to paint government as wasteful and meddling. Rights advocates incline to accusations of oppression and exclusion. But both sets of charges repeatedly flash the message: Government is bad! Government is bad! The "rights-regarding citizen" and the "citizen as consumer" can frequently have different ambitions but they are in many ways aligned in their veneration of Choice.

One More Task for the Courts?

Representative politics in Canada needs rehabilitation. The central purpose of this book has been to plead that case. But how in this age of markets and this time of rights can politics and a positive role for government in people's lives be resuscitated? The momentum seems clearly in favour of markets and rights and away from politics and government. There is no quick fix; there may not even be a longer term solution. The receding of representative politics, at least as we know it, may be already too far gone. Nevertheless, here is a more hopeful scenario.

There is much talk of the "democratic deficit." Responses on offer involve everything from reforming the process of appointments to the Supreme Court of Canada;[34] to proportional representation;[35] to thoughtful, cautious proposals about the potential of cyberspace and citizen participation.[36] In Ontario, the Attorney General is also the minister responsible for "democratic renewal." A tall order. There is much to be discussed regarding these and other initiatives; they are easily the subject of another book. The point here is that if we do not bring positive attitudes to discussions of any of these possibilities, they are likely to be warped by the corrosiveness that is enfeebling politics at present.

Solutions for the disarray in representative politics must start with a reversal of attitudes. The public must, again, have the critical level of confidence in that institution that it once had. A critical step in that direction is recognizing the limits of courts and of markets. Until the public (re)embraces the idea that government has a positive role to play in their lives, almost any initiative involving legislatures and their agents is likely to be greeted by mistrust.[37]

An increase in confidence in representative politics is probably not going to come from overtures from legislators. Such admonitions, however well founded, are likely to be reacted to as special pleading. What is more, some of those of a right-wing cast are all too content to have representative politics and any kind of proactive government seen as the enemy. Disenchanted democrats, at this point, have little patience for their representatives, and even less for exhortations from them that seem ill-disguised rationalizations for a feckless institution not worthy of the public's trust.

An initial reaction might be that the market could never be the source of support for politics and for more active government. For those embracing laissez-faire, proactive government almost always spells the mangling of the market. Thus, the sagging fortunes of representative politics is viewed as mostly a good thing. A weakened politics is not likely to undertake any bold ventures, is unlikely to confront abuses of the market in the lives of citizens.

At the same time, there are many in this country who are supporters of a more robust role for markets but who retreat from such an unqualified embrace of laissez-faire. They recognize that good public goods – education, health care, a decent social safety net, protection of the environment, safeguarding of human rights – are not drags on economic progress but necessary elements of a competitive, knowledge-based economy. Such a workforce makes for good citizens in a good society. A healthy, well-educated workforce with a sense of security against economic deprivation, functioning in a clean environment, and protected in its human rights is not easily attained. Yet, it is one of the best ways to equip this society to be a leader in a globalizing economy. Achieving such a workforce requires boldness on the part of representative politics and its agents. More business leaders need to publicly and emphatically bolster such efforts.

In some ways, hope for rehabilitating politics lies with the judges. The roles of courts and politics have always been linked; they have been closely connected since the introduction of the *Charter*. The judiciary is the institution people trust the most. When judges speak, from the Chief Justice of Canada on down, people listen. Judges themselves have embraced the need for dialogue between the courts and legislatures for the realizing of fundamental values and the workings of democracy.

The courts need to go farther. If the discussion in these pages resonates with judges, I ask them to say so. They should speak out: in their judgments, in their public addresses, individually and collectively. Judges are citizens. The donning of robes does not fundamentally alter that fact. The curial office should not silence their concerns, as citizens, about this society. Justices have accepted many tasks over the last decades. Will they accept another? If so, what should they say?

They need to emphasize the limits of litigation and the boundaries of the market in tackling complex social, economic, and political issues. They ought to say that rights are essential to a free and democratic society but that rights are not enough. They should declare the critical value of good public goods. They should emphasize that they can do little to bring them about, dispelling myths that they can. They need to assert that there is no substitute – not courts, not the market – for a vibrant representative politics employing government for the common good. They should do what they can to restore such participatory democracy. They can acknowledge that the judiciary is something in which all Canadians can take pride: a brilliant ensemble. As such, they should emphasize that the orchestration for the "dance of adjustment," no matter how dissonant at times, lies elsewhere. That momentous task resides with the elected representatives of the people.

"We are in the rapids and must go on."[38]
– *D'Arcy McGee, Confederation debates, 1865*

Notes

Introduction

1 M. Schudson, *The Good Citizen: A History of American Civic Life* (New York: Free Press, 1998).
2 *Ibid.* at 273.
3 W.A. Bogart, *Consequences: The Impact of Law and Its Complexity* (Toronto: University of Toronto Press, 2002).
4 Schudson, *supra* note 1 at 8.
5 *Ibid.* at 295.
6 W.A. Bogart, *Courts and Country: The Limits of Litigation and the Social and Political Life of Canada* (Toronto: Oxford University Press, 1994).
7 Section 91 of the *Constitution Act, 1867,* admonished the powers that be to strive for "peace, order, and good government."
8 C. Epp, *The Rights Revolution: Lawyers, Activists and Supreme Courts in Comparative Perspective* (Chicago: University of Chicago Press, 1998). The phrase in the text is the title of Chapter 10 of that book. See also M. Ignatieff, *The Rights Revolution* (Toronto: House of Anansi, 2000).
9 F. Cairncross, *The Death of Distance: How the Communications Revolution Is Changing Our Lives,* 2nd ed. (Cambridge, MA: Harvard Business School, 2001).
10 D. McKenzie, "69% Say Government Corrupt" *National Post* (22 April 2002) A1, A8.
11 T. Flanagan, *First Nations? Second Thoughts* (Montreal and Kingston: McGill-Queen's University Press, 2000).
12 *Report of the Royal Commission on Aboriginal Peoples* (Ottawa: Canada Communication Group Publishing, 1996).
13 A. Cairns, *Citizens Plus: Aboriginal Peoples and the Canadian State* (Vancouver: UBC Press, 2000).
14 M. Margolis and D. Resnick, *Politics as Usual: The Cyberspace "Revolution"* (Thousand Oaks, CA: Sage Publications, 2000).
15 C. Sunstein, *Republic.com* (Princeton, NJ: Princeton University Press, 2001).
16 A. Shapiro, *The Control Revolution: How the Internet Is Putting Individuals in Charge and Changing the World We Know* (New York: Public Affairs, 1999) describes these possibilities while expressing substantial reservations.
17 Cairncross, *supra* note 9; D. Tapscott, "Outdated Democracy: We Vote, They Rule" *Globe and Mail* (27 May 2004) A21.
18 D. Gutstein, *E.con: How the Internet Undermines Democracy* (Toronto: Stoddart, 1999); R. Davis, *The Web of Politics: The Internet's Impact on the American Political System* (New York: Oxford University Press, 1999).
19 J. Hiebert, *Charter Conflicts: What Is Parliament's Role?* (Montreal and Kingston: McGill-Queen's University Press, 2002).
20 N. Des Rosiers, "Rights Are Not Enough: Therapeutic Jurisprudence Lessons for Law Reformers" (2002) 18 Touro L. Rev. 443.
21 L. Weinrib, "The Activist Constitution" in P. Howe and P. Russell, eds., *Judicial Power and Canadian Democracy* (Montreal and Kingston: McGill-Queen's University Press, 2001) 80 at 86.
22 J. Gross Stein, *The Cult of Efficiency* (Toronto: House of Anansi, 2001).

Chapter 1: Before the Transformation

1 E. Paris, *Long Shadows: Truth, Lies and History* (Toronto: Alfred A. Knopf Canada, 2000) at 1.
2 *Ibid.* at 5.
3 P. Russell, "The Political Role of the Supreme Court of Canada in Its First Century" (1975) 53 Can. Bar Rev. 576 at 593.
4 This section of the chapter is based on one of my earlier books, W.A. Bogart, *Courts and Country: The Limits of Litigation and the Social and Political Life of Canada* (Toronto: Oxford University Press, 1994); see c. 1, "Preserving Its Identity by Having Many Identities."
5 A phrase used by the late Barbara Frum even as she worried that we were losing that special ability: "My view of Canada was that you shift it around and make it work. I liked the non-explicit adjustments we were making – but now we're into a cold, crass explicit trading of advantages. We've lost that dance of adjustment." See S. Godfrey, "Frum on Frum" *Globe and Mail* (1 February 1992) C7.
6 S.M. Lipset, *Continental Divide: The Values and Institutions of the United States and Canada* (Toronto: C.D. Howe Institute and Washington, DC: National Planning Association, 1989) at 2.
7 W. Watson, "Distinct Society?" c. 15 in *Globalization and the Meaning of Canadian Life* (Toronto: University of Toronto Press, 1998) at 143.
8 M. Atwood, *The Journals of Suzanna Moodie: Poems* (Toronto: Oxford University Press, 1970) at 62.
9 Lipset, *supra* note 6 at xiv-xv.
10 L. Hartz, *The Founding of New Societies* (New York: Harcourt, Brace and World, 1969) at 34; Lipset, *supra* note 6 at 9-10, contrasts his thesis with Hartz. See also D. Bell, "The Loyalist Tradition in Canada" (May 1970) 5 Journal of Canadian Studies 22-23; and K. McRae, "Louis Hartz' Concept of the Fragment Society and Its Application to Canada" (1978) 5 Etudes Canadiennes 17-30.
11 G. Horowitz, *Canadian Labour in Politics* (Toronto: University of Toronto Press, 1968) c. 1 and 3.
12 W. Christian and C. Campbell, *Political Parties and Ideologies in Canada*, 2nd. ed. (Toronto: McGraw-Hill Ryerson, 1983) at 27-28.
13 Horowitz, *supra* note 11 at 18.
14 C. Taylor, "Can Canada Survive the Charter?" (1992) 30 Alta. L. Rev. 427 at 429.
15 For example, R. Brym with B. Fox, *From Culture to Power: The Sociology of English Canada* (Toronto: Oxford University Press, 1989) at 61-66. By contrast, see H. Forbes, "Hartz – Horowitz at Twenty: Nationalism, Toryism and Socialism in Canada and the United States" (1987) 20 Can. J. Pol. Sc. 287, reviewing the substantial literature on these ideas, evaluating the criticisms, and basically agreeing with Horowitz's contentions when linked to Canadian nationalism.
16 Taylor, *supra* note 14 at 429.
17 For the history of the development of medicare, see Commission on the Future of Health Care in Canada, "Values and How They Shape Canadians' Views," c. 3 in *Shape the Future of Health Care: Interim Report* (Saskatoon: The Commission, 2002); D. Bricker and E. Greenspon, "The Canadian Exception," c. 6 in *Searching for Certainty: Inside the New Canadian Mindset* (Toronto: Doubleday, 2001).
18 On the Socreds and former premier Bill Vander Zalm, see L. Graham, *Breach of Promise: Socred Ethics under Vander Zalm* (Madeira Park, BC: Harbour Publishing, 1991); S. Persky, *Fantasy Government: Bill Vander Zalm and the Future of the Social Credit* (Vancouver: New Star Books, 1989). On the Reform Party see S. Sharpe, *Storming Babylon: Preston Manning and the Rise of the Reform Party* (Toronto: Key Porter, 1992).
19 On the concentration of wealth in Canada into the 1980s, see *The Distribution of Wealth in Canada, 1984* (Ottawa: Statistics Canada, 1986); C. McWatters, *The Changes behind Canada's Income Distribution: Cause for Concern?* (Kingston, ON: Industrial Relations Centre, Queen's University, 1989).
20 Christian and Campbell, *supra* note 12 at 3.
21 G. Ball, *The Discipline of Power: Essentials of a Modern World Structure* (Boston: Little, Brown, 1968) at 113.
22 W. Morton, *The Canadian Identity*, 2nd ed. (Toronto: University of Toronto Press, 1972) at 131.
23 Lipset, *supra* note 6 at xiv.
24 See also Morton, *supra* note 22 at 88; and see C. Bissell, "The Place of Learning and the Arts in Canadian Life" in R. Preston, ed., *Perspectives on Revolution and Evolution* (Durham, NC:

Duke University Press, 1979) 208, arguing that novels in Canada are more a part "of European than American literature."

25 N. Frye, *The Bush Garden* (Toronto: House of Anansi, 1971).

26 M. Atwood, *Survival* (Toronto: House of Anansi, 1972).

27 J. Moss, *Patterns of Isolation* (Toronto: McClelland and Stewart, 1974) at 109.

28 Frye, *supra* note 25 at 220.

29 C. Berger, "The True North Strong and Free" in P. Russell, ed., *Nationalism in Canada* (Toronto: McGraw-Hill, 1966) at 5. See also R. Gwyn, *The 49th Paradox: Canada in North America* (Toronto: McClelland and Stewart, 1985) at 11; and see Fall 1988 issue of *Daedalus* for a series of articles about Canada.

30 J. Mitgang, "Robertson Davies, A Novelist of the North" *New York Times* (29 December 1988) 11.

31 M. Barlow and B. Campbell, *Take Back the Nation* (Toronto: Key Porter, 1991); and M. Hurtig, *The Betrayal of Canada*, 2nd ed. (Toronto: Stoddart, 1992).

32 P. Berton, *The National Dream: The Last Spike* (Toronto: McClelland and Stewart, 1974).

33 *Royal Commission on the Economic Union and Development Prospects for Canada* (Ottawa: Ministry of Supply and Services, 1985) (informally known as the Macdonald Report; named after its chair) [hereafter *Royal Commission*].

34 R. Naylor, "The Rise and Fall of the Third Commercial Empire of the St. Lawrence" in G. Teeple, ed., *Capitalism and the National Question in Canada* (Toronto: University of Toronto Press, 1972).

35 Gwyn, *supra* note 29 at 197.

36 Hurtig, *supra* note 31; and G. Laxer, *Open for Business: The Roots of Foreign Ownership in Canada* (Toronto: Oxford University Press, 1989).

37 Lipset, *supra* note 6 at 120-21, quoting Pierre Berton from the 1986 TV documentary "O Canada, Eh!"

38 Gwyn, *supra* note 29 at 221.

39 Lipset, *supra* note 6 at 133.

40 Gwyn, *supra* note 29 at 197.

41 J. Mercer and M. Goldberg, "Value Differences and Their Meaning: Urban Development in the United States," working paper no. 12, Faculty of Commerce, UBC Research in Land Economics, Vancouver, 1982, 27.

42 K. Banting, "Images of the Modern State" in K. Banting, ed., *State and Society: Canada in Comparative Perspective* (Toronto: University of Toronto Press, 1986) at 3-4.

43 Gwyn, *supra* note 29 at 222.

44 Watson, *supra* note 7.

45 Lipset, *supra* note 6 at 125.

46 R. Brym, "Canada" in T. Bottomore and R. Brym, eds., *The Capitalist Class: An International Study* (New York: New York University Press, 1989) 186.

47 S. Ostry, "Government Intervention; Canada and the United States Compared" in R. Londes, ed., *Canadian Politics: A Comparative Reader* (Scarborough, ON: Prentice-Hall Canada, 1985) 261.

48 P. Nemetz, W. Stanbery, and F. Thompson, "Social Regulation in Canada: An Overview and Comparison with the American Model" (June 1986) 14 Policy Studies Journal 594.

49 S. Lipset, "Revolution and Counter-Revolution: The United States and Canada" in T. Fond, ed., *The Revolutionary Theme in Contemporary America* (Lexington, KY: University of Kentucky Press, 1965) at 38-44.

50 *Ibid.* at 20-24.

51 S. Clark, *The Developing Canadian Community* (Toronto: University of Toronto Press, 1962) at 192-98.

52 E. McInnis, *The Unguarded Frontier* (Garden City, NY: Doubleday, Doran, 1942) at 307; Lipset, *supra* note 49 at 49-53.

53 Lipset, *supra* note 6 at 16.

54 S. Clark, "The Frontier and Democratic Theory" (1954) Transaction of the Royal Society of Canada 48, 72. See also Morton, *supra* note 22 at 105-6.

55 C. Backhouse, *Colour-Coded: History of Racism in Canada, 1900-1950* (Toronto: University of Toronto Press, 1999); C. Backhouse, "What Is Access to Justice?" in W.A. Bogart et al., eds., *The Way Forward: Access to Justice for a New Century* (forthcoming, 2005).

56 K. McRoberts, *Quebec: Social Change and Political Crisis*, 3rd ed. (Toronto: McClelland and Stewart, 1988) at 200-2.

57 Lipset, *supra* note 6 at 94 and 110-12.
58 S. Beer, "The Modernization of American Federalism" (1973) 3 Publics: The Journal of Federalism 52.
59 D. Smiley, "Public Sector Politics, Modernization and Federalism: The Canadian and American Experience" (1984) 14 Publics: The Journal of Federalism 59.
60 R. Simeon, "Some Questions of Governance in Contemporary Canada" departmental memo, School of Public Administration, Queen's University, Kingston, ON, 1987, 17; Lipset, *supra* note 6 at 194.
61 P. Boswell, "The Atlantic Provinces" in Michael Whittington and Glen Williams, eds., *Canadian Politics in the 1990s* (Toronto: Nelson, 1990) 119.
62 *Ibid.* at 125.
63 *Ibid.* at 126.
64 M. Whittington, "Canada's North in the 1990s" in Whittington and Williams, *supra* note 61.
65 *Ibid.* 35.
66 M. Marchak, "British Columbia: 'New Right' Politics and a New Geography" in Whittington and Williams, eds., *supra* note 61 at 45. See also N. Ruff, "Pacific Perspectives on the Canadian Confederation: British Columbia's Shadows and Symbols" in D. Brown, ed., *Canada: The State of the Federation 1991* (Kingston, ON: Institute of Intergovernmental Relations, 1991) 183.
67 Marchak, *ibid.* at 56.
68 D. Owram, "Reluctant Hinterland" in L. Pratt and G. Stevenson, eds., *Western Separatism: The Myths, Realities and Dangers* (Edmonton: Hurtig Publishers, 1981) as reproduced in R. Blair and J. McLeod, eds., *The Canadian Political Tradition: Basic Readings* (Toronto: Methuen Publications, 1987) at 106-7.
69 D. Smiley, *Canada in Question: Federalism in the Eighties*, 3rd ed. (Toronto: McGraw-Hill Ryerson, 1980) at 264 and 261-69.
70 *Ibid.* at 263; see also D. Smiley, *The Federal Condition* (Toronto: McGraw-Hill Ryerson, 1987) at 158-62.
71 *Ibid.* 263-64.
72 D. Elton and R. Gibbins, "Western Alienation and Political Culture" in R. Schultz et al., eds., *The Canadian Political Process,* 3rd ed. (Toronto: Holt, Rinehart and Winston of Canada, 1979) 83.
73 A. Malcolm, "Beyond Plain Vanilla: Immigration Has Accentuated Canada's Diversity" *New York Times* (8 July 1990) E2.
74 B. Etherington et al., *"Preserving Identity by Having Many Identities": A Report on Multiculturalism and Access to Justice* (Windsor: 1991) a report prepared for the Department of Justice, Canada; *Report of the Special Committee on Visible Minorities in Canadian Society: Equality Now!* (Ottawa: Supply and Services, 1984).
75 Smiley, *Canada in Question: Federalism in the Eighties*, *supra* note 69 at 215-17, and Smiley, *The Federal Condition*, *supra* note 70 at 126.
76 *Parliamentary Debates on the Subject of the Confederation of the British North American Province, 1865* (Ottawa: King's Printer, 1951) at 108.
77 Section 133 guaranteed the use of both French and English in Parliament and the Quebec legislature; section 93 gave the provinces control over education provided that they did not override rights of Protestant or Roman Catholic minorities then existing or subsequently established – particularly significant since, then, the cleavage between the English and French was seen much more in terms of religion than of language; section 94 assumed the law relating to property and civil rights in provinces other than Quebec would become uniform in a code. The section was never implemented, but its inclusion highlighted the differences that the civil code in Quebec presented.
78 Smiley, *Canada in Question: Federalism in the Eighties*, supra note 69 at 218-19; and Smiley, *The Federal Condition*, *supra* note 70 at 128.
79 When Manitoba became a province in 1870, official-language status for French and separate schools were guaranteed in the *Manitoba Act*. The Manitoba legislature passed legislation contrary to these guarantees; see J. Staples, "Consociationalism at the Provincial Level: The Erosion Of Dualism in Manitoba, 1870-1890" in K. McRae, ed., *Consociational Democracy: Political Accommodation in Segmented Societies* (Toronto: McClelland and Stewart, 1974).
80 Smiley, *Canada in Question: Federalism in the Eighties*, *supra* note 69 at 219-21.
81 *Ibid.* at 222-25.
82 H. Guindon, "The Modernization of Quebec and the Legitimacy of the Canadian State" in D. Glendon et al., eds., *Modernization and the Canadian State* (Toronto: Macmillan, 1978) 212.

83 A 1988 survey asked those in Quebec to identify themselves: "above all Québécois" was the selection of 49 percent of Quebec francophones; 39 percent chose "French Canadian," while a mere 11 percent selected "Canadian." For non-francophones the results were in the opposite direction; that is, "Canadian," 75 percent; "Québécois," 10 percent; "English Canadian," 10 percent: see "Le francophone est Québécois, l'anglophone 'Canadien'" *Le Devoir* (25 June 1988) 1.

84 N. Bradford, "Governing the Canadian Economy: Ideas and Politics" in M. Whittington, *Canadian Politics in the 21st Century* (Toronto: Nelson, 2000) 193 at 200.

85 B. Besner et al., "Ontario's Agencies, Boards, Commissions, Advisory Bodies and Other Public Institutions: An Inventory" in *Government Regulation* (Toronto: Ontario Economic Council, 1978) at 207.

86 V. Wilson and O. Dwivedi, "Introduction" in O. Dwivedi, ed., *The Administrative State in Canada: Essays in Honour of J.E. Hodgetts* (Toronto: University of Toronto Press, 1982) at 10-11.

87 *Ibid.* at 4.

88 See introduction to this chapter.

89 Wilson and Dwivedi, *supra* note 86 at 4.

90 A. Brady, "The State and Economic Life" in George W. Brown, ed., *Canada* (Berkeley: University of California Press, 1950) at 353.

91 *Ibid.*

92 V. Fowke, "The National Policy: Old and New" (1952) 18 Canadian Journal of Economics and Political Science 271.

93 W. MacKintosh, "Canadian Economic Policy: Scope and Principles" (1950) 16 Canadian Journal of Economics and Political Science at 317.

94 Wilson and Dwivedi, *supra* note 86 at 9.

95 R. Schultz, "Comments for Panel Discussion on Regulation" (1979) 4 Can. Pub. Pol'y at 486-90.

96 G. Reschenthaler, "Direct Regulation in Canada: Some Policies and Problems" in W.T. Stanbury, ed., *Studies on Regulation in Canada* (Montreal: Institute for Research on Public Policy, 1978) 37.

97 Wilson and Dwivedi, *supra* note 86 at 10.

98 Bradford, *supra* note 84 at 201 and following.

99 P. Monahan, "The Supreme Court and the Economy" in I. Bernier and A. Lajoie, eds., *The Supreme Court of Canada as an Instrument of Political Change* (Toronto: University of Toronto, 1986) at 109. See, generally, Bogart, *supra* note 4, c. 1.

100 *Ibid.*

101 B. Cheffins, "The Development of Competition Policy, 1890-1940: A Re-evaluation of a Canadian and American Tradition" (1989) 27 Osgoode Hall L.J. 449 at 470.

102 *Ibid.* at 479-80.

103 B. Dunlop et al., *Canadian Competition Policy: A Legal and Economic Analysis* (Toronto: Canada Law Book, 1987) at 280-81.

104 Cheffins, *supra* note 101 at 487-88, citing *Transport Oil Ltd. v. Imperial Oil Ltd.*, [1935] 2 D.L.R. 500 (Ont. C.A.) and *Direct Lumber Co. v. Western Plywood*, [1962] S.C.R. 646. See also *General Motors of Canada Ltd. v. City National Leasing* (1989) 93 N.R. 326 (S.C.C.).

105 *Report of the Royal Commission on the Economic Union and Development Prospects for Canada*, vol. 2 (Ottawa: Ministry of Supply and Services Canada, 1985) at 172.

106 Cheffins, *supra* note 101 at 486.

107 W. Stanbury, *Business Interests and the Reform of Canadian Competition Policy, 1971-75* (Toronto: Carswell/Methuen, 1977) at 45.

108 *Competition Tribunal Act*, S.C. 1986, c. 26, Part I, ss. 1-17, discussed in Dunlop et al., *supra* note 103 at 284-85.

109 Gwyn, *supra* note 29 at 221.

110 G. Pitts, "Porter Report Stokes Nationalistic Fires" *Financial Post* (9-11 November 1991) 1; G. Gherson, "Porter Study Takes a Chilling Look at Our Competitive Failings" *Financial Times of Canada* (28 October 1991) 7.

111 *Royal Commission*, *supra* note 33 at 220; Dunlop et al., *supra* note 103 at 59-60.

112 Bogart, *supra* note 4, c. 3, "The Forms of Litigation."

113 *Ibid.*, c. 5, "Women and the Courts: '... How Things Must Be, Forever?'"

114 Backhouse, *supra* note 55 at both sources.

115 Bogart, *supra* note 4, c. 4, "The Administrative State and Judicial Review."

116 *Ibid.*, c. 6, "The Judges and Tort: Purpose and Limit."

117   H. Arthurs, "Jonah and the Whale: The Appearance, Disappearance, and Reappearance of Administrative Law" (1980) 30 U.T.L.J. 225 at 225. Arthurs also developed this theme in more detail in his book *"Without the Law": Administrative Justice and Legal Pluralism in Nineteenth-Century England* (Toronto: University of Toronto Press, 1985).
118   Bogart, *supra* note 4, c. 7, "The Courts and Two Models of the Criminal Law."
119   K. Roach, "Judicial Activism before the *Charter*," c. 3 in *The Supreme Court on Trial: Judicial Activism or Democratic Dialogue* (Toronto: Irwin Law, 2001).
120   Bogart, *supra* note 4, c. 8, "Nation Building, Regionalism, and Federalism Litigation."
121   *Ibid.* at 6.
122   R. Fulford, "Newsletter for a Man of Letters" *Globe and Mail* (14 June 1990) A18.
123   See *supra* note 5.
124   D. McKenzie, "69% Say Government Corrupt" *National Post* (22 April 2002) A1, A8.

Chapter 2: The Ascendance of Courts

1   See Chapter 1, this volume, at 17-18; see also Chapter 4, this volume, at 89-91.
2   On federalism review, see J. Saywell, *The Lawmakers: Judicial Power and the Shaping of Canadian Federalism* (Toronto: University of Toronto Press, 2002).
3   This section draws on one of my earlier books: W.A. Bogart, "So Decried, So Demanded," c. 1 in *Consequences: The Impact of Law and Its Complexity* (Toronto: University of Toronto Press, 2002).
4   N. Bradford, "Governing the Canadian Economy: Ideas and Politics" in M. Whittington and G. Williams, eds., *Canadian Politics in the 21st Century* (Toronto: Nelson, 2000) at 193.
5   D. Vogel, "The 'New' Social Regulation in Historical and Comparative Perspective" in T. McCraw, ed., *Regulation in Perspective: Historical Essays* (Cambridge, MA: Harvard University Press, 1981) 155.
6   B. Bresner et al., "Ontario's Agencies, Boards, Commissions, Advisory Bodies and Other Public Institutions: An Inventory (1977)" in *Government Regulation: Issues and Alternatives* (Toronto: Ontario Economic Council, 1978) 207.
7   See C. Sunstein, *After the Rights Revolution: Reconceiving the Regulatory State* (Cambridge, MA: Harvard University Press, 1990); J. Evans et al., *Administrative Law: Cases, Text, and Materials*, 4th ed. (Toronto: Emond Montgomery, 1995) at 1-5.
8   G. Doern et al., "Canadian Regulatory Institutions: Converging and Colliding Regimes" in G. Doern, ed., *Changing the Rules: Canadian Regulatory Regimes and Institutions* (Toronto: University of Toronto Press, 1999) at 3.
9   Bogart, *supra* note 3 at 46 and following.
10   H. Arthurs and R. Kreklewich, "Law, Legal Institutions, and the Legal Professions in the New Economy" (1996) 34 Osgoode Hall L.J. 2.
11   See R. Abel, "Lawyers in the Civil Law World" in R. Abel and P. Lewis, eds., *Lawyers in Society: The Civil Law World* (Berkeley: University of California Press, 1988).
12   M. Galanter, "Law Abounding: Legalisation around the North Atlantic" (1992) 55 Mod. L. Rev. 1 at 4, citing R. Abel, *The Legal Profession in England and Wales* (Oxford: Basil Blackwell, 1988).
13   B. Curran, *Supplement to the Lawyer Statistical Report: The U.S. Legal Profession in 1985* (Chicago: American Bar Foundation, 1986); W. Glaberson, "Lawyers Contend with State and Federal Efforts to Restrict Their Rising Power" *New York Times* (5 August 1999) A15.
14   D. Stager and H. Arthurs, *Lawyers in Canada* (Toronto: University of Toronto Press, 1990) at 149; J. Melnitzer, "Size of Ontario Bar Grows 30 Per Cent" *Law Times* (29 March-4 April 1999) 1.
15   O. Lippert, "Consumer Demand for Legal Services" *Canadian Lawyer* (November/December 1996) at 14.
16   *Ibid.*
17   F. Zemans and P. Monahan, *From Crisis to Reform: A New Legal Aid Plan for Ontario* (North York, ON: York University Centre for Public Law and Public Policy, 1997) at 19.
18   *Ibid.* at 20.
19   J. McCamus et al., *Report of the Ontario Legal Aid Review: A Blueprint for Publicly Funded Legal Services*, vols. 1-3 (Toronto: Ontario Legal Aid Review, 1997); *Legal Aid Services Act,* S.O. 1998, c. 26.
20   Lippert, *supra* note 15 at 16.
21   This allegation was repeatedly made in the United States throughout the 1990s. See, for example, W. Olson, *The Litigation Explosion: What Happened When America Unleashed the Lawsuit*

(New York: Truman Talley-Dutton, 1991); P. Howard, *The Death of Common Sense: How Law Is Suffocating America* (New York: Random House, 1994); M. Glendon, *A Nation under Lawyers: How the Crisis in the Legal Profession Is Transforming American Society* (New York: Farrar, Strauss, and Giroux, 1994).

22 Galanter, *supra* note 12 at 7.

23 Consultative Group on Research and Education in Law, *Law and Learning* (Ottawa: Social Sciences and Humanities Research Council of Canada, 1983) at 82.

24 Galanter, *supra* note 12 at 7. The title of the article is "Law Abounding: Legalisation Around the North Atlantic." This part of this chapter is especially indebted to the Galanter article.

25 M. Schudson, *The Good Citizen: A History of American Civic Life* (New York: Free Press, 1998) at 264-73.

26 D. Dewees, M. Trebilcock, and P. Coyte, "The Medical Malpractice Crisis: Comparative Empirical Perspective" (1991) 54 Law & Contemp. Probs. 217.

27 Galanter, *supra* note 12 at 13.

28 I. Jenkins, *Social Order and the Limits of Law* (Princeton, NJ: Princeton University Press, 1980) at 215.

29 This section draws on the analysis in Bogart, *supra* note 3.

30 T. Burke, *Lawyers, Lawsuits, and Legal Rights: The Battle over Litigation in American Society* (Berkeley and Los Angeles: University of California Press, 2002) at 8-13; Schudson, *supra* note 25 at 255-64.

31 Bogart, *supra* note 3 at 25-35.

32 P. Williams, "Alchemical Notes: Reconstructing Ideals from Deconstructed Rights" (1987) 22 Harv. C.R.-C.L.L. Rev. 401 at 431.

33 C. Sunstein, "Rights and Their Critics" (1995) 70 Notre Dame L. Rev. 727.

34 M. Glendon, *Rights Talk: The Impoverishment of Political Discourse* (New York: Free Press, 1991) at 7.

35 J. Handler, *Social Movements and the Legal System: A Theory of Law Reform and Social Change* (New York: Academic Press, 1978). See also A. Sarat and S. Scheingold, eds., *Cause Lawyering: Political Commitments and Professional Responsibilities* (New York: Oxford University Press, 1998).

36 S. Scheingold, "Constitutional Rights and Social Change: Civil Rights in Perspective" in M. McCann and G. Houseman, eds., *Judging the Constitution: Critical Essays on Judicial Lawmaking* (Boston: Scott, Foresman/Little, Brown, 1989) at 87.

37 M. Minow, "Interpreting Rights: An Essay for Robert Cover" (1987) 96 Yale L.J. 1860, 1876, 1880 [footnotes omitted].

38 A. Hutchinson, *Waiting for Coraf: A Critique of Law and Rights* (Toronto: University of Toronto Press, 1995).

39 S. Holmes and C. Sunstein, *The Cost of Rights: Why Liberty Depends on Taxes* (New York: W.W. Norton, 1999) at 24-25.

40 W. Novak, "Conclusion: The Invention of American Constitutional Law" *The People's Welfare: Law and Regulation in Nineteenth-Century America* (Chapel Hill, NC: University of North Carolina Press, 1996).

41 Scheingold, *supra* note 36 at 85.

42 S. Walker, *The Rights Revolution: Rights and Community in Modern America* (New York: Oxford University Press, 1998).

43 Schudson, *supra* note 25 at 309.

44 Peter Hogg, the noted constitutional scholar and supporter of the *Charter*, asserted in 1977 (shortly before the entrenchment process began): "In Canada.... civil liberties are better respected than in most other countries." See P. Hogg, *Constitutional Law of Canada* (Toronto: Carswell, 1977) at 418.

45 R. Romanow et al., *Canada Notwithstanding: The Making of the Constitution 1976-1982* (Toronto: Carswell/Methuen, 1984) at xv.

46 R. McMurtry, "The Canadian Charter of Rights and Freedoms" (2001) 14 Sup. Ct. L. Rev. (2d) 243.

47 Romanow, *supra* note 45 at 211.

48 A summary of developments under the *Charter* is contained in R. Jhappan, "Charter Politics and the Judiciary" in Whittington and Williams, *supra* note 4 at 217.

49 C. Epp, *The Rights Revolution: Lawyers, Activists, and Supreme Courts in Comparative Perspective* (Chicago: University of Chicago Press, 1998). The quotes are taken from the titles to Chapters 9 and 10, dealing with Canada.

50   P. Monahan, "The Supreme Court of Canada in the 21st Century" (2001) 60 Can. Bar Rev. 374 at 382. In the 1990s *Charter* and other constitutional cases represented between 20 and 25 percent of the Supreme Court's caseload: P. Monahan, "The Supreme Court of Canada in 1999: The Year in Review" *Canada Watch* 8:1 (October 2000) 3.

51   Epp, *supra* note 49 at 196.

52   See J.M. Weiler and R.M. Elliot, eds., *Litigating the Values of a Nation: The Canadian Charter of Rights and Freedoms* (Toronto: Carswell, 1986).

53   Brochure advertising the Conference on the Tenth Anniversary of the Charter (14-15 April 1992) sponsored by the Canadian Bar Association and the Federal Department of Justice.

54   S. Fine, "The Rights Revolution: The Courts Lead the Charge," a two part series, *Globe and Mail* (24 and 25 November 1992) A1, A8.

55   J. Sallot, "Top Court Becomes Supreme Player" *Globe and Mail* (6 April 1992) A1; "How the Charter Changes Justice," interview J. Sallot with Chief Justice Lamer, *Globe and Mail* (17 April 1992) A11.

56   John Sopinka, quoted in "Limited Value in Confirmation Ritual" *Financial Post* (15 August 1989) 14.

57   D. Beatty, *Talking Heads and the Supremes: The Canadian Production of Constitutional Review* (Toronto: Carswell, 1990) vii.

58   P. Macklem, "First Nations Self-Government and the Borders of the Canadian Legal Imagination" (1991) 36 McGill L.J. 382 at 393.

59   D. Dyzenhaus, "The New Positivists" (1989) 39 U.T.L.J. 361 at 378.

60   D. Coyne, "Commentary" in D. Smith et al., eds., *After Meech Lake: Lessons for the Future* (Saskatoon: Fifth House, 1991) at 140.

61   J. Whyte, "On Not Standing for Notwithstanding" (1990) 28 Alta. L. Rev. 347 at 351.

62   S. Lipset, *Continental Divide: The Values and Institutions of the United States and Canada* (Toronto: C.D. Howe Institute and Washington, DC: National Planning Association, 1989) at 225-26.

63   C. Manfredi, "The Judicialization of Politics: Rights and Public Policy in Canada and the United States" in K. Banting et al., *Degrees of Freedom: Canada and the United States in a Changing World* (Montreal and Kingston: McGill-Queen's University Press, 1997) at 310.

64   *Ibid*. at 326.

65   *Ibid*. at 339.

66   See Chapter 4, this volume, at 87-89.

67   This section continues the analysis in Bogart, *supra* note 3, c. 4, "Six Ideas about the Impact of Law – America the Outlier," and c. 6, "The Impact of Litigation regarding Social Change – 'American Exceptionalism' II."

68   Epp, *supra* note 49; N. Tate and T. Vallinder, *The Global Expansion of Judicial Power* (New York: New York University Press, 1995).

69   R. Kagan, *Adversarial Legalism: The American Way of Law* (Cambridge, MA: Harvard University Press, 2001).

70   H. Jacob, "Conclusion" in H. Jacob et al., eds., *Courts, Law and Politics in Comparative Perspective* (New Haven, CT: Yale University Press, 1996) at 394.

71   L. Kalman, *The Strange Career of Legal Liberalism* (New Haven, CT: Yale University Press, 1996).

72   See, for example, M. Galanter, "Why the 'Haves' Come Out Ahead: Speculations on the Limits of Legal Change" (1974) 9 Law & Soc'y Rev. 95; R. Mnookin and L. Kornhauser, "Bargaining in the Shadow of the Law: The Case of Divorce" (1979) 88 Yale L.J. 950; M. Galanter, "The Radiating Effects of Courts" in K. Boyum and L. Mather, eds., *Empirical Theories about Courts* (New York: Longan, 1983); H. Kritzer and S. Silbey, eds., *In Litigation Do the "Haves" Still Come Out Ahead?* (Stanford: Stanford University Press, 2003).

73   G. Rosenberg, *The Hollow Hope: Can Courts Bring About Social Change?* (Chicago: University of Chicago Press, 1991) at 171.

74   *Ibid*. at 36.

75   For example, see C. Sunstein, "How Independent Is the Court?" *New York Review of Books* (22 October 1992) 47; J. Simon, "'The Long Walk Home' to Politics" (1992) 26 Law & Soc'y Rev. 923; and see the critical reviews of M. Feeler and M. McCann and Rosenberg's response in "Review Section Symposium: The Supreme Court and Social Change" (1993) 17 Law and Social Inquiry 715; and N. Devils, "Judicial Matters," Book Review of *The Hollow Hope: Can Courts Bring About Social Change?* by G. Rosenberg (1992) 80 Cal. L. Rev. 1027.

76   Rosenberg, *supra* note 73 at 338 [emphasis in original].

77 M. Feeley and E. Rubin, *Judicial Policy Making and the Modern State: How the Courts Reformed America's Prisons* (New York: Cambridge University Press, 1998).

78 D. Reed, "Twenty-Five Years after *Rodriguez:* School Finance Litigation and the Impact of the New Judicial Federalism" (1998) 32 Law & Soc'y Rev. 175.

79 B. Canon and C. Johnson, *Judicial Policies: Implementation and Impact*, 2nd ed. (Washington, DC: Congressional Quarterly Press, 1999) at 211 ff.

80 P. Schuck, "Public Law Litigation and Social Reform" (1993) 102 Yale L.J. 1763.

81 See also D. Schultz and S. Gottlieb, "Legal Functionalism and Social Change: A Reassessment of Rosenberg's *The Hollow Hope*" in D. Schultz, ed., *Leveraging the Law: Using Courts to Achieve Social Change* (New York: Peter Lang Publishing, 1998) 169, and especially "Social Science and Historical Positivism" at 190-91.

82 Schuck, *supra* note 80 at 1785-86.

83 *Ibid.* at 1786. See also the important exchange between Rosenberg and McCann in G. Rosenberg, "Positivism, Interpretivism, and the Study of Law" (1996) 21 Law & Soc. Inquiry 435, and M. McCann, "Causal versus Constitutive Explanations (or, On the Difficulty of Being So Positive) 457.

84 This section is based on and develops the analysis in Bogart, *supra* note 3 at 304.

85 *Brown v. Board of Education* 347 U.S. 483 (1954).

86 A. Gold, "The Legal Rights Provisions: A New Vision or Déjà Vu" (1982) Sup. Ct. L. Rev. 4 at 108, quoted in C. Manfredi, *Judicial Power and the Charter* (Toronto: McClelland and Stewart, 1993) at 27.

87 S. Powers and S. Rothman, "Brown, Bussing and the Consequences of Desegregation," c. 2 in *The Least Dangerous Branch: Consequences of Judicial Activism* (Westport, CT: Praeger Publishers, 2002).

88 Rosenberg, *supra* note 73 at 52.

89 For an even stronger statement on the ineffectiveness of *Brown*, see M. Klarman, "*Brown*, Racial Change, and the Civil Rights Movement" (1994) 80 Va. L. Rev. 7. See also the critical comments on Klarman: M. McConnell, "The Originalist Justification for *Brown*: A Reply to Professor Klarman" (1995) 81 Va. L. Rev. 1937; M. Tushnet, "The Significance of *Brown v. Board of Education*" (1994) 80 Va. L. Rev. 173; G. Rosenberg, "*Brown* Is Dead! Long Live Brown! The Endless Attempt to Canonize a Case" (1994) 80 Va. L. Rev. 161; D. Garrow, "Hopelessly Hollow History: Revisionist Devaluing of *Brown v. Board of Education*" (1994) 80 Va. L. Rev. 151. But see M. Klarman, "*Brown*, Originalism, and Constitutional Theory: A Response to Professor McConnell" (1995) 81 Va. L. Rev. 1881.

90 Rosenberg, *supra* note 73 at 111, 118, 155.

91 *Ibid.* at 341-42.

92 Sunstein, *supra* note 75 at 47.

93 R. Flemming et al., "One Voice among Many: The Supreme Court's Influence on Attentiveness to Issues in the United States, 1947-1992"; K. McMahon and M. Paris, "The Politics of Rights Revisited: Rosenberg, McCann, and the New Institutionalism"; D. Schultz and S. Gottlieb, "Legal Functionalism and Social Change: A Reassessment of Rosenberg's *The Hollow Hope*," all in Schultz, *supra* note 81.

94 Rosenberg, *supra* note 73 at 94-106.

95 P. Burstein and M. Edwards, "The Impact of Employment Discrimination Litigation on Racial Disparity in Earnings: Evidence and Unresolved Issues" (1994) 28 Law and Soc'y Rev. 79.

96 J. Donohue, J. Heckman, and P. Todd, "Social Action, Private Choice, and Philanthropy: Understanding the Sources of Improvements in Black Schooling in Georgia, 1911-1960" (paper presented at the University of Wisconsin Poverty Research Institute, Madison, June 1997).

97 D. Bell, *Silent Covenants: Brown v. Board of Education and the Unfilled Hopes for Racial Reform* (New York: Oxford University Press, 2004); S. Cashin, *The Failures of Integration: How Race and Class Are Underscoring the American Dream* (New York: Public Affairs, 2004); C. Clotfelter, *After Brown* (Princeton, NJ: Princeton University Press, 2004); C. Ogletree, *All Deliberate Speed: Reflections on the First Half Century of Brown v. Board of Education* (New York: W.W. Norton, 2004). See also S. Freedman, "Still Separate, Still Unequal" *New York Times Book Review* (16 May 2004) 8.

98 Bell, *ibid.* at 2.

99 S. Wasby, *Race Relations Litigation in an Age of Complexity* (Charlottesville, VA: University Press of Virginia, 1995) at 332.

100 D. Reed, "Twenty-Five Years after *Rodriguez:* School Finance Litigation and the Impact of the New Judicial Federalism" (1998) 32 Law & Soc'y Rev. 175, 181.
101 *Ibid.* at 214-15.
102 J. Hochschild, *The New American Dilemma: Liberal Democracy and School Desegregation* (New Haven, CT: Yale University Press, 1984).
103 E. Frankenberg et al., *A Multiracial Society with Segregated Schools: Are We Losing the Dream?* (Cambridge, MA: The Civil Rights Project, Harvard University, 2003) online at <http://www.civilrightsproject.harvard.edu/research/reseg03/resegregation03.php>.
104 G. Winter, "Schools Resegregate, Study Finds" *New York Times* (21 January 2003) A14; Editorial, "Fighting School Resegregation" *New York Times* (27 January 2003) A26.
105 D. Armor, *Forced Justice: School Desegregation and the Law* (New York: Oxford University Press, 1995) at 231; J. Patterson, *Brown v. Board of Education: A Civil Rights Milestone and Its Troubled Legacy* (New York: Oxford University Press, 2001).
106 Armor, *ibid.*, 232; see also S. Halpern, *On the Limits of the Law: The Ironic Legacy of Title VI of the 1964 Civil Rights Act* (Baltimore: Johns Hopkins University Press, 1995) at 315-16.
107 Sunstein, *supra* note 75 at 50; see also J. Simon, "'The Long Walk Home' to Politics" (1992) 26 Law & Soc'y Rev. 923; I. Holloway, "Book Review: *The Hollow Hope*" (1992) 15 Dal. L.J. 664.
108 A. Lewis, "50 Years after Brown," Letters [to the editor], *New York Times Book Review* (13 June 2004) 4.
109 Kagan, *supra* note 69.
110 Epp, *supra* note 49.
111 For earlier variations of this argument, see H. Fairley, "Enforcing the Charter: Some Thoughts on an Appropriate and Just Standard for Judicial Review" (1982) 4 Sup. Ct. L. Rev. 217; P. Monahan, "Judicial Review and Democracy: A Theory of Judicial Review" (1987) 21 U.B.C. L. Rev. 87.
112 See *supra* notes 52 to 61 and accompanying text.
113 P. Hogg and A. Bushell, "The *Charter* Dialogue between Courts and Legislatures" (1997) 35 Osgoode Hall L.J. 75.
114 *Ibid.* at 81.
115 For example, Justice Iacobucci's comments in *Vriend v. Alberta*, [1998] 1 S.C.R. 493, 565; and those of retired Justice Wilson in B. Wilson, "We Didn't Volunteer" in P. Howe and P. Russell, eds., *Judicial Power and Canadian Democracy* (Montreal and Kingston: McGill-Queen's University Press, 2001) 73 at 75-76.
116 K. Roach, "Dialogue between Courts and Legislatures" c. 10, *The Supreme Court on Trial: Judicial Activism or Democratic Dialogue* (Toronto: Irwin Law, 2001).
117 *Ibid.* at 67, quoting J. Waldron, *Law and Disagreement* (Oxford: Clarendon Press, 1999) at 291.
118 L. Eisenstat Weinrib, "The Activist Constitution" in Howe and Russell, *supra* note 115 at 80, 81.
119 *Ibid.*, at 81.
120 C. Manfredi and J. Kelly, "Six Degrees of Dialogue: A Response to Hogg and Bushell" (1999) 37 Osgoode Hall L.J. 513.
121 C. Manfredi, *Judicial Power and the Charter: Canada and the Paradox of Liberal Constitutionalism*, 2nd ed. (Toronto: Oxford University Press, 2001) at 176-81.
122 *Ibid.*; M. Tushnet, "Policy Distortions and Democratic Debilitation: Comparative Illumination of the Countermajoritarian Difficulty" (1995) 94 Mich. L. Rev. 245.
123 J. Hiebert, *Charter Conflicts: What Is Parliament's Role?* (Montreal and Kingston: McGill-Queen's University Press, 2002) at xiii; M. Dawson, "Governing in a Rights Culture" (2001) 14 Sup. Ct. L. Rev. (2d) 251.
124 Manfredi, *supra* note 121.
125 T. Kahana, "Comment" *Globe and Mail* (19 September 2003) A17, quoting P. Monahan.
126 P. Hogg and A. Thornton, "Reply to 'Six Degrees of Dialogue'" (1999) 37 Osgoode Hall L.J. 529; Roach, *supra* note 116; Monahan, "The Supreme Court of Canada in the 21st Century," *supra* note 50.
127 Roach, *supra* note 116.
128 F. Morton and R. Knopff, *The Charter Revolution and the Court Party* (Peterborough, ON: Broadview Press, 2000).
129 T. Bateman, "Crashing the Party: A Review of F.L. Morton and R. Knopff's The Charter Revolution and the Court Party" (2000) 33 U.B.C. L. Rev. 859, para. 18, articulating this view but not necessarily agreeing with it.
130 Morton and Knopff, *supra* note 128 at 166.

131 *Ibid.* at 162, citing R. Tatalovich, *The Politics of Abortion in the United States and Canada: A Comparative Study* (Armonk, NY: M.E. Sharpe, 1997) Table 4.1, III.

132 *Ibid.* at 162-64.

133 *Ibid.* at 158.

134 For example, D. Beatty, *Constitutional Law in Theory and Practice* (Toronto: University of Toronto Press, 1995); P. Macklem, *Indigenous Difference and the Constitution of Canada* (Toronto: University of Toronto Press, 2001); Weinrib, *supra* note 118 at 80; Roach, *supra* note 116.

135 For example, J. Bakan, *Just Words: Constitutional Rights and Social Wrongs* (Toronto: University of Toronto Press, 1997); A. Hutchinson, *Waiting for Coraf: A Critique of Law and Rights* (Toronto: University of Toronto Press, 1995); M. Mandel, *The Charter of Rights and the Legalization of Politics in Canada*, rev. ed. (Toronto: Thompson Educational Publishing, 1994).

136 For example, R. Moon, *The Constitutional Protection of Freedom of Expression* (Toronto: University of Toronto Press, 2000); K. Roach, *Due Process and Victims' Rights: The New Law and Politics of Criminal Justice* (Toronto: University of Toronto Press, 1999).

137 W.A. Bogart, *Courts and Country: The Limits of Litigation and the Social and Political Life of Canada* (Toronto: Oxford University Press, 1994).

138 For example, S. Burt, "What's Fair? Changing Feminist Perceptions of Justice in English Canada" (1993) 12 Windsor Y.B. Access Just. 337; A. Cairns, *Citizens Plus: Aboriginal Peoples and the Canadian State* (Vancouver: UBC Press, 2000); J. Hiebert, *Limiting Rights: The Dilemma of Judicial Review* (Montreal and Kingston: McGill-Queen's University Press, 1996); C. Manfredi, *Judicial Power and the Charter: Canada and the Paradox of Liberal Constitutionalism* (Toronto: Oxford University Press, 2001); P. Russell, "The Political Role of the Supreme Court of Canada in its First Century" (1975) 53 Can. Bar Rev. 576.

139 For example, R. Fulford, "The Charter of Wrongs" *Saturday Night* (December 1986) 7; L. Martin, *Pledge of Allegiance* (Toronto: McClelland and Stewart, 1993); J. Simpson, "How the Courts Expand Rights and Whittle Away at Government" *Globe and Mail* (12 August 1992) A10.

140 A. Borovy, *When Freedoms Collide: The Case for Our Civil Liberties* (Toronto: Lester and Orpen Dennys, 1988) 213.

141 Morton and Knopff, *supra* note 128 at 149.

142 Schudson, *supra* note 25.

143 *Ibid.* at 8.

144 *Ibid.* at 273.

145 *Ibid.* at 295.

146 *Ibid.* at 308.

147 P. Ryscavage, *Income Equality in America: An Analysis of Trends* (Armonk, NY: M.E. Sharpe, 1999); "Cutting the Cookie" *The Economist* (11 September 1999) 26.

148 D. Kirp, "So, Is It Back to Bowling Alone?" *The Nation* (8 March 1999) 25, 27 (reviewing *The Good Citizen*).

149 P. Russell, "The Political Purposes of the Canadian Charter of Rights and Freedoms" (1983) 61 Can. Bar Rev. 30.

150 H. Arthurs, "More Litigation, More Law? The Limits of Litigation as a Social Justice Strategy" in W.A. Bogart et al., eds., *The Way Forward: Access to Justice for a New Century* (forthcoming, 2005).

151 This point is returned to in Chapter 3, this volume, at 89-91.

152 R. Mackie, "Eves Endorses Death Penalty as Shift to the Right Continues" *Globe and Mail* (4 September 2003) A1, A10; see Bogart, *supra* note 3, c. 5, "Punishment – and Capital Punishment."

153 Roach, *supra* note 136 at 3.

154 *Ibid.* and accompanying text.

155 *Ibid.* at 318.

156 R. Mackie and G. Galloway, "McGuinty Routs Tories" *Globe and Mail* (3 October 2003) A1, A8.

157 "Canada: The Quiet Way" *The Economist* (4 September 1999) 41. Saskatchewan and Manitoba elected moderate social democratic governments in the 1990s.

158 Ryscavage, *supra* note 147, c. 7, "International Comparisons."

159 S. Lipset, *American Exceptionalism: A Double-Edged Sword* (New York: W.W. Norton, 1996) at 146 ff; J. Maxwell, "Don't Be Seduced by the US Boom: Averages Lie" *Globe and Mail* (30 August 1999) A13.

160 Ryscavage, *supra* note 147.

161 Weinrib, *supra* note 118 at 85.
162 *Ibid.* at 81.
163 M. Ignatieff, *The Rights Revolution* (Toronto: House of Anansi, 2000) at 24.
164 J. Gross Stein, *The Cult of Efficiency* (Toronto: House of Anansi, 2001) at 218-19.
165 Weinrib, *supra* note 118 at 86.
166 Quoted in F. Siegel, "Nothing in Moderation" *Atlantic Monthly* (May 1990) 108, 110.
167 R. Hughes, *Culture of Complaint: The Fraying of America* (New York: Oxford University Press, 1993) at 29, quoting Václav Havel.
168 Roach, *supra* note 116, c. 1, "The Supreme Court on Trial."
169 See *supra* notes 52 to 61 and accompanying text.

Chapter 3: Representative Politics in Disarray
1 P. Norris, "Conclusions: The Growth of Critical Citizens and Its Consequences" in P. Norris, ed., *Critical Citizens: Global Support for Democratic Government* (Oxford: Oxford University Press, 1999) at 269.
2 D. Zolo, *Democracy and Complexity*, trans. by D. McKie (Cambridge, UK: Polity Press, 1992) at 54.
3 R. Putnam, S. Pharr, and R. Dalton, "Introduction: What's Troubling the Trilateral Democracies?" in S. Pharr and R. Putnam, eds., *Disaffected Democracies: What's Troubling the Trilateral Countries?* (Princeton, NJ: Princeton University Press, 2000) at 6-8. The figures in the text are taken from Putnam et al. and the sources they cite.
4 Other public institutions have also suffered a decline in support over the last decades; for example, support for universities has dropped from 61 to 30 percent. In 1996, 30 percent of those polled agreed that they had hardly any confidence in the press: J. Nye, "Foreword" in P. Norris, ed., *Critical Citizens: Global Support for Democratic Government* (Oxford: Oxford University Press, 1999) at i.
5 A. Nagourney, "Bush Celebrates Victory" *The New York Times* (4 November 2004) A1, P2. G. Perlin, "The Constraints of Public Opinion: Diverging or Converging Paths?" in K. Banting, G. Hoberg, and R. Simeon, *Degrees of Freedom: Canada and the United States in a Changing World* (Montreal and Kingston: McGill-Queen's University Press, 1997) 71 at 106, citing R. Teixeira, *The Disappearing American Voter* (Washington, DC: Brookings Institution, 1992).
6 "What September 11th Really Wrought" *The Economist* (12 January 2002) 23.
7 A. Nagourney and J. Elder, "Public's Backing of Bush Shows a Steady Decline" *New York Times* (24 January 2003) A1, A21.
8 "What September 11th Really Wrought," *supra* note 6.
9 Putnam et al., *supra* note 3 at 10-11. Sweden, an emblem of the "middle way" between laissez-faire and the oppressive state, has also not been spared eroding trust in politics. In 1968, 51 percent of respondents rejected the statement that "parties are only interested in people's votes, not in their opinions"; by 1994 only 28 percent did so. In 1986, 51 percent still expressed confidence in the Swedish legislature; by 1996 only 19 percent did so. With few exceptions, such as in the Netherlands, similar trends of decline are apparent for other countries of Western Europe. Japan, a nation famed for its deference to authority, has witnessed a steady decline in support for government. The proportion of voters who believe they exert at least "some influence" on national politics fell continuously between 1973 and 1993. Trust in the once much respected civil service has also "plummeted over the last decade": *ibid.* at 13.
10 *Ibid.* at 21-22.
11 P. Norris, *Democratic Phoenix: Reinventing Political Activism* (Cambridge, UK: Cambridge University Press, 2001) at 216.
12 Putnam et al., *supra* note 3 at 22.
13 *Ibid.* at 25.
14 *Ibid.*
15 *Ibid.* at 10.
16 Perlin, *supra* note 5 at 100.
17 There have been some promising exceptions. In 2003 Canadians did register high levels of confidence in governments' capacity to fight SARS and other contagions. G. Smith and G. Galloway, "Few Fear Spread of Contagion" *Globe and Mail* (31 May 2003) A8.
18 Putnam et al., *supra* note 3 at 10, citing sources for figures in this text.
19 Perlin, *supra* note 5 at 100, citing sources for figures in this text.
20 D. McKenzie, "69% Say Government Corrupt" *National Post* (22 April 2002) A1, A8.

21 J. Simpson, "Who Would Be an Elected Politician in This Corrosive, Mean Spirited Age?" *Globe and Mail* (28 October 1992) A26.

22 K. Banting, G. Hoberg, and R. Simeon, "Introduction" in K. Banting, G. Hoberg, and R. Simeon, *Degrees of Freedom: Canada and the United States in a Changing World* (Montreal and Kingston: McGill-Queen's University Press, 1997) at 14.

23 A provision also existed for opting out with compensation from federal spending programs if it were established that the provincial substitute was compatible with "national objectives" set by Ottawa. There was a provision allowing provinces to enter into agreements with the federal government concerning immigration, but this, in the main, formalized what had been existing practice. There was some shift concerning the Senate and the Supreme Court, with the provinces providing lists of those from whom the federal government would chose to make appointments.

24 D. Brown, "An Overview" in D. Brown, ed., *Canada: The State of the Federation 1991* (Kingston, ON: Institute of Intergovernmental Relations, 1991) at 4.

25 The earlier attempts to deal with the First Peoples' demands constitutionally are described in P. Russell, *Constitutional Odyssey: Can Canadians Be a Sovereign People?* (Toronto: University of Toronto Press, 1992) c. 9.

26 It was insufficiently responsive to the needs of Quebec to have the constitutional means to protect itself as a distinct and minority society. It gave too much to Quebec and would have privileged it at the expense of the rest of Canada. It was unintelligible in terms of what changes would actually be effected. It was inattentive to the needs of women, particularly minority women and especially First Nations women – possibly depriving them of the protection of the *Charter*. It gave too much discretion to the courts on these and other issues, and so on.

27 Matters were not helped when Premier Jacques Parizeau blamed the defeat of the referendum on "money and the ethnic vote": "Canada Survey: Holding Its Own" *The Economist* (24 July 1999) 1, 15 [hereafter "Canada Survey"].

28 *Ibid.*

29 D. Bricker and E. Greenspon, *Searching for Certainty: Inside the New Canadian Mindset* (Toronto: Doubleday Canada, 2001) at 291.

30 Perlin, *supra* note 5 at 102-3.

31 K. McRoberts, "Quebec: Province, Nation, or Distinct Society?" in M. Whittington and G. Williams, eds., *Canadian Politics in the 21st Century* (Toronto: Nelson, 2000) at 356.

32 R. Mackie, "Sovereignty Support Near Low, Poll Finds" *Globe and Mail* (26 October 2001) A1, A9. The horrors of 11 September 2001 sent support for independence even lower. A survey in Quebec taken in October 2001 revealed that 72 percent of respondents agreed that they felt more secure with the province being part of Canada. At the same time, in November of that year, Premier Landry caused an uproar by suggesting that blunting the forces of nationalism could lead to terrorism of the kind perpetrated on 11 September 2001: R. Mackie, "Many Quebeckers Crave Stability" *Globe and Mail* (27 October 2001) A9; Editorial, "Mr. Landry, Please Explain" *Globe and Mail* (20 November 2001) A18.

33 "Canada Survey," *supra* note 27 at 17.

34 *Reference re Secession of Quebec*, [1998] 2 S.C.R. 217.

35 C. Doran, *Why Canadian Unity Matters and Why Americans Care: Democratic Pluralism at Risk* (Toronto: University of Toronto Press, 2001).

36 These various statistics are taken from P. Macklem, "First Nations Self-Government and the Borders of the Canadian Legal Imagination" (1991) 36 McGill L.J. 383, 386, and A.J. Siggner, "The Socio-Demographic Conditions of Registered Indians" in J.R. Ponting, ed., *Arduous Journey: Canadian Indians and Decolonization* (Toronto: McClelland and Stewart, 1986) at 57.

37 Macklem, *ibid.* at 454-55.

38 This analysis is based on the "Text of the Charlottetown Agreement: Revised Draft: 2:30 p.m., August 28, 1992" *Globe and Mail* (1 September 1992) A1, A8-9 [hereafter Charlottetown text].

39 M. Cernetig, "Natives Envision Breaking Vicious Cycle" *Globe and Mail* (14 July 1992) A1.

40 Charlottetown text, *supra* note 38 at s. IV.A.42.

41 *Ibid.* at s. IV.A.41.

42 *Ibid.* at s. IV.A.43.

43 S. Delacourt, "Text Being Altered Native Women Say" *Globe and Mail* (19 September 1992) A4; M. Landsberg, "Unity Deal Will Rob Native Women of Key Rights" *Toronto Star* (22 September 1992) B1; S. Fine, "Native Women Aim to Block National Referendum in Court" *Globe and Mail* (13 October 1992) A10.

44 Charlottetown text, *supra* note 38 at s. IV.A.41(a).
45 *Ibid.* at s. IV.C.50.
46 S. Venne, "Treaty Indigenous Peoples and the Charlottetown Accord: The Message in the Breeze" (1993) 4 Const. Studies 43.
47 Canada, *Report of the Royal Commission on Aboriginal Peoples* (Ottawa: Canada Communications Group Publishing, 1996) [hereafter *Report*].
48 Reaction to the report was limited. See A. Cairns, *Citizens Plus: Aboriginal Peoples and the Canadian State* (Vancouver: UBC Press, 2000) at 237 n. 1 for a listing of the few academic and media commentaries.
49 J. Stackhouse, "Canada's Apartheid" *Globe and Mail*, various dates in November and December 2001.
50 K. Banting and R. Simeon, "Changing Economies, Changing Societies" in Banting, Hoberg, and Simeon, *supra* note 22 at 67.
51 Banting, Hoberg, and Simeon, *supra* note 22 at 10.
52 A. Malcolm, "Beyond Plain Vanilla: Immigration Has Accentuated Canada's Diversity" *New York Times* (8 July 1990) E2.
53 Banting, Hoberg, and Simeon, *supra* note 22 at 56-57.
54 Bricker and Greenspon, *supra* note 29 at 297; G. Galloway, "Toronto Most Ethnically Diverse in North America" *Globe and Mail* (22 January 2003) A6.
55 E. Anderssen, "Immigration Shifts Population Kaleidoscope" *Globe and Mail* (22 January 2003) A6.
56 Bricker and Greenspon, *supra* note 29 at 298.
57 *Ibid.* at 296-97.
58 R. Bibby, *Mosaic Madness: The Poverty and Potential of Life in Canada* (Toronto: Stoddart, 1990) at 92 cited in Banting, Hoberg, and Simeon, *supra* note 22 at 68, and see additional discussion at 59.
59 B. Etherington et al., "Preserving Identity by Having Many Identities: A Report on Multiculturalism and Access to Justice" (Windsor, ON: 1991) an unpublished report for the Department of Justice, Canada.
60 E. Anderssen and C. Alphonson, "Immigrants Losing Ground on Income" *Globe and Mail* (12 March 2003) A6.
61 K. Banting, "Social Citizenship and the Multicultural Welfare State" in A. Cairns et al., *Citizenship, Diversity and Pluralism: Canadian and Comparative Perspectives* (Montreal and Kingston: McGill-Queen's University Press, 1999) at 108.
62 Bricker and Greenspon, *supra* note 29 at 296.
63 R. Simeon and E. Willis, "Democracy and Performance: Governance in Canada and the United States" in Banting, Hoberg, and Simeon, *supra* note 22 at 150, 159.
64 J. Simpson, "So, Really, What's the NDP?" *Globe and Mail* (23 November 2001) A15.
65 "Canada: The Quiet Way" *The Economist* (4 September 1999) 41.
66 Editorial, "Can a New Leader Kick-Start the NDP?" *Globe and Mail* (22 January 2003) A18; L. Davies et al., "After the Labour Pains, a New NDP?" *Globe and Mail* (22 November 2001) A27.
67 H.G. Betz, "Introduction" in H.G. Betz and S. Immerfall, eds., *The New Politics of the Right: Neo-Populist Parties and Movements in Established Democracies* (New York: St. Martin's Press, 1998) at 3-6.
68 On the rise of the Reform Party and the development of the new right in Canada, generally, see N. Nevitte et al., "The Populist Right in Canada: The Rise of the Reform Party" in Betz and Immerfall, *ibid.* at 173.
69 *Ibid.* at 174.
70 Betz and Immerfall, *supra* note 67 at 7.
71 P. Boyer, *"Just Trust Us": The Erosion of Accountability in Canada* (Toronto: Dundurn Press, 2003); J. Gross Stein, "When Trust Is Turned Over to the Accountants" *Literary Review of Canada* (June 2003) at 10-11.
72 J. Simpson, *The Friendly Dictatorship* (Toronto: McClelland and Stewart, 2002) at 75.
73 D. Savoie, *Governing from the Centre: The Concentration of Power in Canadian Politics* (Toronto: University of Toronto Press, 1999).
74 *Ibid.* at 7.
75 *Ibid.* at 9-11.
76 *Ibid.* at 10.

77 Simpson, *supra* note 72 at 69.
78 *Ibid.* at 23-24.
79 *Ibid.* at xiii-xiv.
80 Quoted in T. Kent, "He Must Pluck His Power" *Globe and Mail* (29 January 2004) A19.
81 H. Arthurs and R. Kreklewich, "Law, Legal Institutions, and the Legal Profession in the New Economy" (1996) 34 Osgoode Hall L.J. 2.
82 P. Boothe and D. Purvis, "Macroeconomic Policy in Canada and the United States: Independence, Transmission, and Effectiveness" in Banting, Hoberg, and Simeon, *supra* note 22 at 189. It was a misplaced assumption that the economic boom following the Second World War would continue indefinitely. In thirteen of the twenty-two years from 1953 to 1974, Canada's annual GDP grew by 5 percent or more. Yet, in only three of the subsequent nineteen years did it do so. Canada's comfortable standard of living, so far as the government had a role, was maintained by borrowing. Total government debt rose from 18 percent of GDP in 1974 to 70 percent in 1993. In 1993 net external debt had risen to 44 percent, which was clearly the highest in the G7. "Canada Survey," *supra* note 27 at 6-7.
83 *Ibid.* at 6.
84 L. Phillips, "The Rise of Balanced Budget Laws in Canada: Legislating Fiscal (Ir)responsibility" (1996) 34 Osgoode Hall L.J. 681.
85 R. Howse and M. Chandler, "Industrial Policy in Canada and the United States" in Banting, Hoberg, and Simeon, *supra* note 22 at 231, 238-40.
86 The extent of such activity, at its peak in the 1970s, is illustrated by a brief comparison with the United States. Then public enterprises in Canada employed almost 5 percent of the workforce and their investments represented 15.7 percent of gross capital formation; comparative figures for America were 1.6 percent of the workforce and 4.7 percent of gross capital formation: *ibid.* at 239.
87 R. Daniels and M. Trebilcock, "Private Provision of Public Infrastructure: An Organizational Analysis of the Next Privatization Frontier" (1996) 46 U.T.L.J. 375.
88 W.A. Bogart, *Consequences: The Impact of Law and Its Complexity* (Toronto: University of Toronto Press, 2002) at 25-35.
89 Howse and Chandler, *supra* note 85 at 239.
90 "The Big Chill" *The Economist* (24 November 2001) 59.
91 Compas Inc., *The Business Agenda* (Ottawa: Compas Inc., 1995) cited in Howse and Chandler, *supra* note 85 at 264.
92 G. Doern et al., "Conclusion" in G. Doern, ed., *Changing the Rules: Canadian Regulatory Regimes and Institutions* (Toronto: University of Toronto Press, 1999) 389 at 404.
93 I. Ayres and J. Braithwaite, *Responsive Regulation: Transcending the Deregulation Debate* (New York: Oxford University Press, 1992).
94 M. Wilhelmson, "Public Still Trusts the Judiciary, Iacobucci Tells Conference" *The Lawyers Weekly* (25 May 2001) 3.
95 J. Fletcher and P. Howe, "Public Opinion and Canada's Courts" in P. Howe and P. Russell, eds., *Judicial Power and Canadian Democracy* (Montreal and Kingston: McGill-Queen's University Press, 2001) at 255.
96 *Ibid.* at 257.
97 *Ibid.* at 258.
98 *Ibid.* at 260.
99 *Ibid.* at 261.
100 *Ibid.* at 265-66.
101 *Ibid.* at 266.
102 K. Makin, "Canadians Feel Supreme Court Tainted by Partisan Politics" *Globe and Mail* (3 July 2001) A1, A4; C. Schmitz, "Poll Shows Canadians Want Judges to Become More Accountable" *Lawyers Weekly* (17 September 2004) 1.
103 J. Sallot, "Public against Judges Making Laws, Poll Says" *Globe and Mail* (11 August 2003) A5.
104 R. Dahrendorf, "Afterword" in Pharr and Putnam, *supra* note 3 at 311.
105 Norris, "Introduction: The Growth of Citizens?" in Norris, *Critical Citizens, supra* note 1 at 27.
106 See *supra* notes 6 to 8 and accompanying text.
107 Dahrendorf, *supra* note 104 at 312.
108 *Ibid.* at 312.
109 *Ibid.*

110 Norris, *Critical Citizens, supra* note 1 at 27.
111 *Ibid.* at 27.
112 Norris, *supra* note 11 at 215-25.
113 Norris, *Critical Citizens, supra* note 1 at 24-25.
114 R. Putnam, *Bowling Alone: The Collapse and Revival of American Community* (New York: Simon and Schuster, 2000) at 46.
115 *Ibid.* at 47.
116 *Ibid.*
117 Norris, *Critical Citizens, supra* note 1.
118 Simpson, *supra* note 21.
119 A. Cairns, "Introduction" in A. Cairns et al., *Citizenship, Diversity, and Pluralism: Canadian and Comparative Perspectives* (Montreal and Kingston: McGill-Queen's University Press, 1999) 3 at 12.
120 M. Mackinnon et al., "Citizens' Dialogue on Canada's Future: A 21st Century Social Contract" (Ottawa: CPRN, 2003) online at <http://www.cprn.org>.
121 B. Porter, "Claiming and Enforcing Social and Economic Rights" (paper presented at the Conference on Social and Economic Rights, Toronto, December 1991) at 4.
122 *Ibid.*: "Our current set of rights is simply an incomplete set of rights. By omitting all of the social and economic rights that were contained in the Universal Declaration and the International Covenant on Economic, Social and Cultural Rights, our *Charter* denies rights to those who most need them."
123 See "The Politics of Human Rights" and "Righting Wrongs" *The Economist* (18 August 2001) 9 and 18.
124 N. Fraser, "From Redistribution to Recognition? Dilemmas of Justice in a 'Post Socialist' Age" *New Left Review* 212 (1995): 68; and "Rethinking Recognition" *New Left Review* 3 (2000) (2nd ed.) 107.
125 Of course, these two kinds of claims and their respective remedies are analytical types. In the real world, distinctions between both the claims and the remedies can blur in different contexts.
126 For example, the Supreme Court's unwillingness to interfere with legislative determinations concerning social assistance. *Gosselin v. Quebec (Attorney General)* [2002] 4 S.C.R. 429.
127 J. Fudge, "The Canadian Charter of Rights: Recognition, Redistribution, and the Imperialism of the Courts" in T. Campbell et al., *Sceptical Essays on Human Rights* (Oxford: Oxford University Press, 2001) at 335.
128 *Canada (Attorney General) v. Mossop,* [1993] 1 S.C.R. 554; *M. v. H.,* [1999] S.C.R. 3.
129 K. Roach, *The Supreme Court on Trial: Judicial Activism or Democratic Dialogue* (Toronto: Irwin Law, 2001) at 195-200; J. Hiebert, *Charter Conflicts: What Is Parliament's Role?* (Montreal and Kingston: McGill-Queen's University Press, 2002) at 180-90.
130 *Hendricks v. Quebec (Attorney General)* [2002] J.Q. No. 3816 (S.C.); *EGALE Canada Inc. v. Canada (Attorney General)* [2003] B.C.J. No. 994 (B.C.C.A.); *Halpern et al. v. Attorney General of Canada et al.,* [2003] O.J. No. 2268, (2003) 225 D.L.R. (4th) 529.
131 W.A. Bogart, *Courts and Country: The Limits of Litigation and the Social and Political Life of Canada* (Toronto: Oxford University Press, 1994) at 89-91.
132 *Family Law Act,* R.S.O. 1990, c. F.3; *M. v. H., supra* note 128.
133 *Egan v. Canada,* [1995] 2. S.C.R. 513.
134 See Chapter 2, this volume, at 31-37, discussing G. Rosenberg, *The Hollow Hope: Can Courts Bring About Social Change?* (Chicago: University of Chicago Press, 1991).
135 M. Smith, *Lesbian and Gay Rights in Canada: Social Movements and Equality Seeking, 1971-95* (Toronto: University of Toronto Press, 1999).
136 *Ibid.* at 151.
137 See *supra* note 130.
138 B. Laghi et al., "Liberals Could Lose Same-Sex Free Vote" *Globe and Mail* (14 August 2003) A1, A14; J. Simpson, "Why Don't We Just Turn Policy Over to the Courts?" *Globe and Mail* (22 July 2003) A15.
139 M. Raphael, "Who Says All Gays Want to Marry?" *Globe and Mail* (7 April 2004) A11; S. Cole, "I Do's: We Just Might" *Now* (4-10 March 2004) 21; K. Browne, "Will the Tories Force Me to Marry?" *Globe and Mail* (16 June 2004) A22.
140 C. Krauss, "Now Free to Marry, Canada's Gays Say, Do I?" *New York Times* (31 August 2003) A1, A6.
141 See Chapter 2, this volume, at 37-40; Roach, *supra* note 129; and Hiebert, *supra* note 129.

142 Innocenti Report Card, *A League Table of Child Poverty in Rich Nations* (Florence, Italy: UNICEF, 2000) at 3 [hereafter Innocenti Report Card].

143 *Ibid.*

144 M. Corak, "Are the Kids All Right? Intergenerational Mobility and Child Well-Being in Canada" in K. Banting, A. Sharpe, and F. St-Hilaire, eds., *The Review of Economic Performance and Social Progress: The Longest Decade: Canada in the 1990s* (Montreal: Institute for Research on Public Policy, 2001) 273 at 275.

145 Innocenti Report Card, *supra* note 142 at 3.

146 S. Fine, "How Canada Broke Its Pledge to Poor Children" *Globe and Mail* (30 November 1999) A14.

147 S. McCarthy, "Ottawa Trumpets Drop in Child Poverty" *Globe and Mail* (30 April 2001) A4; M. Philp, "Mother and Girls Enjoy Better Times" *Globe and Mail* (26 November 2002) A1, A4. E. Broadbent, "Our Poor Record Fighting Child Poverty Just Got Worse" *Globe and Mail* (24 November 2004) A27.

148 Innocenti Report Card, *supra* note 142 at 6.

149 *Ibid.* at 7.

150 *Ibid.* at 4. Of the wealthy countries, only the United States and the United Kingdom had worse rates of relative poverty among children. Indeed, since 1994 figures for Canada were used for comparisons, our ranking may actually be worse because our numbers of poor kids increased, for some period, in the 1990s. The top five countries had rates of relative poverty below 5 percent; Sweden, in top place, had a rate of 2.6 percent.

151 S. Stroick and J. Jenson, *What Is the Best Policy Mix for Canada's Young Children?* (Ottawa: Canadian Policy Research Networks, 1999) online at <http://www. cprn.org>. The same countries, for example, Sweden, Norway, and Finland, had the lowest rates for both absolute and relative rates of child poverty. These societies combine a high degree of economic development with a reasonable degree of economic equity. These countries are prepared to allocate substantial proportions of GNP to social expenditures. They are also inclined to responsibly experiment with a variety of policies to aid families so that they will have adequate income, engage in effective parenting, and benefit from supportive community environments in raising thriving children.

152 Innocenti Report Card, *supra* note 142 at 3.

153 A. Bielfeld et al., "Dear Mr. Martin: But What about the Children?" *Globe and Mail* (26 March 2004) A19; S. McCarthy, "Social Spending Preferable to Tax Cuts, Poll Finds" *Globe and Mail* (17 February 2003) A1, A4; F. Graves, "The Economy through a Public Lens: Shifting Canadian Views of the Economy" in K. Banting, A. Sharpe, and F. St-Hilaire, *supra* note 144 at 81-83.

154 Editorial, "Plucking Children from Poverty" *Globe and Mail* (26 November 2002) A8.

155 J. Galbraith, "Canada Customs" *Saturday Night* (January 1987) 118.

156 As cited in M. Lind, "Buchanan, Conservatism's Ugly Face" *New York Times* (19 August 1992) A21.

157 See *supra* note 20 and accompanying text.

158 See *supra* note 18 and accompanying text.

159 See *supra* note 102 and accompanying text.

Chapter 4: Chasing Choice

1 See Chapter 1, this volume, at 7-9 and 14-17.

2 R. Howse and M. Chandler, "Industrial Policy in Canada and the United States" in K. Banting, G. Hoberg, and R. Simeon, eds., *Degrees of Freedom: Canada and the United States in a Changing World* (Montreal and Kingston: McGill-Queen's University Press, 1997) 231 at 238-43.

3 L. Friedman, *The Republic of Choice* (Cambridge, MA: Harvard University Press, 1990); and *The Horizontal Society* (New Haven, CT: Yale University Press, 1999).

4 K. Banting and R. Simeon, "Changing Economies, Changing Societies" in Banting, Hoberg, and Simeon, *supra* note 2 at 23, 25-48. This section of the chapter relies to a great extent on this essay.

5 Howse and Chandler, *supra* note 2 at 243-61.

6 H. Arthurs and R. Kreklewich, "Law, Legal Institutions, and the Legal Profession in the New Economy" (1996) 34 Osgoode Hall L.J. 3 at 5.

7 *Ibid.* at 4-16.

8 F. Cairncross, *The Death of Distance: How the Communications Revolution Is Changing Our Lives*, 2nd ed. (Boston: Harvard Business School, 2001).

9 Banting and Simeon, *supra* note 4 at 31, and sources cited.
10 R. Simeon, G. Hoberg, and K. Banting, "Globalization, Fragmentation, and the Social Contract" in Banting, Hoberg, and Simeon, *supra* note 2 at 389, 392.
11 Banting and Simeon, *supra* note 4 at 32.
12 *Ibid.* at 32.
13 L. MacDonald, ed., *Free Trade: Risks and Rewards* (Montreal and Kingston: McGill-Queen's University Press, 2000); "Free Trade on Trial" *The Economist* (3 January 2004) 13.
14 Howse and Chandler, *supra* note 2 at 244-47.
15 Banting and Simeon, *supra* note 4 at 35-36.
16 Cairncross, *supra* note 8.
17 Banting and Simeon, *supra* note 4 at 36, and sources cited.
18 *Ibid.* at 38.
19 R. Martin and M. Porter, "Canadian Competitiveness: Nine Years after the Crossroads," January 2000, unpublished [on file with the author].
20 Banting and Simeon, *supra* note 4 at 39-40.
21 *Ibid.* at 41-42.
22 Martin and Porter, *supra* note 19 at 2.
23 Banting and Simeon, *supra* note 4 at 44, and sources cited.
24 See Chapter 3, this volume, at 67-69.
25 Banting and Simeon, *supra* note 4 at 44-46.
26 J. Gross Stein, *The Cult of Efficiency* (Toronto: House of Anansi, 2001) at xi.
27 Friedman, *The Republic of Choice, supra* note 3 at 74. For a harsh review of *The Republic of Choice* and Friedman's response see D. Herzog, "I Hear a Rhapsody: A Reading of *The Republic of Choice*" (1992) 17 Law & Soc. Inquiry 147, and L. Friedman, "I Hear Cacophony" (1992) 17 Law & Soc. Inquiry 159 at 162. See also J. Kaplan, [Review] (1990) 27 Harv. J. on Legis. 613.
28 Friedman, *supra* note 3 at 61.
29 *Ibid.* at 206.
30 Stein, *supra* note 26 at 199-200.
31 D. Brooks, "The Triumph of Hope over Self-Interest" *New York Times* (12 January 2003) 15.
32 L. Cohen, *A Consumers' Republic: The Politics of Mass Consumption in Postwar America* (New York: Alfred A. Knopf, 2003).
33 Stein, *supra* note 26 at 200.
34 See Chapter 3, this volume, at 50-62.
35 Stein, *supra* note 26 at 201.
36 *Ibid.* at 3.
37 *Ibid.* at 3-4.
38 *Ibid.* at 6
39 J. Heath, *The Efficient Society: Why Canada Is As Close to Utopia As It Gets* (Toronto: Penguin/Viking, 2001).
40 *Ibid.* at xviii, 300.
41 Stein, *supra* note 26. She quotes Heath in several places in her book. For the quotes in her text see pages 68 and 191.
42 *Ibid.* at 191.
43 Heath, *supra* note 39 at xv.
44 Stein, *supra* note 26 at 51.
45 R. Gwyn, *Nationalism without Walls: The Unbearable Lightness of Being Canadian* (Toronto: McClelland and Stewart, 1995) at 78 and 42.
46 S. Clarkson, "Continental and Global Governance," c. 3, and "NAFTA and WTO as Supraconstitution," c. 4 in *Uncle Sam and Us: Globalization, Neoconservatism, and the Canadian State* (Toronto: University of Toronto Press, 2002).
47 C. Summers, "The Battle in Seattle: Free Trade, Labor Rights and Societal Values" (2001) 22 U. Pa. J. Int'l Econ. L. 61.
48 K. Banting, G. Hoberg, and R. Simeon, "Introduction" in Banting, Hoberg, and Simeon, *supra* note 2 at 19.
49 Stein, *supra* note 26 at 57-58; Banting, Hoberg, and Simeon, "Introduction," *ibid.*; and Heath, *supra* note 39 at 287-91.
50 W. Watson, *Globalization and the Meaning of Canadian Life* (Toronto: University of Toronto Press, 1998).
51 *Ibid.*, c. 1-7.
52 *Ibid.*, c. 4, "Convergence?" and especially, 37.

53 J. Slemrod, "Tax Cacophony and the Benefits of Free Trade" in J. Bhagwate and R. Hudec, eds., *Fair Trade and Harmonization: Prerequisites for Free Trade*, vol. 1, *Economic Analysis* (Cambridge, MA: MIT Press, 1996) c. 6, cited in *ibid.* at 59.

54 Slemrod, *ibid.* at 299, 305, quoted in Watson, *supra* note 50 at 59.

55 Watson, *supra* note 50 at 40.

56 *Ibid.* at 42.

57 D. Rodick, "Why Do More Open Economies Have Bigger Governments?" (1998) 106 Journal of Political Economy, 998.

58 D. Cameron and J. Gross Stein, "Street Protests and Fantasy Parks" in D. Cameron and J. Gross Stein, eds., *Street Protests and Fantasy Parks* (Vancouver: UBC Press, 2002) 1 at 9.

59 *Ibid.* at 49-50.

60 R. Gordon and A. Bovenberg, "Why Is Capital So Immobile Internationally? Possible Explanations and Implications for Capital Income Taxation" (1996) 86 American Economic Review 1057.

61 J. Helliwell, "Globalization: Myths, Facts, and Consequences" (paper presented at the Benefactors Lecture, C.D. Howe Institute, October 2000).

62 T. Courchene, *A State of Minds: Toward a Human Capital Future for Canadians* (Montreal: Institute for Research on Public Policy [IRPP]) at 51.

63 *Ibid.* at 289, note 9.

64 J. McCallum, "National Borders Matter: Canada-US Regional Trade Patterns" (1995) 85 American Economic Review 615.

65 *Ibid.* at 622.

66 Watson, *supra* note 50 at 53.

67 *Ibid.* at 54.

68 *Ibid.* at 55.

69 Parts of this section of this chapter are based on W.A. Bogart, *Consequences: The Impact of Law and Its Complexity* (Toronto: University of Toronto Press, 2002) c. 7, "The Environment: Sunshine or Apocalypse," 242 and following.

70 S. Charnovitz, "The North American Free Trade Agreement: Green Law or Green Spin?" (1994) 26 Law & Pol'y Int'l Bus. 1; B. McAndrew, "NAFTA Criticized on Environment" *Toronto Star* (13 August 1997) C3.

71 Clarkson, *supra* note 46, c. 17, "The (Un)sustainable State: Deregulating the Environment" at 329; K. Day and R. Grafton, "Economic Growth and Environmental Deregulation in Canada" in K. Banting, A. Sharpe, and F. St-Hilaire, eds., *The Longest Decade: Canada in the 1990s: The Review of Economic Performance and Social Progress* (Montreal: IRPP, 2001) at 293.

72 D. Vogel, *Trading Up: Consumer and Environmental Regulation in a Global Economy* (Cambridge, MA: Harvard University Press, 1995).

73 *Ibid.* at 269-70.

74 *Ibid.* at 256. Vogel also indicates that in 1993 the German government modified its recycling standards because German firms complained that some of these requirements were disadvantaging them competitively.

75 N. Kada, "Book Review: *Trading Up*" (1996) 5 Journal of Environment and Development 120.

76 R. Peduzzi, "Book Review: *Trading Up*" (1996) 23 Ecology L. Q. 499.

77 D. Caldwell and D. Wirth, "Trade and the Environment: Equilibrium or Imbalance?" (1996) 17 Mich. J. Int'l L. 563 at 579-80.

78 See also R. Howse, "The Appellate Body Rulings in the Shrimp/Turtle Case: A New Legal Baseline for the Trade and Environment Debate" (2002) 27 Colum. J. Envtl. L. 491.

79 Vogel, *supra* note 72 at 269-70.

80 K. Harrison, "Paper Trails: Environmental Regulation in a Global Economy" (paper presented at the annual meeting of the American Political Science Association, August-September 2002).

81 C. Runge, "Book Review" (1997) 35 Journal of Economic Literature 143 at 144.

82 J. Stiglitz, *Globalization and Its Discontents* (New York: W.W. Norton, 2003).

83 Cameron and Stein, *supra* note 58 at 142.

84 Stein, *supra* note 26 at 58.

85 M. Barlow and D. Robinson, "Another Take on the Effects of Free Trade" *Globe and Mail* (15 December 1995) A23.

86 J. Bakan, *The Corporation: The Pathological Pursuit of Profit and Power* (Toronto: Viking Canada, 2004); R. Walker, "The Alienation Market" *New York Times Magazine* (13 June 2004) 32.

87   Bakan, *ibid*. The phrase in quotation marks is the subtitle of the book.
88   K. Banting, "The Social Policy Divide: The Welfare State in Canada and the United States" in Banting, Hoberg, and Simeon, *supra* note 2 at 267.
89   *Ibid*. at 268-69.
90   *Ibid*. at 268.
91   *Ibid*. at 268.
92   *Ibid*. at 303.
93   *Ibid*. at 297-99.
94   *Ibid*. at 303.
95   *Ibid*. at 305.
96   *Ibid*. at 305-6.
97   *Ibid*. at 306.
98   *Ibid*. at 309.
99   K. Banting, A. Sharpe, and F. St-Hilaire, "The Longest Decade: Introduction and Overview" in Banting, Sharpe, and St-Hilaire, *supra* note 71 at 1.
100 J. Stanford, "The Economic and Social Consequences of Fiscal Retrenchment in Canada in the 1990s" in Banting, Sharpe, and St-Hilaire, *ibid*. at 141 and 155-56.
101 T. Courchene, *A State of Minds: Toward a Human Capital Future for Canadians* (Montreal: IRPP, 2001) at 12.
102 *Ibid*. at 10.
103 W.A. Bogart, "The Forms of Litigation," c. 3 in *Courts and Country: The Limits of Litigation and the Social and Political Life of Canada* (Toronto: Oxford University Press, 1994).
104 *Ibid*., c. 5, "Women and the Courts: '... How Things Must Be, Forever?'"
105 C. Backhouse, *Colour-Coded: A Legal History of Racism in Canada, 1900-1950* (Toronto: University of Toronto Press, 1999).
106 Bogart, *supra* note 103, c. 4, "The Administrative State and Judicial Review."
107 *Ibid*., c. 6, "The Judges and Tort: Purpose and Limit."
108 H. Arthurs, "Jonah and the Whale: The Appearance, Disappearance, and Reappearance of Administrative Law" (1980) 30 U.T.L.J. 225 at 225; Arthurs has developed this theme in more detail in his book *"Without the Law": Administrative Justice and Legal Pluralism in Nineteenth-Century England* (Toronto: University of Toronto Press, 1985).
109 P. Monahan and A. Petter, "Developments in Constitutional Law: 85-86 Term" (1987) 9 Sup. Ct. L. Rev. 69 at 71, 178, and 180, quoted in K. Roach, *The Supreme Court on Trial: Judicial Activism or Democratic Dialogue* (Toronto: Irwin Law, 2001) at 70. See also M. Mandel, *The Charter of Rights and the Legalization of Politics in Canada*, rev. ed. (Toronto: Thomson, 1994); A. Hutchinson, *Waiting for Coraf: A Critique of Law and Rights* (Toronto: University of Toronto Press, 1995); and J. Bakan, *Just Words: Constitutional Rights and Social Wrongs* (Toronto: University of Toronto Press, 1997).
110 For an analysis of these decisions and further legislative attempts to protect victims, see Roach, *ibid*. at 268-73 and J. Hiebert, *Charter Conflicts: What Is Parliament's Role?* (Montreal and Kingston: McGill-Queen's University Press, 2002) c. 5, "Sexual Assault Trials."
111 *RJR MacDonald Inc. v. Canada, (A.G.)* [1994] 1 S.C.R. 311. For a discussion of the effects of law in suppressing smoking see Bogart, *supra* note 69, c. 6, "Smoking – and Waves of Cultural Antagonism."
112 Roach, *supra* note 109 at 161-63 and 184-87. See also Hiebert, *supra* note 110, c. 4, "Tobacco Advertising."
113 *Eaton v. Brant County Board of Education*, [1997] 1 S.C.R. 241, discussed in Chapter 7, this volume; and *Law v. Canada* [1999] 1 S.C.R. 497, discussed in Chapter 8, this volume.
114 *Delgamuukw v. British Columbia*, [1997] 3 S.C.R. 1010; see also Chapter 5, this volume.
115 See Chapter 2, this volume, at 40-42.
116 See Chapter 3, this volume, at 64-67.
117 See Chapter 2, this volume, at 43-44.
118 Arthurs and Kreklewich, *supra* note 6 at 20.

Chapter 5: Aboriginals
1   L. Friedman, *The Horizontal Society* (New Haven, CT: Yale University Press, 1999); this book builds on his earlier one, *The Republic of Choice* (Cambridge, MA: Harvard University Press, 1990).
2   *Ibid*., *The Horizontal Society* at 20.

3 *Ibid.* at 23.
4 *Ibid.* at 18-19.
5 *Ibid.* at 18.
6 *Ibid.* at 17.
7 R.S.C. 1985, c. I-5.
8 J. Stackhouse, "First Step: End the Segregation" *Globe and Mail* (15 December 2001) F1, F9. This article was the conclusion to a fourteen-part series that ran during November and December 2001.
9 C. Krauss, "Native Canadians Bask in New Business Climate" *New York Times* (26 October 2002) A3.
10 J. Richards, "Neighbors Matter: Poor Neighborhoods and Urban Aboriginal Policy" (Toronto: C.D. Howe Institute, 2001) 13.
11 *Ibid.* at 16.
12 J. Stackhouse, "The Young and the Restless" *Globe and Mail* (5 December 2001) A10.
13 L. Chwialkowska, "PM Set to Overhaul Native Policy" *National Post* (8 December 2001) A1, A10.
14 J. Richards, "Let's Get Past Our Reservations" *Globe and Mail* (19 December 2001) A19.
15 T. Flanagan, *First Nations? Second Thoughts* (Montreal and Kingston: McGill-Queen's University Press, 2000) at 197.
16 Chwialkowska, *supra* note 13.
17 Flanagan, *supra* note 15 at 91-92 and the sources he cites for the statistics and quotations set out in the text.
18 Chwialkowska, *supra* note 13.
19 Bill C-7, *An Act Respecting Leadership Selection, Administration and Accountability of Indian Bands, and to Make Related Amendments to Other Acts*, 2d Sess., 37th Parl., 2003.
20 Editorial, "If He Differs with Nault, What Is Martin's Plan?" *Globe and Mail* (8 May 2003) A18; C. Clark and K. Lunman, "Martin Softens His Opposition to Aboriginals Bill" *Globe and Mail* (9 May 2003) A7.
21 R. Jamieson, "Building New Relationships" *Law Times* (28 July 2003) 7.
22 K. Lunman and S. McCarthy, "Chiefs Intimidating Natives, Minister Says" *Globe and Mail* (8 May 2003) A4; Editorial, "Martin Is Sliding Past Tough Aboriginal Issues" *Globe and Mail* (20 April 2004) A16.
23 Quoted in A. Fleras and J. Elliott, *The "Nations Within"* (Toronto: Oxford University Press, 1992) at 39, cited in A. Cairns, *Citizens Plus: Aboriginal Peoples and the Canadian State* (Vancouver: UBC Press, 2000) at 17.
24 Quoted in *Report of the Royal Commission on Aboriginal Peoples*, vol. 2 (2) *Restructuring the Relationship* (Ottawa: Canada Communication Group Publishing 1996) at 553 [hereafter RCAP], cited in Cairns, *ibid.* at 18.
25 M. Whittington, "Aboriginal Self-Government in Canada" in M. Whittington, ed., *Canadian Politics in the 21st Century* (Toronto: Nelson, 2000) 105 at 109.
26 RCAP, *supra* note 24, vol. 1, *Looking Forward, Looking Back*, c. 11, "Relocation of Aboriginal Communities."
27 N. Dyck, *What Is the Indian "Problem"?* (St. John's, NF: Institute of Social and Economic Research, 1991) at 27, cited in Cairns, *supra* note 23 at 50.
28 H. Hawthorn, ed., *A Survey of the Contemporary Indians of Canada*, 2 vols. (Ottawa: Queen's Printer, 1966 and 1967) online at <http://www.ainc-inac.gc.ca/pr/pub/srvy/sci_e.html> (accessed 6 October 2003) [hereafter Hawthorn Report].
29 Canada, *Statement of the Government of Canada on Indian Policy*, presented to the First Session of the Twenty-Eighth Parliament by the Honourable Jean Chrétien, minister of Indian Affairs and Northern Development (Ottawa: Department of Indian Affairs and Northern Development, 1969) (the White Paper).
30 *Ibid.* at 11.
31 The Right Honourable Pierre Elliott Trudeau, remarks on the Indian, Aboriginal, and treaty rights, Vancouver, 8 August 1969, cited in Cairns, *supra* note 23 at 52.
32 Quoted in M. Watkins, ed., *Dene Nation: The Colony Within* (Toronto: University of Toronto Press, 1977) at 3-4, cited in Cairns, *supra* note 23 at 166.
33 Friedman, *supra* note 1.
34 F. Abele, "Small Nations and Democracy's Prospects: Indigenous Peoples in Canada, Australia, New Zealand, Norway and Greenland" (2001) 10 Inroads 137.

35 See also section 25 of the *Charter*: "[T]his *Charter* ... shall not be construed so as to abrogate or derogate from any aboriginal, treaty or other rights or freedoms"; see T. Isaac, *"Canadian Charter of Rights and Freedoms:* The Challenge of Individual and Collective Rights of Aboriginal People" (2002) 21 Windsor Y.B. Acess Just. 431.

36 Cairns, *supra* note 23 at 172.

37 The Charlottetown Accord's provisions relating to Aboriginal people are summarized in Cairns, *supra* note 23 at 81-83.

38 RCAP, *supra* note 24.

39 The recommendations of RCAP are summarized in Cairns, *supra* note 23 at 199-220.

40 *Ibid.* at 117.

41 National Association of Friendship Centres (NAFC) and Law Commission of Canada (LCC) *Urban Aboriginal Governance in Canada: Re-Fashioning the Dialogue* (Ottawa: NAFC and LCC, 1999) at 16 [hereafter NAFC and LCC]; see also P. Hogg, *Constitutional Law of Canada, 2003* student ed. (Toronto: Carswell, 2003) c. 27, "Aboriginal Peoples"; and B. Morse, "Twenty Years of *Charter* Protection: The Status of Aboriginal Peoples under the *Canadian Charter of Rights and Freedoms"* (2002) 21 Windsor Y.B. Access. Just. 385. In November 2004, the Supreme Court reinforced the importance of governments' obligations to consult with Aboriginals regarding any use of disputed lands: see K. Makin, "Landmark Claims Ruling Made" *Globe and Mail* (19 November 2004) A7.

42 See also M. Ignatieff, *The Rights Revolution* (Toronto: House of Anansi, 2000) at 58-62 and 80-81.

43 Cairns, *supra* note 23 at 175.

44 P. Macklem, "First Nations Self-Government and the Borders of the Canadian Legal Imagination" (1991) 36 McGill L.J. 382 at 394-95. See also P. Macklem, *Indigenous Difference and the Constitution of Canada* (Toronto: University of Toronto Press, 2001) [hereafter *Indigenous Difference*].

45 *Ibid.*, "First Nations Self-Government" at 393.

46 *Ibid.* at 394.

47 *Ibid.* at 387.

48 W. Pentney, "The Rights of the Aboriginal Peoples of Canada in the Constitutional Act, 1982: Part I – The Interpretive Prism of Section 25" (1982) 22 U.B.C. L. Rev. 21 at 59.

49 J. Borrows, *Recovering Canada: The Resurgence of Indigenous Law* (Toronto: University of Toronto Press, 2002) at xii.

50 M. Glendon, *Rights Talk: The Impoverishment of Political Discourse* (New York: Free Press, 1991) at 7.

51 K. Roach, *The Supreme Court on Trial: Judicial Activism or Democratic Dialogue* (Toronto: Irwin Law, 2001) at 172; L. Dufraimont, "From Regulation to Recolonization: Justifiable Infringement of Aboriginal Rights at the Supreme Court of Canada" (2000) 58 U.T. Fac. L. Rev. 3.

52 See Chapter 3, this volume, at 64-67.

53 *R. v. Marshall*, [1999] 3 S.C.R. 456.

54 L. Rotman, "Marshalling Principles from the *Marshall* Morass" (2000) 23 Dal. L.J. 5 at 46.

55 Roach, *supra* note 51 at 172.

56 Cairns, *supra* note 23 at 187.

57 Macklem, *Indigenous Difference*, *supra* note 44 at 287.

58 J. Mahoney, "Numbers on the Rise as Language on the Wane" *Globe and Mail* (22 January 2003) A6; Richards, *supra* note 10 at 3.

59 Western Landscapes, "Urban Aboriginals: Opportunities and Challenges" (Calgary: Canada West Foundation, 2001) [hereafter Western Landscapes]. See also the Final Report: A Western Cities Project Report, *Shared Responsibility: Final Report and Recommendations of the Urban Aboriginal Initiative* (Calgary: Canada West Foundation, 2003).

60 Cairns, *supra* note 23 at 128-29, and sources cited.

61 Flanagan, *supra* note 15 at 176.

62 Richards, *supra* note 10.

63 Stackhouse, *supra* note 8, and J. Stackhouse, "Welcome to Harlem on the Prairies" *Globe and Mail* (3 November 2001) F2.

64 C. Hanselmann, *Urban Aboriginal People in Western Canada: Realities and Policies* (Calgary: Canada West Foundation, 2001) at 4-9.

65 Cairns, *supra* note 23 at 126, citing figures in RCAP, *supra* note 24.

66 *Ibid.* at 100, and source cited.
67 Mahoney, *supra* note 58.
68 M. Wente, "In Whose Best Interest?" *Globe and Mail* (13 September 2003) A27.
69 Cairns, *supra* note 23 at 101.
70 *Ibid.* at 126.
71 *Ibid.* at 124.
72 Canada, RCAP, *Partners in Confederation. Aboriginal Peoples, Self-Government and the Constitution* (Ottawa: Canada Communication Group, 1993) at 44.
73 J. Simpson, "Just What Is a 'Nation' and How Can It Work Like a Province?" *Globe and Mail* (25 February 1997) A18.
74 Cairns, *supra* note 23 at 124.
75 NAFC and LCC, *supra* note 41.
76 *Ibid.* at 44-50.
77 *Ibid.* at 44.
78 *Ibid.* at 50-54.
79 *Ibid.* at 50.
80 *Ibid.* at 55-58.
81 *Ibid.* at 55.
82 *Ibid.* at 25-26.
83 *Ibid.* at 9.
84 *Ibid.*
85 Macklem, *Indigenous Difference*, *supra* note 44.
86 *Ibid.* None of the chapters, in whole or in part, address urban issues. The words "city," "off reserve," and "urban" do not appear in the index.
87 Hanselmann, *supra* note 64 at 9-10.
88 Government of Canada, *Gathering Strength: Canada's Aboriginal Action Plan* (Ottawa: Minister of Indian Affairs and Northern Development, 1997) online at <http://www.ainc-inac.gc.ca/gs/chg_e.html> (accessed 6 October 2003).
89 Western Landscapes, *supra* note 59 at 2.
90 Indian and Northern Affairs Canada, "Budget 2003 Highlights," online at <http://www.ainc-inac.gc.ca/nr/wc/bdg2k3hl_e.html> (accessed 6 October 2003).
91 C. Hanselmann, *Enhanced Urban Aboriginal Programming in Western Canada* (Calgary: Canada West Foundation, 2002).
92 *Ibid.* at 10.
93 *Ibid.* at 9.
94 *Ibid.* at 12.
95 *Ibid.*
96 O. Mercredi and M. Turpel, *In the Rapids: Navigating the Future of First Nations* (Toronto: Viking/Penguin, 1993) at 35.
97 Cairns, *supra* note 23 at 143.
98 *Ibid.* at 154.
99 *Ibid.* at 158.
100 Canada, *Gathering Strength: Canada's Aboriginal Action Plan*, *supra* note 88.
101 Cairns, *supra* note 23 at 122.
102 *Ibid.* at 121.
103 J. Simpson, "A View of Life That Harkens to a Golden Age for Aboriginal Peoples" *Globe and Mail* (26 February 1997) A16.
104 J. Simpson, "The Words Are Magnificent, but Can They Be Realistically Implemented?" *Globe and Mail* (28 February 1997) A18.
105 Canada, *Indian and Native Programs: A Study Team Report to the Task Force on Program Review* (Ottawa: Supply and Services, 1986).
106 S. Weaver, "Indian Policy in the New Conservative Government, Part 1: The Nielsen Task Force of 1985" (1986) 2 Native Studies Review 1 at 15, quoted in Cairns, *supra* note 23 at 71.
107 *Ibid.* at 19, quoted in Cairns, *supra* note 23 at 72.
108 P. Manning, *The New Canada* (Toronto: Macmillan, 1992) at 304.
109 M. Smith, *Our Home or Native Land?* (Victoria, BC: Crown West, 1995) at 264.
110 Flanagan, *supra* note 15.
111 *Ibid.* at 5.

112 *Ibid.* at 194-95.
113 Letter from A. Cairns to T. Flanagan (24 February 2001) in "Flanagan and Cairns on Aboriginal Policy" (2001) Policy Options 43, 46; L. Rotman, Review (Spring 2001) Isuma 130.
114 D. Bricker and E. Greenspon, *Searching for Certainty: Inside the New Canadian Mindset* (Toronto: Doubleday, 2001) 276-78.
115 *Ibid.* at 277.
116 *Ibid.* at 277, quoting a 1998 Angus Reid survey.
117 K. Makin, "Canadians Hold Charter Ideals High" *Globe and Mail* (20 November 2002) A6.
118 S. McCarthy, "Social Spending Preferable to Tax Cuts, Poll Finds" *Globe and Mail* (17 February 2003) A1, A4.
119 Bricker and Greenspon, *supra* note 114 at 278.
120 Cairns, *supra* note 23.
121 *Ibid.* at 28.
122 A. Parkin, "Introduction: 'What Will Hold Us Together?'" in the CRIC Papers, *Bridging the Divide between Aboriginal Peoples and the Canadian State* (Montreal: Centre for Research and Information on Canada, 2001) at 2 [hereafter CRIC Papers].
123 Cairns, *supra* note 23 at 210.
124 *Ibid.* at 199.
125 *Ibid.* at 102.
126 *Ibid.* at 143 and 168.
127 Hawthorn Report, *supra* note 28, discussed above, at 100-1.
128 Cairns, *supra* note 23 at 9.
129 CRIC Papers, *supra* note 122 at "Preface," 1.
130 Letter from T. Flanagan to A. Cairns in "Flanagan and Cairns on Aboriginal Policy," *supra* note 113 at 43.
131 K. Brock, "*Citizens Plus:* Old Debates, New Understandings" in CRIC Papers, *supra* note 122 at 15 and 15.
132 B. Rae, "*Citizens Plus:* A Review" in CRIC Papers, *supra* note 122 at 5.
133 P. Monture-Angus, "*Citizens Plus:* Sensitivities versus Solutions" in CRIC Papers, *supra* note 122 at 8 and 10.
134 Rae, *supra* note 132 at 7.
135 *Ibid.* at 7.
136 W. Kymlicka, "Paddling on a Parallel Course" *National Post* (10 June 2000) B12.
137 Letter from T. Flanagan to A. Cairns in "Flanagan and Cairns on Aboriginal Policy," *supra* note 113 at 44.
138 *Ibid.* at 45.
139 Brock, *supra* note 131 at 15.

Chapter 6: Citizens in Cyberspace

1 All quoted in F. Cairncross, *The Death of Distance: How the Communications Revolution Is Changing Our Lives*, 2nd ed. (Boston: Harvard Business School, 2001): the British Admiralty and the telegraph, 6; *New York Times*, 60; Olsen and the computer, 32.
2 Good histories of the Internet and explanations of its components are contained in A. Terrett and I. Monaghan, "The Internet: An Introduction for Lawyers" in L. Edwards and C. Waelde, eds., *Law and the Internet,* 2nd ed. (Oxford: Hart Publishing, 2000) 1; M. Smith and P. Kellock, "Communities in Cyberspace" in M. Smith and P. Kellock, *Communities in Cyberspace* (London. Routledge, 1999) 3.
3 Cairncross, *supra* note 1 at 37.
4 See, generally, P. Norris, *Digital Divide: Civic Engagement, Information Poverty, and the Internet Worldwide* (Cambridge, UK: Cambridge University Press, 2001) at 23.
5 However, in terms of overall technological development, it is a laggard among the best: S. Edwards, "Canada Eighth in Technology Race" *National Post* (10 July 2001) A8, reporting on the technology index published by the United Nations.
6 B. Ebo, "Cyberglobalization: Superhighway or Superhypeway?" in B. Ebo, ed., *Cyberimperialism? Global Relations in the New Electronic Frontier* (Westport, CT: Praeger Publishers, 2001) 1 at 3.
7 "Broadband Blues" *The Economist* (23 June 2001) 62.
8 Cairncross, *supra* note 1 at 90-91.
9 Ebo, *supra* note 6 at 3.
10 Online: <http://www.ntia.doc.gov>, as cited in Cairncross, *supra* note 1 at 308 n. 33.

11 Cairncross, *supra* note 1 at 286; K. Hafner, "For Some Internet Users, It's Better Late Than Never" *New York Times* (25 March 2004) E1.

12 A. Wilhelm, *Democracy in the Digital Age: Challenges to Political Life in Cyberspace* (New York: Routledge, 2000) at 150-51.

13 Cairncross, *supra* note 1 at 287.

14 P. Woodall, "Survey: The New Economy: Untangling the e-conomics" *The Economist* (23 September 2000).

15 Ebo, *supra* note 6 at 2.

16 *Ibid.* at 2-3.

17 See discussion of this point and related ones in A. Shapiro, *The Control Revolution: How the Internet Is Putting Individuals in Charge and Changing the World We Know* (New York: Public Affairs, 1999) at 65.

18 *Ibid.* at 3.

19 *Ibid.* at 4-5.

20 "Canyon or Mirage" *The Economist* (24 January 2004) 69.

21 Cairncross, *supra* note 1 at 2.

22 "The Internet, Untethered" *The Economist* (13 October 2001) 3.

23 Cairncross, *supra* note 1 at 7. K. Hafner "The Future of Cellphones Is Here – Sort Of" *New York Times* (14 February 2002) D1; J. Selingo, "Talking More but Enjoying It Less" *New York Times* (14 February 2002) D1.

24 Cairncross, *ibid.* at 9 and 125.

25 *Ibid.* at 61.

26 "Fading" *The Economist* (8 March 2003) 53.

27 C. Sunstein, *Republic.com* (Princeton, NJ: Princeton University Press, 2001) at 13.

28 "Pass the Pulitzers" *The Economist* (7 July 2001) 33. See also S. Elliott, "Altered Reality: ABC's New Show 'All American Girl' Will Work In the Products of Sponsors" *New York Times* (12 March 2003) C7.

29 Usenet is a computer conferencing network that permits a user to read and post messages on an electronic bulletin board. The bulletin board can be read by any other person who subscribes to that bulletin board. Thousands of Usenet groups exist, covering a multitude of topics.

30 Shapiro, *supra* note 17 at 42.

31 Wilhelm, *supra* note 12 at 139, referring to D. Holmes, "Virtual Identity: Communities of Broadcast, Communities of Interactivity," in D. Holmes, *Virtual Politics: Identity and Community in Cyberspace* (London: Sage, 1997). More generally, see N. Postman, *Amusing Ourselves to Death* (New York: Penguin Books, 1986); and R. Putnam, *Bowling Alone: The Collapse and Revival of American Community* (New York: Simon and Schuster, 2000).

32 A. Hamon, "Exploration of World Wide Web Tilts from Eclectic to Mundane: Routine Visits Are Replacing Cyberspace Surfing" *New York Times* (26 August 2001) A1, A8.

33 Cairncross, *supra* note 1 at 3.

34 D. Gallagher, "New Economy: In the 'Google Economy' Businesses Thrive by Appearing Prominently on the Search Engine's Free Listings" *New York Times* (9 December 2002) C6.

35 Cairncross, *supra* note 1 at 116.

36 Shapiro, *supra* note 17 at 98.

37 S. Hansell, "Internet Losing Ground in Battle against Spam" *New York Times* (22 April 2003) A1, C6; G. Johnson, "That Gibberish in Your In-Box May Be Good News" The Week in Review, *New York Times* (15 January 2004) 16.

38 Shapiro, *supra* note 17 at 99-100, quoting the original WebTV advertisement.

39 Wilhelm, *supra* note 12 at 139.

40 J. Naughton, *A Brief History of the Future: The Origins of the Internet* (London: Weidenfeld and Nicolson, 1999) at xii.

41 "When Terrorists Log On" *New York Times* (21 October 2001) A14; J. Schwartz, "Cyberspace Seen as Potential Battleground" *New York Times* (23 November 2001) B5.

42 Quoted in Shapiro, *supra* note 17 at 30.

43 K. Hafner, "The Internet's Invisible Hand: At a Public Utility Serving the World, No One's Really in Charge. Does It Matter?" *New York Times* (10 January 2002) D1; P. Brethour, "New Rules to Track Internet Traffic Unveiled" *Globe and Mail* (16 January 2002) B1.

44 Shapiro, *supra* note 17 at 63-64.

45 "Developments in the Law: The Law of Cyberspace" (1999) 112 Harv. L. Rev. 1574; J. Boyle, "Foucault in Cyberspace: Surveillance, Sovereignty, and Hard-Wired Censors" (1997) online at <http://www.law.duke.edu/boylesite/fouc1.htm>.

46 L. Lessig, "The Law of the Horse: What Cyberlaw Might Teach" (1999) 113 Harv. L. Rev. 501; see also F. Easterbrook, "Cyberspace and the Law of the Horse" (1996) U. Chicago Legal F. 207.

47 M. Geist, "Internet Jurisdiction: The Shifting Adjudicatory Approach" (Spring 2002) Isuma 87; M. Richtel, "Courts Are Split on Internet Bans: Some Judges Say Cybercrime Justifies Limits on Convicts" *New York Times* (21 January 2003) A1, C2.

48 Government of Canada, *Illegal and Offensive Content on the Internet* (Ottawa: Industry Canada, February 2001) online at <http://www.connect.gc.ca/cyberwise>.

49 "The Internet's New Borders" *The Economist* (11 August 2001) 9; M. Geist, "E-Borders Loom, for Better or Worse" *Globe and Mail* (28 June 2001) B15.

50 R. Diebert, "The Internet and the 'Borderless' World" (Spring 2002) Isuma 113.

51 Cairncross, *supra* note 1 at 83-86.

52 C. Mann and D. Orejas, "A NAFTA Approach to Internet Governance" (Spring 2002) Isuma, 113.

53 Editorial, "The Next Microsoft Windows" *New York Times* (13 July 2001) A18.

54 "Broadband Blues," *supra* note 7 at 62.

55 Information Advisory Council, *Connection, Community, Content: The Challenge of the Information Highway* (Ottawa: Industry Canada, 1995) online at <http://strategis.gc.ca/SSG/ih01070e.html> and *Preparing Canada for a Digital World* (Ottawa: Industry Canada, 1997).

56 Report of the National Broadband Task Force, *The New National Dream: Networking the Nation for Broadband Access* (Ottawa: Industry Canada, 2001) online at <http://broadband.gc.ca>; Information Highway Advisory Council, *Building the Information Society: Moving Canada into the 21st Century* (Ottawa: Industry Canada, 1996).

57 CRTC, *New Media*, Broadcasting Public Notice, CRTC 1999-84.

58 Sunstein, *supra* note 27. For a critical review of Sunstein, see "Web Phobia" *The Economist* (24 March 2001) 99.

59 D. Gutstein, *E.con: How the Internet Undermines Democracy* (Toronto: Stoddart, 1999).

60 Regarding the problems determining the outcomes produced by law see W.A. Bogart, *Consequences: The Impact of Law and its Complexity* (Toronto: University of Toronto Press, 2002).

61 E. Turner, *Why Things Bite Back: Technology and the Revenge of Unintended Consequences* (New York: Alfred A. Knopf, 1996).

62 "E-commerce Takes Off" Special Report, *The Economist* (15-21 May 2004) 9. Canadians may be laggards in some respects in this regard: see B. Tedeschi, "E-Commerce Report" *New York Times* (26 January 2004) C5.

63 Even job searching may not be particularly aided by the Net: M. Ligos, "In Job Search, Warm and Fuzzy Beats Online and All-Business" *New York Times* (2 February 2003) 10-11.

64 Sunstein, *supra* note 27 at 7, discussing the ideas of MIT technology specialist Nicholas Negroponte.

65 Sunstein himself may have retreated somewhat from his original position. See his subsequent essay and various comments on it: C. Sunstein, "The Daily We: Is the Internet Good for Democracy?" (2001) online at <http://boston review>. See also J. Fallows, "He's Got Mail" *New York Review of Books* (14 March 2002) 4.

66 Shapiro, *supra* note 17 at 113.

67 Report of Special Rapporteur Abid Hussain to the United Nations Commission on Human Rights, "Promotion and Protection of the Right to Freedom of Opinion and Expression," 28 January 1998, section 3(C), quoted in Shapiro, *supra* note 17 at 14 and 239 n. 4.

68 J. Davidson and W. Rees-Mogg, *The Sovereign Individual: How to Survive and Thrive During the Collapse of the Welfare State* (New York: Simon and Schuster, 1997) at 320.

69 Shapiro, *supra* note 17 at 84-85.

70 *Ibid.* at 21.

71 J.-J. Rousseau, *Emile,* trans. A. Bloom (New York: Basic Books, 1979) at 120, quoted in *ibid.* at 86.

72 L. Grossman, *The Electronic Republic: Reshaping Democracy in the Information Age* (New York: Viking, 1995) at 4.

73 Wilhelm, *supra* note 12 at 3-4.

74 R. Davis, *The Web of Politics: The Internet's Impact on the American Political System* (New York: Oxford University Press, 1999) at 33, quoting H. Howard, *Multiple Ownership in Television Broadcasting* (New York: Arno Press, 1979) at 219.

75 Davis, *ibid.* at 34.
76 S. Rosell, *Renewing Governance: Governing by Learning in the Information Age* (Toronto: Oxford University Press, 1999). The book contains the report and commentary.
77 *Ibid.* at 7.
78 *Ibid.* at 170.
79 *Ibid.* at 170 and see c. 5, "Governing in an Information Society."
80 E. Richard, "Lessons from the Network Model for Online Engagement of Citizens." A project by Canadian Policy Research Networks with Public Works and Government Services Canada (2000) online at <http://www.cprn.org/pubs/files/pubs-e.html>.
81 Deloitte Consulting and Deloitte and Touche, "At the Dawn of E-Government: The Citizen as Customer" Report (New York: Deloitte Research, 2000) at 4, online at <http://www.dc.com/research>.
82 *Ibid.* at 16.
83 Cairncross, *supra* note 1 at 166-67.
84 Deloitte, *supra* note 81 at 6.
85 *Ibid.* at 12.
86 "A Survey of Government and the Internet" Insert, *The Economist* (24 June 2000) 1.
87 Deloitte, *supra* note 81 at 15.
88 Though self-diagnosis and self-treatment based on information gleaned from the Net can pose real hazards: S. Qaadri, "The Best Prescription: Surf with Caution" *Globe and Mail* (19 February 2002) R5.
89 Cairncross, *supra* note 1 at 174-75.
90 Deloitte, *supra* note 81 at 11.
91 Cairncross, *supra* note 1 at 175.
92 Broadband Task Force, *supra* note 56 at 29; W. Immen, "Healing without the Human Touch" *Globe and Mail* (7 August 2001) R5.
93 R. Downey and L. Berdahl, "E-Municipalities in Western Canada" Report (Calgary: Canada West Foundation, 2001) at 19.
94 *Ibid.* at 2.
95 *Ibid.* at 3.
96 "A Survey of Government and the Internet," *supra* note 86 at 4.
97 Quoted in Cairncross, *supra* note 1 at 158.
98 W. Lippman, *The Public Philosophy* (New York: New American Library, 1955) quoted in Shapiro, *supra* note 17 at 153.
99 H. Rheingold, *Smart Mobs: The Next Social Revolution* (Cambridge, MA: Perseus Books Group, 2003) at xviii [emphasis in original].
100 Only 50.7 percent of Americans eligible to vote did so in the 1996 presidential elections, Cairncross, *supra* note 1 at 162.
101 *Ibid.* at 159-64.
102 D. Tapscott, "Outdated Democracy: We Vote, They Rule" *Globe and Mail* (27 May 2004) A21.
103 "Digital Dilemmas" and "Power to the People" *The Economist* (25 January 2003) 17-23.
104 Cairncross, *supra* note 1 at 164.
105 Shapiro, *supra* note 17 at 157. See above discussion about disintermediation, at 126-27.
106 M. Margolis and D. Resnick, *Politics as Usual: The Cyberspace "Revolution"* (Thousand Oaks, CA: Sage Publications, 2000) 66.
107 Margolis and Resnick, *ibid.* at 73, discussing the study that they conducted.
108 *Ibid.* at 54.
109 *Ibid.* at 56-57.
110 *Ibid.* at 73.
111 R. Fairley Raney, "E-Mail Finds the Rare Ear in Congress" *New York Times* (13 December 2001) D11.
112 Margolis and Resnick, *supra* note 106 at 54.
113 *Ibid.* at 65.
114 R. Berke, "A New Movement Logs on to the Democratic Party and May Reshape It" The Week in Review, *New York Times* (28 December 2003) 5; G. Justice and J. Wilgoren, "Kerry Said to Have Raised $50 Million in Last Quarter" *New York Times* (3 April 2004) A11.
115 For a study of New Zealand politics and the Internet which reaches similar conclusions, see J. Roper, "New Zealand Political Parties Online: The World Wide Web as a Tool for

Democratization or for Political Marketing?" in C. Toulouse and T. Luke, eds., *The Politics of Cyberspace: A New Political Science Reader* (New York: Routledge, 1998) at 69.

116 G. Segell, "A People's Electronic Democracy and an Establishment System of Government: The United Kingdom" in Ebo, *supra* note 6 at 111.

117 *Ibid*. at 119.

118 R. Gibson and S. Ward, "Introduction" in R. Gibson and S. Ward, *Reinvigorating Democracy? British Politics and the Internet* (Aldershot, UK: Ashgate, 2000) 1 at 3.

119 R. Gibson and S. Ward, "Conclusions: Modernising without Democratising" in *ibid*. at 210.

120 *Ibid*. at 211. See also S. Coleman, "The Westminster Model in the Information Age" in S. Coleman et al., eds., *Parliament in the Age of the Internet* (Oxford: Oxford University Press, 1999) 9 at 25: "[the Internet and related technologies have] so far been relatively untested and regarded with traditional caution."

121 K. Magarey, "The Internet and Australian Parliamentary Democracy" in Coleman, *ibid*. at 42.

122 Norris, *supra* note 4 at 23.

123 *Ibid*. at 22.

124 S. Ostry, "A Clarion Call to Whatever" *Literary Review of Canada* 9:6 (Summer 2001) 5; W. Rashbaum, "Protestors and Police Using Internet" *New York Times* (1 February 2002) A15.

125 J. Lee, "How Protesters Mobilized So Many and So Nimbly" The Week in Review, *New York Times* (23 February 2003) 3.

126 R. Diebert, "Civil Society Activism on the World Wide Web: The Case of the Anti-MAI Lobby" in D. Cameron and J. Gross Stein, eds., *Street Protests and Fantasy Parks* (Vancouver: UBC Press, 2002) 88 at 103.

127 Gutstein, *supra* note 59 at 275-81, providing other examples of Canadian groups and their use of cyberspace.

128 Cairncross, *supra* note 1 at 160-61.

129 B. Wellman et al., "Does the Internet Increase, Decrease or Supplement Social Capital? Social Networks, Participation and Community Involvement" (2001) 45:3 American Behavioural Scientist 437-56, rev. version. The evidence comes from a National Geographic Society website survey; respondents included Canadians. The study challenges many of the assertions of Putnam, *supra* note 31.

130 Information on the government initiative Volnet can be obtained online at <http://www.volnet.org>.

131 Davis, *supra* note 74 at 82-84.

132 Margolis and Resnick, *supra* note 106 at 71.

133 See *supra* note 111 and accompanying text.

134 For a study of the English courts, see C. Walker, "The Courts, the Internet and Citizen Participation" in Gibson and Ward, *supra* note 118 at 81.

135 *Ibid*. at 88.

136 Davis, *supra* note 74 at 142.

137 M. Poster, "Cyberdemocracy: Internet and the Public Sphere" in D. Porter, ed., *Internet Culture* (New York: Routledge, 1997) 201 at 206.

138 J. Brown, chief scientist at Xerox, quoted in Davis, *supra* note 74 at 175.

139 Margolis and Resnick, *supra* note 106 at 100 (articulating but not agreeing with the position set out in the quote).

140 *Ibid*. at 109-11.

141 Davis, *supra* note 74, c. 6, "The Virtual Public."

142 *Ibid*. at 167; A. Harman, "Politics of the Web; Meet, Greet, Segregate, Meet Again" The Week in Review, *New York Times* (25 January 2004) 16.

143 L. Sproull and S. Faraj, "Atheism, Sex, and Databases: The Net as Social Technology" in B. Kahin and J. Keller, eds., *Public Access to the Internet* (Cambridge, MA: MIT Press, 1995) at 62.

144 Wilhelm, *supra* note 12, c. 5, "Virtual Sounding Boards: How Deliberative Is Online Discussion?" Wilhelm observes, 11: "The data show that these gathering places are in general home to an array of overlapping, short-lived conversations, usually among like-minded individuals. Sustained deliberation is rare in these forums, which means that, as currently designed and used, they may not be effective sounding boards for solving problems, engaging in collective action, and articulating issues to be addressed by government." See also K. Hill and J. Hughes, *Cyberpolitics: Citizen Activism in the Age of the Internet* (Lanham, MD: Rowman and Littlefield, 1998). Based on their empirical analyses of Usenet groups, websites, and "chat rooms" the authors observe: "Politics on the Internet is dominated by a relatively small, vociferous and technologically savvy, conservative minority. While Internet activists as a group

may not be overwhelmingly conservative, a conservative subset of these people is very active posting messages, engaging in political chats, and creating Web pages" (180).

145 C. Hanselmann, *Electrically Enhanced Democracy in Canada* (Calgary: Canada West Foundation, 2001).
146 *Ibid.* at 5-6.
147 *Ibid.* at 10.
148 *Ibid.* at 10.
149 *Ibid.* at 13.
150 *Ibid.* at 14.
151 Margolis and Resnick, *supra* note 106 at 100.
152 Wilhelm, *supra* note 12 at 132-38.
153 Speech from the Throne, 23 September 1997.
154 Report of the Panel on Smart Communities, *Smart Communities* (Ottawa: Industry Canada, 1998) at 1, online at <http://smartcommunities.ic.gc.ca/english/index2.htm>.
155 L. Roth, "How Comfortably Does the Internet Sit on Canada's Tundra? Reflections on Public Access to the Information Highway in the North" in L. d'Haenens, *Cyberidentities: Canadian and European Presence in Cyberspace* (Ottawa: University of Ottawa Press, 1999) at 83. This paper describes some unsuccessful efforts, including Nunavik.net, to connect the North and the First Peoples.
156 P. Hoffert, *All Together Now: Connected Communities – How They Will Revolutionize the Way You Live, Work, and Play* (Toronto: Stoddart, 2000) c. 8, "Rankin Inlet: A Community Net."
157 *Ibid.* at 68; taken from the list of objectives of the elementary school's website.
158 "Netville" is a fictitious name given to that community for reasons of confidentiality.
159 K. Hampton, "Living the Wired Life in the Wired Suburb: Netville, Globalization and Civil Society" (PhD thesis, University of Toronto, Department of Sociology, 2001) at 172.
160 Gutstein, *supra* note 59 at 269.
161 *Ibid.* at 270-72.
162 Hoffert, *supra* note 156 at 59.
163 See "Digital Dilemmas," *supra* note 103, "Caught in the Net," at 23.
164 "'The New Wealth of Nations': A Survey of the New Rich" *The Economist* (16 June 2001).
165 *Ibid.*, regarding "fuck-you money"; "patrician gypsies" is mine.

Chapter 7: The Youngest Citizens and Education as a Public Good?
1 R. Manzer, *Public Schools and Political Ideas: Canadian Educational Policy in Historical Perspective* (Toronto: University of Toronto Press, 1994) at 3.
2 J. Murphy, "Good Students and Good Citizens" *New York Times* (15 September 2002) section 4 at 15.
3 J. Saul, *The Unconscious Civilization* (Toronto: House of Anansi, 1995) at 65.
4 J. Gross Stein, *The Cult of Efficiency* (Toronto: House of Anansi, 2001) at 208.
5 J. Boyston, ed., *The Collected Works of John Dewey: Later Works, 1925-1953*, vol. 2: *1925-1927* (Carbondale, IL: Southern Illinois University Press, 1987) at 240.
6 Manzer, *supra* note 1 at 263.
7 Stein, *supra* note 4 at 155.
8 Manzer, *supra* note 1 at 269.
9 *Ibid.* at 258.
10 *Ibid.*
11 Extended funding in the early 1980s to the Roman Catholic Church was required by Bill C-30 passed in 1986: *An Act to Amend the Education Act*, S.O. 1986, c. 21.
12 Manzer, *supra* note 1 at 267.
13 M. Winzer, "Inclusion Practices in Canada: Social, Political, and Educational Influences" in S. Vitello and D. Mithaug, eds., *Inclusive Schooling: National and International Perspectives* (Mahwah, NJ: Lawrence Erlbaum Associates Publishers, 1998) at 132.
14 D. Bricker and E. Greenspon, *Searching for Certainty: Inside the New Canadian Mindset* (Toronto: Doubleday, 2001) at 172.
15 *Ibid.* at 159; See C. Alphonso, "Canadians Are Now World's Best Educated" *Globe and Mail* (12 March 2003) A6.
16 H. Skoloff, "Canada in Top 5 in Schools Study" *National Post* (4 December 2001) A2, 18.
17 G. Galloway, "Canada Ranks 4th in Schooling Study" *Globe and Mail* (26 November 2002) A7.
18 *Ibid.*
19 Stein, *supra* note 4 at 90.

20 Bricker and Greenspon, *supra* note 14 at 151.
21 *Ibid.* at 157.
22 *Ibid.*
23 See *supra* notes 15 to 18 and accompanying text.
24 M. Fullan, "Schools: Failing Grades" *Globe and Mail* (3 September 2002) A11.
25 M. Campbell, "For Most Canadians, Our History Is a Mystery" *Globe and Mail* (30 June 2001) A1, A7.
26 H. Stevenson, "A TIMSS Primer" (1998) 2:7 Fordham Report 1-28.
27 Stein, *supra* note 4 at 90; G. Smith and R. Mackie, "25 Percent Fail Grade 10 Literacy Test" *Globe and Mail* (1 October 2002) A1, A9; R. Mackie, "Witmer Considers Options for Students Who Fail Literacy Tests" *Globe and Mail* (2 October 2002) A8.
28 Bricker and Greenspon, *supra* note 14 at 160.
29 Editorial, "Rozanski's Prescription" *Globe and Mail* (12 December 2002) A24.
30 J. Mintz, "A Textbook Case of Success" *Globe and Mail* (6 February 2004) A19; A. Mitchell, "School Britannia" *Globe and Mail* (1 May 2004) F4.
31 Stein, *supra* note 4 at 91.
32 Bricker and Greenspon, *supra* note 14 at 156.
33 Stein, *supra* note 4 at 95.
34 Stevenson, *supra* note 26 at 1.
35 Bricker and Greenspon, *supra* note 14 at 165.
36 "A Special Interest Supplement on Private Schools" *Globe and Mail* (4 November 2002) section F.
37 Statistics Canada, "Trends in the Use of Private Education" *The Daily* (4 July 2001).
38 Editorial, "Rozanski's Prescription," *supra* note 29.
39 Bricker and Greenspon, *supra* note 14 at 162.
40 Statistics Canada, "University Tuition Fees" *The Daily* (25 August 1999 and 27 August 2001).
41 R. Birgeneau, "President's Message: The Noise about Rising Tuition Fees" *U of T Magazine* (Summer 2002).
42 *Post Secondary Choice and Excellence Act 2000*, S.O. 2000, c. 36.
43 *The Manitoban*, 17 January 2001, online at <http://www.umanitoba.ca>, quoting D. Cunningham, Minister of Training (Colleges and Universities).
44 *Ibid.*, quoting M. Mancuso, associate vice-president, University of Guelph.
45 Birgeneau, *supra* note 41.
46 R. Martin, "A Bright Light on a Bad Strategy" *Globe and Mail* (18 May 2004) A19.
47 Statistics Canada, "University Tuition Fees," *supra* note 40.
48 *Ibid.*; J. Gray, "Arts Tuition Increases Leveling Off, Statistics Reveal" *Globe and Mail* (28 August 2001) online at <http://www.globeandmail.com/series/school/tuition.html>.
49 D. Guyatt, "Exploding Tuition Fees: A Disaster for Medical Students" *Straight Goods* (23 September 2002) online at <http://www.hwcn.org/link/mrg/guyatt.2002.htm>; B. Feldthusen and M. Geist, "Canada's Law Schools: High Tuition v. Academic Excellence" *Globe and Mail* (20 December 2001) A23; S. Goldberg, "Wealthy and Wise: Law School Tuition Fees" *CBA Magazine* (December 2001) online at <http://www.cba.org>.
50 J. Kwong et al., "Effects of Rising Tuition Fees on Medical School Composition and Financial Outlook" (2002) 166 Canadian Medical Association Journal 1023.
51 R. Daniels, "The Price of Excellence" *National Post* (17 December 2001) A18.
52 Editorial, "Law-School Math" *Globe and Mail* (3 March 2003) A12; D. Gambrill, "Study Shows Debt Doesn't Determine Career Path" *Law Times* (10 March 2003) 5. See also A. King et al., *Study of Accessibility to Ontario Law Schools* (Kingston: Social Program Evaluation Group, Queen's University, October 2004).
53 Bricker and Greenspon, *supra* note 14 at 162.
54 Manzer, *supra* note 1 at 266.
55 Stein, *supra* note 4 at 101. For this part of this chapter, I am particularly indebted to Professor Stein's discussion.
56 *Zelman v. Simmons-Harris* [2002] SCT-QL 155.
57 Quoted in E. Bumiller, "Bush Calls Ruling about Vouchers a 'Historic Move'" *New York Times* (2 July 2002) A1.
58 Editorial, "The Wrong Ruling on Vouchers" *New York Times* (28 June 2002) A26.
59 J. Witte, *The Market Approach to Education: An Analysis of America's First Voucher Program* (Princeton, NJ: Princeton University Press, 2000).

60 Stein, *supra* note 4 at 102. The results of some other voucher experiments have been even more controversial; see M. Winerip, "What a Voucher Study Truly Showed and Why" *New York Times* (7 May 2003) A27.
61 *Ibid.* at 104.
62 M. Trebilcock, R. Daniels, and M. Thorburn, "Government by Voucher" (2000) 80 B.U.L. Rev. 205.
63 C. Finn, B. Manno, and G. Vanourek, *Charter Schools in Action: Renewing Public Education* (Princeton, NJ: Princeton University Press, 2000) 71.
64 Stein, *supra* note 4 at 116.
65 P. Berman et al., *The State of Charter Schools 2000: Fourth Year Report* (Washington, DC: US Department of Education, Office of Educational Research and Development, 2000).
66 M. Winerip, "When It Goes Wrong at a Charter School" *New York Times* (5 March 2003) A23; S. Rimer, "Study Finds Charter Schools Lack Experienced Teachers" *New York Times* (9 April 2003) A12.
67 Stein, *supra* note 4 at 118.
68 *Ibid.* at 120.
69 *Ibid.*; M. Schneider, "Institutional Arrangements and the Creation of Social Capital: The Effects of Public School Choice" (1997) 91 American Political Science Review 82.
70 Stein, *ibid.* c. 3 at note 54. See B. Fuller, ed., *Inside Charter Schools: The Paradox of Radical Decentralization* (Cambridge, MA: Harvard University Press, 2000) at 37.
71 D. Bositis, "School Vouchers along the Colour Line" *New York Times* (15 August 2001) A27.
72 M. Buechler, *Charter Schools: Legislation and Results after Four Years* (Bloomington, IN: Indiana Education Policy Centre, 1995) cited in L. Bosetti, "The Dark Promise of Charter Schools" (1998) 19 Policy Options 63 at 64.
73 Fuller, *supra* note 70 at 24 and 28.
74 Manzer, *supra* note 1, c. 10, "Ethical Liberalism and Cultural Community: Religion and Language in Person-Regarding Public Education."
75 T. Riddell, "The Impact of Section 23 of the *Charter of Rights* on Official Minority-Language Education Policy outside Quebec Since 1982" (2001) 21 Windsor Y.B. Access Just. 277.
76 W.A. Bogart, *Courts and Country: The Limits of Litigation and the Social and Political Life of Canada* (Toronto: Oxford University Press, 1994) at 266-71.
77 (1990) 1 S.C.R. 342.
78 Riddell, *supra* note 75 at 278-85.
79 *Reference Re the Education Act and Minority Language Education Rights* (1984) 47 O.R. (2d) 1 (Ont. C.A.).
80 *Education Act*, R.S.O. 1980, c. 129, ss. 258 and 261.
81 *Mahé v. Alberta, supra* note 77 at 344-47.
82 Riddell, *supra* note 75 at 288.
83 *Ibid.* at 288-89.
84 *Arsenault-Cameron v. Prince Edward Island* (2000) 1 S.C.R. 3.
85 *Doucet-Boudreau v. Nova Scotia (Minister of Education)* (2000) 185 N.S.R. (2d) 246 (N.S.S.C.).
86 C. Gillis, "Today's Lesson: Segregation" *National Post* (5 October 2000) A3.
87 See Chapter 2, this volume, at 31-37; *Doucet-Boudreau v. Nova Scotia (Minister of Education)* [2003] 3 S.C.R. 3.
88 Riddell, *supra* note 75 at 295.
89 *Ibid.* at 295-96.
90 Commissioner of Official Languages, *Annual Report 2000-01* (Ottawa: Minister of Government Services, 2001).
91 Riddell, *supra* note 75 at 297-98.
92 *Ibid.* at 298-99.
93 *Ibid.* at 299.
94 Winzer, *supra* note 13 at 133.
95 M. Philp, "Parents Say School Locked Up 7-Year-Old" *Globe and Mail* (25 February 2003) A1, A2.
96 G. Abate, "Judge Lets Suspended Boy Sue Principal" *Globe and Mail* (30 June 2001) A1, A6.
97 Winzer, *supra* note 13 at 133.
98 US, Public Law 94-142 – *Education of All Handicapped Children Act*, 1975. This act is now codified as IDEA (Individuals with Disabilities Education Act).
99 Bill 82, *An Act to Amend the Education Act,* 4th Sess., 31st Leg., Ontario, 1980.

100   Winzer, *supra* note 13 at 137-38.
101   G. Porter and D. Richler, "Changing Special Education Practice: Law, Advocacy, and Innovation" (1990) Can. J. of Comm. Mental Health 65.
102   A. MacKay and V. Kazmierski, "And on the Eighth Day, God Gave Us ... Equality in Education: *Eaton v. Brant (County) Board of Education* and Inclusive Education" (1998) 7 N.J.C.L. 1.
103   M. Williams and R. Macmillan, "Litigation in Special Education" (2000) 10 Education L.J. 259.
104   *Eaton v. Brant County Board of Education,* [1997] 1 S.C.R. 241 [hereafter *Eaton SCC*].
105   *Eaton v. Brant County Board of Education* (1995) 22 O.R. (3d) 1, 123 D.L.R. (4th) 43 (C.A.)
106   *Eaton SCC, supra* note 104, paras. 78-80.
107   Winzer, *supra* note 13 at 139-40; J. Morris, "Disabled Angry over Court Ruling" *Chronicle Herald* (10 October 1996) A14; V. Galt, "Teachers Support Disabled in Classes: Fiscal, Social Realities Prevent Student Integration" *Globe and Mail* (23 August 1997) A1.
108   For a more nuanced approach, see M. Williams and R. MacMillan, "Litigation in Special Education between 1996-1998: The Quest for Equality" (2002-3) 12 Educ. & L.J. 293.
109   See Chapter 2, this volume, at 31-33.
110   O. Reg. 181/98, Amendment to O. Reg. 137/01 Identification and Placement of Exceptional Pupils. The treatment and education of children with autism also raises very difficult issues: see C. Krauss, "Canada Suit Seeks Aid for Autism Victims" *New York Times,* International (8 November 2004) A7; K. Makin, "Court Won't Force Provinces to Pay for Autism Treatment" *Globe and Mail* (20 November 2004) A1, A11 and Editorial, A26.
111   A. Picard, "Boris, 7, Isn't Welcome at Local School" *Globe and Mail* (4 February 2000) A21.
112   Editorial, "Rozanski's Prescription," *supra* note 29.
113   A. Jordan, "Ontario, Canada: Reversing the Gains Made in Special Education" (paper prepared at "Including the Excluded," International Special Education Congress, University of Manchester, 2000) unpublished, online at <http://www.isec2000.org.uk/abstracts/papers_j/jordan_1.htm>.
114   Winzer, *supra* note 13 at 148.
115   Manzer, *supra* note 1 at 169-70.
116   *Reference Re Bill 30, An Act to Amend the Education Act (Ont.)* [1987] 1 S.C.R. 1148.
117   *Adler v. Ontario,* [1996] 3 S.C.R. 609.
118   *Ibid.* at para. 29. See paras. 29-33.
119   United Nations, Human Rights Committee, 67th Sess.: Communication No. 694/1996, 13, as quoted in L. Johnston and S. Swift, *Public Funding of Private and Denominational Schools in Canada* (Toronto: Ontario Legislative Library, 2000) at 2-3.
120   M. Valpy, "Not Our Problem, Ottawa Responds to the Ruling of Bias" *Globe and Mail* (4 February 2000) A8.
121   Johnston and Swift, *supra* note 119 at 8.
122   M. Landsberg, "Public Shouldn't Pay for Any Religious Schools" *Toronto Star* (19 February 2000) T1.
123   K. Reid, "Canadians Debate Education Tax Credits" *Education Week* (14 November 2001) online at <http//:www.edweek.org/eco/newstory/cfm?slug=11international.h21>.
124   Editorial, "How to Undermine the Public Schools" *Globe and Mail* (22 May 2001) A16.
125   O. Reg. 1498/01, Amendment to O. Reg. 340/03 Equity in Education Tax Credit (*Income Tax Act*).
126   L. Robson and C. Hepburn, *Learning from Success: What Americans Can Learn from School Choice in Canada* (Toronto: Fraser Institute, 2002).
127   M. Taube, "Ontario Shows the Way on School Choice" *Wall Street Journal* (9 August 2001) A9.
128   A. Bayefsky, "It Was the Right Thing to Do" *Globe and Mail* (18 May 2001) A15.
129   M. Nelson, "Private School Debate Grows: Proposed Legislation Amounts to a Subsidy for Rich Parents, Opponents to Bill 45 Say" *Globe and Mail* (25 May 2001) A10.
130   J. Smyth, "60% Support Tax Relief for Private Schooling" *National Post* (2 June 2001) A1.
131   Johnston and Swift, *supra* note 119 at 3-8.
132   Statistics Canada, "Trends in the Use of Private Education," *supra* note 37.
133   Bayefsky, *supra* note 128, in the context of applauding the vouchers' availability for religious schools.
134   Stein, *supra* note 4 at 105.
135   Statistics Canada, "Trends in the Use of Private Education," *supra* note 37.

136 *Fiscal Responsibility Act,* S.O. 2003, c. 7, ss. 9-13.
137 Editorial, "Rozanski's Prescription," *supra* note 29; M. Philp, "Ontario to Unveil School Child-Care Plan" *Globe and Mail* (24 November 2004) A1, A13.

Chapter 8: Ever More Citizens Who Are Senior

1 S. Page, "Boom, Bust & Conflict" *Citizens' Weekly* (24 March 2002) C3; Toronto Star Staff, "Code Zero" *Toronto Star* (27 and 28 May 2002) A1, A10; J. Lewington, "Canada Facing Age Crunch" *Globe and Mail* (17 July 2002) A1, A15.
2 I was a Virtual Scholar in Residence with the Law Commission of Canada (LCC) in 2002-3. I was heavily involved with the LCC's project on "generational justice." In this regard see the Discussion Paper: Law Commission of Canada, *Does Age Matter? Law and Relationships between Generations* (Ottawa: Law Commission of Canada, 2004). The support of the LCC and the Social Science and Humanities Research Council for the Virtual Scholar in Residence Program is gratefully acknowledged. The opinions expressed in this chapter are mine alone.
3 Health Canada, *Federal Report on Aging,* "Who Are Canada's Seniors? Demographic Profile of Canada's Aging Population" (Ottawa: Health Canada Division of Aging and Seniors, 2002) online at Health Canada <http://www.hc.sc.gc.ca/seniors-aines/pubs/fed-paper/fedreport1_01_e.htm> [hereafter *Federal Report on Aging*].
4 M. Beaulieu and C. Spencer, *Older Adults' Personal Relationships and the Law in Canada: Legal, Psycho-Social and Ethical Aspects* (Ottawa: Law Commission of Canada, 1999) online at <http://www.lcc.gc.ca/en/themes/pr/oa/spencer.pdf>.
5 *Federal Report on Aging, supra* note 3, "The Health of Older Canadians: Health Status."
6 *Ibid.,* "Who Are Canada's Seniors: Senior Women and Senior Men."
7 D. Foot with D. Stoffman, *Boom, Bust and Echo 2000* (Toronto: Stoddart, 2000) at 144.
8 M. Wolfson et al., "Generational Accounting and Government Policy with Heterogeneous Populations" in M. Corak, ed., *Government Finances and Generational Equity* (Ottawa: Statistics Canada, Catalogue no. 68-513-XPB, 1998) 107 at 119.
9 *Old Age Security Act,* R.S.C. 1985, c. O-9.
10 J. Tuokko and F. Hunter, "Using 'Age' as a Fitness-to-Drive Criterion for Older Adults" (Ottawa: Law Commission of Canada, 2002) online at <http://www.lcc.gc.ca/en/ress/rr.afp>.
11 *Income Tax Act,* R.S.C. 1985, c. I (5th Supp.) s. 146(13.3).
12 D. Poirier and N. Poirier, *Older Adults' Personal Relationships: Final Report. Why Is It So Difficult to Combat Elder Abuse and, in Particular, Financial Exploitation of the Elderly?* (Ottawa: Law Commission of Canada, 1999) at 68-72. Online at <http://www.lcc.gc.ca/en/themes/pr/on/poirier/index.htm/>.
13 Ontario Human Rights Commission, *Time for Action: Advancing Human Rights for Older Ontarians – Final Report* (Toronto: Ontario Human Rights Commission, 2001) at 32-44 [hereafter OHRC].
14 OHRC, *supra* note 13 at 24-27.
15 *Federal Report on Aging, supra* note 3, "The Health of Older Canadians: Health Status."
16 *Ibid.,* "The Health of Older Canadians: Health Care Utilization."
17 OHRC, *supra* note 13 at 51-67.
18 *Ibid.* at 51-67.
19 *Federal Report on Aging, supra* note 3, "Independence and Quality of Life – Caregiving and Social Support."
20 Foot, *supra* note 7 at 223.
21 S. Hogan et al., "Life Expectancy, Health Expectancy, and the Life Cycle," *Horizons* 6, 2 (2003): 17.
22 Foot, *supra* note 7 at 143-45.
23 "Over 60 and Overlooked" *The Economist* (10 August 2002) 51, 51 [hereafter "Overlooked"].
24 J. Brooke, "Japan Seeks Robotic Help in Caring for the Aged" *New York Times* (5 March 2004) A1, A4.
25 "Overlooked" *supra* note 23 at 52.
26 D. Hayes, "So Immature" *Globe and Mail, Report on Business Magazine* (June 2004) 48.
27 "Forever Young: A Survey of Retirement" *The Economist* (27 March 2004) 3, 8.
28 "Overlooked" *supra* note 23 at 51.
29 W.A. Bogart, *Consequences: The Impact of Law and Its Complexity* (Toronto: University of Toronto Press, 2002).
30 OHRC, *supra* note 13 at 20.

31 *Ibid.* at 15.
32 *An Act Respecting Labour Standards,* R.S.Q., c. N-1.1; *An Act to Amend Chapter 377 of the Revised Statues, 1989, the Public Service Superannuation Act,* R.S. 2003, C. 6.
33 Richard Mackie, "Ontario to Ban Mandatory Retirement at 65" *Globe and Mail* (30 August 2003) A1.
34 OHRC, *supra* note 13 at 38.
35 *McKinney v. University of Guelph* [1990], 3 S.C.R. 229, S.C.J. No. 122.
36 OHRC, *supra* note 13 at 32.
37 H. Grant and G. Grant, *Age Discrimination and the Employment Rights of Elderly Canadian Immigrants* (Ottawa: Law Commission of Canada, 2002).
38 OHRC, *supra* note 13 at 38-40.
39 *Ibid.* at 36-38.
40 T. Kirkwood, 2001 *Reith Lectures,* BBC Radio.
41 Ontario Human Rights Commission, *Discrimination and Age: Human Rights Issues Facing Older Persons in Ontario,* Discussion Paper (Ontario Human Rights Commission: Toronto, 2000) at 7.
42 G. McGregor, *Unemployment Protection for Older Workers: A Case Study of Systemic Bias in a Statutory Regime* (Ottawa: Law Commission of Canada, 2002).
43 P. Drucker, "Survey: The Near Future (Part I)" *The Economist* (2 November 2001) 1, 4.
44 *Ontario Human Rights Commission v. Ontario Ministry of Health* (1989) 10 C.H.R.R. D/6353 (Ont. Bd. Inq.) aff'd 14 C.H.R.R.D.11 (Ont. Div. Ct.) rev'd 21 C.H.R.R. D/259 (C.A.).
45 OHRC, *supra* note 13 at 59-60.
46 M. Beaulieu and C. Spencer, *Older Adults' Personal Relationships and the Law in Canada: Legal, Psycho-Social and Ethical Aspects* (Ottawa: Law Commission of Canada, 1999) online at <http://www.lcc.gc.ca/en/themes/pr/on/spencer/>.
47 Commission on the Future of Health Care in Canada, *Building on Values: The Future of Health Care in Canada – Final Report,* Commissioner Roy J. Romanow, November 2002, at 171, online at <http://www.hc-sc.gc.ca/english/care/romanow/index1.html>.
48 OHRC, *supra* note 13.
49 *Ibid.* at 32-73.
50 Health Canada, online at <http://www.hc-sc.gc.ca/seniors-aines/nfa-cnv>. Quebec did not participate in the development of the principles.
51 OHRC, *supra* note 13 at 77.
52 *Ibid.* at 66.
53 *Ibid.* at 60.
54 See Chapter 3, this volume, at 67-69.
55 *Federal Report on Aging, supra* note 3, "Financial Security Later in Life: Income Later in Life."
56 *Ibid.*
57 *Ibid.,* "Financial Security Later in Life: Seniors with Low Income."
58 *Ibid.*
59 *Ibid.,* "Income and Labour Force Issues: Canada's Retirement Income System."
60 *Income Tax Act,* R.S.C. 1985, c. 1, S. 180.2.]
61 *Old Age Security Act,* R.S.C. 1985, c. O-9, S. 11(1).
62 *Ibid.*
63 *Canada Pension Plan Act,* R.S.C. 1985, c. C-8, S. 44(1); *An Act respecting the Québec Pension Plan,* R.S.Q., c. R-9, S. 106-3.
64 K. Howlett, "Early Retirees Putting a Strain on CPP" *Globe and Mail, Report on Business* (14 April 2003) B1.
65 *Income Tax Act,* R.S.C. 1985, c. 1, S. 146(1).
66 Foot, *supra* note 7 at 65-66.
67 J. Daly, "Mind the Gap" *Globe and Mail, Report on Business* (April 2003) 38; W. Immen, "Retirees' Benefits under Siege" *Globe and Mail* (19 May 2004) C1.
68 *Law v. Canada* (1999) 170 D.L.R. (4th) 1.
69 *Ibid.,* paras. 108, 106, and 95.
70 K. Roach, *The Supreme Court on Trial: Judicial Activism or Democratic Dialogue* (Toronto: Irwin Law, 2001) at 130-31, but compare D. Greschner, "Does *Law* Advance the Cause of Equality?" (2001) 27 Queen's L.J. 299.
71 F. Blais, *Ending Poverty: A Basic Income for All Canadians* (Toronto: James Lorimer, 2002).
72 K. Battle, "Relentless Incrementalism: Deconstructing and Reconstructing Canadian Income Security Policy" in K. Banting et al., *The Review of Economic Performance and Social Progress: The*

Longest Decade: Canada in the 1990s (Montreal: Institute for Research on Public Policy [IRPP], 2001) 183 at 186.

73 See Chapter 4, this volume, at 88-89.

74 *Ibid.* at 76-79.

75 T. Courchene, *A State of Minds: Toward a Human Capital Future for Canadians* (Montreal: IRPP, 2001) at 175, citing various definitions of social cohesion found in Standing Senate Committee on Social Affairs, Science and Technology, *Final Report on Social Cohesion* (Ottawa: Senate of Canada, 1999).

76 Courchene, *ibid.*

77 E. Gee and G. Gutman, "Introduction" in E. Gee and G. Gutman, *The Overselling of Population Aging: Apocalyptic Demography, Intergenerational Challenges, and Social Policy* (Toronto: Oxford University Press, 2000) at 1; see also D. Cheal, "Aging and Demographic Change in Canadian Context" *Horizons* 6:2 (2003) 21; and D. Cheal, ed., *Aging and Demographic Change in Canadian Context* (University of Toronto Press, forthcoming).

78 E. Anderson, "Paycheques Show Generational Split" *Globe and Mail* (12 March 2003) A6.

79 Drucker, *supra* note 43 at 4.

80 S. McDaniel, "'What Did You Ever Do for Me?': Intergenerational Linkages in the Restructuring of Canada" in Gee and Gutman, *supra* note 77 at 130 and 147.

81 Gee and Gutman, *supra* note 77 at 1 and 2.

82 Foot, *supra* note 7 at 77.

83 M. Prince, "Apocalyptic, Opportunistic, and Realistic Demographic Discourse" in Gee and Gutman, *supra* note 77 at 100 and 101.

84 "Forever Young," *supra* note 27 at 11-17.

85 Drucker, *supra* note 43 at 3.

86 P. Clark, "Public Policy in the United States and Canada: Individualism, Family Obligations, and Collective Responsibility in the Care of the Elderly" in J. Hendricks and C. Rosenthal, eds., *The Remainder of Their Days: Domestic Policy and Older Families in the United States and Canada* (New York: Garland, 1993) at 38-39.

87 F. Graves, "The Economy through a Public Lens: Shifting Canadian Views of the Economy" in Banting et al., *supra* note 72 at 63.

88 P. Hicks, "The Policy Implications of Aging: A Transformation of National and International Thinking" *Horizons* 6:2 (2003) 12.

Conclusion

1 S. Rubin, "Canada's Top 25 Women Lawyers: At the Top of Their Game" *Financial Post* (10 September 2003) FP9.

2 F. Cairncross, *The Death of Distance: How the Communications Revolution Is Changing Our Lives,* 2nd. ed. (Boston: Harvard Business School, 2001).

3 W.L. Mackenzie King, House of Commons *Debates,* 18 June 1936, as quoted in R.M. Hamilton and D. Shields, eds., *The Dictionary of Canadian Quotations and Phrases* (Toronto: McClelland and Stewart, 1979) at 394. See Chapter 1, this volume, at 10-11.

4 "Canada's New Spirit" *The Economist* (27 September-3 October 2003) 13.

5 Conference Board of Canada, *Performance and Potential 2003-4: Defining the Canadian Advantage* (9 October 2003).

6 B. Little, "Canada's Latest Report Has Disappointing Marks" *Globe and Mail, Report on Business* (4 October 2003) B1, B4.

7 Editorial, "Cool Canada? Why Not, Eh?" *Globe and Mail* (30 September 2003) A22.

8 S. Godfrey, "Frum on Frum" *Globe and Mail* (1 February 1992) C7.

9 D. McKenzie, "69% Say Government Corrupt" *National Post* (22 April 2002) A1.

10 J. Galbraith, "Canada Customs" *Saturday Night* (January 1987) 113.

11 J. Heath, *The Efficient Society: Why Canada Is As Close to Utopia As It Gets* (Toronto: Penguin/ Viking, 2001).

12 J. Gross Stein, *The Cult of Efficiency* (Toronto: House of Anansi, 2001); see also Chapter 4, this volume, at 76-79.

13 See Chapter 2, "The Ascendance of Courts," notes 52 to 61 and accompanying text.

14 G. Rosenberg, *The Hollow Hope: Can Courts Bring About Social Change?* (Chicago: University of Chicago Press, 1991); R. Kagan, *Adversarial Legalism: The American Way of Law* (Cambridge, MA: Harvard University Press, 2001); T. Burke, *Lawyers, Lawsuits and Legal Rights: The Battle over Litigation in American Society* (Berkeley and Los Angeles: University of California Press,

2002); and S. Powers and S. Rothman, *The Least Dangerous Branch: Consequences of Judicial Activism* (Westport, CT: Praeger Publishers, 2002).

15 *Brown v. Board of Education* 347 U.S. 483 (1954).
16 A. Gold, "The Legal Rights Provisions: A New Vision or Déjà Vu?" (1982) Sup. Ct. L. Rev. 4, 108, quoted in C. Manfredi, *Judicial Power and the Charter* (Toronto: McClelland and Stewart, 1993) at 27; see also Chapter 2, this volume, at 31-37.
17 K. Makin, "Canadians Feel Supreme Court Tainted by Partisan Politics" *Globe and Mail* (3 July 2001) A1, A4.
18 See *supra* note 9 for the "corrupt" figures.
19 For example, C. Krauss, "Now Free to Marry, Canada's Gays Say, Do I?" *New York Times* (31 August 2003) A1, A6; see also Chapter 3, this volume, at 64-67.
20 C. Krauss, "Gay Wedding Bells. Why No Hubbub? It's Canada" *New York Times* (24 September 2003) A4.
21 A. Cairns et al., eds., *Citizenship, Diversity and Pluralism: Canadian and Comparative Perspectives* (Montreal and Kingston: McGill-Queen's University Press, 1999).
22 P. Norris, ed., *Critical Citizens: Global Support for Domestic Government* (Oxford; Oxford University Press, 1999); see also Chapter 3, this volume, at 48-49 and 62-64.
23 R. Beiner, ed., *Theorizing Citizenship* (Albany, NY: State University of New York Press, 1995).
24 M. Schudson, *The Good Citizen: A History of American Civic Life* (New York: Free Press, 1998) at 295; see also Chapter 2, this volume, at 42-46.
25 *Ibid.*
26 Though see "Digital Dilemmas" and "Caught in the Net" *The Economist* (25 January 2003) 23.
27 Stein, *supra* note 12 at 191.
28 *Eaton v. Brant County Board of Education,* [1997] 1 S.C.R. 241, discussed in Chapter 7, this volume; and *Law v. Canada,* [1999] 1 S.C.R. 497, discussed in Chapter 8, this volume.
29 See Chapter 5 at 101-5.
30 See Chapter 2 at 40-42.
31 See Chapter 3 at 64-67.
32 See Chapter 2 at 44.
33 See Chapter 7at 166-70.
34 J. Taber, "Liberal Says MPs Will Vet Top-Court Nominees" *Globe and Mail* (30 January 2004) A1, A4.
35 L. Gordon, "Time to Shed an Old Political Skin" *Globe and Mail* (14 April 2004) A15.
36 D. Tapscott, "Outdated Democracy: We Vote, They Rule" *Globe and Mail* (27 May 2004) A21.
37 J. Maxwell, "Hear, Hear for Citizen Input" *Globe and Mail* (30 April 2004) A21; see also Ontario Panel on the Role of Government, *Investing in People: Creating a Human Capital Society for Ontario* (Toronto: n.p., 2004).
38 Quoted in O. Olive, "An Honours List for Canada, on the Eve of Its 125th" *Globe and Mail* (27 June 1992) D4.

Index

Dewey, John, 145
Dominion Law Reports, 26
Durham, Lord, 12

E The People, 136
Eaton v. Brant County board of Education
(1997), 165
economy: business liberalism, 6; Canada-
US trade, 72-73, 83-84; competition
policies, 4, 8-9, 15-17; concentration of
wealth tolerated, 4, 7-8, 15; dependence
on US, 73; "economic passivity," 8,
15-16; employment and incomes,
75-76; government involvement pre-
transformation, 5-6, 7-9, 10, 15, 71;
government regulation, 8, 14-15, 24-25,
60-61; market orientation, 72; "new
economy," 72; productivity trends, 74-
75; regional differences, 10-11; resource-
dependent, 7, 15-16, 73; taxes and
public spending vs US, 82-83; technological change, 73-74; transformation
(1980s-1990s), 72-76; unions in Canada
and US, 75. *See also* globalization; markets
education: Aboriginal situation, 98, 100;
Canadian vs other nations, 147-48;
charter schools and myth of exit, 155,
157-59; choice, rights, and markets, 144,
147, 150, 154-59, 166-70; civic purposes
of, 144-47; competition and the markets,
152, 168-70; confidence in, 143, 147-50;
educational models and testing, 149-50;
global competitiveness and, 145, 146,
148-49; goals, different viewpoints, 145-
47; government funding, 146, 148-49,
151-52, 166-70; individual development
and "ethical liberalism," 145-47, 154;
judicial activity (*Brown* case, 1954), 33-
37, 197; minority-language rights, 143,
145-46, 150, 159-63; private schools
and myth of exit, 150-51, 166-70; as
public good, 144, 170; public support
for public school system, 147-50, 154,
169; religious schools, rights of, 143-44,
145-46, 150, 166-70; resource problems,
148-49; special needs students' rights,
143-44, 150, 159, 163-66; subsidies for
private education (Ontario), 166-70; tax
credits (Ontario), 168-69; university
tuition deregulation and markets as exit,
150, 151-54; vouchers and myth of exit,
155-57, 158-59, 168
Education Amendment Act (Ontario, 1980),
164
efficiency, cult of, 78-79, 196
Efficient Society, The (Heath, 2001), 79
EGALE (Equality for Gays and Lesbians
Everywhere), 66
Egan v. Canada (1995), 66

elderly. *See* seniors
employment insurance, 60, 73, 88, 179, 182
environment and globalization, 84-86, 199
Equity in Education Tax Credit (Ontario),
168-69
"ethical liberalism," 145-47, 154
exit. *See* myth of exit

First Nations Governance Act, 99
First Nations? Second Thoughts (Flanagan,
2000), 113-14
First Peoples: assimilation argument, xii,
95; assimilation as government policy,
100-101, 111, 113-15; *Charter* and
Aboriginal rights, 54, 97, 102, 104-5;
as "citizens plus," xiii, 95-96, 111-13,
115-17; constitutional accords and,
52, 53-54, 102; as nations and rights
holders, xiii, 53-54, 95, 101-5, 111; self-
government, xiii, 53-54, 103; Supreme
Court decisions, 90-91, 103-4, 200; two
row wampum, 111-13; urban Aboriginals,
105-11, 115, 200; wardship under *Indian
Act*, 97-98, 100. *See also* Aboriginals
Flanagan, Tom, 113-14, 117
free trade: borders' continuing importance,
83-84, 199; environmental protection
and, 84-86; impact on economy, 72-73;
markets and, 16-17; NAFTA, 3, 72-73,
83-84; symbol of markets and of choice,
3. *See also* NAFTA
Friedman, Lawrence, 77, 96-97, 102
Friendship Centres, 110-11
Frye, Northrop, 6, 19
Fudge, J., 65

Galanter, Marc, 26
Galbraith, John Kenneth, 69, 196
Gallagher, Jack, 8
*Gathering Strength: Canada's Aboriginal
Action Plan* (1997), 112-13
GATT (General Agreement on Tariff and
Trade), 72
gay relationships. *See* same-sex marriage
Gitxsan Health Authority, 99
globalization: environmental protection
and, 84-86; "hollow state" and, 81-84;
impact on individual societies, 79-81;
market orientation of society and, 19,
71-73, 86-87, 195; meanings, 80; politicians' ability to respond to citizens'
interests and, 50; tax rates and public
spending, 82-83; transnational institutions, 81. *See also* free trade
*Good Citizen, The: A History of American Civic
Life* (Schudson, 1998), x-xi, 42
government: Aboriginal assimilation as
policy, 100-101, 111, 113-15; courts'
ascendance over, 43-44, 45-46, 61-62,